Muslims in Global Societies Series

Volume 3

Series Editors
Gabriele Marranci
National University of Singapore, Singapore

Bryan S. Turner
Wellesley College, Wellesley, USA

For further volumes:
http://www.springer.com/series/7863

Mark Woodward

Java, Indonesia and Islam

Springer

Mark Woodward
Department of Religious Studies
Arizona State University
Tempe, AZ 85287-4302
USA
mark.woodward@asu.edu

ISBN 978-94-007-0055-0   e-ISBN 978-94-007-0056-7
DOI 10.1007/978-94-007-0056-7
Springer Dordrecht Heidelberg London New York

Library of Congress Control Number: 2010937672

Printed on acid-free paper

Springer is part of Springer Science+Business Media (www.springer.com)

Preface

The essays included in this volume were written between 1985 and 2010. They are based on three decades of ethnographic research in the Sultanate of Yogyakarta and other regions of the Indonesian island of Java and on close readings of contemporary and historical Indonesian Islamic texts. Versions of all but two have been published previously. Those which have appeared previously have been greatly revised and expanded to reflect, and attempt to explain, the ways in which Javanese and Indonesian religions, cultures and societies have changed since I first came to Yogyakarta, and in response to more recent scholarship. They also reflect the development my own theoretical interests in nationalisms and problems of religion and violence. Many are nearly double the length of the originals. I have also included occasional references to others parts of Muslim Southeast Asia I have had to opportunity to visit over the years, especially Jakarta, East Java, Lombok and Sumatra in Indonesia as well as Malaysia and Singapore. All are informed by comparisons with other lived and mediated Islams and by Pan-Islamic Arabic textual traditions that have shaped the development of Javanese and Indonesian Islams.[1]

All of these essays are products of a research program that commenced in the late 1970s with a study of the local Islams of the Yogyakarta *Kraton* (palace) and the *kampung* (named residential quarters) surrounding it that resulted in my first book: *Islam in Java: Normative Piety and Mysticism in the Sultanate of Yogyakarta*. With interludes that have taken me to Burma and Singapore, I have continued to visit Yogyakarta, the *Kraton* and the *kampung* for more than 30 years. The young children who crowded around me yelling "Hello mister!" nearly every morning as I left home, now have children of their own, who greet me in much the same way. Friends of my own age are now grandparents. Many of my elderly teachers, from whom I learned most of what I know about Java and Islam, have now, as Indonesians often put it, "Returned home to the mercy of God." I can now only bring flowers and incense to their final resting places and continue to ask their blessing and guidance, in keeping with the most Javanese and most Muslim tradition of *ziyarah*. Others,

---

[1] I use the term mediated rather than print Islam because developments in electronic communications media ranging from audio cassettes, which have been popular since the 1970s, to DVDs and the Internet have rendered the former obsolete.

whose views of this life and the next were shaped by modernist Islamic currents that swept Indonesia and much of the rest of the Muslim World in the twentieth century, would not have approved of what they believed to be among the "non-Islamic" elements of Javanese and other Muslim cultures. While respecting their sometimes explicitly stated requests that I not visit their graves, which are in many cases unmarked, I hold their memories in equal regard.

While I have returned to Yogyakarta, the *Kraton* and the *kampung* more times than I can now recall, my interests in religions as constantly emerging cultural systems and the course of Javanese and Indonesian history have led to shifts in the geographic and social locations of my research. During the final years of the New Order and the early days of the Reformation Era I found myself in the Indonesian capital Jakarta, almost as often as in Yogyakarta. During those years I found myself almost as often in the crowed streets of Jakarta as in the narrow alleyways of Yogyakarta *kampung*. Even after returning to Yogyakarta for an extended and indefinite time in 2008, I find myself sitting in chairs in offices and classrooms as often as I do on the floors of mosques and small houses. Indonesian politics at the end of the twentieth century and the beginning of the twenty-first led me to become increasing interested in the life of the Muslim World's youngest and largest democracy. In addition to Yogyakarta princes I now count Indonesian religious, political and academic figures as friends and research partners. It has been a privilege to be in the company of Javanese Sultans and Indonesian Presidents and every bit as much to have shared the company of Javanese and other Indonesian *wong cilik* (common people) in their homes and mosques and the *warung* (food stalls) that crowd the streets of cities and in the villages that surround them. When I first began my intellectual and personal journey into the worlds of Java, Indonesia and Islam, I could not have anticipated these developments. But that is why ethnography is never boring and always challenging. In the 1970s none could have foreseen that after having had only two presidents between 1945 and 1998, Indonesia would have four between 1998 and 2008 and that Sultan Hamengkubuwana X would be twice nominated for the office of President of Indonesia, or that just as it had been the "Mother City" of the struggle for independence in the 1940s, that Yogyakarta would become the "Mother City" of the democratic revolution of the 1990s. It was not difficult to expect that when this change came that many Javanese would interpret it in terms of local, religiously based, concepts of authority and power. None could have predicted that of these four presidents the first would be an eccentric Islamic Modernist technocrat, the second one of the nation's most prominent and charismatic conservative Islamic scholars, the third the daughter and heir apparent to the charisma of Indonesia's first president Sukarno, and the fourth a decidedly uncharismatic, secularist retired army general with the unusual habit of singing in his own campaign commercials. But then while Anthropology, Religious Studies and other Human Sciences are explanatory, they are predictive only in the sense of pointing to possibilities. Human agency and creativity are such that more precise predictions are impossible. This is again, what makes ethnography exciting, especially in times of change.

Despite these shifts in focus, the question I ask myself today is the same as it was when I first arrived in Yogyakarta on a May morning in 1977, that is: "How is Islam understood and lived in Java?" though now I am increasingly interested in how Java and Indonesia are conceptual categories as much as they are geographic and political entities, how each informs and shapes the other and how this interaction influences the understanding and experience of Islam among people who find themselves inhabiting both worlds simultaneously. It is in sense ironic that I write these words sitting in an office at Gajah Mada University in Yogyakarta which is located in the northern portion of the city in an area that in many respects is more Indonesia than Java, but whose original campus was located in an audience hall in the northern portion of the *Kraton*.

Yogyakarta, Indonesia   Mark Woodward
May 2, 2010

Acknowledgments

So many people in so many places have contributed to my thinking about Yogyakarta, Indonesia, Islam and nationality that it is impossible to mention, or unfortunately even to remember, them all. The following teachers, colleagues, friends and students are the ones who have been most influential in bringing this volume to its present form. F.K. Lehman and Clark Cunningham of the University of Illinois and Frank Reynolds of the University of Chicago were the most important of the many fine teachers I had in the United States. I have had equally remarkable teachers in Indonesia including Taufik Abdullah, Nurcholish Madjid and G.P.H. Poerwokoesoemo. I have now been at Arizona State University for more than 25 years. The list of people from ASU who have challenged my thinking and in other ways made this project possible is very long. In no particular order, people who are now, or who were once, on the faculty include: Richard Wentz, Richard Martin, Peter Suwarno, Christopher Duncan, Kenneth Morrison, Carolyn Warner, Sani Umar, Anne Feldhaus, Joel Gereboff, Linell Cady, Sheldon Simon, Tom Taylor, Carolyn Warner, Miriam Elman, Juliane Schober, Norbert Samuelson, James Rush, Shala Talebi, David Jacobson, David Damrel, Miriam Elman, Eugene Clay, Steven McKinnon, John Carlson, Pori Park, James Eder, Hasan Davulcu, Alexander Henn and James Foard have been as marvelous a group of scholars to work with and to know as one could possibly imagine. Former and current students at Arizona State, Nanyang Technological University in Singapore and Universitas Gadjah Mada in Yogyakarta, many of who know have well established careers of their own, have been equally import. Those who have contributed most to this project are, again in no particular order, Inayah Rohmaniyah, Ronald Lukens-Bull, Mariani binte Yahya, Miriam Cohen, Elizabeth Ursic, Nanjiyah Jim Martian, Doe Daugherty, Anna Gade, Hermawan Sulystio, Rohani Mohammed, Diana Coleman, Ali Amin and Syamsul Ma'arif. Conversations with Sita Hidayah of the Anthropology Department at UGM led me to rethink and rewrite Chapter 1 long after I thought that it was finished. Seven marvelous support staff people moved mountains and did other impossible things to make this project possible: again in no particular order, they are Patricia Hutton, Carolyn Forbes, Maria Ingrid Nabubhoga, Cynthia Carsten, Marsha Schweitzer, Sandy Leong Mee Yit and Carol Withers. There are people who made especially important contributions to several of the chapters that follow. They are mentioned individually in footnotes.

To you all: *Terima Kasih Banyak!*

Contents

Chapter 1
Yogyakarta: Religion, Culture and Nationality

> *We the President of the Republic of Indonesia confirm Ingkang Sinuwan Kanjeng Sultan Hamengkubuwana Senopati Ing Nagala Abdurrakhman Sayidin Panatagama Kalifatull ingkang Kaping IX of Ngayogyakarta Hadiningrat in his position in the belief that he will devote all of his thoughts, energy, spirit and deeds to the establishment of tranquility (keselamatan) to the region of Yogyakarta as a territory of the Republic of Indonesia.*

Jakarta, August 19, 1945
President of the Republic of Indonesia
Soekarno

> *We Sultan Hamengku Buwono IX of the nation of Ngajogjokarto Hadiningrat proclaim:*
>
> *1. That the nation of Ngajogjokarta Hadiningrat is a special region of the nation of the Republic of Indonesia with the attributes of a kingdom.*
> *2. That We, as head of the region, hold all powers internal to the nation of Ngajogjokarta Hadiningrat and therefore, in light of current conditions, all matters of government, from this time forward, are in Our hands and we retain all other powers.*
> *3. That relationships between Ngajogjokarto Hadiningrat and the central government of the Republic of Indonesia are direct and that We are responsible for Our nation directly to the President of the Republic of Indonesia. We command all inhabitants of Ngajogjokarta Hadiningrat act in accordance with Our proclamation.*

Nga Jogjokarto Hadiningrat
28 Pasa, Ehe, 1878
(5 September, 1945)
Hamengku Buwono

This exchange of letters, or from a Yogyakarta perspective, diplomatic notes, between Indonesia's first President Soekarno and Sultan Hamengkubuwana IX set the tone for relationships between the Sultanate of Yogyakarta and the Republic of Indonesia. President Soekarno's note was sent two days after he and Vice President Mohammad Hatta declared Indonesia's independence from the Netherlands.[1] The

---

[1] Soekarno and Hatta were complimentary opposites. Soekarno was the consummate revolutionary. He was flamboyant, charismatic and a spell binding orator. Hatta was a brilliant, cool headed rationalist. Hamengkubuwana IX was a flamboyant, highly charismatic, cool headed rationalist.

M. Woodward, *Java, Indonesia and Islam*, Muslims in Global Societies Series 3,
DOI 10.1007/978-94-007-0056-7_1, © Springer Science+Business Media B.V. 2011

Sultan's note is dated more than two weeks later. Both men spoke as head of state. Both used the regal "We". In other respects the two notes are very different.

Soekarno spoke in vague terms, confirming the Sultan in his position with unspecified powers and authority and declaring "Yogyakarta", an Indonesian word, to be part of Indonesia. The Sultan was more precise. He describes both Indonesia and Ngajogjokarto Hadiningrat, a self referential Javanese term, as nations. Indonesia is a Republic, Yogyakarta a kingdom with all internal power and authority remaining in the hands of the Sultan. Soekarno's note is dated according to the International Calendar, the Sultan's primarily according to the Javanese Islamic Calendar and only secondarily in accord with international reckoning. Ironically, Soekarno refers to the Sultan by his full title which translates, "Supreme Military Commander, Servant of the Merciful (God) Descendent of the Prophet Muhammad, Regulator of Religion, Caliph (representative) of God. The Sultan refers to himself only as "Sultan of the Nation of Ngajogjokarto Hadiningrat". In Yogya, however, the second designation implies the first,

The tone of Soekarno's note was in keeping with colonial usage. The "political contract" which specified the nature of relationships between the Sultanate and the Netherlands Indies government was sometimes renegotiated, and at others simply confirmed at the beginning of a new reign. Soekarno's note confirms the colonial relationship.[2] But in August of 1945 the polarity between Batavia, now Jakarta, and Yogyakarta was reversed. The "new reign" was Soekarno's presidency of the Republic of Indonesia. The Sultan had no interest is reaffirming the colonial relationship. In his note to Soekarno he abrogated the colonial political contract that he had negotiated with the Dutch in 1940, reclaiming many of the powers the *kraton* (palace) had possessed during the reign of his ancestor Hamengkubuwana I (reigned 1755–1792), nearly two centuries earlier. It seemed likely at the time, and would soon become clear, that the British and Dutch would respond to Indonesia's unilateral declaration of independence with force and that Indonesia needed Yogyakarta as much, if not more, than Yogyakarta needed Indonesia. Even during the Japanese occupation the young Sultan had taken steps toward political and economic modernization and felt that he could negotiate with the Indonesian Republic from a position of strength.[3]

Issues of religion, culture and nationality were all at stake in this exchange.[4] They have reverberated through the histories of both nations for more than 60 years,

---

On Soekarno see B. Hering, *Architect of a Nation*, Leiden: KTLV, 2002. On Hatta, G. Kahin, "In Memoriam: Mohammad Hatta,: Indonesia, 1980, pp. 13–20 and M. Hatta, *Portrait of a Patriot: Selected Writings*, The Hague: Mouton, 1972. On Hamengkubuwana IX see S. Kutoyo, *Sri Sultan Hamengku Buwono IX, Riwayat Hidup dan Perjuangan*, Jakarta: Mutiara Sumber Widay, 1996.

[2] On the political contracts see S. Hardjodipoero, *Kasultanan Yogyakarta, Satu Tinjauan Kontrak Politic (1877–1940)*, Yogyakarta: Gadjah Mada University Press, 1985.

[3] K.P.H. Poerwokoesoemo, personal communication and S. Soemarjan, *Social Changes in Yogyakarta*, Ithaca: Cornell University Press, 1962, J. Monfries, "The Sultan and the Revolution," *Bjidragen to de Taal, Land- en Volkenkunde*, vol. 164, no. 2/3, pp. 269–297, 2008.

[4] My understanding of these issues, and the ways in which they play out in the histories of Yogyakarta and Indonesia has benefited enormously from conversations with Sita Hidayah of the Department of Anthropology at Gadjah Mada University.

surfacing most recently in 2008 in debates concerning the still unresolved status of the Sultanate in the Indonesian Republic.[5] Both documents are inscribed on marble plaques enshrined in the Yogyakarta *Kraton*.[6] That on which Soekarno's words are engraved is adorned with the Indonesian national coat of arms. The one preserving the words of Hamengkubuwana IX is adorned with the national coat of arms of Ngajogjokarto Hadiningrat. The meanings and significance of this barely post-colonial discourse will emerge throughout this volume and especially in Chapter 7 which describes the ways in which the identities of both nations were contested in the Indonesian democratic transition of 1998, when once again it seemed that the survival of Indonesia depended on what transpired in Yogyakarta.

Religion, Culture and Nationality

The triad of religion, culture and nationalism, though not necessarily in exactly these terms, as interacting concepts for the analysis of post-colonial societies and states is entirely conventional. It has been a staple of anthropological and political science analysis of post-coloniality for more than a generation.[7] In Yogyakarta the balance is thrown some what off kilter not only by the complex interrelations of *kebudayaan* (culture) and *agama* (religion) as *emic* categories in Indonesian, and to a lesser extent, Javanese, discourse, but also by the fact that there are competing nationalisms: Indonesian nationalism and Yogyakarta nationalism. The Indonesian terms *agama, kebudayaan* and *kebangsaan* are only roughly translated as religion, cultural and nationality. All three are socially and politically constructed categories the boundaries of which have shifted considerably over time and which are still very much in flux and at issue.

Kebangsaan refers to a nation, people or ethnic group and in contemporary Indonesian discourse has all three connotations. The use of the Malay/Indonesian root *bangsa* in reference to the population of the nation state Indonesia suggest an

---

[5]On the political status of Yogyakarta and the Sultan in the Republic of Indonesia see Chapter 7. Following the democratic transition of 1998, the status of the Sultan as provincial governor was confirmed for a period of ten years. In 2008 it was extended for three additional years after an extended struggle between royalist forces in Yogyakarta and some, including Islamist political parties, in the national parliament that attempted to disestablish the monarchy, see, M. Woodward, "Resisting Wahhabi Colonialism in Yogyakarta," *COMPS Journal: Analysis, Commentary and News from the World of Strategic Communications*, pp. 1–8, 2008.

[6]These are the sources of the texts translated here. On hearing of this Ronald Lukens-Bull of the University of North Florida suggested that in this case the texts were, in this case, "literally carved in stone". On the 30th of October 1945 the Sultan issued a second proclamation stating the powers formerly held by the Netherlands Indies Government had reverted to him, *Kedaulatan Rokyat*, October 31, 1945. This proclamation is more technical in nature and is not "carved in stone".

[7]S. Alatas, *Alternative Discourses in Asian Social Science: Responses to* Eurocentrism, New Delhi, SAGE Publications, 2006, C. Breckenridge. and P. Van der Veer (eds.), *Orientalism and the Postcolonial Predicament. Perspectives on South Asia*, Philadelphia University of Pennsylvania Press, 1993, N. Dirks, *Colonialism and Culture*, Anne Arbor, University of Michigan Press, 1995. Rita Kipp has addressed similar issues in her study of religion, ethnicity and identity among the Karo people of Sumata, *Dissociated Indentities. Ethnicity, Religion and Class in an Indonesian Society*, Ann Arbor: The University of Michigan Press, 1993.

ethnic and cultural unity that is far more imagination than reality. The Malays of
East Sumatra are, for example, much more similar to those of West Malaysia than
they are to Javanese. Many of the peoples of Eastern Indonesia are culturally entirely
distinct from the Malay (in the broadest sense of the term) cultures of Java and other
parts of Western Indonesia.

Agama and *kebuayaan* are more complex still. Analytically speaking, religions
are concerned with, among other things, relationships between humans and non-
human (some of which may be non-material) entities possessing some measure of
consciousness, power and agency. Many, probably most, religions are located in
fixed cultural and geographic spaces. Others transcend culture and place. Trans-
cultural religions are simultaneously more and less than culture.[8] They are more
than culture in the sense that they transcend cultural, ethnic and national boundaries
and are lived and interpreted in very different cultural contexts They are less than
culture in the sense that, the claims of some "fundamentalists" not withstanding,
there are some elements of culture that have little, if any, religious significance.
Javanese and Saudi Arabians are Muslims but are very different in most other
respects. Hoisting caged song birds on poles is an element of Javanese culture
but has nothing to do with Islam. Nor does camel racing: a sport beloved in Saudi
Arabia. More significantly, young Indonesian men who wear Pakistani style clothing
are no more "Islamic" than others, though they claim to be because they, incorrectly,
think that these outfits resemble the clothing worn by the Prophet Muhammad.
Rather they have shifted elements of Pakistani, and more specifically Pashtun,
culture into a variant of Indonesian Islam.

In some societies "religion" is not a salient *emic* category, or at least was not
until it was introduced as one in colonial or neo-colonial contexts. This seems to
be the case in Japan and among most American Indian People.[9] Many Japanese are
convinced that they do not have a religion because "religion" is defined as exclusive adherence to a particular sectarian group.[10] In the American Southwest many
Navajo people call what non Indian people would call their "religion" simply the
"Navajo way" and use the term religion to refer to varieties of Christianity, Islam,
Buddhism and other trans-cultural religions with which they are familiar. In places
where religion and culture *are* salient categories, and Indonesia is one of them, their
boundaries are permeable and shift over time.

Questions of what is "religion" and what is "culture" may, at times, be bitterly contested. In the 1970s much of what is described in this book was often
referred to as "Javanese Religion" (*Agama Jawa*). Prior to the advent of Muslim
modernism, with its puritanical inclinations, in the early years of the twentieth
century, and among individuals untouched or untroubled by this development, this

[8]My thinking on these definitional issues has profited enormously from many years of conversation with Professors Emeritus James Foard and Kenneth Morrison of the Department of Religious
Studies at Arizona State University.
[9]I use the term Indian rather than the more politically correct "Native American" because my Pima
and Navajo friends in Arizona prefer to be called "Indian People".
[10]I would like to thank James Foard for this observation.

complex of knowledge and praxis was, and still is, simply "Islam". Today the prayer meals, traditional medicine and palace rituals are commonly referred to as "Javanese Culture" (*Kebudayaan Jawa*) even though the nature of these phenomena have not changed substantially, no matter what one calls them. This reflects the diminution of religious polarization over the past 30 years, and a strategy for avoiding it. Proponents of what was formerly Javanese Religion are willing to accept the designation Javanese Culture to avoid antagonizing orthoprax, and especially modernist and Islamist, Muslims.[11] The logic is that if these practices are defined as being not religion they are also not heresy.[12] Similarly, many orthoprax Muslims have sought to describe this complex as "Javanese Islamic Culture" for similar reasons. But, as is shown in Chapter 7, shifts in the boundaries between "culture" and "religion," can have important consequences for understanding the dynamics of power in Javanese and Indonesian society. The Yogyakarta *Kraton* now routinely refers to itself as a "center of Javanese culture".[13] Here *Kebudayan Jawa* and *Kebudayaaan Yogyakarta*, refer not only to the fine and performing arts, and to things that anthropologists would typically refer to as culture, but also to elements of Javanese culture that scholars would generally consider to be religion, and that Javanese understand as being highly charged with power (*kesekten*).[14] These

---

[11] A similar dynamic tension can be found in many Indonesian Christian societies. Ambon is a particularly striking and complex example. There is a distinction between *Kristen Ambon* or Ambonese Christianity and *Kristen Belanda* or Dutch Christianity. *Kristen Ambon* includes many elements of traditional belief and ritual practice. *Kristen Belanda* is a more "orthodox" form of Dutch Calvinism. *Kristen Ambon* is practiced and supported exclusively by native Ambonese. During the colonial period Dutch missionaries discouraged this hybrid form of Christianity. Today *Kristen Belanda* is supported by Ambonese ministers who have studied in the Netherlands and by the large diaspora community most of who migrated the Netherlands in the 1950s because of their support for the Dutch during the Indonesian Revolution. Some Indonesian Ambonese Christians consider them to be "imperialists" or "colonialists". This closely resembles the way in which many traditional Javanese Muslims think of Islamists affiliated with Saudi Arabian and other Wahhabi groups. On Wahhabi colonialism see M. Woodward, "Contesting Wahhabi Colonialism in Yogyakarta," *COMPOS Journal: Analysis, Commentary and News from the World of Strategic Communications,* November, 2008, pp. 1–8.

[12] This strategy does not always work. In October of 2008 the Islamist *Front Pembela Islam* (Front for the Defense of Islam) attacked the headquarters of Javanist *kebudayaan* groups they considered to be "un-Islamic". In Yogyakarta they targeted the modernist mystical organization Sapta Dharma, which, analytically speaking, is a religious organization.

[13] This is, of course, a hegemonic discourse that is strongly contested by the neighboring court of Surakarta, which also claims to be the center of Javanese culture. The intensity with which these rival claims remain contested became clear to me in January of 2008 when I delivered an address at ceremonies inaugurating the Center for the Study of Religion and Javanese Culture at the National Higher School of Islamic Studies in Surakarta in which I spoke primarily about Yogya. The audience, of approximately 300 found this more than a bit disturbing. Several pointed out that "Surakarta is the older of the two kingdoms and the real center of Javanese culture". Both claims are contested because in Yogya it is believed that Surakarta ceased to be a genuine kingdom when Ngajogjokarto Hadiningrat was established. It is also contested by Javanese living out side the territories of *both* kingdoms.

[14] On the Javanese theory of power see Chapter 2.

include state ceremonies, pilgrimages to graves and other sacred places, traditional medicine, and the veneration of sacred heirlooms (*pusaka*) whose powers are so great that they can be fatal. Thus when the *kraton* describes itself as a "center of *kebudayaan*" it is making very significant claims about its religious (in the analytic sense) legitimacy. To avoid confusion I will use the English words culture and religion to refer to analytic or etic concepts and the Indonesian *kebudayaan* and *agama* to refer to Javanese cultural categories in this and the chapters that follow.

Many Javanese and other Indonesian intellectuals now blame the cultural/religious polarization of earlier periods of post-colonial Indonesian history on the divide and rule policies of the Dutch and the research of Orientalists, Colonialist and Neo-Colonialist Anthropologists and Historians. Even the neo-fundamentalist journal *Panjimas* published a special issue describing the Islamic character of aspects of Javanese Culture that in the late 1970s it would have denounced in the harshest possible terms.[15] My own works, including some included in this volume, but more frequently those that have appeared in Indonesian translation, are sometimes cited in this discourse.[16] This does not, however, mean that relationships between *agama* and *kebudayaan* have reached a point of stable equilibrium. The lines of conflict have shifted because of the emergence of neo-Wahhabi Islamist groups supported by the Saudi state and private foundations in Saudi Arabia and elsewhere in the Middle East who seek to replace even the most Islamic forms of Javanese culture with *what they consider to be* the *sunnah* or social practice of the Prophet Muhammad and his close companions. They see themselves as proponents of "pure" Islam. Many other Javanese call them Arab, Saudi or Wahhabi "colonialists" bent on destroying *kebudayaan local* (local culture).

The Javanese and larger Indonesian discourse about *agama* and *kebudayaan* is also of more general methodological and theoretical significance. It suggests that while the manner in which emic cultural categories are structured is of significance for Anthropologists, and especially for Cognitive Anthropologists, who are concerned with the logic of conceptual categories, it may be of less importance for Religious Studies scholars. Indeed, while in the study of religion it is essential to take account of these categorizations, it is equally important not to limit our analysis to what is locally defined as "religion". It is especially important given the inherent tendency of religions to segment. To accept what one sectarian or political group claims about others and the category religion is a fatal analytic error. Throughout this volume it is argued that this is what led Clifford Geertz and others to seriously misunderstand and misrepresent Javanese Islam – accepting the definition of "Islam" proposed by neo-fundamentalists as an analytic category. This is

---

[15] *Panjimas*, vol. 1, no. 12, May 2007.

[16] Throughout the issue of *Pajimas* cited above and particularly in the editor's introduction to most recent edition of the Indonesian translation of *Islam in Java* (*Islam Jawa*, Yogyakarta: LKiS, 2006) in which the book is compared with Edward Said's *Orientalism* for exposing the anti-Islamic biases of Anglo-Dutch Orientalism and American Anthropology. In Indonesia the book is frequently read as inclusivist Islamic theology. While this was not my intent when I wrote it, that is what it has become.

equally important in the study of religion in contemporary Indonesia because for slightly more than three decades *agama* was a central component of the ideological structure of an authoritarian state. Every Indonesian was required to be a member of an *agama* which was defined as a social group having:

- An all encompassing way of life governed by fixed statutes
- Belief in the oneness or unity of God
- A Holy Book
- A Prophet to whom knowledge of the above was revealed

The officially sanctioned *agama* were Islam, Protestant Christianity, Roman Catholic Christianity, Hinduism and Buddhism. Hinduism and Buddhism were reimagined in ways that brought them into correspondence with these criteria and made them into monotheisms.[17] Some indigenous religions were redefined as variants of Hinduism, which became something of a residual category. This was very clearly an Islamic understanding of what "religion," in the generic sense of the term, is. It suggests that while Indonesia is not an "Islamic" state, that it is a religious state based on Islamic concepts which others disregard at their peril. This is clearly a hegemonic theological discourse. Hidayah shows that various formulations of this definition have been used to distinguish between "genuine" religion that supports and is entitled to support from the state and "irrational superstition" the continued existence of which impedes "modernization". She puts it this way: "any religious belief that contravenes the State's definition of "*agama*" is considered per se superstition – *and therefore, necessarily, irrational and illegal*".[18] Religion that is not religion is not only irrational, it has been defined in practice, though not at law as dangerous and evil. Much of what Anthropologists and other scholars of religion would define as religion, but falls outside the official Indonesian definition, is defined as what is, in Javanese, called *gawat* – powerful, dangerous and at least potentially evil. This places Indonesians whose beliefs and practices fall into this category is precarious positions and even more so because not having a "religion" was among the characteristic of the most feared and despised political enemy of the state – "Godless Communism". It also enabled the state to define Communists and those accused on being Communists as being immoral, dangerous and evil.

Stanley has shown that in the wake of the abortive "Communist coupe" of 1965 the Indonesian military depicted party members and especially women who were members of the leftist *Gerakan Wanita Indonesia* (Indonesian Women's

---

[17]Prior to the consolidation of the New Order regime in the early 1970s the list of "religions" was more open. Confucianism was originally included, but was dropped in 1978 because the category "Chinese" was associated with "Communism". For a discussion of debates concerning the extent and boundaries of the category *agama* see: S. Hidayah, *Religion in the Proper Sense of the Word: The Discourse of Agama in Indonesia*, unpublished MA thesis, Center for Religious and Cross-Cultural Studies, Gadjah Mada University, 2007, pp. 58–59.

[18]Ibid., p. 7.

Organization) as murderous, sexually depraved evil spirits.[19] This made killing them not only politically expedient, morally imperative. By a strange and perverse twist of fate efforts to define *agama* provided a religious mandate for state terrorism on a massive scale.

Yogyakarta nationalism is *not* ethno-nationalism in anything like the conventional sense of the term. Yogyanese are a small fraction of the total Javanese population and the Sultanate occupies a small part of the territory inhabited by Javanese. And yet, many Yogyanese consider themselves to be fundamentally different from other Javanese, almost as much as they are from other Indonesians simply because they are subjects (*kuwala*) of the Yogyakarta *Kraton*. Yogya nationalism is not an attempt to carve an ethnic enclave out of an existing state nor is it an attempt to redefine the state in terms of a uniquely local ethno-religious identity or to subordinate others.[20] It is rather an insistence that a state far older than Indonesia, the Sultanate of Ngayogyakarta Hadiningrat, is the primary locus of authority and collective identity for its subjects-citizens. Very few people think that Yogyakarta ever will be or should be independent. A substantial number of people think of Yogyakarta as a nation within a nation. For many in Yogyakarta democracy means the right of subject-citizens to have their Sultan as their governor. Yogya is surely one of the few places where given the opportunity to vote for a chief executive, the legislature *voted not to vote*.[21] The people of Yogya cherish their newfound democracy. Many also cherish their Sultan and the concept of sacral kingship. This

---

[19] Stanley, *"Penggambaran Gerwani sebagai Kumpulan Pembunnuh dan Setan (Fitnah dan Fakta Penghancuran Organisasi Perempuan Terkemuka)"*. in, *Sejarah. Pemikiran, Rekonstrucksi, Persepsi,* no. 9, pp. 23–32, n.d.

[20] On ethno-religious nationalisms see, P. Brass, *Ethnicity and Nationalism: Theory and Comparison,* Sage Publications: New Delhi, 1991; W. Connor, *Ethnonationalism and the Quest for Understanding,* Princeton: Princeton University Press, 1994 and J.L. Comaroff, "Ethnicity, Nationalism and the Politics of Difference in an Age of Revolution," L. Danforth, *The Macedonian Conflict: Ethnic Nationalism in a Transnational World,* Princeton: Princeton University Press, 1995 and S. Tambiah, "The Nation State in Crisis and the Rise of Ethno-Nationalism," In: E. Wilmsen and P. McAllister (eds.), *The Politics of Difference,* Chicago: The University of Chicago Press, 1996, pp. 144–162 and 124–143. Unfortunately, in most of the literature on these hybrid nationalisms, the concepts of religion and ethnicity are conflated. Yogyakarta nationalism is far more religious than it is ethnic. In terms of the local discourse about *kebudayaan* (culture) and *agama* (religion), it is as much, if not more, cultural than religious because the term *agama* refers to transnational and trans-cultural religious traditions such as Islam and Christianity. In October of 2008, in the midst of a national level debate about the political future of the Sultanate one observer of the political scene commented: "There is no other place in Indonesia where traditional culture (*kebudayaan*) is so politically important as it is here. In Yogya *kebudayaan* is almost like what *agama* is in other places".

[21] See Chapter 7. There are, of course, others who reject the idea of Yogyakarta nationalism and consider is to a relic of the "feudal" past. These views are most common in new, middle class areas, especially Seleman in the northern part of the city where there are many universities and colleges. The area is home to many who are not Yogyakarta natives and do not have strong attachments to its distinctive culture and history. It is sometimes said that there is a *perang dingin* (cold war) between the *kraton* and Seleman. It is also said that Seleman is Indonesia and the older parts of Yogyakarta are Java.

seeming paradox runs through every chapter of this volume, but is most apparent in the concluding chapter which I have, in all seriousness, called "The Kraton Revolution: Religion, Culture, Regime Change and Democracy in Yogyakarta". If anything, the national level democratic transition of 1998, increased in intensity of royalist nationalism in Yogyakarta.[22]

In this chapter I have three basic purposes. The first is to provide readers for whom Yogyakarta, Java and/or Indonesia are *terra incognito* with cultural, religious and historical positioning systems to locate these cultural subsystems within the larger Javanese, Indonesian and Islamic cultural and trans-cultural landscapes. The second is to locate my readings of Javanese religion and culture in scholarly discourse concerning Java, Indonesia and Islam. The third is locate this analysis within contemporary theoretical discourse concerning the study of religion in general and more specifically that concerned with local, culturally specific, variants of trans-cultural religions. I apologize in advance to specialist readers who may find these brief treatments of complex subjects simplistic. To such critics I can say only that the global community of Java specialists is extremely small and that such an exercise is essential if accounts of this rich and multifaceted civilization are to contribute to the larger academic discourse concerning religion, power, history and colonialism. This chapter is not intended as a comprehensive treatment of any of these topics. Rather, it is a *bricolage* of history and theory that will hopefully bring some order to the complexities of nationality, religion and culture in Yogyakarta described in the chapters that follow.

Historical and Political Contexts: Java, Yogyakarta, and Indonesia

The aspects of religion and culture in Yogyakarta described in this volume are located at the intersection of Indonesia and Java understood as both conceptual categories and geographic territories. Among the salient features of Javanese and Indonesian political history that figure significantly in these essays are the rivalry between Yogyakarta and the neighboring city of Surakarta which dates to the Dutch colonial era, Yogyakarta's unique political position as a kingdom within the Republic of Indonesia, its history as the "Mother City" (*Ibu Kota*) of the Indonesian Revolution and what are understood by Indonesians as distinctions among the three major eras of their common history: the *Order Lama* (Old Order) of the country's first president Soekarno (1945–1966), the *Order Baru* (New Order) of the second president Suharto (1966–1998) and the and the *Order Reformasi* (Reformation

---

[22]In a certain sense Yogyakarta nationalism resembles Thai nationalism where the king is highly revered by the masses of the people. But because Yogyakarta is far smaller than Thailand the Sultan is in far more frequent contact with his subjects than the king. He is also far more actively involved in day to day governance.

Order 1998- present) in which there have been four presidents in rapid succession following the end of more than 30 year of authoritarian rule.[23]

Javanese civilization has a long and complex history. It has rich literary and artistic traditions that have assimilated elements of many trans-cultural religions: Hinduism, Buddhism, Islam and most recently Christianity.[24] While the overwhelming majority of Javanese are Muslims, there are significant Protestant and Roman Catholic communities and small numbers Hindus and Buddhists.[25] There have been many Javanese states and empires some of which brought other ethnic groups and islands under their dominion. Yogyakarta, or more properly Ngayogyakarta Hadiningrat, is a Sultanate of approximately 3,200 km^2 and slightly more than 3 million people in south central Java.[26]

Yogyakarta is one of two royal cities in south central Java. It was founded in 1755 in accordance with the terms of the treaty of Giyanti that divided the kingdom of Mataram between rival claimants to the throne. The treaty was brokered by the Dutch East India Company which, at the time, could influence, but not yet control Javanese politics. The other is Surakarta. Until the time of the Java War

---

[23] The democratic transition of 1998 is discussed in Chapter 7.

[24] For introductions to Old Javanese Hindu and Buddhist civilization see: see R. Jordaan (ed.), *In Praise of Prambanan. Dutch Essays on the Loro Jonggrang Temple Complex*, Leiden, KITLV, 1996; N. Krom, *Hindoe-Javansche Gescheidenis*, 's-Gravenhage: Nijoff, 1931; W. Stutterheim, *Rama-legenden und Rama-reliefs in Indonesien*, Munchen: Georg Muller, 1925; T. Pigeaud, *Java in the Fourteenth century*, The Hague: Martinus Nijhoff, 1960 and P. Zoetmulder, *Kalawangan. A Survey of Old Javanese Literature*, The Hague: Martinus Nijoff, 1974.

[25] On Christianity in Indonesia see P. Van Akkeren, *Sri and Christ; a Study of the Indigenous Church in East Java*, London: Trinity Press, 1970; L. Aragon, *Fields of the Lord: Animism, Christian Minorities and State Development in Indonesia*. Honolulu: University of Hawaii Press, 2000 and R. Kipp, "Conversion by Affiliation: the History of the Karo Batak Protestant Church," *American Ethnologist* vol. 22 no. 4, pp. 868–882, 1995. On Hinduism see: R. Hefner, "Ritual and Cultural Reproduction in Non-Islamic Java," *American Ethnologist* vol. 10 no.4, pp. 665–683, 1983 and *Hindu Javanese: Tengger Tradition and Islam*, Princeton: Princeton University Press, 1985 and M. Ramstedt, *Hinduism in Modern Indonesia*. New York: Routledge Curzon 2004 During the New Order "Buddhism" was a politically acceptable label for traditional Chinese Folk Religion, which includes elements of Mahayana Buddhism, Daoism, Confucianism and local forms of ancestor veneration. Today there are small Mahayana and Theravada Buddhist communities. Almost all Mahayana Buddhists are ethnic Chinese. The Theravada community includes ethnic Chinese and some Javanese converts. Non Muslim religions expanded rapidly during the New Order as former "Communists" "ran to religion" in hopes of escaping persecution and who, because of the role that Muslim organizations played in the mass killings of 1965 and 1966, found continuing to refer to themselves as "Muslim" unpalatable. Some other Javanese have converted to Theravada Buddhism for more purely religious reasons and have undertaken serious study of Theravada teachings and Pali, the language of the Theravada scriptures, in Thailand and Burma. There is now a Theravada monastery in Mendut near the ancient Mahayana Buddhist monument Borobudur. I would like to thank Yulianti and Willis Rengganiasih Ekowati Endah, both of whom are Javanese Theravada Buddhists and Buddhist scholars at the Center for Religious and Cross-cultural Studies at Gadjah Mada University in Yogyakarta, for informing me of these developments.

[26] On the founding and early history of Yogyakarta see M. Ricklefs, *Jogjakarta under Sultan Mangkubumi, 1749–1792: A History of the Division of Java*, London: Oxford University Press, 1974.

(1825), Yogyakarta was a center of resistance to Dutch colonial rule.[27] However, as Dutch colonial power grew, it became more and more of a theater state in which ritual replaced military and economic power as the foundation of royal prestige and authority. Of the many indigenous states included within the Netherlands Indies at the beginning of the Second World War, Yogyakarta is the only one to have survived the transition to Indonesian independence.[28] In Yogyakarta the Sultan remains a prominent religious and political figure. Yogyakarta nationalism is a significant factor in the politics of the Sultanate. As one long time friend and research partner put it during the transition from authoritarian to democratic rule in the late 1990s: "We are all in favor of democracy and we have to remember that this is still a kingdom".[29] Yogya nationalism transcends religion. Even Christians and many members of the modernist Islamic organization Muhammadiyah, which has strong fundamentalist tendencies, are devoted subjects.[30] So much so that *Muhammadiyah* members from other parts of Indonesia often say things like: "*Muhammadiyah* can never really be Muhammadiyah until it stops being part of Yogyakarta".

The rivalry between the two courts is deeply felt and at times bitter. Both, for example, claim that theirs are the genuine spiritually powerful heirlooms (*pusaka*) and that those of the other court are less powerful, if not out right forgeries. This rivalry has been simultaneously a research topic and has limited the locus of my research for the entire time that I have been traveling to Java. It was not, and still is not, possible to conduct intensive research in both courts. This was apparent from the beginning of my time in Java and as my works have appeared in

---

[27] On the Java War see P. Carey, *Babad Dipanagara: an account of the outbreak of the Java War (1825–30): the Surakarta court version of the Babad Dipanagara*, Kuala Lumpur: Royal Asiatic Society of Great Britain and Ireland, Malaysian Branch, 1991.

[28] It is difficult to say exactly how many "Native States" there were in the Netherlands Indies because of the imprecise use of the term *kerajan* (kingdom) in colonial discourse. In some parts of Ambon and other areas in what is now Eastern Indonesia every village was referred to as a kingdom (*kerajaan*) and every village chief as a king (*raja*).

[29] On monarchist tendencies in contemporary Yogyakarta see Chapter 7.

[30] With more than 30 million members Muhammadiyah is Indonesia's, and the worlds, largest Muslim modernist organization. It also has branches in Singapore and Malaysia. Its teachings build on those of the early twentieth century Egyptian reformers Muhammad Abduh and Rashyid Riddah, On developments in Middle Eastern Muslim thought that influenced the development of Muhammadiyah and other modernist movements in Southeast Asia see A. Hourani, *Arabic Thought in the Liberal Age, 1798–1939,* Cambridge: Cambridge University Press, 1983. Muhammadiyah was founded by Kyai Achmad Dhalan, an official of the Grand Mosque of Yogyakarta, which is located within the palace walls, in 1912. On the history and teachings of Muhammadiyah see: Alfian, *Muhammadiyah. The Political Behavior of a Muslim Modernist Organization under Dutch Colonialism,* Yogyakarta: Gadjah Mada University Press, 1989, M. Nakamura, 1983. *The Crescent Arises over the Banyan Tree: A Study of the Muhammadiyah Movement in a Central Javanese Town.* Yogyakarta, Gadjah Mada University Press, 1978. D. Noer, *The Modernist Muslim Movement in Indonesia, 1900–1942* Kuala Lumpur: Oxford University Press, 1973 and J. Peacock, *Muslim Puritans: Reformist Psychology in Southeast Asian Islam*, Berkeley: University of California Press, 1978. The seeming contradiction between Muhammadiyah's reformist theological orientation and acceptance of many aspects of Javanese culture is explored in Chapters 5 and 6.

Indonesian translation I have become increasingly associated with Yogyakarta –
to the point that in some circles I am known as the *"bule dari Yogya"* (the foreigner from Yogyakarta). This opens many doors in Yogya and closes some in
Solo. It is also simply impossible to be at the same ritual in a different city at the
same time.

It is somewhat ironic, though entirely understandable, that Yogyakarta was able
to establish its special status as a kingdom within a republic and to preserve the
charisma of the throne precisely because of its contributions, and particularly those
of Sultan Hamengkubuwana IX, to Indonesian independence and nationhood.[31]
Despite clear legal foundations for its internal autonomy, the power of the Sultanate
waned as that of the Indonesian central authority grew in the post-colonial era,
and especially during the New Order.[32] The Sultan was an important figure in
Indonesian national politics, but less of one in his own realm. Suharto ruled all of
Indonesia with an iron hand. As his authority grew, that of all regional and provincial governments decline proportionately. When I first visited Yogyakarta in the late
1970s the Sultan was revered but seemingly powerless even though he was Vice
President of Indonesia. The *kraton* (palace) was among the city's primary attractions for Indonesian as well as foreign "tourists".[33] Few would have guessed that at
the end of the New Order the spirit of resistance – so evident in the early years of
the Sultanate and those of the Indonesian independence struggle – would re-emerge,
or that the *kraton* would once again become the stage on which high political drama
was played out. Three decades later, it is clear that the spirits of resistance and that
of Yogyakarta nationalism never really died. They took different forms in the colonial era and in that of the New Order of the Indonesian Republic. It is argued in
Chapter 4 that during the colonial period state ceremonies were used as mode of
symbolic resistance of colonial hegemony.

Yogyakarta holds a special place in the mystical world of Indonesian political culture and history. It was the cradle of Indonesian nationalism. Many
of the early nationalist and modernist movements that have shaped Indonesian
thought and history, including the modernist Islamic *Muhammadiyah* and the cultural nationalist *Taman Siswa*, were founded within the walls of the Yogyakarta
kraton.[34] Yogyakarta was also known as the "Mother City" of the revolution.
The revolution was fought, very nearly lost and ultimately won, not from Jakarta,

---

[31] On Yogyakarta and Surakarta during the Indonesian Revolution see B. Anderson, *Java in a Time
of Revolution: Occupation and Resistance 1944–1946*, Ithaca: Cornell University Press, 1972. On
the political transformation of Yogyakarta during this period see, S. Soemardjan, *Social Changes
in Yogyakarta*, Ithaca: Cornell University Press, 1962.

[32] See Chapter 7.

[33] For Indonesians visiting the *kraton*, and other historic or holy places in the Sultanate and
elsewhere in Java, the line between tourism and pilgrimage is very fine.

[34] Taman Siswa (The Garden for Students) is a cultural nationalist movement. It promotes traditional Javanese culture, especially the performing arts. It also established a network of schools,
which now include universities. See K. Tsuchiya, *Democracy and Leadership. The Rise of the
Taman Siswa Movement in Indonesia* Honolulu: University of Hawaii Press, 1987.

which was rapidly reoccupied by the Dutch, but from Yogyakarta.[35] It is also known as the "City of Struggle" (*Kota Perjuangan*) – a concept that is strongly associated with the Islamic concept of *jihad* (struggle in the cause of God). Ironically Sultan Hamengkubuwana IX and not President Soekarno represented Indonesia at ceremonies marking the formal transfer of sovereignty from the Netherlands.

In Yogyakarta it is widely believed that the city, and more specifically the *kraton*, is the mystical center of the Indonesia. A study of the constitutional history of the Sultanate by K.P.H. Soedirman Poerwokoesoemo provides a telling example of the transformation of traditional concepts of sacred geography in modern Indonesia.[36] Poerwokoesoemo was a Dutch educated lawyer who was mayor of Yogyakarta from 1946 to 1967. He was also a high ranking *kraton* official. The purpose of his history of Yogyakarta is to explain the position of the Sultanate in the Indonesian Republic. The greater part of his work consists of a painstaking account of the legal foundations of the Sultanate's status as a "special region" within the Indonesian Republic. It draws heavily on Dutch as well as Indonesian sources. One would not necessarily know that the author was Javanese or that the work could be read as a religious text until nearly the end of the book. The authorial voice of the final chapter shifts from that of Soedarisman Poerwokoesoemo, legal scholar, to that of Kangeng Pangeran Hario Poerwokoesoemo, Yogyakarta prince and Javanese mystic. Here he speaks of Yogyakarta as the sacred center and *axis mundi* of Indonesia, and of the Indonesian revolution as the continuation and culmination of the struggle between Sultan Agung (reigned 1613–1645) and the Dutch East India Company. He describes Yogyakarta as the "Land of Mataram" and the cradle of Indonesian civilization.[37] He associates the ancient Buddhist and Hindu monuments Borobudur and Prambanan with the past glory of the sacred territory, and the modernist organizations Muhammadiyah and Taman Siswa as evidence of its continued glory. I had the privilege of discussing this theory of history with Pak Poerwo at considerable length in the late 1970s. He explained to me that the centrality of the Yogyakarta region in Indonesian history was in no sense accidental. He believed it to have been selected by God as the region from which new ideas, ranging from Hinduism and Buddhism to the modernism of *Muhammadiyah* and *Taman Siswa*, would flow into the embryo of the Indonesian nation.[38] In post New

---

[35] The Republican government fled advancing Dutch forces, retreating to Yogyakarta in January of 1946, less than 6 months after the August 17, 1945 declaration of independence. On the role Yogyakarta played in the Indonesian Revolution see Monfries, op. cit.

[36] S. Poerwokoesoemo, *Daerah Istimewa Yogyakarta*, Yogyakarta: Gajah Mada University Press, 1984,

[37] Mataram is the name of the kingdom prior to its division into Yogyakarta and Surakarta both of which claim to be its sole legitimate successor.

[38] A clearer example of what Mircea Eliade terms the "symbolism of the center" in which the structure of traditional states mirrors that of the cosmos, and that of their historical narratives cosmogonic mythology would be harder to imagine. See: Eliade, *The Myth of Eternal Return or Cosmos and History*, Princeton: Princeton University Press, 1954.

Order Indonesia there is an increasing concern with not only ethnic and religious tolerance but with pluralism and multi-culturalism. Because it home to a large number of universities, colleges and other educational institutions Yogyakarta has one of the most diverse populations in Indonesia and now prides itself on being a model for the rest of the nation.

In Surakarta the situation is very different. A the critical juncture in the revolutionary struggle when the Dutch recaptured central Java, Sultan Hamengkubuwana IX locked himself in the *kraton* and informed the Dutch that the only thing he had to discuss with them was when and how they were going to leave. Pakubuwana XII of Surakarta greeted them with open arms and, according to sources in Yogyakarta that may not be entirely reliable, gave them expensive presents. Today many in Surakarta consider the court to be an irrelevant anachronism – a view shared even by some members of the royal family. Others view it as a repository of Javanese culture that should be preserved, despite its political irrelevance. One sign of its decline is that the Surakarta court now bestows titles on those who provide it with financial and other forms of support. Even non Javanese, and non Indonesians, have received such honors. It was also heavily dependent on patronage from the presidential family throughout the New Order. Many consider the close relationships between the Surakarta court and the Suharto family to have been nothing short of shameful.[39]

Javanese and Indonesian: Language, Nationality and Identity

Indonesia and Java are overlapping social, linguistic, cultural, conceptual and religious as well as geographic spaces and political entities. Indonesia has acquired, willingly or unwillingly, much from Java. To be Javanese is to be Indonesian but the reverse is clearly not the case. Anderson observes the emergence of "Indonesia" as an idea and Indonesian as a national langue were significantly influenced by Javanese cultural, linguistic and religious concepts.[40] Javanese culture occupies a position of "first among equals," or hegemony depending on one's perspective, in the larger Indonesian society because the Javanese are the largest ethnic community and have been politically dominant since the beginning. But at the same time, Java has borrowed much from Indonesia, perhaps most importantly, the idea if not the reality, of social equality.

Language and language use offer important insights into the imbrication of "Javaneseness," "Yogyaness" and "Indonesianess" and of the ways in which Indonesia is a hybridity shaped by local cultures, nationalism and colonialism. Faruk describes Indonesian as an "imperialist language".[41] He argues that after Dutch

---

[39] In Yogyakarta at least, this is not a new development. In the late 1970s there were many in Yogyakarta ho found their neighbor's near complete dependence on the New Order deeply disturbing.

[40] B. Anderson, "The Languages of Indonesian Politics", *Indonesia* vol. 1:1, pp. 89–116, 1966.

[41] Faruk, *Belenggu Paasca-Kolonial. Hegemoni dan Resistensi dalam Sastra Indonesia*, Yogyakarta, Pustaka Pelajar, p. 8.

merchants learned that Malay was the *lingua franca* of the region, scholars in their employ set themselves to the tasks of mastering, transforming and standardizing it. As the economic and political power of the Dutch East India Company grew, so did the hegemonic character of the emerging "Indonesian" language because the Dutch insisted that it be their primary means of communication with indigenous subject communities.[42] While Dutch scholars were fluent in local languages, particularly Javanese, the only Asian language that most colonial officials understood was Malay. Standardizing and encouraging the use of Malay was, therefore, among the means through which colonial hegemony was established and strengthened. It was a foreign tongue for both the Dutch and indigenous peoples and the bridge language in which the discourse of colonialism was conducted.[43] Standard Malay and modern Indonesian were not derived entirely from dialects spoken in commercial districts. In their efforts to standardize the language Dutch philologists relied heavily on the literary Malay of the Riau and Johor kingdoms in territories that are now included in both Malaysia and Indonesia. To this day Malay speakers in Jambi in northern Sumatra refer to their native tongue as the "real Indonesian language" and consider others dialects to be somewhat sub-standard. One result of colonial language policy was that "High Malay" grew into standard Indonesian. An important difference between Malay and Javanese is that the former is less hierarchically structured. While Malay/Indonesian makes use of honorifics it does not have the elaborate series of speech registers that Javanese does.[44] For this reason it is often described as a "democratic" or "egalitarian" language.

The use of a non-native language as the language of colonialism was of particular importance in Java, owing to the complex ways in which social and political hierarchy are encoded and expressed in Javanese. Javanese has a complex system

---

[42] On the history and development of Indonesian see, J. Snedden, *The Indonesian Language: Its History and Role in Modern Society*, Sydney: University of New South Wales Press, p. 19

[43] There were, and still are, numerous distinct dialects of Malay/Indonesian some of which are barely mutually intelligible. "Standard Indonesian" is the language of politics, education commerce and the media, but is not well understood in many of the more remote regions of the country. It is understood, but not usually spoken in others, including Kudus in east Java. Because it was the language of colonialism in a multi-ethnic and multi-linguistic colonial state Malay/Indonesian acquired large numbers of words and phrases from regional languages, as well as from Dutch, Portuguese, Chinese and Arabic. In the post colonial era English has replaced Dutch as the source of European borrowings. In the past thirty years the number of Arabic words in common use has increased substantially.

[44] The dialect of Javanese spoken in Yogyakarta and Surakarta, and which has come to be considered "standard" Javanese in Indonesia and the global academic community is especially hierarchical. Dialects spoken in areas that were not subject to the control of Mataram and its successor states are decidedly less hierarchical. This indicates that the linguistic hierarchies of the Javanese Muslim courts were created as elements of *kraton* centered hegemonic discourse. Javanese who do not speak the court centered dialects are often reluctant to speak Javanese with those for whom this dialect is a native tongue for fear of making mistakes and being taken as "rustics". I would like to thank Inayah Rohmaniyah and Sita Hidayah, both of whom are native speakers of the decidedly less hierarchical Banyumas dialect, for insisting on the cultural and political salience of this linguistic distinction.

of speech registers and perhaps even more complex, and often subjective, system of rules and habits governing the ways in which these are used in various social contexts.[45] There are three basic registers, *ngoko,* spoken with children, social inferiors and equals in some contexts and most animals, *kromo* used in polite conversation and with superiors and *kromo ingill* spoken to superiors, including some animals, where status differences are extreme. There are still higher levels that are used only to address members of the royal family with which few outside *Kraton* circles are familiar. Differences in age, gender, social status and educational attainment and the social context is which a conversation is conducted influence the selection of the speech level appropriate for both self and other. To speak Javanese is to speak in hierarchy as well as in language. Linguistic considerations were, therefore, important elements of colonial policy. Javanese was singularly inappropriate for colonial discourse, particularly in the systems of indirect rule that were a basic element of Dutch colonial strategy. To speak to native elites in *ngoko,* the level appropriate level with which to address inferiors would have been extremely insulting and would have undermined their authority with local populations on which Dutch rule depended. To speak to them in *kromo* or even more so in *kromo ingill,* the levels in which elite status in Javanese culture mandates, would have undermined colonial authority. To have spoken Dutch would have been to accept them as equals.[46] This left Malay/Indonesian as the only viable alternative through which to maintain the legitimating fiction and irresolvable contradiction of local authority and colonial power.

Faruk has also noted that during the colonial era Indonesian was simultaneously a language of compliance and a language of resistance.[47] To the extent that is was the medium through which colonial authority was conveyed and enforced it was a language of domination, for the Dutch, and of acquiescence for the native peoples of the Netherlands Indies. By supplanting local languages in public and particularly political discourse it defined speakers and readers as colonial subjects. At the same time, in the context of Indonesian nationalism, it was, to the extent that it transcended ethnic and linguistic identities, a language of resistance. Because it was, and is, almost no one's native language, and at the same time was not the internal language of colonialism, it was an ideal venue for redefining or in Anderson's terms "reimagining" the Netherlands Indies as Indonesia in linguistic and cultural as well as political, economic and administrative ways.

Soemardjan observes that in the final days of colonialism, when many of the Yogyakarta elite spoke Dutch with native or near native fluency and more Dutch people at least understood Javanese, the situation was somewhat different, but

---

[45] See J. Errington, *Language and Social Change in Java: Linguistic Reflexes of Modernization in a Traditional Royal Polity,* Athens, Ohio: Ohio University Center for International Studies, 1985.

[46] Very few colonial subjects spoke Dutch. After the establishment of independence English rapidly became the international language of choice. For a time teaching Dutch, even to ones children, was criminal. Here the contrast between Indonesia and former British colonies in South and Southeast Asia where English in the *defacto Lingua Franca* is striking. It has had lasting consequences for Indonesia because of the emergence of English as the global *Lingua Franca* in the post World War Two era.

[47] Op. cit., p. 69

equally complex but equally stratified.[48] While formal communication with the Sultan was conducted in Javanese, most other government documents were written in "Malay" (as it was then known). To have referred to the language as "Indonesian" would have been to have recognized and legitimized nationalist aspirations which, of course, the Dutch were not prepared to do. Communication among Javanese and Dutch civil servants was conducted in either Malay or Dutch, because many Javanese elites spoke Dutch with greater fluency than Dutch spoke Malay. Some Dutch people understood, but *never* used *kromo ingill* even in contexts where, were it not for the status differences inherent in colonial society is would have been appropriate. At the same time many required subordinates and household servants to address them in *kromo ingill* and to observe other forms of deference including keeping their heads at a lower level than their "masters" at all times.

This complex hierarchy changed with the Japanese occupation because Malay was the only means through which Javanese and the new colonialists could communicate. With the coming of the Indonesian Revolution, all official business, including communication with the Sultan began to be conducted in Indonesian, though among themselves Javanese continued to speak their native language even in government offices.

The establishment of Indonesian as a national language and the establishment of mass education are among the nation's most important accomplishments. Today Indonesian is the primarily language of education, government, mass communications, political, intellectual and increasingly religious discourse. Language policy and practice have been and remain important parts of the work of nation building. For the last 30 years signs posted outside the Provincial Governor's office in Yogyakarta have encouraged people to use "*Bahasa Indonesia yang baik dan benar*" (Good and Correct Indonesian) as their "primary means of communication".[49] Almost all the street signs are in Indonesian though many now make considerable use of English.[50] Public discourse is almost entirely in Indonesian.[51] Today,

---

[48]S. Soemardjan, *Purubahan Sosial do Jogyakarta*, Jakarta: Kommunitas Bambu, 2009, pp. 150–157. Translation of *Social Change in Yogyakarta*, Ithaca: Cornell University Press, 1962. My own conversations with members of the Javanese elite in the late 1970s were very similar.

[49]Policies aimed at the establishment of linguistic uniformity are nearly universal aspects of nationalist projects. France provides a striking example. In his classic, *Peasants into Frenchmen, The Modernization of France. 1870–1914*, Stanford: Stanford University Press, 1976, pp. 303–339, E. Weber shows that schools played a central role is almost eliminating distinctive local languages and establish the Parisian dialect as the national language. The United Stated employed similar policies to effectively eliminate German, Polish, Italian and other non-English European languages after the First World War. China and Singapore have employed similar strategies in attempts to establish Mandarin Chinese as a national language.

[50]In older sections of Yogyakarta street signs are also in Javanese, in Javanese script, even though few can now read it. They are emblematic of the "Javaneseness" of these parts of the city. Their function is more cultural than informational.

[51]This trend has been somewhat reversed as a consequence of the Post-New Order policy of decentralization. Yogya TV, which was founded in 2004, broadcasts a significant portion of its programs, ranging from local, national and international news to comedies and variety shows, in Javanese. It is argued in Chapter 7 that it is also a media vehicle for resurgent Yogyakarta Nationalism and that it is entirely appropriate to refer to it as Yogyakarta Kraton TV. The fact that many non-Javanese residents of Yogyakarta find Yogya TV very boring supports this view.

in government and university settings, Indonesian is the dominant language, even when Javanese are speaking with other Javanese. There are at least three reasons for this. The first is simply that Indonesian is "official". the second is that many consider it to be difficult, if not impossible, to determine who should speak to who in what level. Relationships based on notions of equality are much easier to conduct in Indonesian.

Javanese has in this sense been privatized, but for most, remains the language in which they think and dream. It is less and less of a public language. Little is now written and very few people, despite lessons in school, can read or write in Javanese script. High Javanese is increasingly an esoteric mode of communication, thought by many to contain the wisdom of the past accessible only to those with the skills and increasingly the spiritual attainment required. Low Javanese remains the language of household and family communication. To a certain extent Javanese has become Indonesianized in that it has become less hierarchical. There is a consensus among older people that the young lack the skills necessary to move effortlessly through its hierarchies. This was the case in the late 1970s when I was first in Yogyakarta. Such sentiments are even more pronounced today. Many younger people agree and some find the scope of these hierarchies absurd. When I was discussing these issues, in English, with a woman in her mid thirties in July of 2007 she said: "What's the point? Why do I need to know how to say "baby water buffalo" in *kromo ingill?*" When I replied that in the Surakarta kraton there is a family of sacred albino water buffalo for who such usage would be appropriate, she replied: "Those *kraton* people, they are just living in the past". There are also increasing numbers of young people who prefer to speak Indonesian, even with their parents and grandparents. This is especially true of Javanese who were raised outside of Java and those of mixed ethnic backgrounds. A considerable number now think of themselves as "Indonesian" rather than Javanese. Married couples who speak different dialects of Javanese often speak to each other, and their children in Indonesian. The result is a growing number of ethnic Javanese whose "native" language is Indonesian.

In a subtle way my friend was right. "Java" is increasingly linked to the past, the ancestors and to Javanese traditional performing arts and *kraton* culture. "Indonesia" on the other hand is associated with the nationalism, modernity and public discourse. Nearly 30 years ago an elderly palace official told me that: "Java is the past, Indonesia is the future and today we are someplace in-between". We are much closer to Indonesia today than we were in the 1970s. And yet, Java and Indonesia are intertwined in complex ways. Today Yogyakarta is an array of hybridities in which pre-colonial, colonial and post colonial Java and Indonesia all figure significantly. Nowhere are these hybrid tendencies clearer than in the ways in which the Yogyakarta *Kraton* has been transformed since I first visited it. As is explained in Chapter 4, it remains the ceremonial center of the Javanese state but it is also an Indonesian and trans-national tourist destination. In a clear nod towards modern "Indonesianess" one of the long disused kitchens has been transformed into a modern coffee shop and restaurant, and a branch of a leading Jakarta department store. The old Dutch Fort Vredeburg, located just outside the *kraton* walls, was used by the Indonesian armed forces during the revolutionary and early Republican periods, between 1965 and 1971 it was used as a political prison where thousands of actual and suspected "Communists" were held following the "abortive coupe" of September 30, 1965. It was then abandoned and allowed to fall into ruins and in 1991 was restored to house a museum of the Indonesian Revolution. In ruins, it was a symbol of the humiliation of the Dutch at the hands of Republican revolutionary forces. Restored, and with the Indonesian flag flying at the gate, it is a triumphalist visual narrative of the revolutionary struggle. Today it is both a representative of the cosmogonic myth of Indonesian nationalism and a not very subtle symbolic statement that in the end Java and Indonesia triumphed over colonialism. The fact that former officer's quarters just to the east of the fort now house a center for Indonesian-Javanese performing arts center and a children's playground amplify this message. What was once Dutch political and military space is now Indonesian-Javanese recreational space. Today, there is nothing that recalls its role in the politicide of the mid 1960s.

Yogyakarta, the New Order and *Reformasi*

Much of he field work on which this volume is based was carried out during the second half of the "New Order". It is supplemented by additional research at the time of the democratic transition of 1997 and 1998 and in the years that have followed. The topics considered are extremely diverse, ranging from popular and imperial ritual, to architectural symbolism and from traditional healing to the fast of Ramadan. However, they all are concerned with systems of religious knowledge and praxis, that, while situated in Indonesian and trans-cultural Islamic contexts, are distinctively Javanese and in some instances Yogyanese. All of them concern, in some sense or another, the imbrication of religion, culture, power, nationalism and history. The modes of religious thought and praxis they describe are situated in post-colonial, and, in a sense, "post-Javanese" contexts. In every case the analysis presented presumes the agency of Javanese actors of all religious orientations and socio-political locations and the importance of Dutch colonialism and subsequently Indonesian nationalism and nation building in the development of religion in Yogyakarta in the last three decades of the twentieth century and the first decade of the twenty-first.[52]

---

[52] As Talad Asad has noted, some Anthropologists and Historians, to which one might add particularly those concerned with the societies and cultures of colonial and post-colonial South Asia, have found concepts of agency and resistance to be powerful analytic devises. Many have been very nearly obsessed with the desire to "give subordinate peoples what they think of as 'their own agency.'" T. Asad, *Formulations of the Secular. Christianity, Islam and Modernity*, Stanford: Stanford University Press, 2003, p. 216. I find this discourse to be well intentioned, but naïve, presumptuous and most of all elitist and even neo-colonialist. Human agency, in the sense of attempting to define the course of one's life, regardless of the contexts in which it is located is characteristic of human beings, no matter what their circumstances. While the "agency of the oppressed" can sometimes be "recovered" by scholars where it has been inadvertently or deliberately ignored in the representation of events, it is by no means the task of scholars to "give"

The New Order, and the terror with which is began and ended, are among the contexts within which the subjects of these ethnographic portraits are located and have shaped the ways in which Muslims and others in Yogyakarta understand and experience religion, nationality and culture. The New Order was a military dominated, managerial state focused on development and political stability. Despite the repressive, undemocratic character of the regime, its accomplishments in economic development and education were remarkable. While friends and relatives of the president and ranking officials made huge fortunes at the people's expense, it is also clear that ordinary Indonesians are much better off than they were in 1965. Changes in Yogyakarta over the three decades that I have known it make this abundantly clear. In the *kampung* where I first lived, and which I still visit regularly, people who once lived in bamboo houses now have brick houses. Streets that were dust during the dry season and mud during the rains, are now paved with concrete or asphalt. Motorcycles have replaced bicycles as the most common mode of transportation. Ox carts have almost entirely disappeared and horse carts now serve domestic and foreign tourists rather than those in need of basic transportation. There is now a substantial urban middle class and malls and supermarkets that cater to middle class tastes. Basic education is now almost universal. The system of government and private secular, Islamic and Christian colleges and universities has expanded enormously. These changes have influenced the ways in which religion in Yogyakarta has developed. So has the violence with which the New Order began, and which continued, albeit at much lower levels, throughout its rule. Economic development and social change expanded the opportunity space within which religion in Yogyakarta is located. Memories of terror and ongoing fear of its recurrence constrained the social and religious agency of many.

The New Order began and ended with horrific episodes of collective violence that appear to have orchestrated by elements of the military. In the wake of an abortive coupe in 1965 hundreds of thousands of members and supporters of the Communist party were murdered.[53] Other victims had tenuous, at most, links to the party and

---

people what is a simple fact of human existence. What the scientific study of religion, culture and history requires is that scholars endeavor to capture the multiple agencies present in any social situation. The concept of agency is often associated with that of resistance. This linkage betrays an ideological rather than analytic orientation as acquiescence to power is as much a behavioral manifestation of agency as is resistance. The contrast between the political strategies of the two Javanese courts of Yogyakarta and Surakarta in the early days of the Indonesian national revolution provides a cogent example. The Surakarta court *chose* acquiescence to Dutch power, in the expectation that imperialism would emerge triumphant and with the hope of regaining territory lost to Yogyakarta in the eighteenth century. The Yogyakarta court *chose* the path of resistance to the Dutch and acquiescence with Indonesian claims of sovereignty, describing itself as a kingdom within the Republic of Indonesia. Agency is readily apparent in both cases. Neither was a passive subject in the political and military struggles of the Indonesian nationalist revolution.

[53]Exactly who was responsible for the 1965 coupe remains the most controversial topic in modern Indonesian history. There is an extensive and controversial literal on the subject. Some scholars, particularly Anderson and McVey, maintain that it was an internal military feud, that the Communist Party (*Partai Komunis Indonesia*/PKI) was not directly involve, but that it was used as excuse for mass slaughter,. B. Anderson and R. McVey, A *Preliminary Analysis of the October 1*

were labeled "communist" to justify settling other "scores" in the most violent way possible. The violence was not limited to those who were, or who were accused of being communists. The "sins" of the mothers and fathers very literally vested unto the children, and subsequent descendants who were denied opportunities for public education and employment and other rights of citizenship for seven generations.[54] In central Java and Bali most of the killing was conducted by conservative factions of the Nationalist Party who opposed the communists for economic reasons. In east Java most of the killing was done by *Ansor* the youth wing of the traditionalist Islamic organization, and at that time political party, *Nahdlatul Ulama*. It was orchestrated by the organization's senior leadership. The military did nothing to stop the killings and often provided logistical support.[55]

Indonesians who can remember the slaughter often speak of headless and/or limbless corpses floating in streams and the stench of decaying, unburied bodies. This is a powerful symbolic statement to Muslims because of the requirement that corpses be ritually purified and buried quickly. The desecration of corpses robs them of their Muslim identities. It suggests that victims were apostates deserving of death. It also denied the families of the victims the ability to mourn in culturally and religiously appropriate ways and to perform pilgrimage to their graves before and after Ramadan. This is an important element of the local Islam practiced by most of the victims and their families. The killings were, in a perverse way, religious acts. Denying victims proper funerals was a ritual of negation. Many Javanese affirm this negation by avoiding sites associated with the killings in fear that victims have become dangerous ghosts. Some of the victim's families attempt to negate the negation by describing the dead as martyrs.

More than 40 years later Indonesians continue to struggle to come to terms with this unspeakable slaughter. As Herman observes "The ordinary response to atrocities is to banish them from consciousness".[56] The New Order did not encourage collective amnesia about the violence that accompanied its birth. Indeed, it constantly reminded Indonesians of its own mythologized version of it. The propaganda

---

1965 Coupe in Indonesia, Ithaca: Cornell University Southeast Asia Program, 1971. An English translation of the Indonesian government's account of the coup is *The September 30th Movement, the Attempted Coup by the Indonesian Communist Party: Its background, Actions and Eradication,* Jakarta: State Secretariat of the Republic of Indonesia, 1995. Hermawan Sulistyo provides a detailed account of the killings in East Java and the role of the conservative Muslim organization *Nahdlatul Ulama* in planning and carrying them out, H. Sulistyo, *The Forgotten Years: The Missing History of Indonesia's Mass Slaughter (Jobang-Kediri 1965–1966),* Unpublished Ph.D. Thesis, Arizona State University, 1997. On violence and the fall of the new order see Chapter 7 and K. Van Dijk, *A Country in Despair. Indonesia Between 1997 and 2000,* Leiden: KITLV, 2001.

[54] This is remarkably perverse but culturally significant because seven is the number of generations considered to be the limit of affinity in Javanese kinship reckoning.

[55] J. Bresnan, *Managing Indonesia. The Modern Political Economy.* New York Columbia University Press, 1993, pp. 7–28.

[56] Herman, Judith, *Trauma and Recovery: The aftermath of Violence from Domestic Abuse to Political Terror,* New York: Basic Books, 1997, p. 6.

film/documentary *Gestapu 30 SPKI* is a graphic depiction of the New Order interpretation of these events. It was shown annually on the anniversary of the coup on
state Television and on other occasions to school children. This misremembering has
had profound impacts on many whose friends, neighbors and relatives are portrayed,
almost literally, as archetypes of evil, inhuman monsters and enemies of the nation
and whose murderers are depicted as national heroes. Most have suffered this terror in silence, some with pent up rage and bitterness. Others suffer from "survivor's
guilt", asking why they should have lived or avoided the stigma of being labeled "X"
(PKI) on their national identity cards, while others did not. Tragically, some victims
even believe the lies of the New Order. This is denial at a national level. Herman has
also show that denial does not bring healing and that remembering and truth telling
are essential for the restoration of genuine social solidarity at the national level and
psychological healing for individual victims. The politics of post 1965 Indonesia
and the complicity of the military in the killings made truth telling impossible for
33 years. The process has now only begun. To carry it forward will require not only
telling the truth of about the killings, but also about the lies that were told about
them for more than a generation.

The New Order was as concerned with the management of ideology and religion
as it was with that of the economy.[57] Leftist, Islamic, Feminist, ethnic and religious
nationalisms and other opposition voices were silenced by death, imprisonment or
fear. For 32 years there were many questions that could not be asked, let alone
answered. Publicly at least the imagination of Indonesia was monopolized by the
forces of the New Order. Religious and secular intellectuals, journalists and other
writers engaged in a great deal of self censorship because they fully understood what
the consequences of more overt criticism of the regime and especially of the president and his family would be.[58] The imagination of Indonesia as a highly centralized
unitary, state dedicated to neo-liberal development policies and a carefully defined
understanding of religious tolerance and based on the national ideology *Panca Sila*
(Five Principles) could not be debated or questioned publicly. The five components
of *Panca Sila* are:

---

[57] On the centrality of management in New Order politics see Bresnan, op. cit., pp. 293–95.

[58] From the time I first visited Indonesia until the fall of the New Order harsh criticism of the regime
circulated in the form of rumors. One of the most extreme of these was that Suharto and his family were secretly Christian and were conspiring with Chinese Roman Catholics to "Christianize"
Indonesia Another than circulated widely after the death of Suharto's wife Siti Hartinah 1996 is
that people do not want to visit her grave because they could hear her crying – a sure sign that she
is already suffering the pains of Hell. The same is now said of Suharto. One friend told me that
he knew someone who had video-taped the grave site and that while he heard nothing at the time
when he played the tape back he could hear the former president screaming *Tolong! Tolong!* (Help!
Help!), which suggests that he too is suffering the pains of Hell. In 1997 freedom of speech and
the press came to Indonesia in ways that they never had before. Nowhere was this more apparent
than in accounts of the former president and his family. Much that had long been spoken in private
began to appear in print. Several of these works are discussed in Chapter 7. One of these is a vitri-
olic Islamist critique of his "sins". The others explain his rise and fall in the language of Javanese
Islamic mysticism.

- *Ketuhanan Maha Esa* – Devotion to the principle of divine oneness
- *Kemanusiaan yand adil dan berahad* – Human society which is just and characterized by mutual respect
- *Persatuan Indonesia* – The unity of Indonesia
- *Kerakyatan yang dipimpin oleh hikmat kebijaksanaan dalam bermusyawararan/ perwakilan* Society governed with wise justice in the context of mutual consultation and assistance
- *Keadilan social bagi seluruh rakyat Indonesia* – Social justice for all of the people of Indonesia.

Nurcholish Madjid has shown the vocabulary of *Panca Sila* is primarily Arabic and that it can be understood best as being a deconfessionalized variant of common Islamic social and political principles.[59] It was also the subject of intense negotiation at the time of the founding of the republic. The wording of the first principle was chosen to indicate clearly that the meaning is monotheism and not simply religiousness and as Madjid observes the "Unity of Indonesia" was chosen instead of nationalism because of the suspicion with which some observant Muslims viewed this concept. Muslim leaders advocated the inclusion of what came to be known as the Jakarta Charter, "with the obligation for Muslims to live in accordance with *Shari'ah* in the first principle, but relented when Christians, who are the majority in portions of Eastern Indonesia, threatened to establish their own state if they were included. Indonesia's president Soekarno wanted "the unity of Indonesia" to be the first principle, which Muslim leaders could not accept. As a whole, what has come to be known as the "Birth of *Panca Sila*" required the negotiation of religion, culture and nationality.[60]

As originally formulated, *Panca Sila* was a pluralistic ideology that, as many Indonesians observe with considerable pride, is neither secular, because it promoted religion in general, nor religious, in the sense that it did not establish an official religion. Throughout the New Order, and especially as it became increasingly consolidated in the late 1970s and 1980s, it became the core of a repressive, hegemonic discourse in which nationality was of paramount importance.[61] The New Order strategy for managing religion was complex. It included suppression of all but the vestiges of political Islam, the promotion of pluralistic theologies and personal piety

---

[59] See Nurcholish Madjid, "In Search of the Islamic Roots for Modern Pluralism: The Indonesian Experiences". In: M. Woodward (ed.), *Toward a New Paradigm. Recent Developments in Indonesian Islamic Thought.* Tempe AZ: Arizona State University Program for Southeast Asian Studies Monograph series, 1998, pp. 89–116

[60] R. Abdoelgani, Roeslan (ed.), *Sejarah Lahirnya Pancasila.* Jakarta: Yayasan Soekarno-Hatta dan Yayasan Pembela Tanah Air, 1984 and Soekarno, The *Birth of Panca Sila*, Ithaca: Cornell Modern Indonesia Project, 1972.

[61] For a discussion of the religious roots of this discourse and Muslim responses to it see M. Woodward, "Textual Exegesis as Social Commentary: Religious, Social and Political Meanings of Indonesian Translations of Arabic Hadith Texts", in, *The Journal of Asian Studies* vol. 52, no. 3, 1993, 565–583.

and the heavy handed manipulation of the national ideology.[62] The threat of force was ever present.[63] Even those who actually had relatively little to fear lived in fear of the police and the military. An Indonesian joke that could be told openly only after the fall of the New Order goes as follows:

> Two men are sitting next to each other on a train. One asks the other: "Are you a member of the military or the police?" "No," the other replies. "Then is a member of your family in the military or the police?" "No". "Are any of your friends in the military or the police?" "No" "Do you know anyone in the military or the police?" "No". "Then will you please take your foot off of mine!"

Javanese political and mystical thought provided something of a velvet glove for the iron fist of the New Order. New Order justifications for authoritarianism close resemble interoperations of "democracy and leadership" developed by Ki Hajar Dewantara.[64] Dewantara was a Javanese aristocrat and the founder of the nationalist educational organization *Taman Siswa*. He based his political and educational philosophy on the Javanese and more general Sufi concept of the "union of servant and lord". The concept of the union of servant and lord is among the most basic principles of Javanese religious and political thought. As a mystical principle, it refers to the attainment of union with Allah. As a political principle, it refers to the unity of interests of ruler and subject.[65] Moertono (characterizes the servant/lord relationship as follows:

> The ruler (and his officials), in terms of practical administrative policy, must care for his subjects as a parent cares for his children; thus the ruler assumes in fact an attitude of protective superiority, and the ruled an attitude of acquiescent subservience.[66]

---

[62] D. Porter, *Managing Politics and Islam in Indonesia*, London, Routledge 2002: D. Ramagae, *Politics in Indonesia: Democracy, Islam and the Ideology of Tolerance*, London: Routledge, 1995. The emergence of a vibrant critical and very nearly "post-modernist" Muslim theological discourse was the almost certainly unintended, consequence of New Order attempts to depoliticize Islam and simultaneously develop Islamic education. This discourse has been referred by terms including *"Islam Libera,l" "Islam Inklisif,"* "Neo-Modernism," and "Neo-Traditionalism". See, G. Barton, "Neo-Modernism: A Vital Synthesis of Traditionalist and Modernist Islamic Thought in Indonesia", *Studia Islamika*, vol. 2, pp. 175–196, 1995, R. Marin, M. Woodward and D. Atmaja, *Defenders of Reason in Islam. Mutazilism from Medieval School to Modern Symbol,* Oxford: One World, 1997 and M. Woodward (ed.) *Towards a New Paradigm: Intellectual Developments in Indonesian Islam,* Tempe: Arizona State University Program for Southeast Asian Studies Monograph Series, 1996

[63] On the role of role of violence and the threat of violence in governance during the New Order see B. Anderson (ed.), *Violence and the State in Suharto's Indonesia*, Ithaca: Cornell Southeast Asia Publications, 2001.

[64] H. Schulte Nordholt, *State-Citizen Relations in Suharto's Indonesia: Kawula-Gusti.* Rotterdam: Comparative Asian Studies Program, Erasmus University, 1987.

[65] On the Quranic and Sufi origins of the concept of the union of servant and lord, see Woodward, op. cit., *Islam in Java...*, pp. 73–75.

[66] S. Moertono, *State and Statecraft in Old Java: A Study of the Later Mataram Period.* Ithaca: Modern Indonesia Project, Southeast Asia Program, Department of Asian Studies, Cornell University, 1968, p. 27.

Dewantara emphasized the importance of a wise leader who would guide his people in a collective quest for spiritual tranquility and material well-being.[67] He opposed Western Democracy because of the value it accords to individual freedom, contrasting it with Eastern Democracy which values "establishing a unity of all individuals".[68] New Order intellectuals described the union of servant and lord as the essence of *Panca Sila*. Ki Ranajuda puts it this way:

> Let us hope that in this way the New Order period will gradually achieve the ideal of our ancestors: The *keris (J.* dagger) enters the scabbard, that is a period of mutual responsi- bility and destiny between the Leadership and its People beneath the spreading rays of *manunggaling kawula gusti.*[69]

As McVey observes, the practical application of the concepts of "union of servant and lord" and "democracy and leadership" and the "family principle" allows leaders to assume dictatorial powers to overcome disagreement within the sacred family.[70] She wrote in 1967, at the very beginning of the New Order. There have been few instances in which a scholar has so accurately foreseen the path a regime would take.

In the 1970s and 1980s the "fatherly teachers" of the New Order introduced a series of policies and bills in the legislature that most observant Muslims, and many other Indonesians, found to be deeply offensive.[71] Beginning in the early 1970s the New Order instituted what Hasan and Hidyah describe as a "Foucaultian," and I would add "Orwellian" project of ideological manipulation and indoctrination.[72] The "extreme left" (Communists and other leftists) and the "extreme right" (Political Islam) were declared to be enemies of the emerging *Panca Sila* Democracy. Suspected "leftists" and "rightists" were put under surveillance, and harassed. As late as the 1990s suspected "Communists" simply disappeared. Following the first New Order "elections" in 1971 Islamic parties were forcibly "fused" into the *Partai Persatuan Pembangunan* (United Development Party) and Christian and Nationalist Parties into the *Partai Demokrasi Indonesia* (Indonesian Democratic Party). Elections continued throughout the New Order period. The were often described as *Pesta Demokrasi* or "Festivals of Democracy". They were not always very festive and hardly democratic. The only question at issue was by what per cent- age the government party GOLKAR would win. In 1970 the government introduced

---

[67]On the *Taman Siswa* movement, see Tsuchiya, op. cit., On the centrality of the concept of the unity of servant and lord in Dewantara's thought, see B. Dewantara, *100 Tahun Ki Hajur Dewantara.* Jakarta: Pustaka Kartini, 1989, 93–95. Dewantara was also influenced by Theosophical thought.

[68]Tuschiya, op. cit., p. 141.

[69]Reeve, op. cit., p. 312.

[70]R. McVey, "Taman Siswa and the Indonesian National Awakening, *Indonesia,* No. 4, 1967.

[71]S. Prawiranegara, "Pancasila as the Sole Foundation," *Indonesia* 38:74–84, 1984; D. Reeve, *Golkar of Indonesia: An Alternative to the Party System.* Singapore: Oxford University Press, 1985 and N. Tamara, *Indonesia in the Wake of Islam.* Kuala Lumpur: Institute of Strategic and International Studies, 1986;

[72]N. Hasan, *Laskar Jihad. Islam, Militansi dan Pencarian Identitas di Indonesia Pasca-Orde Baru,* Jakarta: LP3ES, 2008, p. 48 and S. Hidayah, op. cit.

a *Panca Sila* education/indoctrination program known as *Pedoman, Penghayatan dan Pengamalan Pancasila* (P4). One would have allowed secular marriage. A second would have afforded official recognition to *Aliran Kebatin* – Javanese mystical groups that most observant Muslims consider to be heretical because the reject the ritual program mandated by *Shari'ah* and teach the doctrine of the unity of God and the human soul. In the late 1970s leaders of these groups hoped and expected that they would be recognized as "religions" along side Islam, Protestant and Roman Catholic Christianity, Hinduism and Buddhism.[73] A third required that all social organizations adopt *Panca Sila* as their *Asas Tungall* (sole organizing principle).[74] All of the major Muslim organizations held the view that these bills promoted adultery and apostasy and were intended as a blow against Islamic organizations if not against Islam itself.[75] The government ultimately compromised on the issues of secular marriage, which was not put into practice, and the *Aliran Kepercayaan,*

---

[73] *Alran Kepercayaan* are formalized and in the Weberian sense, rationalized organizations that promote mystical teachings and modes of ritual practice rooted in Javanese Sufism, Theosophy and rediscovered pre-Islamic Javanese Hindu and Buddhist traditions. They began to appear in the 1920s and continue to figure significantly in the Javanese religious landscape. While they are primarily urban and middle class, some have extended their reach into rural communities in East and Central Java. They are the product of the interaction of modernity and Orientalism. Unlike more traditional Javanese mystical groups, including one described in Chapter 2, they are not strongly tied to locality or specifically Javanese historical narrative. Most teach that they are modes of belief and practice that are independent of, but can be combined with any "religion". Like Theosophy they are concerned primarily with the psychological and experiential dimensions of mysticism. Many of the leaders of these movements I interviewed in the late 1970s were familiar with the writings of Hellena Blavatsky, the founder of Theosophy, and had Dutch translations of her works in their personal libraries. Many also teach that there have been Prophets and revelation after the Prophet Muhammad. For this reason, and because they teach "mystical truths" in public contexts, they are regarded as heretical by most Javanese Muslims. In 2008 many were targeted for attack by the extremist, and violent *Front Pembela Islam* (Front for the Defense of Islam) in Yogykarta and elsewhere in Indoneisa. It is a serious error to consider these groups to be representative of Javanese mystical thought and practice. It is, however, for many of these same reasons that some *Aliran Kepercayaan,* especially *Subud,* have a global appeal. The spread of groups like *Subud* to the United States and Europe, like that of Tibetan Buddhism, provides an example of the globalization or universalisation of local religion. Many *Aliran Kepercayaan* leaders I interviewed in the late 1970s believed that they were supported by Suharto, his wife or other important New Order figures. So did many of their opponents. For studies of this variety of Javanese religion see: A. Geels, *Subud and the Javanese Mysitcal Tradition,* London: Cruzon 1997; C. Geertz, *Religion of Java,* op. cit., pp. 339–59, J. Howell, "Indonesia: Searching for Consensus". In: C. Caldarola (ed.), *Religions and Societies, Asia and the Middle East,* The Hague: Mouton, 1982 pp. 497–48; P. Stange "The Logic of Rassa in Java" *Indonesia,* no. 38, pp. 113–34, 1984 and "Legitimate Mysticism in Indonesian" *Review of Indonesian and Malaysian Affairs,* vol. 20, no. 2, pp. 76–117, 1986. On the influence of Theosophy on the development of religious and nationalist thought among the Javanese elite of the later colonial period see L. Sears, *Shadows of Empire: Colonial Discourse and Javanese Tales,* Durham: Duke University Press, 1996.

[74] President Suharto announced this policy initiative in a speech delivered August 16, 1982. For a critique by a leading conservative Muslim scholar see D. Noer, *Islam pancasila dan Asas Tunggal,* Jakarta: Yayasan Perkhidmatan, 1983.

[75] M. Djadijono, "The 28th Congress of Nahdlatul Ulama," *The Indonesia Quarterly* 9, 1:10–14, 1990. and L. Harun, *Muhammadiyah dan Asas Puncasila,* Jakarta: Pustaka Panjimas, 1986.

supervision of which was assigned to the Ministry of Education and Culture instead of the Ministry of Religion. It would not budge on the *Panca Sila* question.[76]

The Social Organizations Act allowed the government to disband any organization that did not "accept" *Panca Sila*. The leaders of Indonesia's two largest organizations, *Nahdlatul Ulama* (NU) and *Muhammadiyah* seriously considered active resistance but concluded that the cost in human life could be very high and that the probability of success minimal.[77] Liberal, democracy oriented intellectuals including Nurcholish Madjid did not support the government's policies, but did devise Islamic apologies for *Panca Sila*.[78] The following statement by Kyai Hajji Muslich, a leading NU figure, is typical:

> In Indonesia, even though it is a *Panca Sila* state, Muslims may carry out the commands of Islamic law in any way. They are not blocked by government regulations. On the contrary the government provides assistance. The origin of this is *Panca Sila* and the 1945 constitution.[79]

With the collapse of the New Order and the establishment of democratic governance and a greatly enhanced concern for freedom of speech and other human rights, Indonesia faces new challenges. Clearly the management of religious, ethnic and national sources of collective identity in the new open and democratic context are among them, particularly in light of the fact that there are individuals and groups who would use religion to incite communal violence and others who seek to impose *Shari'ah* based social norms by legislative means at local and national levels. In 2006 Minister of Defense Juwono Sudarsono put it this way:

> Being an Indonesian Muslim, therefore, necessitates a tolerant expression of one's sense of being an Indonesian citizen, with all its rich nuances arising from family, ethnic and racial heritage including enrichment of Islam through understanding the beliefs and precepts of other faiths.[80]

This is little more than a restatement of the New Order ideology of tolerance and the subordination of religion to nationality. But the state no longer has the means or the will to silence opposing voices. Questions about the future of Indonesia are being asked again today in increasingly complex ways. Federalism and regional autonomy, the degree to which "Islamic" law, norms and values should be embodied in national and/or regional law, socialism and Marxism and their roles in the future

---

[76] See D. Weatherbee, "Indonesia in 1984: Pancasila, Politics and Power". *Asian Survey* 25, p. 190, 1985 and M. Woodward, "Textual Exegesis as Social Commentary: ..." op. cit.

[77] This observation is based on conversations with NU and Muhammadiyah leaders in 1998, after the fall of the New Order. Several stated that the only reason that *jihad* was not required in this case was that it could not possibly have been successful and that according to Islamic teachings tyranny is preferable to chaos.

[78] For an English language example, based on a previously published Indonesian article see Madjid op. cit.

[79] K. Muslich 1987, "Dakwah Dengan Kasih Sayang". *Pesantren* vol.4, no. 4, pp. 4:29–32, p. 32, 1987.

[80] Jakarta Post, June 20, 2006.

of Indonesia are now topics that not only can be, but are discussed, especially among intellectuals.

Theorizing Religion

Theoretically this volume is located at the intersection of two disciplines, Cultural Anthropology and Religious Studies, which share common empirical concerns and increasingly methodologies, but have very different intellectual pedigrees.[81] Both disciplines grew out of post-Enlightenment European encounters with, and attempts to understand, the cultural and religious others of the Americas, Africa, the Pacific Islands and Asia. Both disciplines are linked directly or indirectly, and in very complex ways, to the two principle modes of European expansion: colonialism and Christian missionization which together provided the material base and ideological superstructure for the establishment of what Wallerstein describes as the "sixteenth century world system" – a hegemonic world order that persists, with modifications, to the present day.[82] Anthropology emerged as a consequence of European encounters with non-literate, "tribal" societies of Africa, the Americas, the Pacific and the economic and political peripheries of Asia. Prior to the emergence of ethnographic fieldwork as the defining methodology of the discipline, it drew heavily on the evolutionary paradigm first fully articulated by Darwin in the biological sciences. It attempted to place the then known human societies on a cultural "Great Chain of Being" starting with what were considered to be the vestiges or survivals of the earliest stages of human cultural history and culminating with nineteenth century secular industrial capitalism. Religious Studies emerged from the philological study of the sacred texts of East and South Asia and the Middle East, a field of study that has subsequently been described by Edward Said and others as "Orientalism". As has become increasing apparent in recent decades Orientalism and Religious Studies have deep roots in Biblical Criticism and Liberal variants of Christian, and particularly Protestant, theology.[83]

As they have shed, or are at least in the process of shedding, their colonial and theological baggage, the theoretical orientations, the methodologies and objects of study of the two disciplines have converged. In some sense each has encroached upon the intellectual space traditionally occupied by the other. Anthropologists have become increasing concerned with the study of religion itself, and with societies in which the textual traditions of local and/or trans-cultural religions occupy central positions in social, political and economic life. Religious Studies scholars, for their part, have become increasingly concerned with the social, political and economic

---

[81] This discussion builds on that included in my earlier book, *Islam in Java: Normative Piety and Mysticism in the Sultanate of Yogyakarta*, Tucson: University of Arizona Press, 1989.

[82] I. Wallerstein, *The Modern World System: Capitalist Agriculture and the Origins of the European World Economy in the Sixteenth century*, New York: Academic Press, 1974

[83] E. Said, *Orientalism*, New York: Vintage Books, 1979.

contexts within which religious texts, life and experience are located and with the religious systems of non-literary cultures.

As even a brief perusal of recently published books and articles will reveal, many Religious Studies scholars have adopted the methodologies of Cultural Anthropology, ethnographic fieldwork chief among them. Even scholars whose research agendas render fieldwork unnecessary or impossible have mined the works of Cultural Anthropologists for analytic tools and theoretical inspiration.

Even some Christian theologians have come to rely on concepts and modes of analysis borrowed from Cultural Anthropology in assembling their interpretive "toolkits". Worgul, for example, draws on the now conventional anthropological understanding of ritual as a behavioral medium though which systems of meaning are publicly articulated and that can be "read" and "interpreted" as texts by detached scholars, if not by those for whom its performance is a vitally important part of social and religious life. Asad quotes the following passages in his account of the historical development of the anthropological understanding of ritual as a representational medium:

> Any rebuttal to our theological contentions must also critique the findings of psychology, sociology and anthropology which support our theological contentions. The lines of convergence between a behavioral and a theological understanding of ritual's operation and meaning are too strong to dismiss ...

> Ritual is a medium or vehicle for communicating or sustaining a particular culture's root metaphor, which is the focal point and permeating undercurrent for its worldview. ... A people's ritual is a code for understanding their interpretation of life.[84]

These points could just as well have been made by an anthropologist writing about contemporary Christian theology as by a theologian invoking anthropology and other social sciences to advance a religious position. As will be argued later in this chapter, Worgul has the causal arrow in the equation very nearly reversed. Anthropological understandings of ritual support those of modern theology because both emerged from post-Enlightenment understandings of religion. This seemingly unlikely convergence is the result of the widely accepted view that ritual, and religion more generally, are not what people who have escaped the Enlightenment critique of religion think them to be: factual accounts of the universe inhabited by human beings and others and instrumental means for establishing or altering the characteristics of these beings and/or relationships obtaining among them. Those who hold this view would have us accept the position that because religion and ritual are not what they claim to be, and because they are very nearly human universals, they must have a disguised representational reality of which indigenous people are ignorant, but which Enlightenment oriented others may discern. My own view is that religion is located in social and political contexts, but is not merely a reflection of some combination of them. This is an important point, and is among the theoretical propositions in which this volume is rooted. But here, what is more important

---

[84]G. Worgul, *From Magic to Metaphor: A Validation of Christian Sacraments.* New York: Paulist Press, 1980, p. 234.

is that Worgul's work provides an example of the ways in which scholars in sub-fields of Religious Studies most distant from Cultural Anthropology have made use of the conclusions of anthropological research for their own purposes without compromising their commitments to an "insiders" understanding of religion.

Similarly, Cultural Anthropologists concerned with the study of literate cultures are increasingly attuned to the importance of texts for the study of local variants of trans-cultural religions. Jack Goody, for example, has argued that because of the significance of writing and literary formulation of religions, villages, and I add would urban communities as well, can not be treated as cultural isolates that can be understood apart form the analysis of religious texts.[85] I have argued elsewhere that in Java, because lived religion is informed by the reading, recitation and performance of religious, historical and literary texts it can not be understood in the absence of close attention to these traditions.[86] My view of the interconnectedness of textual and ethnographic research in the analysis of local variants of trans-cultural religions resembles that of Religious Studies Scholar Richard King, who, in a study of the Orientalist construction of Hinduism and Buddhism as "World Religions," has written that:

> While scholars should certainly be aware of the distorting lenses of literacy and the "textualist" presuppositions of Religious Studies, these findings should not deter philologically and philosophically inclined scholars from studying religious texts. It is clear that such texts can never be totally divorced from the historical reality in which they are produced, and they do, in fact, provide important insights into the nature of the religion under consideration. To argue that "textual Buddhism" for instance, bears no relation to actual Buddhist religious belief and practice is to overstep the mark widely. There is much of practical significance that can be gleaned from religious texts as one of the many potential source materials for the study of religion. Attempts to establish a polarized opposition between "ideal" religious texts and "actual" religious beliefs drives a false wedge between two facets of the total religious phenomena, which, in practice, interact with one another in a dynamic fashion.[87]

King is a Religious Studies scholar who is sensitive to the limitations of textual analysis as a method for understanding religion as a total phenomenon. While I share his view that commitment to textual hegemony, or what might be termed the tyranny of the written word, impedes scholarly understanding of religion, I come to this position form the opposite direction. As a Cultural Anthropologist, my concern is primarily with contemporary and historical variants of lived religion. I am, however, cognizant of the incompleteness of ethnography as a method for understanding this reality. The anthropological study of religion in literary societies requires textual analysis both because people engage texts – and in the twentieth-first century this includes electronic as well print and manuscript documents – by reading, viewing, discussing and debating them, and equally as important because many who do not engage texts directly are influenced by those who do, so much so, that as will be pointed out in Chapter 6, what many Javanese consider to be local proverbs are, in

---

[85] J. Goody, *Literacy in Traditional Societies*, Cambridge: Cambridge University Press, 1986, p. 5.
[86] Woodward, *Islam in Java*. op.cit.
[87] King, op. cit., p. 71.

fact, Javanese paraphrases of Arabic religious texts. King's position and my own are, therefore, opposite sides of the same analytic coin, reflecting the convergence of Cultural Anthropology and Religious Studies.

My own approach to the study of religion is fundamentally Anthropological in that it is firmly rooted in ethnography. I am in total agreement with Sherry Ortner who argues that Cultural Anthropology is unique among the social sciences because field work provides an *entrée* into the lives of "real people". She observes that:

> It is our location "on the ground" that puts us in the position to see people not simply as passive reactors to enactors of some "system," but as active agents and subjects in their own history.[88]

To this I would add that not only does field work locate research in the midst of lived experience, it is simultaneously discursive and dialectical. One can not engage a text, document, icon or corpus of statistical data in the same sense that one can engage human beings who are capable of responding to and correcting the observations, impressions, representations and hypotheses of the researcher. Field work also provides the researcher with the opportunity to ask not only What?, but also Why? It establishes a dialectical hermeneutic in which analytic representations are subject to revision in response to "insider" critiques. It is also possible to test and revise hypotheses in conversations with research partners. An example is the characterization of the *Kraton Garebeg Malud* as a *slametan* (prayer meal). By observing the two rituals I had come to the conclusion that they were extremely similar and was able to confirm that the *Garebeg* is an imperial *Slametan* in conversations with palace informants.

Ethnography can make important contributions to textual studies. Even when I am concerned with the analysis of textual materials, they are viewed through an ethnographic lens. The knowledge of Javanese and Indonesian religion and culture that enables me to make sense of these materials I have acquired almost exclusively through conversations with Javanese and other Indonesians. In the case of contemporary local texts it can make unique contributions to textual analysis because it is possible to discuss the significance of a work with local readers and sometimes with authors.

For the most part, Anthropologists have been less inclined to turn to Religious Studies scholarship for theoretical guidance and analytic tools. The reasons for this asymmetry are, I think, rooted in a debate concerning the epistemological foundations of Religious Studies internal to the discipline and how it is perceived elsewhere in the academy. Religious Studies as an academic discipline is suspect in the eyes of many scholars in the Social Sciences because of its historical links with theology and Christian institutions. Many Anthropologists associate it with missionaries, who many regard as their traditional enemies. As an Anthropologist who has taught in a Religious Studies department for many years, I have often been asked if I am actually a closet Christian missionary. Nothing could be further from the truth.

---

[88] S. Ortner, "Theory in Anthropology Since the Sixties," *Comparative Studies in Society and History*, vol. 26, no. 1, 1984, 143.

As important as debates concerning the relative merits of scientific and religious or quasi-religious orientations may be for the future of Religious Studies as a discipline, they have little bearing on questions about the academic merits of appropriating more specific theoretical and analytic constructs rooted in this system of discourse for application in fields external to it. My use of concepts such as the repetition of archetypes developed in the writings of Mircea Eliade and others in the field of Religious Studies does not in any sense presuppose or suggest a commitment to the transcendentalist agendas underlying many of their works. The analyses presented here are firmly rooted in what Richard King has described as "methodological agnosticism" – a somewhat softer version of what Peter Berger calls "methodological atheism[89] I prefer King's formulation to Berger's because it requires the analyst to disavow any concern with the truth claims of religious phenomena rather than operating with the assumption that they are necessarily false. My purpose here is to move analytic discourse about religion as far away from religious or anti-religious discourse as possible. Among my purposes in this chapter, and in those that follow, is to explore the nature of, and hopefully foster the further development of this disciplinary convergence.

Some scholars from both disciplines may question my reliance on Eliade's theory of the myth of eternal return and the repetition of the repetition of archetypes for any of at least four reasons. The first is that his work can be, and often is, read theologically. Particular in the concluding chapter of *The Myth of Eternal Return,* Eliade suggests that Christianity may be the appropriate religion for the modern age because it, unlike the other traditions he considers is set with a linear rather than cyclic theory of time.[90] In a more general sense Timothy Fitzgerald describes Eliade's use of the concept of the "sacred" as: "theological transcendentalism".[91] Daniel Wiebe presents a nearly identical critique, stating that:

... the object of Eliade's creative hermeneutic is not to provide us with knowledge about religions or even the values held by a given religious community, but rather to recover the abandoned transcendental values and meanings once provided to their devotees by those traditions.[92]

---

[89]P. Berger,. *The Sacred Canopy: Elements of a Sociological Theory of Religion*, Garden City, 1967; Doubleday, *Rumor of Angels*. Garden City: Doubleday, 1970, King, op. cit.

[90]Eliade, op. cit., I do find it curious that Eliade wrote very little about Islam which approaches the question of relationships between time and religion in very similar ways. On Islam's self location in linear history see W Smith, *Islam and Modern History*, New York, The New America Library, 1969, p.14 and N. Shiddiqi, "Sejarah: Pisau Bedah Ilmu Keislaman", In: T. Abdulah and M. Karim (eds.), *Metodologi Penelitian Agama*, Yogyakarta, Tiara Wacana, 2004, pp. 83–108.

[91]T. Fitzgerald, *The Ideology of Religious Studies*, New York: Oxford University Press, 2000, p. 12.

[92]D. Wiebe, *The Politics of Religious Studies*, New York: Palgrave, 1999, p. 60. I do not accept Wiebe's op. cit., pp. 100–01, more general conclusion that the Divinity School at the University of Chicago, as a whole pursued a theological agenda during Eliade's tenure there. I studied there in the 1970s and 1980s as well as in theAnthropology Department at the University of Illinois, which was then and is now, entirely secular. I have subsequently served on one Ph.D. committee at Chicago. Some people very clearly and self consciously pursued various theological agendas. Others, particularly graduate students, employed a variety of text critical, historical and social

The second is that, as McCucheon and Manea observe, his emphasis on cosmogonic mythology and celestial archetypes *may* have been motivated by a perhaps unconscious desire to flee from terrors of his childhood and youth growing up in Romania during the First World War and the turbulent inter-war period.[93] The third is his association with the Romanian Fascist and anti-Semitic Iron Guard. The fourth, perhaps most strongly articulated by the anthropologist Edmund Leach, is that Eliade pays insufficient attention to the social and political contexts in which religion is located.[94]

I have one general and other more specific, response. I am not concerned with the ontological status of archetypes and the religious character of their repetition. For analytic purposes, if a theoretical construct helps to explain a corpus of data, there is no reason to ignore it because of the ideological, theological, social or political contexts from which it emerged. Eliade formulates his theory of the replication of cosmology in sacred geography in the most general possible terms. Other scholars, whose work is more narrowly focused on Southeast Asian cultures, have arrived at all most identical conclusions independently.[95] I have little doubt that there are aspects of the biographies of many scholars that influence the fields of study they chose to adopt and the methodologies they employ. I suspect that this is as true of Chemists and Medical Researchers as it is of Anthropologists and Historians of Religion. In the interest of full disclosure I am a Cultural Anthropologist, but unlike many of my colleagues in the field, and in some cases against their advice, I have never conducted prolonged research in a village, and never will. I was raised in a village, or rather on a farm near one, know what toiling in the fields is like, and spent my youth struggling to escape from it. Unlike some of my colleagues I do not find village life idyllic or romantic.[96] I would be the last to apologize for Eliade's

---

science methodologies in the analysis of both the sacred texts and lived religions of Hinduism, Buddhism and Islam. I can state with absolute certainty that none of my mentors there, among who Frank Reynolds was the most important, and who Wiebe associates with Eliade's theological agenda, did not encourage those of us who were not inclined towards theological perspectives to adopt them. I think that few of us associated with that segment of the Divinity School would associate ourselves with Wiebe's position.

[93] R. McCutcheon, *Manufacturing Religion. The Discourse on Sui Generis Religion and the Politics of Nostalgia*, New York, Oxford University Press, 1997, p. 79 and on this discourse concerning the historical and political contexts of his scholarship more generally, pp. 74–100 and Norman Manea, "Happy Guilt: Mircea Eliade, Fascism and the Unhappy Fate of Romania," in: *The New Republic*, 1991, 5 August, pp. 27–36.

[94] E. Leach, "Sermons by a Man on a Ladder," in, *The New York Review of Books*, 1966, 20 October, pp. 28–31. While he wrote extensively on religion, Leach (personal communication) was a secular person who took a dim view of it.

[95] See, for example, S. Moertono, *State and Statecraft in Old Java: A Study of the Later Mataram Period, 16th to 19th centuries,* Monograph Series, Modern Indonesia Project. Ithaca: Cornell University S. Tambaiah, *World Conqueror and World Renouncer*, Cambridge, Cambridge University Press, 1974.

[96] My rural background influenced my research on Javanese Islam in two other less significant ways. It enabled me to determine that the sheep and goats slaughtered at the Feast of Sacrifice were all approximate a year old as I know how to judge the age of a ruminant by examining its

youthful flirtations with Fascism. At the same time those of us who are children of the 1960s and were in our own youths apologists for Mao Ze Tung and Ho Chi Min, and scholars of Eliade's generation who were apologists for or supporters of the Joseph Stalin, live in political glass houses and should not throw stones at those whose youthful indiscretions were on the opposite extreme of the political spectrum. As an anthropologist I could not agree more fully with Leach's objection to the decontextualized study of religion. All of this being said, the analysis of Javanese myths and rituals presented here strongly supports the position that Eliade provides powerful analytic tools, even for studies of religious phenomena that do not share his larger epistemological perspective or cultural/religious agenda.

Each of the essays included in this volume is, in one sense, theoretically free standing. Most were conceived as journal articles or as papers for presentation at conferences in the United States or Indonesia. In writing them my choice of theoretical tools was dictated not by a grand design, but rather by what I found useful in the task of attempting to explain elements of Javanese and Indonesian Islamic discourse, thought and praxis. They are, however, united by a common set of meta-theoretical assumptions concerning the nature of religion and culture. First and foremost among these is that while local variants of trans-cultural religious traditions share texts and other narratives, symbols, images, and modes of religious practice including, but not restricted to, ritual, that attempts to define an "essence" or "pure form" of Islam or any other transcultural-religion is, or at least should be, a theological, rather than analytic endeavor. To paraphrase Congressman Tip O'Neil, in this sense, all religion is local. Trans-cultural religions exist and are lived in myriad variants each of which is located in time, space and culture and in locally defined historical contexts and configurations of power and authority. None can be privileged or used as a benchmark against which the "purity" or "authenticity" of others is judged. To do so is confuse academic discourse about religion with religious discourse itself. It is also to trivialize the religious self understandings of adherents of locally defined variants of trans-cultural religions for whom their own beliefs and practices are coterminous with the religious truths of the larger tradition, and in instances, such as Java, where there are deep religious divisions, privilege one as authentic and others as somehow corrupt. This same analytic caveat applies to the study of the internal variants of local religion. In this sense my approach to the study of religion resembles that of Talal Asad who characterizes the anthropological study of religion in the following terms:

---

teeth – they acquire one set of permanent incisors per year. My neighbors were also very surprised to learn that I could and would be a participant as well as an observer in the sacrifice as I had slaughtered sheep and goats on many previous occasions. I also did not come to Asian Studies by accident. When I decided to become an Anthropologist in my senior year in high school, the choice of "areas" was entirely obvious. My paternal grandparents were "Old China Hands" who had spent much of the period between the two World Wars with the US Army in China and the Philippines. When I was a child visiting their house was like going to a museum which was filled with "priceless Oriental antiques," which I did not discover for many years bore a striking resemblance to the "art objects" one finds in Hong Kong and Singapore curio shops.

My argument, I must stress, is not just that religious symbols are intimately linked to social life (and so change within it), or that they usually support dominant political power (and occasionally oppose it). It is that different kinds of practice and discourse are intrinsic to the field in which religious representations (like any representation) acquire their identity and their truthfulness. From this is does not follow that the meanings of religious practices and utterances are to be sought in social phenomena, but only that their possibility and their authoritative status are to be explained as historically distinctive disciplines and forces. The anthropological student of particular religions should therefore begin from this point, in a sense unpacking the comprehensive concept which he or she translates as "religion" into heterogeneous elements according to its historical character.[97]

I have not addressed these issues in any of my previous writings – most of which have been conducted in what, at the time, I believed to be what Thomas Kuhn terms a "normal science" voice.[98] This was in some sense a silent protest against the debates concerning the nature and even the possibility of scholarly representation of religion and other cultural phenomena that filled the pages of scholarly journals during the period in which most of these essays were written.[99] None of the essays included in this volume addresses these issues theoretically. All of them are detailed representations of elements of Indonesian and Javanese Islam and strive for descriptive adequacy as a first step towards theoretically driven explanation. In this sense I place my self firmly in the company of those Anthropologists and Historians of Religion who consider the study of religion and culture to be scientific endeavors and in opposition to those who would maintain that representation is so inevitably colored by the social, cultural religious and political positions or prejudices of the observer that objective representation, let alone scientific explanation, are impossible and attempts to undertake them naïve.

One of the problems with much recent scholarship on the problem of representation of religion and the search for a non theological foundation for Religious Studies is that Fitzgerald, McCutcheon, Weibe, among others, are inextricably bound to the very post-enlightenment demons they seek to exorcise. Individually and collectively their works show that much of what has passed for "objective" and "comparative" analysis of religion is rooted in at least implicit and at times quite explicit, theological agendas and truth claims concerning universalist, individualistic, salvation oriented, post-Christian ecumenical theologies that understand all forms of religion as being manifestations of a single, underlying Truth. At the same time they seem incapable of offering a solution to the problem, other than to advocate abandoning the category religion as being hopelessly polluted with at the very least the tropes

---

[97] T. Asad, *Genealogies of Religion. Discipline and Reasons of Power in Christianity and Islam.* Baltimore: The Johns Hopkins University Press, 1993, pp. 53–54.

[98] T. Kuhn, *The Structure of Scientific Revolutions*, Chicago: University of Chicago Press, 1996 (3rd edition)

[99] Cultural Anthropology underwent a similar epistemological crisis in the 1980s. For a summary of this literature see G. Marcus and M. Fischer, Anthropology *as Cultural Critique. An Experimental Moment in the Human Sciences*: Chicago: University of Chicago Press, 1986. For a critique of the extreme cultural relativism this approach motivated see the papers included in J. Dougherty, *Directions in Cognitive Anthropology*, Urbana: University of Illinois Press, 1986.

of Western Christianity. Their point would seem to be that over the course of the Nineteenth Century the representation of the religious "other" as some combination of heathenism, paganism, idolatry and depravity became increasingly untenable as knowledge of these "others" expanded, and that as the truth claims of Biblically based Christianity became increasingly indefensible, Western intellectuals turned from deprecating to domesticating the religious "other".

Throughout this volume, I use the term "trans-cultural religions" to distance myself from debates concerning the Christian theological origins of the more conventional "World Religions" and its use as an analytic "cover" for a broad ecumenical assumption that, whatever their differences may be, that religions, or at least the "Big Five" (Hinduism, Buddhism, Judaism, Christianity and Islam) and presumably others, including Sikhism, Baha'i, Daoism and Jainism, that make universal truth claims and are open to all humans regardless of ethnicity, are man-ifestations of a single religious reality or "Truth". I could not disagree with this view more strongly. By trans-cultural religions I mean simply those that make universal truth claims and are located in ethnically and linguistically diverse set-tings. Anthropologists may find this distinction unnecessary and indeed peculiar. However, the sheer volume of works on the topic published by Religious Studies scholars in recent years, and the acrimonious character of the debate makes it essential in a work straddling the two disciplines.[100]

While I find much of the critique of Religious Studies convincing, the proposed solution of abandoning the category "religion," is, in my view untenable. Even soci-eties in which something like "religion" is not an emic category there is almost invariably some complex of beliefs and practices that resemble what is referred to as religion in scholarly discourse. It is my contention that the academic study of religion requires more, and not less, theory. Most theories of religion are either rep-resentationalist, in the sense that they are rooted in the assumption that religion is a symbolic reflection of some complex of social, natural or psychological phenom-ena or they are driven by theological assumptions. Theories of both types can be criticized as reductionist: The first in the sense that they trivialize what empirical studies have shown to be the central role of religion in human societies the world over; the second because they would trivialize the impact of other social and natural realities on the religious imagination. The claim that religion can only be explained in its own terms is tautological. To make such a claim is a religious not a scientific venture.

---

[100]On these debates and their significance in the discourse of *Religious Studies* see: R. King, *Orientalism and Religion. Post Colonial Theory and the Mystic* East, London: Routledge, 1999; F. Timothy, *The Ideology of Religious Studies*, Oxford: Oxford University Press, 2000: McCalla, Authur, "When is History not History?" in, *Historical Reflections* vol. 20: 435–52, 1994; McCutchen, Russell, *Manufacturing Religion. The Discourse on Sui Generis Religion and the Politics of Nostalgia*. Oxford, Oxford University Press, 1997; P. Samuel, *Explaining Religion: Criticism and Theory from Bodin to Freud*. New Haven, Yale University Press, 1987; M. Tomoko, *The Invention of World Religions*, Chicago: University of Chicago Press, 2005; and D. Wieber, *The Politics of Religious Studies*, New York: Palgrave, 1999.

What Skorupski terms the "literalist" approach to the study of religion offers the possibility of greater explanatory power while avoiding the problem of claiming that religions can not be what they claim to be: accounts of the nature of existence and the place of humans and other beings in it. He summarizes this approach in the following way:

> a) that traditional religious beliefs are to be interpreted at face value as beliefs about the natural world and its underlying dynamic principles (b) that they are deployed for purposes of explaining, and providing the rationale for attempts to control the natural environment; and yet still believe that these goals are not the only ones to be grasped if traditional religious thought is to be understood – that there are important needs and preoccupations, significantly different from the activist, this worldly ones of explanation and control, which from the first shape and form the content of religious thought.

Sperber offers a related perspective when he states that for the Dorze a leopard is a member of the Ethiopian Orthodox Church.[101] He continues that in this cultural context this statement is not a metaphor or symbol, but rather a statement of fact. A conversation I had with one of my Javanese/Indonesian students in the summer of 2007 points to a similar conclusion and to the utility of this approach in the study of religion. We were discussing the spirits which most Javanese *know* to inhabit dilapidated buildings. I asked if there could be a *setan* living in the abandoned house across the street from the one in which I was living. His reply was: "No, not a *setan,* but perhaps a *demit. Setan* and *demit* are different. *Demit* can bother you if you bother them, but *setan* are completely evil". This was not a conversation about representations or symbols. For my friend *setan* and *demit* are real – just as real as humans. They are part of the world in which Javanese live. This perspective allows us to capture both the practical aspects of religion and more abstract and ethereal metaphysical reflection Evans Pritchard, Hallowell and Morrison have shown to be characteristic not only of literary trans-cultural religions but those of exclusively oral cultures as well.[102] It also allows for a multi-variant theorization of religion in which factors including observation of the natural environment, social structure and emotion isolated in the classical theories of religion help to shape the religious imagination.

Chomsky, Keesing, Lehman, Piaget and other Cognitive Psychologists and Anthropologists have argued that cultures and other human knowledge systems are hierarchically organized.[103] The principle of hierarchy makes it possible to explain

---

[101] D. Sperber, *Rethinking Symbolism*, Cambridge: Cambridge University Press, 1975.

[102] E. Evans-Pritchard, Nuer *Religion*, Oxford: Clarendon Press, 1956; A. Hallowell, "Ojibwa Ontology, Behavior and World View," In: D. Tedlock and B. Tedlock (eds.), *Teachings from the American Earth*, New York: Liveright, 1975, pp. 141–78; K. Morrison, "The Cosmos as Intersubjective: Native American Other-Than-Human Persons," in G. Harvey (ed.), *Indigenous Religions: A Companion*. London: Cassell, 2000, pp. 23–36.

[103] N. Chomsky, *Syntactic Structures*, The Hague: Mouton, 1957;R. Keesing, "Linguistic Knowledge and Cultural Knowledge: Some Doubts and Speculations," in: *American Anthropologist*, 1979, vol. 81: pp. 14–37; F. Lehman, "Cognition and Computation: On Being Sufficiently Abstract". In: J. Dougherty,. (ed), *Directions in CognitiveAnthropology*, Urbana:, University of Illinois Press, 1985, pp. 19–48.

relationships among a set of cultural domains with out resorting to reductionist theories positing unidirectional causal relationships. It is, however, not sufficient to consider relationships obtaining among named or identifiable cultural domains. As defined by Keesing culture is a system of knowledge including:

> Specific routines and understandings appropriate to particular contexts and *more general assumptions* about the social and natural worlds (my italics).

It is not, therefore, necessary to theorize that one cultural domain, for example religion, is determined by another, for example political economy, simply because the two exhibit structural similarities. It is equally possible that the similarities derive from the fact that both are governed by a single set of overarching assumptions. Lehman has described culture as resembling language in that it has seemingly infinite generative capacity and that a common set of assumptions and generative rules can give rise to a diversity of surface form. In this volume and especially in Chapter 2 which concerns traditional medical practice and Chapter 3 which concerns the Javanese *slametan* or ritual meal, it is suggested that this generative process often takes the form of what Levi Strauss called *bricolage*.[104] The term originally referred to sudden and unseen events and subsequently to craftsmen working with only the tools and materials at hand. He describes this process as being the ways in which mythological principles are used in the interpretation of nature (however defined).

> The characteristic feature of mythological thought is that it expresses itself by means of a heterogeneous repertoire which, even if extensive, is never the less limited. It has to use this repertoire, however, whatever the task in hand because it has nothing else at its disposal. Mythological thought is therefore a kind of intellectual "bricolage" – which explains the relation which can be perceived between the two. Like bricolage of the technical plane, mythical reflection can reach brilliant unforeseen results on the intellectual plane.

Applied to the study of religion this makes it possible to provide a logical account of variation within both culturally specific and trans-cultural religions. Public expression, if not the formulation, of variant modes of religiosity is constrained by power relations. This links the cognitive approach to the study of religion to Asad's insistence that it must be studies in social and political contexts. This suggests that "orthodoxy" can be maintained only by coercion and that under conditions of religious freedom the proliferation of variant myths, rituals and theologies is to be expected. It is orthodoxy or orthopraxy that requires explanation not variety. Here, Asad's emphasis on the political location of religion is critically important.

The differences between pilgrimage traditions of Yogyakarta and East Java provide a cogent example. The purposes of pilgrimage (*ziyarah*) in both regions are identical. Pilgrims seek the blessing (*berkat*) of saints and their assistance with a wide variety of worldly problems, ranging from healing to passing university

---

[104]C. Levi Strauss, *The Savage Mind*, Chicago: University of Chicago Press, 1966, p. 167. "Shade tree mechanics" are a contemporary American example. Burmese mechanics I knew in the early 1980s, who seemed to do everything with anything, including installing a 1970s Toyota transmission in a 1951 English Ford are even better examples.

entrance exams. Others come in quest of mystical experience and the saint's assistance in drawing closer to God. The differences derive from the patterns of authority prevalent in the two regions. In Yogyakarta (and in Surakarta) the most important pilgrimage sites are the graves of the monarchs of the Mataram dynasty.[105] Access to them is strictly controlled by the courts. Other than nobility and palace officials, people are allowed to approach the graves only on a few specified days and hours. At other times they may only approach the closed and barred gates. They must wear costumes prescribed for palace servants by arcane sumptuary regulations. Women do not cover their heads and must wear strapless breast cloths – a symbolic statement that they are the property of the court.[106] Men in full regalia are required to leave their *keris* (ceremonial daggers) outside the gates – also a sign of submission. Commoners are allowed to place flowers on the graves and burn incense only by presenting to a *juru cunci* (literally guardian of the keys) employed by one of the two courts who does it for them. The process is brief. Crowds are not allowed to congregate around the tombs for extended periods. This is an Imperial Islam in which rulers, who themselves are thought of as saints, control accesses to the blessings that can be imparted by their ancestors. Pilgrimage resembles a ceremonial audience with a living monarch – for which opportunities are even rarer.[107]

Pilgrimage in East Java is far less restricted and regulated. The most important shrines are the tombs of the legendary *wali* (Muslim saints) believed to have been responsible for the establishment of Islam in the region and the great mosque at Demak, which is said to have been the first in Java, and, with its distinctive three tiered roof, is the archetype for traditional Javanese mosque architecture. Each of these shrines defines both a *wilayah* (territory) and an *ummah* (Muslim community) Thousands of people visit these shrines every day. Today they come in tour buses from throughout Java and other parts of Indonesia, but are particularly revered by local residents. There are no formal dress codes, though most wear clothing deemed

---

[105] Yogyakarta and Surakarta are both successor states of Mataram. There has been an intense rivalry between the two courts since the kingdom was divided in the late eighteenth century. The royal cemetery at Imogiri is divided into three sections: one for undivided Mataram, one for Surakarta and One for Yogyakarta. The ceremonial costumes of the two courts are quite distinct and it is, therefore quite easy to identify someone as the subject of one of the two rivals. People wearing either costume may visit the Mataram graves. Only those in the politically appropriate attire may visit those of Surakarta and Yogyakarta.

[106] It is for this reason that many Javanese women will not visit these places. In October of 2008. I and colleagues at the Center for Religious and Cross-cultural Studies at Gadjah Mada University attempted to arrange a "field trip" for students to visit some of the important religious sites near the university. We initially thought of the royal cemetery at Imo Giri but found that many of our female Muslim students were literally horrified about what they would have to (not) wear. We visited a Roman Catholic shrine instead. Some were very surprised to discover that Catholic nuns cover their hair "just like Muslim girls" as one put it (English in the original).

[107] This is why the practice of making frequent public appearances and mingling with the *wong cilik* (little people) instigated by Hamengkubuwana IX and continued by the present Sultan is of such great symbolic importance. Hamengkubuwana X now holds "open houses" at the end of Ramadan which are attended by thousands of people and are of course, featured on the news on Kraton TV.

appropriate for communal prayer.[108] Most men wear sarongs and almost all women conform with customs that they cover their hair and arms. People are free to wander through the cemeteries surrounding the central shrine to place flowers on the graves. Large crowds gather around the tomb of the *Wali*. Many sit for extended periods reciting or reading the *Qur'an*, especially *Surah Yasin* The emphasis is not on individual submission to royal/saintly authority but on collective veneration of a teacher/saint.

These modes of pilgrimage are equally Islamic and equally Javanese. The difference can be attributed to the fact that in East Java religious and, considerable political, authority are in the hands of *kyai* (Islamic scholar/teachers), while in Yogyakarta, at least in principle, the Sultan is the ultimate religious and political authority. Significantly at shrines in Yogyakarta and Surakarta that are not controlled by the courts, the East Javanese custom prevails. In all my experience in Java I have not encountered a clearer example of the ways in which the structure of power relations shapes religious conduct. At the same time they are based on nearly identical concepts concerning the nature of blessing and sainthood.

Local Cultures and Trans-cultural Religions

An Analytic Framework for the Study of Local Variants of Trans-cultural Religion

The study of local variants of trans-cultural religions presents challenges to both Religious Studies scholars and Cultural Anthropologists. It necessarily involves tacking between the two disciplines in order to capture the complexities of the multifaceted imbrications of trans-cultural and local texts and modes of religious practices. It requires both knowledge of universals and particulars and analytic tools suitable to the task. What follows is a schema that is intended to capture the complex relationships between "Universalist" and local variants of trans-cultural religions. Though it focuses primarily on "Islams" it is intended as a method of more general applicability. It includes four categories: Universalist, Essentialist, Received, and Local, all but the first of which are subject to change and development in the course of history Eickelman has written that:

> ...the main challenge for the study of Islam in Local contexts is to describe and analyze how the universalist principles of Islam have been realized in various social and historical contexts without presenting Islam as a seamless essence on the one hand or as a plastic congeries of beliefs and practices on the other.[109]

---

[108] In 2006 I visited the Shrine of the *wali* Sunan Kudus wearing jeans and a western style shirt. This would have been utterly impossible at Imo Giri.

[109] C. Geertz, *Islam Observed: Religious Development in Morocco and Indonesia*, Chicago: University of Chicago Press, 1968.

The observations apply to other religions with equal force. Eickelman isolates pre-existing religious and cultural patterns, class and other configurations of social and economic power as factors influencing the formulation and reproduction of Local Islams and is critical of Geertz's theory that culture patterns or "classical styles" are the dominant factors shaping the interpretation of Islamic texts and tradition.[110] Geertz treats classical styles as constants that are extremely resistant to change. In short, his analysis stresses local cultural continuity and minimizes the transformative effect that Islam (and other trans-cultural religions) may have on culture. The analysis presented in this volume indicates that, at least in central Java, Islam has had a profound impact on culture and that religious debate is between groups committed to distinct modes of Muslim piety and not between committed and nominal Muslims.

This suggests that if we are to understand the varieties of Islam and other transcultural religions found within and across local contexts, it is essential to pay greater attention to the vicissitudes of the textual tradition itself. It is also necessary to consider relationships between imperial, peasant, and urban formulations local religion in any given context. But there is also, as Eickelman observes, an equally significant and perhaps more vexing problem, that is, that of defining the other side of the "Universalist"/"Local" coin. This problem is particularly difficult because there are, in almost every case competing voices about what should be included and what excluded for the Universalist canon. As Rahman has noted, the "great traditions" of Islam and other trans-cultural religions are far from monolithic. What some consider to be normative, others view as heterodox. Rahman's own view was to see the *Qur'an* and the "Prophet's definitive conduct" as a normative "criterion-referent" against which philosophical interpretations and local traditions can be judged.[111] Martin's perspective is that "Essentialist" Islam is an intertextual discourse including "principal texts and the literary deposits they have left in Islamic cultures since the rise of Middle Arabic in the eighth century".[112]

Even when combined with Eickelman's set of contextual considerations, neither of these orientations is sufficient to explain the variety of Islams found in Java and I suspect in other Muslim cultures as well. Rahman's view was shaped by a theological concern with what he considered to be the fundamental truths of the tradition. This made it difficult for him to handle the question of how it is that participants in Local Islams, despite a tendency toward "orthodoxification," firmly believe in the "truth" of their own traditions. To put it bluntly, everyone considers her or his particular understanding of religion to be the correct one. An analytic approach to Local Islam must attempt to determine why this is so. Martin's characterization

---

[110]D. Eickelman, "The Study of Islam in Local Context, *Contributions to Asian Studies*, 17, pp. 1–16, 1982.

[111]F. Rahman, "Approaches to Islam in Religious Studies: Review Essay". In Martin, op. cit., p. 196.

[112]R. Martin, "Islam and Textuality: Aspects of Discourse on the Qur'an in the Buyid Period (945–1055 C.E.)" (paper presented at the Ohio State University Conference on the Origins of Islam, Columbus, 1986).

of Essentialist Islam as intertextual discourse avoids the problem of normativeness but fails to capture the importance of ritual and its interpretation in Islamic history and religious life. As Cantwell Smith and Denny have observed, doctrine and ritual are, in Denny's words, "mutually confirmatory moments in a unified process of religious discovery and discipline".[113] Moreover, a significant portion of the canonical Hadith and subsequent Essentialist literature are about ritual performance. In Ricoure's sense these rites can be understood as texts in that they inscribe meaning and are objects of subsequent interpretation.[114] But from a Muslim perspective, ritual texts differ from written ones as it is performance, not inscription or exegesis, which constitutes submission to Allah which is what they know Islam to be.

Given the importance of ritual in all varieties of Islam, the text based Essentialist (or normative or formal)/local (or popular) distinction can be refined by a more complex typology that includes written and oral texts and ritual. What follows is a tentative schema that is intended to capture the complexity of the Essentialist tradition and the variety of factors influencing the formulation of Local Islams. It includes four categories: Universalist, Essentialist, Received, and Local, all but the first of which are subject to change and development in the course of history. Though it focuses primarily on "Islams" it is intended as a method of more general applicability. It includes four categories: Universalist, Essentialist, Received, and Local, all but the first of which are subject to change and development in the course of history.

Universalist Islam includes the *Qur'an* and Hadith (Rahman's normative Islam) together with rituals including the pilgrimage to Mecca (*hajj*), liturgical prayer (*salat*), the fast of Ramadan and other rites and devotional acts specifically enjoined by Universalist texts.[115] It is primary in the sense that Muslim tradition holds that these materials embody and act upon ultimate truth and, from the perspective of social science, because they are the objects of interpretive programs that give rise to the diverse modes of piety and thought that constitute Islam as a religious tradition. These texts and rituals are out of time and out of space. While they originated in particular contexts they now transcend them and are in this sense also "eternal" and "unbounded". The Universalalist category can be applied in a relatively straightforward way to the study of Judaism, Christianity and other religions in which there is a core body of texts and rituals. It is more difficult to employ in the study of Buddhism and Hinduism in which there is no such body of texts and practices. In the case of Buddhism, perhaps all that is universal is the basic outline of the story of the life of the Buddha and belief in the power of his bodily relics. In the case of Hinduism there is perhaps less that is generally shared. Indeed as King has argued, it is not unreasonable to conclude that there actually is no such thing as "Hinduism"

---

[113] W. Cantwell Smith, *Islam in Modern History* Princeton: Princeton University Press 1957, p. 20; F. Denny, "Islamic Ritual: Perceptions and Theories," in Martin, op. cit., pp. 63–77.

[114] P. Ricoure, "The Model of the Text: Meaningful Action Considered as Text," in *Interpretive Social Science: A Reader*, In: P. Rabinow and W. Sullivan (ed.), Berkeley and Los Angeles, 1979.

[115] Hadith are traditions concerning the speech and actions of the Prophet Muhammad and are recognized as being a source of religious law second in importance only to the *Qur'an*.

and that the category is the product of European and Muslim discourse. This is all the more true when one throws Bali into the mix.[116] At best Hinduism can be understood as a family of related religions. There are, however, concepts, if not particular texts and rituals which are broadly shared. Among these are caste, the idea of a great multiplicity of gods and goddesses and *puja* or offerings to them.

My use of the term "Essentialist" Islam derives from Martin's, with the addition of those modes of ritual practice that, while not mandated by Universalist texts, are widely distributed in the Muslim worlds. These would include the *mawlid al-nabi*, commemorating the birth of the Prophet Muhammad, the *dihkr* (remembrance of God) rites of Sufi orders, the Shiah celebration of Muharram, commemorating the martyrdom of Husayn, as well as the modes of ritual action commonly employed in the veneration of saints and local pilgrimage rites. Essentialist Islam is, therefore, and extremely inclusive category. Few, if any, Muslims would find themselves in agreement with all of it. The category is defined not as corpus of texts and rituals but as a system of discourse that extends beyond the borders of local Muslim societies. Essentialist Islam expands as new works are produced and enter into trans-local religious discourse. It contracts as materials are lost or no longer considered to be central elements of Islamic discourse and praxis. Continuing the exploration of the use of this schema in the study of other religion, the veneration of Buddha images and *stupas* (reliquary structures) occupies a similar position in Buddhism. These modes of religious praxis transcend enormous doctrinal differences.

Received Islam is that portion of the Universalist and Essentialist categories present in specific local contexts. Variation across local contexts can be enormous and contributes to the distinctive character of Local Islams as it constitutes the textual/ritual corpus that is the object of local interpretations. Local Islams are determined not only by the qualities of local culture but also by the nature of the Essentialist materials that are the grist for the mill of local interpretation. The fact that Javanese-Received Islam was largely Sufi exerted a powerful influence on the development of Javanese Local Islam. But Received Islam is far from static. It changes as the knowledge of the Essentialist corpus expands or contracts and as new works enter into the discourse of Essentialist Islam. The introduction of fundamentalist reformism into Javanese Islam in the early twentieth century and the theological and political debates it prompted are examples of the effects that the changing parameters of Received Islam may have on local traditions. The application of this element of the schema to other religions is relatively transparent. The use of Chinese Buddhist texts By Japanese, Korean and Vietnamese Buddhists is an example.

Local Islam is that set of oral, written, and ritual texts that are unknown outside of their area of origin. They derive from the interaction of local culture and Received Islam. This does not mean that they are any less complex or sophisticated

---

[116]Bali is the remaining Hindu enclave in otherwise Muslim and Christian Indonesia. Balinese Hinduism shares gods and goddesses with Indian Hinduism, but little else.

that those that are part of the Essentialist corpus – only that they are of local, rather than trans-cultural significance. Nurcholish Madjid's writings are, for example, as intellectually sophisticated as anything that has ever been written in Arabic.[117] They remain elements of Indonesian Local Islam because they are accessible only to those who can read Indonesian. But while Received Islam is interpreted in terms of culture, it may also shape it. The importance of Hadith (traditions concerning the speech and actions of the Prophet Muhammad) in central Java and the fact that significant elements of Javanese culture are derived from non-Javanese Muslim sources are examples of the interaction of local culture and Essentialist and Universalist Islam. Local Islams are also the source of the Essentialist corpus. The distinction is not so much one of content but rather of the degree to which Local Islamic materials are communicated to and come to influence the larger Muslim tradition.

Java, Indonesia, Islam and Orientalism

The remainder of this chapter will be concerned the way in which western understandings of Islam – many of which have deep roots in Christian theology – contributed to the development of a paradigmatic structure that relegates Islam to the periphery of Indonesian society and culture and how it is that over the past three decades a more Islam centered paradigm for understanding Indonesia has emerged. John Bowen characterizes Indonesianist perceptions of Islam in the late 1970s as follows:

> Although my colleagues working in mainland Southeast Asia had immersed themselves in the study of Theravada Buddhism, and all South Asianists were conversant in matters of caste, those of us engaging in Indonesian studies by and large left the systematic study of Islam out of our curricula.[118]

Bowen's research interests and initial fieldwork experience were in north Sumatra. Known as the "gateway to Mecca", it is a region that has long had the reputation of being among the most thoroughly Islamic in Indonesia. His portrayal of the neglect of Islam applies with even greater force to those of us who worked in Java – an area, the literature told us, that was among Indonesia's most nominally Islamic regions. Bowen's contrast between the curricula of students studying the Theravada Buddhist cultures of mainland Southeast Asia and the various Hindu cultures of South Asia and the curricula of Indonesianists is all the more revealing in light of the fact that he was a graduate student at the University of Chicago, a highly regarded center for Middle Eastern studies. During the late 1970s, a significant number of graduate students in anthropology at several institutions – including the University

---

[117]M. binte-Yahya, *Pimikir Islam*, Singapore: Majlis Ugama Islam Singapura, 2005, is one of the few scholars to have appreciated that Madjid and other Southeast Asian Muslim thinkers are "world class" figures.

[118]J. Bowen, *Muslims Through Discourse*, Princeton: Princeton University Press, 1993, p. 3. Most of the time I spent at Chicago was devoted to Buddhist Studies.

of Chicago and the University of Illinois at Urbana- Champaign – availed themselves of Chicago's resources in South Asian and Buddhist studies, working closely
with such renowned scholars as Wendy Doniger and Frank Reynolds. I was one of
them. Very few of us, however, took advantage of the fact that Fazlar Rahman, one
of the great Islamicists of the time, was also at Chicago, or that he had a keen interest
in Islamic theology and education in Southeast Asia, and had worked closely with
Indonesian graduate students. I must admit that I am just as guilty of this intellectual
sin of omission as others. My studies of Hinduism and Buddhism did, however, did
contribute to my contributions to the development of Indonesian Islamic studies in
a rather backhanded way. When I arrived in Yogyakarta it was very clear that what
I was hearing and seeing was *not* Hinduism or Buddhism despite what the literature
said.

The systematic neglect of Islamic studies by Indonesianists has deep roots
in British and Dutch Orientalism. The view that Islam plays a marginal role
in Indonesian religion and culture dates to the earliest periods of Anglo-Dutch
Orientalism. The marginalization of Islam in studies of Indonesia can be attributed
to a complex combination of Protestant understandings of the nature of religion,
colonial policy, and the influence, in recent decades, of Weber's understanding of
Islam as a religion of ethical prophecy.

The emergence of an Islam-centered paradigm in Indonesian studies is also a
movement away from the anti-Islamic Orientalism of the colonial era. What is
now termed "Islamaphobia" has very deep roots in the Christian branch of Western
Civilization. Tropes of the Crusades, or as the are known among Muslims, Wars
of the Cross, helped to shape centuries of European scholarship. Perhaps the clearest statement of this hostile view of Islam can be found in Pope Urban II's call for
Christian armies to recapture the city of Jerusalem, which is holy for both Christians
and Muslims. In one account of his address calling upon Christians to take up the
Crusader's banner he is alleged to have describe the behavior of Muslims in the
Holy City of Jerusalem as follows:

> ... a race from the kingdom of the Persians, an accursed race, a race utterly alienated from
> God, a generation forsooth which has not directed its heart and has not entrusted its spirit
> to God, has invaded the lands of those Christians and has depopulated them by the sword,
> pillage and fire; it has led away a part of the captives into its own country, and a part it
> has destroyed by cruel tortures; it has either entirely destroyed the churches of God or
> appropriated them for the rites of its own religion.[119]

Urban promised to forgive the sins of all who went into battle against Muslims
and urged them to enter the fray with cries of "It is the will of God" on their lips. His
words, or rather inchoate tropes of them continue to haunt the collective memories
of Christians and Muslims. The persistence of this attitude, or at least traces of it,
is revealed in the ways in which Western scholars have represented Islamic history
and contemporary Islamic societies.

---

[119]D. Munro, "Urban and the Crusaders", *Translations and Reprints from the Original Sources of
European History*, vol 1:2, Philadelphia: University of Pennsylvania, 1895, pp. 5–8

Edward Said has observed that

> To the west, Asia had once represented silent distance and alienation; Islam was militantly hostile to European Christianity. To overcome such redoubtable constants the Orient needed first [to] be known, then invaded and possessed, then recreated by scholars, soldiers, and judges who disinterred forgotten languages, histories, races, and cultures in order to posit then – beyond the modern Oriental's ken – as the true classical Orient that could be used to judge and rule the modern Orient".[120]

Said argues that the representation – or, more accurately, the misrepresentation – of Islam was not only associated with, but was an essential component of colonial domination. Islamic "others" were understood initially from the perspective of the Christian concept of heresy as well as from those of classicist and Biblical studies concerned with the search for the original or pure form of religious traditions. Islam was, for many centuries, the dangerous "enemy other" of the Christian west. As Said notes elsewhere, Islam was contrasted to an India that is viewed in a more favorable and romantic light. This is still the popular view to a considerable degree. Put bluntly, in the popular mind, Islam is identified with fanaticism, terrorism, conversion by the sword, and anti-Zionism; India is synonymous with the Upanishads, bathing in the Ganges, silly but harmless "gurus" tending to the spiritual needs of new age flocks, and the Buddha – or more accurately, western (mis)representations of the Buddha.[121]

Said has almost nothing to say about Java, Dutch "Indologie," or its social scientific successors. Ironically, this omission is a powerful argument in favor of his interpretation of the political character of Orientalism. In Indonesia, Orientalism not only misrepresented Islam, it denied its existence. Instead, Orientalists offered the curious explanation that the millions of people who, as Benda put it, "consider themselves to be good and devout Muslims, profoundly attached to their own version of the faith," really are not Muslim or are only marginally so.[122] This is particularly true of studies of religion and culture in Java. Orientalist characterizations of Java mirror Said's observation regarding the contrast between Islam and India in western scholarship. The "real" Javanese religion is portrayed as a generally undefined variety of Hinduism and/or Buddhism articulated in classical dance, the *gamelan*, the *wayang*, and mystical sects.

This understanding of Javanese and other Indonesian cultures dates at least to the time of the British colonial officer and Orientalist Sir Thomas Stamford Raffles. Raffles governed Java during the British interregnum of 1811–1816. He was a man of little formal education but considerable academic talent. His interests were

---

[120]Op. cit., pp. 91–92.

[121]The Reverend Jerry Falwell is an example. In an interview with CBS news that sparked riots throughout the Muslim world he said:. "I think Mohammed was a terrorist. He – I read enough of the history of his life written by both Muslims and – and – non-Muslims, that he was a violent man, a man of war".

[122]H. Benda, "Christian Snouck Hurgronje and the Foundations of Dutch Islamic Policy in Indonesia," in *Continuity and Change in Southeast Asia: Collected Journal Articles of Harry J. Benda* (New Haven: Yale University Center for Southeast Asian Studies, 1972), 86.

largely antiquarian and commercial. His intellectual concerns focused primarily on what he termed the "ancient institutions": art and literature of the pre-Islamic era of Javanese history. His understanding of Islam appears to have been shaped primarily by the virulently anti-Islamic polemics of his day. While many of his observations ring true, they were colored by the Christian fear and distrust of Islam. At times, Raffles appears to have taken his personal affection for Javanese and Malays as a sign that they could not possibly take the religion of the despised enemy other of European Christianity very seriously. He was also an advocate of the "forward policy" of advocating the annexation of ever more territory by the British East India Company. Describing the Javanese as docile, nominal Muslims was as politically expedient as it was romantically attractive. This confusion of themes is apparent in Chapter 9 of his classic work, *The History of Java*.[123] Because of its enormous impact – both direct and indirect – on generations of scholars, Raffles' work merits careful consideration.

Raffles began his description of Javanese religion with a very brief discussion regarding the introduction of Islam in the fifteenth century. He then turned to a lengthy description of ancient Hindu and Buddhist temples and texts, which concluded with a brief account of Hindu Bali:

> The most striking vestige of antiquity ... to be found in the Eastern Seas is the actual state of society in the island of Bali, whither the persecuted Hindus took refuge on the destruction of Majapahit, and where the Hindu religion is still the established worship of the country.[124]

The contrast between Raffles' characterization of Bali as the survival of Javanese Hinduism and his previous account of Islam is striking:

> The natives are still devotedly attached to their ancient institutions, and though they have long ceased to respect the temples and idols of a former worship, they still retain a high respect for the laws, usages, and national observances which prevailed before the introduction of Mahometanism. And though some few individuals among them may aspire to a higher sanctity and closer conformity to Mahometanism than others, it may be fairly stated that the Javans in general, while they believe in one supreme God, and that Mahomet was his Prophet, and observe some of the outward forms of worship and observances, are little acquainted with the doctrines of that religion and are the least bigoted of its followers. Few of the chiefs decline the use of wine, and if the common people abstain from inebriating liquors, it is not from any religious motive. Mahometan institutions, however, are still gaining ground, and with a free trade a great accession of Arab teachers might be expected to arrive. Property usually descends according to Mahometan law; but in other cases, the Mahometan code, as adopted by the Javans, is strangely blended with the more ancient institutions of the country.

Pilgrims to Mecca are common ... Every Arab from Mecca, as well as every Javan who had returned from a pilgrimage thither, assumed on Java the character of a saint, and the credulity of the common people was such, that they too often attributed to such persons supernatural powers. Thus respected, it was not difficult for them to rouse the country to rebellion, and they became the most dangerous instruments in

---

[123] Raffles, *History of Java* op. cit., vol. 2, pp. 1–64.
[124] Ibid., p. 61.

the hands of the native authorities opposed to the Dutch interests. The Mahometan priests have almost invariably been found most active in every case of insurrection. Numbers of them, generally a mixed breed between the Arabs and the islanders, go about from state to state in the Eastern Islands, and it is generally by their intrigues and exhortations that the native chiefs are stirred up to attack or massacre the Europeans, as infidels and intruders.

The commercial monopoly of the Dutch, however injurious to the country in other respects, was in this highly advantageous to the character of the Javans, as it has preserved them from the reception of many of the more intolerable and deteriorating tenets of the Koran

I have already mentioned, that every village has its priest, and that in every village of importance there is a mosque or a building set apart adapted to religious worship. The usual Mahometan service is performed; and the Panghulu, or priest, is consulted and decides in all cases of marriage, divorce and inheritance ...

In their processions and rejoicings on religious festivals and other occasions, the Javans are free from that noisy clamor and uproar, which is usual with the Mahometans of continental India. The ceremony of husen hasen, which on the continent excites such a general noise throughout the country, here passes by almost without notice ...

> The Mahometan religion, as it at present exists in Java, seems only to have penetrated the surface, and to have taken but little root in the heart of the Javans. Some there are who are enthusiastic, and all consider it a point of honour to support and respect its doctrines: but as a nation, the Javans by no means feel hatred towards Europeans as infidels; and this perhaps may be given as the best proof that they are very imperfect Mahometans.[125]

From these statements it is apparent that Raffles, like many of his contemporaries, understood "Mahometanism" as a religion of violence and bigotry. His reference to the Shi'ah celebration of the martyrdom of Imam Husayn as a defining characteristic of Islam, indicates that his understanding of the diversity of the Islamic tradition was faulty at best. He appears to have regarded Islam to be essentially a legal code and to have failed to understand the tension between *Shari'ah* and local custom that is a basic concern in all Muslim civilizations. When viewed from the perspective of pre-Islamic Javanese culture and religion, his observations that the old temples had been entirely abandoned, that there were well-established systems of mosques and Islamic officials, and that the Javanese understood the fundamental Islamic teaching of the unity of God indicate that early nineteenth-century Java was far more Islamic than Raffles realized. On the whole, his work is marred by a strong tension between his obvious affection for the Javanese and his contempt for Islam.

Raffles' understanding of Islam and its role in Javanese and other Indonesian cultures was deeply rooted in theologically charged Christian polemics against Islam that had circulated in Europe for centuries. These polemics had been used by earlier Dutch scholars, and shaped Dutch "Indologie" and policy throughout

---

[125]Raffles cites a memoir by Hogendorp that states: "The Javans, however, are far from bigots in their religion, as other Mahometans generally are".

the colonial period. European interest in, and concern with, Indonesian Islam dates to the seventeenth century, when Dutch theologians and administrators began to confront the problems of understanding and controlling the formidable Islamic communities in Java, Sumatra, and eastern Indonesia. Karel Steenbrink points out that Calvinist polemics against the Papacy and Catholic ritual practices, including fasting and pilgrimage, shaped protestant understandings on Islam in Indonesia and elsewhere.[126] Like Luther, Dutch Calvinists had difficulty deciding who they hated more – Muslims or Roman Catholics. When Voetius (1655) attributed the unwillingness of the Muslims of Ternate (in what is now Eastern Indonesia) to convert to Christianity to ignorant Muslim "priests" with a scant knowledge of Arabic, and when Dutch officials referred to Islamic rulers as "Popes," they were engaging in a highly polemical theological discourse that incorporated factual errors. Priests, and particularly Popes, were understood as being, quite literally, agents of Satan and corrupters of the pristine doctrines of the early Christian community. Calvinists viewed Islam as grossly heretical, associating modes of religious practice – such as pilgrimage, fasting, and the keeping of vigils – with Catholic "idolatry".[127]

Theologically charged polemics depicting Islam as a Christian heresy and the Prophet Muhammad as the anti-Christ date to the eighth century theologian John of Damascus. Orientalism and the study of Arabic began for three reasons: to refute the – generally misunderstood – religious message of Islam, to acquire the scientific and philosophical knowledge that was accessible to medieval Europeans only through the study of Arabic, and to gain a greater understanding of the range of semitic languages that, it was believed, would aid in the interpretation of the Biblical textual corpus. From the beginning, there was a tendency to focus primarily on the *Qur'an* and the life of the Prophet Muhammad. This focus was largely due to the centrality of the gospels and the importance of the sacralized biography of Jesus of Nazareth in the Christian, and particularly Protestant, tradition.

Protestant scholars continued the medieval traditions of denouncing the *Qur'an* and the Prophet Muhammad, but introduced a novel element into the anti-Islamic polemic – the theory that, just as Roman Catholics had perverted the teachings of Christ, contemporary Muslims had departed from the original meaning of Islam. An early version of what was to become a major theme in Orientalist studies of Indonesian Islam can be found in the works of the Dutch scholar Adrian Reland. Reland was more sympathetic to Islam, in general, than most other scholars of his day, and he attempted to refute some of the more blatant medieval imaginations of Islam. His sympathy did not, however, extend to the Muslim communities of his day. When he spoke positively about Islam he meant the "original doctrine of Islam and not . . . the doctrine as it is currently practiced by a number of Muslims".[128]

---

[126] K. Steenbrink, *Dutch Colonialism and Indonesian Islam: Contacts and Conflicts 1596–1950*, Amsterdam and Atlanta: Editions Rodopi B.V., 1993, p. 50.

[127] Ironically, Voetius found common ground with Muslims in their rejection of the veneration of images and icons, and in their ridicule of the Catholic doctrine of transubstantiation as eating God. Cited in Steenbrink, *Dutch Colonialism*, p. 52.

[128] Ibid., p. 55.

Reland's purpose was to present a "realistic" account of Islam, freed from the outrageous polemics of his medieval predecessors. This does not mean, however, that he was any more sympathetic towards Islam, or that he was prepared to consider the diversity of the Islamic tradition. Like other Protestant authors of his time, Reland's understanding of religion was text centered and predicated on the assumption that the earliest variants of the textual tradition represented the "true" version of the faith, from which subsequent generations had deviated.

Reland pointed out that Catholics and Protestants frequently invoked medieval polemics against Islam in debates internal to the Christian tradition. He quoted the Catholic author Vivaldus:

> Mahomet affirmed that he only had the Gospel, and knew what things were to be rejected, and what to be Received out of both the Testaments; So the impious Luther said that the Gospel was never in Germany before him. Mahomet had seventy two sects, so the Evangelicks have as many. Mahomet said that men's opinions were to be judged only according to his writings: So say the Hereticks. He changed the course of Lent: But the Lutherans not only change but abhor all fasts.[129]

Reland maintained that it was necessary to study Islam in order to defeat it. He turned his attention to the refutation of the *Qur'an* because of his frustration with the fact that Muslim interlocutors relied upon scripture to justify their positions rather than entering into the type of theological debates characteristic of eighteenth-century Protestantism. He characterized Muslims as ignorant and fanatical:

> I own that the Mahometans don't lie so near to us as the Papists and others; nor am I for teaching the method of defeating the Muslims before other Adversaries, who are daily amongst us. He that understands me so is in a gross mistake. But have we not a great deal of business with the Mahometans at Constantinople, upon the confines of Hungary and the Turkish Empire, upon the coasts of Africa, in Syria, Persia and the East Indies, where are our Colonies, and the places we frequent to get riches contain an abundance of Mahometans. But they will not dispute about their religion. I grant it, they are not forward to dispute because they keep close to Alcoran [*sic*]; and when a Christian disputes against them, they cannot answer anything, but that they believe or do this because of what God hath commanded. Now since the Mahometans are perfectly fixed in this, and esteem every command in the Alcoran [*Qur'an*] as Divine we cannot dispute with them whether such a doctrine or such a rite be good or convenient but the whole dispute will be about the sole authority of the Alcoran. And when it comes to that, such passages should be drawn out of the Alcoran itself as would show it not to be a divine book.[130]

Despite his attempt to "understand" Islam, Reland was entirely dedicated to its destruction. He was strongly critical of his countrymen who journeyed to the east with the sole purpose of finding riches. He described himself as one committed to saving souls and destroying the enemies of the true faith:

---

[129] A. Reland, *Of the Mahometan Religion, Two Books. The former of which is a short system of Mahometan Theology, Translated from an Arabick Manuscript, and Illustrated with Notes. The latter examines into some Things falsly charged upon the Mahometans* London, 1712, p. 9.

[130] Ibid., p. 13.

> From the time that the Mahometan Doctrine poisoned almost the whole Earth with its
> Infection and Contagion, there were a great many who endeavored to put a stop to a growing
> evil, and confute a most abominable Religion.[131]

He further declared that he was "concerned for this alone, that this and all my other labors may contribute to the triumph of truth, of the Evangelical Faith, and the last end, the Glory of the only God".[132] For all of this, subsequent generations of Dutch missionary scholars considered Reland to have been too liberal and sympathetic toward Islam.

Gibbon's account of Islam, which relied in part on Reland's work, is included in his classic work, *The Decline and Fall of the Roman Empire*. He popularized the distinction between the purity of the *Qur'an* and the corruption of Islam, and he pushed the timeline for that corruption back to the lifetime of the Prophet Muhammad himself. While praising the Quranic teaching on the unity of Allah, Gibbon suggested that Muhammad became increasing cynical and corrupt as his political power grew. The Muhammad of Mecca was a "humble preacher" with motives of "pure and genuine benevolence". Following his emigration to Medina, Muhammad is transformed. He is now a "prince" who "secretly smiled ... at the enthusiasm of his youth and the credulity of his proselytes".[133]

It is not possible to determine precisely the degree to which Raffles views of Javanese Islam were influenced by Reland, Gibbon, and other eighteenth-century scholars. It is clear that he understood Islam as a corrupt, bigoted faith that had lead to the decline of "classical" Javanese civilization. Dutch Indologie was inspired by Raffles' pioneering work and, in a more general sense, by British colonial scholarship that sought to use knowledge of Asian cultures to facilitate colonial administration. From the beginning there was a strong interrelationship between colonial and missionary scholarship. As Day and Florida have observed, the origins of Dutch Indologie can be traced to the Institute of Javanese Language and Literature established in Surakarta in 1832.[134] The founder of the institute, J. F. C. Gericke, was a Bible translator. Day argues that Gericke's fear of and disdain for Islam led him to eliminate "Islamic literature from the spectrum of intellectually recognizable categories," and to ignore the vast majority of Javanese literary and religious texts focusing on explicitly Islamic themes.[135] Florida puts it this way:

As a classical discipline, colonial Javanalogical philology is preoccupied with the question for golden ages, periods of alleged literary florescence succeeded by

---

[131] Ibid., p.47.

[132] Ibid., p.17.

[133] E. Gibbon, *The History of the Decline and Fall of the Roman Empire,* London: Methuen and Co., 1911, pp. 401–402.

[134] A. Day, "Islam and Literature in Southeast Asia: Some Premodern, Mainly Javanese Perspectives," In: M. B. Hooker (ed.), *Islam in Southeast Asia,* Leiden: E. J. Brill, 1988, pp. 130–59. N. Florida, *Writing the Past, Inscribing the Future: History as Prophecy in Colonial Java,* Durham: Duke University Press, 1995.

[135] Day, op. cit., p. 134.

periods of decline or decadence. Such philology teaches that Javanese literature attained the zenith of its sophistication and aesthetic value in the distant pre-Islamic past.[136]

Given this perspective it is hardly surprising that Dutch philology came to focus increasing on Bali in the later colonial period. While Islamic Java was regarded as, in Florida's terms, "derivative and sometimes degenerate,"[137] Bali came to be understood as the last bastion of Hindu-Javanese high culture.

There are, of course, exceptions. The development of Dutch Indologie was paralleled by that of Arabic and Islamic studies. As the nineteenth century wore on, Dutch scholars acquired an increasingly sophisticated understanding of Indonesian Islamic textual and popular traditions. However, advances in empirical understanding did little to change the view that Indonesian Islams were corrupt versions of an essentially foreign religion.[138]

The theme of contemporary Islamic practice as a corruption of the faith and practice of the Prophet Muhammad has become a recurrent one in western studies of Islam and Southeast Asia. This combined with a tendency to glorify those aspects of Indonesian culture that clearly are not derived from Islamic sources, has led some scholars to underestimate the importance of Islam as a religious faith and others to ignore it completely. This orientation lead Snouck Hurgronje and others to understand Indonesian Islam as deviant and corrupt to the extent that popular practice differed from that mandated by *fiqh* (legal) texts. While Snouck Hurgronje was aware of the fact that the distinction between *fiqh* and popular practice applied equally to the Local Islams of South Asia and the Middle East, he took this as an indication of the general corruption and rigidity of nineteenth-century Islam, rather than as an example of the complexity of the Islamic tradition and its ability to adapt itself to local conditions. Steenbrink and Suminto attribute his emphasis on law and corruption to a combination of theological and administrative concerns.[139] As a colonial official, his mission was to limit the political potential of Islam. He brought to this task an understanding of religion shaped by his studies of Protestant theology, as well as by an impressive knowledge of Islamic jurisprudence. His knowledge of *fiqh* enabled him to provide "Islamic" justifications for anti-Islamic colonial policy, including the restriction of mosque construction in rapidly expanding urban areas.[140] His Protestant background probably contributed to his characterization of

---

[136]Florida, op. cit., p. 26.

[137]Ibid., p. 27.

[138]This perspective is apparent even in the works of Drewes whose contributions to scholarly knowledge of early Javanese Islam are enormous. In the introduction to his translation of what is certainly one of the oldest extant Javanese Islamic texts Drewes takes the homiletic character of the text, which is similar to basic ethical texts used throughout the Muslim world as a sign that the "Javanese neophytes did not stand too firmly in their shoes". G. Drewes, *An Early Javanese Code of Muslim Ethics,* The Hague: Martinus Nijhoff, 1978, p. 5.

[139]Steenbrink, op. cit., p. 88. A. Suminto, *Politik Islam Hindia Belanda,*Jakarta: LP3ES, 1985, 117.

[140]Suminto, op. cit., p., 171–73.

Islamic scholasticism as "medieval rubbish which Islam has been dragging along in its wake for too long".[141]

Snouck Hurgronje's policy of "associationism," which was one of the core elements of the Dutch "ethical policy" introduced in the early years of the twentieth century, played a major role in creating the elite that generations of Dutch and English scholars and colonial officers had imagined. Prior to the introduction of the ethical policy, the children of the *priyayi* elite received two types of education. At home and in palace schools, they received training in traditional literature and the performing arts. The sons of the elite were also educated in *pesantren* (Islamic boarding schools). One of the consequences of the "ethical policy" was that the children of the elite were boarded with Dutch families, and received modern, secular educations rather than traditional Islamic educations. Ironically, the term *pondok* was used for both types of boarding schools. As a result of this policy, a generation of elite Javanese received little, if any, formal Islamic education.

The gap between *santri* and *priyayi* (aristocratic) elites, which Geertz described in the early 1950s, is another consequence of this policy. As Ahmad Djajadiningrat observed, many of the *Kyai* (Islamic teachers) of the period were intensely suspicious of the *priyayi* elite because of their close ties to the colonial government, which the thought to be forbidden by Islamic law.[142] In the early twentieth century many *Ulama* believed that attending a Dutch school was *haram* (forbidden by *Shari'ah*). This combined with the obvious material benefits of modern education was one of the factors that motivated the founding of Muhammadiyah. While the vast majority of *priyayi* considered themselves to be Muslims, many did not receive even rudimentary Islamic educations. Some did not even know the Arabic phrases necessary to perform the daily prayers. In the late 1970s, several elderly Javanese *priyayi* explained to me that as youths they had been actively discouraged, if not actually prohibited, from attending mosque services. In its final generation, the Dutch colonial policy had begun to create the Indonesia it desired: one in which Islam was either isolated or domesticated. Edward Said and other students of colonial discourse have argued that the maintenance of social and political hegemony required not only military force and economic domination but also the development of cultural and religious hybridities through which subject peoples, or at least elites, came to identify with the material interests and cultural values of hegemonic powers.[143] This was clearly the goal of Dutch colonial policy in the late nineteenth and

---

[141] C. Snouck Hurgronje, *Mekka in the Latter Part of the Nineteenth century* Leiden: E. J. Brill, 1931.

[142] A. Djajadiningrat, "Reminiscences about Life in a Pesantren," In: C. Peders (ed. and trans.), *Indonesia. Selected Documents on Colonialism and Nationalism, 1830–1942*, Saint Lucia: University of Queensland Press, 1977, pp. 248–52. On relationships between the *Priyayi* elite and Dutch colonial authorities see H. Sutherland, *The Making of a Bureaucratic Elite. The Colonial Transformation of the Javanese Priyayi*, Singapore, The Australian Association for Asian Studies, 1976.

[143] A. Appadurai, Modernity at *Large, Cultural Dimensions of Globalization*. Minneapolis: University of Minnesota Press. 1996, pp. 89–90, T. Asad, *Anthropology and the Colonial*

early twentieth centuries. They failed, instead of loyal colonial subjects, they created a revolutionary nationalist elite who used what they had learned of western political theory against the colonial masters. Especially in the twentieth century Javanese and other Proto-Indonesian elites were fully informed of political developments, and especially the rise of democracy and notions of national self determination in Europe. As one Yogyakarta noble put it in the late 1970s, "We learned about democracy and nationalism from the Dutch, and wondered why, if small countries in Europe could have them, why a country as large as Indonesia could not". On March 18th 1940 Sultan Hamengkubuwana IX spoke for a generation of Dutch educated Javanese and Indonesians when, in his coronation address he said:

"Even though I have had a western education, I am first of all – and will remain – Javanese".[144]

For the most part *santri* elites adopted non-cooperationist attitudes towards the colonial government, which were understood n terms of the Islamic concept of *hijra* or emigration. This term refers to the flight of the Prophet Muhammad and the Muslim community from Mecca to Medina in 622 in the face of severe persecution. It is understood as flight from an area in which Islam can not be practiced and in which struggle against the forces of oppression (*jihad*) can not be conducted successfully. In colonial Java *hijra* was sometimes physical, as many *Pesantren* are located in rural areas or provincial cities such as Kudus. It could also be social in the sense of being in, but not of, the world of colonialism. It either case there was a strong tendency for *santri* to distance themselves from colonial authority and culture. Some prominent *ulama* went so far as to move permanently to Mecca.[145] This was to have long term implications for the development of Indonesian concepts of nationality because "modern" education was not fully accepted by traditional *santri* until nearly the end of the twentieth century because of its association with colonialism and "unbelief".

Encounter, New York: Humanities Books, 1995. J. Comaroff and J. Comaroff, *Of Revelation and Revolution, Vol. II: The Dialectics of Modernity on South African Frontier*, Chicago: University of Chicago Press, 1997, E. Said, op. cit.

[144]These words are engraved on a marble plaque located in *Ghedung Kaca* in the Yogyakarta *Kraton*. The text is in Indonesian and Dutch: "*Walapun saya telah emgenyam pendidikan barat yang sebenarnya namun pertama-tama saya adalah dan tetap adalah orang Java*" and " *Al hebik een uitgesproken westerse opreoding gehad toch been en blijf Ik in de allereerste plaats Javaan*". See Chapter 4 for a more lengthy discussion.

[145]A. Azra, *The Origins of Islamic Reformism in Southeast Asia: Networks of Malay-Indonesian and Middle Eastern 'Ulama' in the Seventeenth and Eighteenth centuries*, Leiden: KITLV, 2004, Snouck Hurgronge *Mekka . . .* op. cit., On the history of Southeast Asian Islamic movements see, B. Boland, *The Struggle of Islam in Modern Indonesia*. The Hague, Martinus Nijhof, 1982. On more recent developments and attempts to bridge this divide see R. Heffner, *Civil Islam. Muslims and Democracy in Indonesia*, Princeton: Princeton University Press, 2004 and N. Ichwan and N. Hasan, *Moving with the Times. The Dynamics of Contemporary Islam in a Changing Indonesia*. Yogyakarta, Center for the Study of Islam and Social Transformation, Sunan Kalijaga State Islamic University, 2008.

Rejection of "modern" education limited the ability of conservative *Santri* to participate in many areas of public life in the colonial state and subsequently in independent Indonesia. This, in turn contributed to the perception, common in the 1970s, and which persist today that Indonesia is somehow "un-Islamic" or even "anti-Islamic". Those *santri* who did embrace western education and other elements of modernity were, for the most part, associated with Muhammadiyah, Persatuan Islam and other "reformist" organizations whose neo-Wahhabi tendencies and especially the rejection of Sufi devotionalism remains a deeply divisive force. Muhammadiyah attempted to fill this gap by establishing a vast network of schools colleges and universities that provide education in "general" subjects in an Islamic context. While this contributed great to the growth of the organization, religiously conservative Muslims were, and many still are, reluctant to send their children to Muhammadiyah schools because of their "reformist" theological orientation. The introduction of secular subjects into the *pesantren* curriculum and the establishment of a system of Islamic higher education by the Ministry of Religion in the 1960s has done much to remedy this situation. This system began with two campuses one in Jakarat and the other in Yogyakarta and has expanded enormously to include hundreds of Islamic colleges (*Sekola Tingii Islam Negri/STAIN* and higher level *Insitut Agama Islam Negeri/IAIN*) and universities (*Universitas Islam Negeri*). Today these institutions provide educational opportunities for young people from conservative Muslim backgrounds who would be reluctant, or even completely unwilling, to attend secular government or Muhammadiyah schools.[146] In 2007 the Rector of STAIN Surakarta explained to me that the purpose of these institutions is to provide students with "life skills" (English in the original) in an Islamic context. In this sense the goals of the system are very similar to those of Muhammadiyah schools, but the Islamic "context" is non-sectarian and if anything tipped in the direction of traditionalist understandings of Islam. Similarly the Rector of the Islamic University in Malang in Central Java described his institution as being "A *pesantren* inside a University and a University inside a *Pesantren*". He was referring to the fact that, unlike most others, the university provides living quarters for female students, which he called "*pondok prempuan*" (women's dormitories). He continued that this reassured parents that their daughters were "safe" at the university.

During the same period in which there were systematic attempts to deny and domesticate Javanese Islam, Dutch Indology, with its focus on Hindu-Javanese and Balinese texts, also came to maturity as a scholarly enterprise and restoration or

---

[146]These observations are based on interviews with students, faculty and administrators at institutions throughout Indonesia between 2000 and 2008. For detailed discussions of these issues see: R. Lukens-Bull, "Two Sides of the Same Coin: Modernity and Tradition in Indonesian Islamic Education". *Anthropology and Education Quarterly.* vol. 32, no. 3, 2001, 350–372 and *A Peaceful Jihad: Negotiating Identity and Modernity in Muslim Java,* New York: Palgrave Mcmillan, 2005 and R. Martin and M. Woodward, *Defenders of Reason in Islam. Mutazilism from Medieval School to Modern Symbol,* Oxford: One World, 1997.

reconstruction of ancient Hindu and Buddhist monuments commenced.[147] At times
the two endeavors overlapped. Groneman, whose account of the *Garebeg Malud* is
discussed in Chapter 5 was also in charge of the initial phases of the "restoration"
of the Hindu-Javanese Prambanan temple complex 15 km east of Yogyakarta.[148]
The development of Dutch structural anthropology provided a "scientific" foundation – as opposed to a political or theological one – for Islam denying Orientalism.
Building largely on the theoretical postulates of Durkheim and the French *Annee
Sociologique* school, Dutch scholars described aspects of Javanese culture and
religion – including divination, architecture, sacred geography, and ritual – as man-
ifestations of pre-Hindu systems of "primitive classification".[149] Rassers, Pigeaud,
and others were particularly concerned with isolating survivals of kinship systems
based on dual organization in Javanese texts, symbols, and material culture. This
orientation facilitated the comparison of Java with other Indonesian cultures, but
tended to discourage the serious consideration of the ways in which Hinduism,
Buddhism, and Islam had shaped Javanese culture. It also contributed to an ahis-
torical understanding of Java in which what could be shown to be the "oldest" was
putatively accepted as the most authentic. It was assumed that the focus of anthropological inquiry was the structural core of numerous ancient Indonesian cultures,
and that the organization of these archaic societies is closely connected with, and to
a large extent determined by, kinship and marriage systems.

While it is difficult to attribute a grand theoretical design or explicit political
agenda to the "Leiden School", and even less so to the Java Society, both were
coherent in their emphasis on pre-Islamic and pre-Hindu "survivals," and their con-
cordant systematic neglect of Islam. The paradigmatic concept that archaic systems
of classification are resistant to change and find expression in subsequent historically conditioned social and religious phenomena made it possible for scholars
like Rassers and Pigeaud to mention Islamic rituals, including circumcision and the
celebration of the birth of the Prophet Muhammad, as examples of primeval dual-
ism.[150] This tendency is illustrative of the theoretical difference between Dutch and
French structuralism. Like Durkheim, Dutch structuralists held the view that religion was a symbolic reflection of "social facts," particularly those of kinship. The
historicized version of Durkheim's sociology, most clearly articulated by Rassers,

---

[147] Raffles was as influential here as he was in setting the course for the study of Islam in Indonesia.
His *History of Java*, op.cit., includes the first scholarly accounts of Javanese Hindu and Buddhist
monumental architecture. For an account his influence and on early Dutch efforts to "restore"
Hindu and Buddhist monuments in the last 19th and early 20th centuries see R. Jordaan, op. cit.

[148] Jordaan describes Groneman's clearing of the site as a "disaster" from the perspective of scientific archeology. R. Jordaan, "Candi Prambanan. An Updated Introduction", p. 14, in Jordaan,
op.cit., See also J. Groneman, "De Vereenining voor Oudheid-, Land-,Taal- en Volkenkunde to
Jogjakarta, en de Tjandi Prambanan," in *Indische Gids*, vol. 9, no. 2, 1887.

[149] On the *Annee Sociologique* and its contributions to European social thought see, N. Yash, *Emile
Durkheim. Contributions to L'Annee Sociologique*, New York: The Free Press, 1980.

[150] W. Rassers, *De Pani-Roman*. Antwerpen, De Vos von Kleff, 1922. English translation, *Panji,
the Culture Hero*. The Hague: Martinus Nijhoff, 1959; Pigeaud, op. cit.

maintained that hypothetical "social facts" of a distant past, rather than of the present, determined the structural core of Javanese religion and culture. Emphasis on this supposed structural core allowed Rassers and others to treat the doctrinal and symbolic systems of Hinduism, Buddhism, and Islam as interchangeable and trivial components of an enduring structural pattern. Stutterheim held a distinct, though related view that ancestor worship provides the key to understanding Java from what he understood as the superficially Hindu and Buddhist societies of the eighth and ninth centuries to the equally superficially Islam of modern Java.[151] He argued, or rather asserted that: "It is known to but a few that the so-called "Hindu temples" on the island of Java are not temples, nor were they built by Hindus".

The Contemporary Legacy of Anglo-Dutch Orientalism

The persistence of Orientalist representations of Javanese and other Indonesian Islams in contemporary scholarship can be attributed, in large measure, to the pervasive influence on Indonesian studies of Clifford Geertz and Benedict Anderson. Both echo common themes in Dutch orientalism, but employ Weberian rather than Orientalist analytic categories. Taken together, Geertz's and Anderson's interpretations of Indonesian religion and culture form what Kuhn calls a paradigm. Paradigms are the assumptions that define the problems addressed in particular fields of study, or as Kuhn puts it, the "puzzles" that define normal science.[152]

Clifford Geertz's *The Religion of Java* replaced Snouck Hurgronje's *The Achehnese* as the standard reference on Indonesian Islam – the work against which all others were, until recently, judged. It does not include a bibliography, and contains only occasional bibliographic footnotes, but Geertz's reliance on Snouck Hurgronje is very clear. Geertz cites Snouck Hurgronje's statement that:

> the building of Islam is still mainly supported by the central pillar, the confession that there is no god but Allah and that Muhammad is the messenger of Allah [however], this pillar is surrounded with a medley of ornamental work quite unsuited to it which is a profanation of its lofty simplicity,

Commenting that: "his simile would have applied even more aptly to Java.[153]

Geertz's "general introduction" to Islam echoes Snouck Hurgronje's *fiqh*-centered approach. Building on Weber's studies of religion and rationality, Geertz describes Islam as "a religion of ethical prophecy" whose message is "rationalization and simplification".[154] While Geertz does not cite Weber, the parallel with Weber's discussion of prophecy in *The Sociology of Religion* is clear. Weber mentions Muhammad as being among a small group of "ethical prophets" whom he characterizes as follows: "Preaching as one who has received a commission from

---

[151] For a more detailed consideration of Sutterheim' views see Jordaan, op.cit., pp. 35–37.

[152] Kuhn, op. cit., pp. pp. 10–11

[153] Geertz, *Religion of Java*, op. cit., p. 24.

[154] Ibid., p.121.

God, he demands obedience as an ethical duty".[155] This understanding of Islam, rationality, and ethical prophecy provides the basis for Geertz's depiction of Islam as the religion of the marketplace, and for his depiction of aspects of the Javanese religion that do not fit Weber's "ideal type" as vaguely defined combinations of animism, Hinduism, and Buddhism. The "failure" of Islam is linked to the failure of rationalization. As Geertz puts it:

> Buddhist mystical practices got Arabic names, Hindu Radjas suffered a change of title to become Moslem Sultans, and the common people called some of their wood spirits jinns; but little else changed.[156]

Geertz mentions that he and other participants in the "Modjokuto project" spent 4 months in the Netherlands "interviewing" otherwise unidentified "Dutch scholars" on Indonesia.[157] His descriptions of the *"abangan"* (lower class *kejawen*) variant of Javanese Islam, when compared with those of Dutch Indologists and missionaries, points to an even more pervasive parallel. His analysis of the Javanese *slametan* is strikingly similar to that of Mayer and van Moll – so much so that both works include detailed discussions of the cost of ritual performance.[158] Even more significant is the fact that the tripartite *santri* (Muslim), *abangan* (Animist), and *priyayi* (Hindu-Buddhist) distinction,[159] made famous by Geertz, was already well known to Dutch missionary scholars. The distinction between orthodox *santri* and heterodox *abangan* was mentioned by Poensen in 1886, who used the term *putihan* (white people) to refer to pious Muslims – now more commonly referred to as *santri*. He described *putihan* as those Javanese who were concerned with Islamic religious teachings and *abangan* (red people) as those Javanese who ignored such teachings.[160] Similar terminology was used by the Yogyakarta court, which divided its

---

[155] M. Weber, *The Sociology of Religion*, Glenco: Free Press, 1963, p. 46.

[156] Geertz, *Religion of Java*, op. cit., p. 125.

[157] Ibid., p. 38.

[158] Ibid., pp. 30–85. L. Mayer, and J. van Moll, *De Sedekahs en Slametans in de Desa de Daarbij Gewoonlijk door den Given Gegeven Festiviteiten*, Semarang: Van Dorp, 1909.

[159] It has never been clear what "Hindu-Buddhist" might mean. Geertz's typology has, by now, fallen out of use. The most basic division in Javanese Islam, that be *shari'ah*-centric and Sufi variants is most commonly referred to as that between *santri* and *Kejawen* Islam. Divisions within the *santri* community are now more complex than they were when Geertz described them in the late 1950s. Today Indonesian and other scholars now speak of traditionalist, modernist, neo-modernist or neo-traditionalist and Islamist variants. The category "traditionalist" is, itself problematical because it is at least implicitly defined in terms of various strains of Islamic "modernism" that emerged in Indonesia and elsewhere in the Muslim world in the late nineteenth and early twentieth centuries. As such it neglects, and indeed trivializes, difference within this community, as as such can be understood as being yet another Orientalist construction. "Traditionalist" Islam is, in fact, extremely diverse. Theological orientations within the Javanese *pesantren* tradition range from those associated with pantheistic Sufis to Shari'ah centric textual literalists. A comprehensive study of the varieties of traditional Javanese Islam remains to be written.

[160] C. Poensen, "Letters about Islam from the Country Areas of Java, 1886". in Penders, *Indonesia*, 241–47.

subjects into *santri putih* and *santri abang*. Missionary scholars tended to emphasize the "non-Islamic" character of Javanese religion because of the widely shared opinion that "orthodox Muslims" were utterly nonconvertible. Javanese mystics were at least willing to discuss religious matters with Christian missionaries, though few were willing to seriously consider conversion. It was necessary for missionaries to deny Javanese Islam in order to classify Java as a proper mission field, one in which the work of spreading the Gospel could be conducted with some hope of success. While Geertz does not share these Islamaphobic missionary sentiments, and describes Java's orthodox Muslim merchants as Indonesia's best hope for a brighter economic future, *The Religion of Java* is best understood as an elegant restatement and theoretical reformulation of a combination of Orientalist and colonial depictions of Islam, Java and Indonesia.

Anderson's "The Idea of Power in Javanese Culture" makes explicit reference both to colonial scholarship and to Weber.[161] He relies heavily on colonial studies of Hindu-Javanese kingship and on Geertz's characterization of Javanese kingdoms as Indic states. He emphasizes Java's *tantric* past, basing much of his argument on close readings of old Javanese texts. In a subsequent essay, Anderson explains that his purpose was to show Weber's analysis of charismatic leadership as flawed to the degree that it accorded priority to the characteristics of persons rather than to the reemergence of traditional, substantive understandings of power during periods of cultural and political crises.[162] His understanding of Islam mirrors that of both Snouck Hurgronje and Geertz. He states that:

> rulers assumed Islamic titles, kept Islamic officials in their entourage, and added Islam to the panoply of their attributes. Yet this overt Islamization of the rulers does not seem to have caused major alternations in their way of life or outlook".[163]

His depiction of traditional Islamic scholars parallels that of his account of Indonesian Muslim rulers:

> The Islam of the *Kyai* was a kind in which traditional elements remained exceedingly powerful: intuitive, personal and mystical in character, it inherited much of the pre-Islamic religion.[164]

---

[161] B. Anderson, "The Idea of Power in Javanese Culture," In: C. Holt (ed.), *Culture and Politics in Indonesia*, Ithaca: Cornell University Press, 1972. While I am deeply indebted to Anderson for his theoretical observations on the nature of nationalism, I could not disagree more strongly with his assessment of the significance of Islam in Javanese history and culture.

[162] B. Anderson, *Language and Power: Exploring Political Cultures in Indonesia,* Ithaca: Cornell University Press, 1990, p. 11.

[163] Anderson, *"The Idea of Power,"* op. cit., pp. 58–59.

[164] Ibid., p. 54. This is simply not the case. Almost all *Kyai* are thoroughly conversant with Muslim legal, theological and/or mystical texts. Geertz's account of *Kyai*, and of traditional Javanese Islam in general is so wide of the mark that it is difficult to see how he could have been more than very superficially acquainted with the *pesantren* tradition. He was also was seemingly unable to distinguish between Sufism, Hinduism and Buddhism. See Z. Dhofier, *Tradisi Pesantren: Studi tentang Pandangan Hidup Kyai.* Jakarta: LP3ES, 1985 and *Pesantren Tradition: The Role of the Kyai in the Maintenance of Traditional Islam in Java.* Tempe, Arizona State University Program for Southeast Asian Studies, 1999 and S. Jones, "The Javanese Pesantren: Between Elite and

The paradigmatic status of the Weberized Orientalism of Geertz and Anderson is exemplified by otherwise excellent scholars taking the marginality of Islam in Indonesian culture as a given. Keeler provides a clear illustration of the ways in which Islam is circumscribed. He states:

> The distinction between *Abangan* (syncretist) and *Santri* (devout, whether orthodox or modernist) is hardly clear-cut – it is rather a spectrum, not an opposition – but I must defer to other scholars on the subject of the more orthodox Muslims in Java.[165]

Having circumscribed Islam, Keeler proceeds with an analysis of the Javanese shadow play that employs a considerable number of Islamic concepts – including the Sufi distinction between *zahir* (outward) and *batin* (inner) modes of piety – which are never identified as being Islamic. James Siegel and Shelly Errington carry the circumscription of Islam even further. Siegel groups "Muslims" with Chinese and foreigners as non-Javanese elements of Javanese society.[166] Errington mentions the fact that the last traditional ruler of the Buginese state she describes was "a very observant Muslim – he prayed five times a day, kept the fast, and had made the hajj to Mecca".[167] She characterizes the Buginese concept of the mystical path in terms of the following proverb:

> If a servant is in a state of intense longing for his master, and his master longs intensively for his servant, the servant will be wrapped in his master's clothing".[168]

It would be difficult to find a clearer example of the influence of Middle Eastern Sufism on Indonesian culture. Yet, in her introduction to the "economy, ethnic groups, languages, and religions of South Sulawesi," the word Islam never appears – nor is it to be found in the index.

Other scholars take an even stronger position, echoing Raffles' opinion that the conversion of Javanese and other Indonesians to Islam was superficial in nature. This position is forcefully articulated by M. C. Ricklefs, who has argued that conversion to Islam did not alter the fundamentally Hindu/Buddhist character of Javanese religious thought:

> ... to be Javanese is, for the majority, to be *Abangan* Javanese; the *Santri* Javanese is perceived by the bulk of Javanese society as a person who has to some extent removed himself from the social and cultural environment.[169]

Peasantry". In: C. Keyes (ed.), *Reshaping Local Worlds: Formal Education and Cultural Change in Rural Southeast Asia,* New Haven: Yale Center for International and Area Studies – Southeast Asia Studies, 1991. On Arabic language Islamic texts studied in *Pesantren* see: M. van Bruinessen, *Kitab Kuning:Ppesantren dan Tarekat: Tradisi-Tradisi Islam di Indonesia,* Bandung, Mizan, 1995.

[165] W. Keeler, *Javanese Shadow Plays, Javanese Selves,* Princeton: Princeton University Press, 1987, p. 23.

[166] J. Siegel, *Solo in the New Order: Language and Hierarchy in an Indonesian City,* Princeton: Princeton University Press, 1986, p. 70.

[167] S. Errington, *Meaning and Power in a Southeast Asian Realm,* Princeton: Princeton University Press, 1989, p. 23.

[168] Ibid., p. 87.

[169] M. Ricklefs, "Six centuries of Islamization in Java," In: N. Levtzion (ed.), *Conversion to Islam,* New York, Holmes and Meier, 1979, p. 127.

Some scholars have gone so far as to claim that Buddhism and Hinduism had an equally weak hold on the Javanese mind, and that the "real" Javanese religion is to be found in the remnants of pre-Indic mythologies. Theodore Pigeaud's statement is an eloquent formulation of this perspective:

> Perhaps it is safe to assume that for many centuries down to A.D. 1500, in large areas of the country (which was sparsely populated), rites connected with ancestor worship and ancient indigenous myth, in addition to cults of local spirits of mountains, sources of rivers, lakes and woods, and the sea, were sufficient religious bonds with the Unseen for Javanese and Balinese country-people, living in the restricted circle of small rural communities. No doubt in Java there is an analogy between the positions of Indian religion and of Islam in the cultural history of the people, both being originally foreign ideologies which for a long time remained the spiritual property of a cultural elite, without spreading to or being appreciated by the common people of the countryside.[170]

From the perspective of either Ricklefs or Pigeaud, "real Muslims" are somehow not quite "real Javanese". This is true only if one makes an *a priori* assumption that it is. Observant Javanese Muslims find such statements preposterous and insulting.

Islamic Studies, Javanese and Indonesian Islams – A New Paradigm

Kuhn has argued that paradigms are defined by, and in turn define, scientific communities. He observes that:

> Both useful and comfortable, paradigms delimit the questions that normal scholarship asks; once established, however, they die slowly. When an established paradigm shifts, it generally does so in response to a crisis relative to its inability to adequately explain empirical data.[171]

The deconstruction of the political underpinnings of existing paradigms can also figure significantly in what Kuhn terms "scientific revolutions," especially in the social sciences. It is not sufficient, however, because a "scientific revolution" also requires the redefinition of communities of scholars. This is often as much a social as it is an intellectual process. The Orientalist paradigm that relegated Islam to the periphery of Javanese and Indonesian cultures and histories served the interests of many generations of scholars. As late as the 1960s, it appeared to explain the cultural and political divisions of Indonesian, and in particular, of Javanese society. It was well established, with recognized authorities, who could be cited in books articles and grant proposals to establish one's own credentials, easily understood and intellectually safe. One could dismiss Islam as the religion of those who were somehow "not really Javanese" and get on with "normal science" and building one's career.

Today such a paradigm has ceased to have even the appearance of explanatory power. The neglect of Islam for political or religious reasons cannot be justified in

---

[170]T. Pigeaud, *Javanese and Balinese Manuscripts and some codices written in related idioms spoken in Java and Bali*, Wiesbaden: Franz Steiner Verlag GMBH, 1975, p. 77.

[171]Kuhn, op. cit., pp. 176–77.

the post-colonial world. Indonesian Islam is a reality that scholars can no longer ignore. The wave of Islamic resurgence that has swept the country in the past three decades makes it increasingly difficult, and even more absurd, to portray Islam as a marginal force located on the edges of Javanese and Indonesian civilizations. This, combined with the convergence of text centered Religious Studies and ethnographically based Anthropological methods which came belatedly to Islamic and Indonesian studies, led to the emergence of a new Islam centered paradigm beginning in the 1980s.

This process began with the emergence of a body of literature deconstructing the old Orientalism and exposing the ways in which it combined missionary fantasies with colonial policy bent on silencing the political voice of Islam. Commentaries on the study of Islam in Indonesia by both William Roff and Karel Steenbrink parallel Edward Said's expose of the hegemonic character of Orientalist discourse concerning the central lands of the Islamic world.[172] Roff observes that through out the history of Indonesian Studies there had been:

> an extraordinary desire on the part of Western social science observers to diminish, conceptually, the place and role of the religion and culture of Islam, now and in the past, in Southeast Asian societies.

He attributes this tendency in part to the desire of colonial powers to vanquish their Muslim subjects by locating "greatness" in a classical Hindu/Buddhist past and depravity in a corrupt Islamic present.[173] A related factor is the often simplistic and legalistic understanding of Islam that has been used in the evaluation of Southeast Asian religious systems. Steenbrink notes that Dutch "Indologie" was influenced by a colonial concern bordering on obsession with the legal dimension of Islam.[174] While this concern is understandable, given the colonial context in which Orientalism was located, it contributed to the formulation of a highly distorted understanding of Islam as a religion, and of the role of Islam in the religious lives of Javanese and other Indonesians.

Colonial scholars greatly underestimated the importance of Islam in Javanese culture, literature, and religion in part because they did not want to see Islam. The Orientalist paradigm was predicated on the assumption that the Javanese *kraton* are bastions of Buddhism and/or Hinduism. Postcolonial studies of the role of Islam in the life of the Javanese royal courts, including those included in this volume, have led to the demise of this paradigm and raised questions concerning the motives of colonial Orientalists. Studies of court literature by Soebardi, and of the role of Islam in the daily life of the courts by Ann Kumar, show that Islam played a central role in pre-modern *priyayi* life. The court *literati* were familiar with a wide range

---

[172]See W. Roff, "Islam Obscured? Some Reflections on Studies of Islam and Society in Southeast Asia," *Archipel*, vol. 29, no. 1, 1985, 7–34; Steenbrink, *Dutch Colonialism*; op. cit., and Said, *Orientalism*, op. cit.

[173]Roff, "Islam Obscured?" op. cit.

[174]Steenbrink, *Dutch Colonialism*, op. cit., pp. 90–91.

of Arabic textual materials.[175] Elderly *priyayi* I have spoken with who escaped the net of Islamaphobic Dutch education find the view that Islam was not important to be important in their religious lives have often declared that these are scandalous misrepresentations of *kraton* life. One wondered how anyone could say such things and explained that when she was growing up in the pre-war Surakarta *Kraton* that it was "*Qur'an* in the morning and *wayang* in the evening".

The Islamicization of Indonesian studies, described by John Bowen, has been the product of both an increased awareness of Islam among Indonesianists and a major shift in the orientation of many scholars who define themselves as Islamicists.[176] John Esposito argues that Islamic studies has, for many decades, been a conservative, philologically oriented discipline.[177] Many traditional Islamicists, therefore, consider the production of a critical edition of a classical text of greater significance than either a translation or a thematic analysis. While critical editions play an essential role in textual scholarship, they often are published in difficult-to-read fragments filled with interpolations, and they often convey little to a wider audience unless accompanied by translations and thematic analyses. Many Arabic and Persian texts, for example, are so complex that even a good translation is unintelligible without extensive commentary – which too few translators provide. This overall philological conservatism of Islamic studies, combined with an Arab and/or Persian centrism, has clearly contributed to the situation Bowen describes.

> While it is true that many Indonesianists have ignored Islam and Islamic studies, it is equally true that many Islamicists have had little or no interest in Indonesian or other Asian Islamic traditions, or in establishing a scholarly dialogue with those who do. Very few, indeed, even have a reading knowledge of any Southeast Asian language.[178]

Islamic studies have, however, changed fundamentally in the past three decades. While the tradition of rigorous, if highly conservative philological scholarship continues, younger scholars have expanded their horizons to include the contemporary understanding and practice of Islam, as well as the study of Islam outside the Middle Eastern "heartland". The Iranian revolution contributed to this development in many parts of the Islamic world by raising the question, "Can it happen here?" The publication of Edward Said's *Orientalism*, coupled with the rise of Islamic fundamentalism, served as a wake-up call more to Islamicists than to Indonesianists. In the 1980s, Islamic studies became a growth industry in much the same way that Southeast Asian studies did in the 1960s and early 1970s. Islam, like Southeast Asia during the Third Indo-China War, has emerged from obscurity to become the daily subject of newspaper headlines, evening television newscasts, and talk radio programs. Khomeini was often been accused (wrongly) of wanting to drive Islam back

---

[175] S. Soebardi, *The Book of Cabolek*, The Hague: Martinus Nijhoff, 1975; A Kumar, "Javanese Court Society and Politics in the Late Eighteenth century: The Record of a Lady Soldier," *Indonesia*, 29: pp. 1–46 and M.Woodward, *Islam in Java,* op. cit.

[176] op. cit., pp. 1–8.

[177] Esposito, op. cit., p. 203.

[178] Op. cit., p. 6. Scholars of South Asian Islam voice similar complaints.

into the thirteenth century. While it was probably the least of his concerns, he played a significant role in driving western Islamic studies into the twentieth. The attacks of September 11, 2001 have only increased interest in Islam and Islamic Studies; though as I often tell my students – for all the wrong reasons.

Public interest in and governmental concern with Islam led to both funding and academic positions.[179] This occurred at a time when there was an increased interest in applying the theoretical approaches of the humanities and social sciences to the study Islamic texts and societies. The deconstruction of Orientalism, accompanied with an increased emphasis on Islam as a living faith, opened the door for more serious attention to the Islams of the "periphery" – Europe, Africa, and Asia east of the borders of Iran. Just as Indonesianists began to pay more serious attention to Islam, classically trained Islamicists began to notice Southeast Asia. Many have traveled to the region on Fulbright lectureships, while others assumed teaching positions at various Indonesian Islamic Academies and Universities. Many of the younger generation of Indonesianists have learned Arabic – something that few of us trained in the 1970s would have dreamed of because we were told that we did not really need to.

Ad yet, paradigms die slowly, especially when they are associated with academic luminaries. The persistence of Orientalist themes in Euro-American Indonesian Studies is due in large measure to the influence Clifford Geertz, whose renown for theoretical contributions to Anthropology and other human sciences is well known and well deserved. Geertz's theoretical acumen was, unfortunately, combined with a simplistic and inaccurate understanding of Islam and its role in the lives of Javanese and other Indonesians. In one of his later works, which offers a retrospective commentary on more than four decades on research and reflection on Indonesian society and religion, Geertz argued that the emergence of the new, Islam-centered paradigm in Indonesian studies can be attributed to the influence of the Indonesian government's program of encouraging religious tolerance and discouraging the Islamic rhetoric of apostasy and unbelief in scholarly characterizations of Islam.[180] Geertz's observation is understandable given the fact that the works of

---

[179]Unfortunately this has also given birth to a vast body of quasi-academic punditry that reincarnates the very worst Orientalist stereotypes of Islam. One need look no further than the front tables of Borders and other chain bookshops for examples. Books that would otherwise pass largely unnoticed have become instant best sellers and their authors propelled to international prominence for no other reason than that they are Islamaphobic in a cultural climate where Islamapobhia is politically acceptable and economically profitable. See, for example, B. Lewis, *What Went Wrong? The Clash Between Islam and Modernity in the Middle East*, New York: Harper Perennial, 2003, D. Pipes, *Militant Islam Reaches America*, New York: W.W. Norton, 2003. Pipes is fond of referring academics who disagree with him as "Jihadi Professors". Most of us on his list consider it an honor to be included. I have argued elsewhere that attempts to attribute the subordinate position of Muslim peoples and countries in the World System are Orientalist fictions masking the military and economic foundations of Western hegemony, "Modernity and the Disenchantment of Life: A Muslim Christian Contrast," in, J. Meuleman (ed.) *Islam in the Era of Globalization. Muslim Attitudes Towards Modernity and Identity.* London: Rutledge Cruzon, 2002, pp. 111–142.

[180]C. Geertz, *After the Fact: Two Countries, Four Decades, One Anthropologist*, Cambridge: Harvard University Press, 1995, pp. 56–57.

many of the (then) younger generation of anthropologists to which he refers (myself included) did not begin to appear until the mid–1980s, by which time an Indonesian Islamic revival was in full swing. But as Bowen observes, most of the participants in this discourse did not originally intend to become Islamicists. We conducted our initial field work in the 1970s before it became fashionable for Indonesian generals, politicians, and public officials to open speeches with Arabic greetings. Mitsuo Nakamura and I shared similar experiences when we arrived in Yogyakarta. I was very surprised to discover that the state ceremonies of the Yogyakarta *Kraton* were Islamic. Nakamura observes that: "While I was living amidst Javanese Muslims I gradually started to feel and realize that there is nothing peculiar for a Javanese to be a pious Muslim".[181] Looking back on it, this was a very strange state of affairs. Nakamura and I were Ph.D. candidates in, what were at the time, two of the premiere Southeast Asian Studies programs in the United States: Cornell University and the University of Illinois. We had both obtained prestigious fellowships to support our dissertation research projects and neither us had the slightest inclination that Javanese *really are* Muslims. That would not happen today.

Geertz was correct when he argued that the Islamic revival that has taken place in Indonesia in the past three decades has influenced the development of Indonesian studies and caused Western scholars to take Islam more seriously. He was also correct in his claim that an increasing number of scholars have come to understand Indonesian texts and oral tradition as "locally encoded Muslim commentaries". Indonesian and Western scholars, on comparing Indonesian materials with those of other Islamic cultures, have come to the *academic* conclusion that this perspective is useful, and indeed, essential for explaining the historical development and contemporary forms of Indonesian cultures and religions. While politics plays a role in paradigm shifts, it rarely determines them. Geertz's suggestion that the emergence of an Islam centered paradigm was a response to Indonesian government policy is absurd. This is torturous, and I must add self serving, logic. It suggests that an entire generation of Indonesian and Western scholars fell so deeply under Suharto's spell that we could not tell the difference between scientific analysis and New Order propaganda![182] Suharto was very powerful, but not *that* powerful. Geertz never acknowledged the works of those whose interpretations Indonesia or Islam differed from his own as scholarly achievements, or as reflecting "on the ground" realities. At a meeting sponsored by the US Indonesia Society in 1998, at which Robert Heffner, Nurcholish Madjid and I were all present, he stated that he had said everything that needed to be said about Islam in Indonesia in the 1950s and that nothing had changed. Out of respect for a senior colleague Cak Nur, Bob and I chose not to

---

[181] M. Nakamura, *The Cresent Arises Over the Banyan Tree,* Yogyakarta, Gadjah Mada University Press, 1983, pp. 182–83.

[182] The list of scholars who would have to be included on this list is too long to recount here. By virtue of the ways in which they have described Islam in Indonesia Western scholars would include John Bowen, Nancy Florida, Anna Gade, Robert and Nancy Smith Heffner and Ronald Lukens-Bull. Indonesian scholars would have to be included are Tuafik Abdullah, Dwi Atmaja, Azurmadi Azra, Nurcholish Madjid, Abdurahman Masud, Amien Rais and Inayah Rochmaniyah. There are many others.

reply – or perhaps it was because of the sheer audacity of his statement – I don't really know and don't think that I ever will.

Geertz's rearguard defenses not withstanding, Islamic Studies, or at least Islamic Studies as conducted in and about Indonesia, has changed fundamentally since the beginning of the paradigm shift in the 1980s. It is now, at least in my view, better suited to the task of understanding the variety of Indonesian Islams than it has ever been. The Old Orientalism has been relegated to the dust bin of history.[183] Fully two generations of scholars committed to the view that Islam must be taken seriously in the analysis of Indonesian cultures, literatures, symbolism, politics and other aspects of individual and collective experience have come to maturity. A third generation is now making their way onto the scholarly stage. Islamic Studies in Indonesia has returned to a "normal science" mode of discourse. Today it can hardly be called a "Western" discipline as Indonesian, Japanese, Malaysian and Singaporean scholars play leading roles. The younger generation of Western scholars are far better suited to the task than those of us who came of age in the 1970s and 1980s because they have not had to play "catch up," recognizing the importance of Islam only when in the final stages of writing Doctoral Dissertations. Many are fluent in Arabic, as, of course, are many Indonesian scholars. This is a vitally important research tool that most of us of the now "older generation" never acquired.

Among the results of this convergence of interests is the inclusion of some discussion of the Islams of Southeast Asia in comparative studies of Islamic societies that formerly made only passing reference, if any at all, to Muslim societies outside the Middle East. The rapid expansion of the number of Indonesian students in and graduates of Islamic studies programs in Australia, Europe and North America has made them, as well as the Islamic traditions they represent, increasingly difficult to ignore. One ironic sign of the heightened awareness of Southeast Asia among the community of scholars defining themselves as Islamicists is that members of the *Middle East Studies Association* can now designate *"Southeast Asia"* as their primary research area! The scholarly literature on Indonesian and Javanese Islam, in both Indonesian and English is now so extensive that a systematic review would require a monograph length study.

These are very positive developments that present new challenges and opportunities for both Indonesian and Western scholars. We can no longer be content to describe Indonesian cultures and Local Islams as separate from the wider Islamic world of which they are a part. The current question should be *how* rather than *if* the Muslim cultures of Indonesia are Islamic. We cannot, however, avoid discussing the Indic and indigenous contributions to Indonesian Islamic cultures for fear of Islamist sensibilities. To do so would be the same as to describe "classical" Islamic thought with out reference to the Hellenistic traditions that informed it. It would

---

[183]This does not mean that works produced within this paradigm are without value. Many contain enormous amounts of data that could not possibly be collected today because of the scale of change that has taken place in Indonesia over the last century. Rather, the information they include must be carefully scrutinized, but can be used in the construction of analyses quite different from those the authors intended.

produce a portrait of Java no less distorted than that of Islam denying Orientalism. The term "Local Islam" consists of two elements – it is as mistaken to neglect the "Local" as it is to ignore the "Islam".

Area studies scholarship can no longer be conducted solely as an enterprise in which western observers describe and hope to explain the cultural, social, and religious systems of nonwestern others. Indonesian studies provides a significant example of the ways in which Eurocentric discourse has begun to give way to conversations that transcend cultures and paradigms to become international, inter-cultural, and inter-religious discourse systems. Some contemporary Indonesian scholarship is "detached" in the sense that it seeks historical or anthropological, and not theological understanding. Much more makes use of social science theory and method in a theological enterprise. It is essential, that Indonesian and western scholars do not loose sight of the fact that we now conduct scholarly discourse across paradigms but that we simultaneously acknowledge and maintain the distinction between normative and analytic scholarly voices. *Detached* scholarship is fundamentally different from *committed* scholarship. Each defines truth in a different way. In a multi-vocal scholarly discourse system each *informs* the other, but neither can determine either the questions addressed or the answers given *by* the other.

It is also essential to acknowledge that in all but the most repressive environments religions do not speak in a single voice and that these voices multiply rapidly when societies and states become more open and the forces of *bricolage* are unchained. This has certainly been the case on Yogyakarta and Indonesia more generally since the democratic transition of 1998. But in societies where religion has not been privatized as it has been in Western Europe, and to a lesser extent in North America, this means that new, religious systems of potentially hegemonic discourse also emerge. One could scarcely imagine a clearer example than the growth of politically engaged Islamism in Indonesia. In the chapters that follow I have attempted to capture some of the Muslim voices that have spoken, and continue to speak in Yogyakarta. I am concerned primarily with Islam as lived religion and with the interaction of what may be termed *kraton* and "popular" voices. There are others, especially theological discourses that presume familiarity with Arabic language textual traditions, which I must leave to others with the requisite knowledge and linguistic skills to consider. The study of any human phenomena as complex and diverse as Islam in Yogyakarta is necessarily a collective endeavor.

Chapter 2
The Javanese Dukun:
Healing and Moral Ambiguity

Healing is an integral component of Local Islams the world over.[1] While some healing techniques, including reciting passages from the *Qur'an* and belief in the healing power of the *barakah* (blessing) of saints and descendants of the Prophet Muhammad are universal or at least nearly so, others are unique to particular cultures. This chapter concerns the religious and cultural foundations of Javanese traditional medicine. Geertz has described curing as being among the central features of what he considers to be the animistic substratum of Javanese religion.[2] Here, it will be shown that Geertz's analysis is deeply flawed, and that Javanese theories of health, illness and curing are based on a Muslim world view and theory of personhood. The pervasive influence of Muslim theology, doctrine and mysticism on Javanese curing indicates that while it is possible to isolate a what can be called a traditional medical system, medical knowledge and practice do not comprise discrete domains in Javanese culture. Many of the abstract concepts of personhood, cosmology, power and knowledge that form the basis of the Javanese medical system derive ultimately from Middle Eastern Muslim scriptural traditions. Others are rooted in older Hindu-Javanese traditions. They cannot, however, be said to belong uniquely to any single cultural domain. Such concepts assume the status of axioms in Javanese culture, and as such are used to analyze, explain and impart meaning to a diversity of empirical phenomena ranging from religious ritual to the problems of health and illness.

Kleinman defines a health care system as:

> a system of symbolic meaning anchored in particular arrangements of social institutions and patterns of personal interaction "including" patterns of belief about the causes of illness,

---

[1] See, for example, E. Doumato, *Getting God's Ear. Women, Islam and Healing in Saudi Arabia and the Gulf*, New York: Columbia University Press 2000, and S. Beckerleg, "Medical Pluralism and Islam in Swahili Communities in Kenya" in *Medical Anthropology Quarterly*, new series vol. 8, no. 3, 1994, 299–313. I would like to thank Ary Budiyanto for information concerning the healing practices of Javanese and other Indonesians of Arabic descent and the early history of commercialized traditional healing, and in general for reintroducing me to the world of the *dukun* and Sarah Krier for sharing her observations concerning the commercialization of *jamu* production.

[2] C. Geertz, *The Religion of Java*, Glencoe: Free Press, 1960.

M. Woodward, *Java, Indonesia and Islam*, Muslims in Global Societies Series 3, DOI 10.1007/978-94-007-0056-7_2, © Springer Science+Business Media B.V. 2011

norms governing the choice and evaluation of treatment, socially legitimated statuses, roles and power relations, interactional settings and institutions.[3]

The Javanese medical system draws on a wide variety of symbols, roles and interactional patterns, none of which may be understood as uniquely medical. Concepts of personhood, cosmology, power and knowledge are melded into a corpus of closely related theories explaining the origins of disease and motivating highly diverse treatment strategies. Medical pluralism is, therefore, and inherent feature of Javanese traditional medicine. There are two primary modes of medical practice. One, rooted in *Sufi* concepts of sainthood (*wali*) is based on Islamic mystical concepts of miracles and gnosis. The other, practiced by *dukun* (curers) involves the use of morally suspect forms of magical power some of which are derived from Hindu-Javanese traditions and others that are uniquely Javanese or at least Malay.[4]

Analysis of the Muslim roots of the Javanese medical system lends support to Keesing's theory that culture comprises a hierarchically ordered system of knowledge.[5] Relations between traditional medicine, mysticism and the Javanese theory of kingship are explained in terms of the Piagetian theory of generative structuralism.[6] This theory holds that the structural congruity of cultural systems is the output of a generative system in which a finite set of axioms and rules of inference structures a multiplicity of surface domains, among which there need be no intrinsic relationship. Examination of the conceptual foundations of the social roles *dukun* and *Wali* and the manner in which individual curers seek to establish their legitimacy reveals that the macro-level patterns of Javanese culture and individual social behavior are the products of a single generative system. It is argued further that Javanese notions of health, illness and health care are constantly evolving and *bricolage* is among the processes through which hybrid, traditional-biomedical systems emerge.

The Javanese Healthcare System

The Javanese health care system includes complex theories of anatomy, the origin and treatment of disease, a large number of herbal and mineral medicines and a system of social interaction directing potential patients towards specialists who treat only a small subset of the culturally recognized ailments. The system is, however, fundamentally paradoxical. While Javanese consult *dukun* concerning medical and other, primarily religious, problems, they rarely trust them. It is often said that most *dukun* are charlatans that their primary goals are the acquisition of wealthy

[3] A. Kleinman, *Patients and Healers in the Context of Culture*. Berkeley: University of California Press, 1980.

[4] Here is use the term Malay in an inclusive sense to refer to the peoples of insular and mainland Southeast Asia who speak one of the many Malayo-Polynesian languages.

[5] R. Keesing, "Linguistic Knowledge and Cultural Knowledge: some Doubts and Speculations," *American. Anthropologist* vol. 81, no. 15, 1979

[6] J. Piaget, *Psychology and Epistemology: Towards a Theory of Knowledge*. New York: Penguin Books, 1977.

and social status, and that many are sorcerers. Many Javanese are afraid of *dukun* considering them to be dangerous as well as powerful.[7] Accusations of sorcery occasionally lead to demands that *dukun* be arrested and charged and sometimes to revenge killings. Many *dukun* agree with these negative evaluations. Of the numerous curers I interviewed in and around Yogyakarta, none thought of himself as a *dukun*, though most were quick to use the term for their rivals. They referred to themselves as "helper" (*pitulung*), "mystic" (*ahli kebatinan*), "expert in Javanese science" (*ahli ngilmu Jawa*), "elder" (*orang tua*), "smart person" (*orang pintar*) or some similar term. Today they are often referred to as "para-normals" (*paranormal*) or practitioners of "alternative medicine" (*pengobatan alternative*). Many, if not most are considered to be *dukun* by their patients and neighbors. A very small number are described as having the powers of *wali* (saints). Traditional healers with strong Islamic orientations call themselves "religious teacher" (*Ustad*), "wise man" (*habib*) or "Arabic physician" (*tabib*). The later two titles are especially common among healers of Arabic descent.[8]

Only a small, though highly respected, minority of curers are not thought of as *dukun* by their patients. Such individuals are know primarily for their religious or mystical attainments and are often thought to be saints (*wali*).[9] *Kyai* are also said to have the ability to heal and exorcise demons. Paradoxically many of these pious men are reluctant to act as healers. Those who do claim to be ignorant of traditional medicine, attributing their healing powers to some combination of divine appointment (*wahyu*), prayer and meditation. Most will heal only their relatives, personal retainers and close friends. The paradox is enhanced by the fact that the number of *dukun* greatly exceeds that of *wali*. This forces the great majority of Javanese to rely almost exclusively on the services of *dukun* who they fear more than trust. This chapter will explore of the varieties of medical, religious and cultural knowledge on which these two modes of medical practice are based and the ways

---

[7]Saliba and Miyazaki report similar finding. Saliba reports that a patient with whom she worked was terrified by the fact that her husband had become a *dukun* even though his reason for doing so was to combat sorcery. M. Saliba, "Story Language: A Sacred Healing". In: *Literature and Medicine*, vol. 19, no.1, 2000, 38–50. Miyazaki writes that in Malaysia *dukun* descendant from Javanese immigrants are some times accused of using their powers to murder people for financial gain. K. Miyazaki, "Javanese-Malay: Between Adaptation and Alienation". In *SOJOURN: Journal of Social Issues in Southeast Asia*, vol. 15, no. 1, 2000, 1–18.

[8]There is a substantial community of Hadrami (Yemini) Arabs in Java and elsewhere in Indonesia. Many Hadrami families have lived in Indonesia, and elsewhere is the Malay world of Southeast Asia, for generations and move easily between Javanese or Malay and Arabic cultures, collective and personal identities. They are clearly distinguished from Saudi Arabian and Gulf Arabs who have come to the region in recent decades and who have scant knowledge of local cultures. There are also many Javanese, especially among aristocratic and clerical families, who claim Arabic descent.

[9]Anyone believed to have mystical powers is thought to have at least the potential to be a healer. Among the recognized signs of mystical attainment are devotion to meditation and pilgrimage, the possession of magical heirlooms (*pusaka*), Islamic learning, and expertise in martial arts or the Javanese fine arts of *gamelan* (percussion orchestra), dance, or *wayang* (show play performance).

in which *dukun* attempt to present themselves as *Wali* through the sponsorship of quasi-medical, quasi-religious spirit cults.

Personhood in Javanese Culture

Geertz has called attention to the complexity and variability of concepts of personhood.[10] He uses the term "personhood" to refer to:

> ...the sorts of labels which one person can apply to another in order to identify him as a unique individual.

Geertz demonstrates that "symbolic orders of person definition" can not be understood as isolated cultural subsystems (kin terminology, personal names, titles, etc.). Rather, they are applied conjointly to define each individual's positions in a wide variety of social networks. In general, Geertz is concerned with the ways in which individuals use systems of social classification in daily life. There are, however, other aspects of personhood which he does not consider. Here, I will be concerned not with the symbolic systems used to distinguish among individuals, but with the symbols and metaphysical postulates which distinguish humans as a class from other beings and entities in the universe and their implications for understanding healing and related activities.

Concepts of health and illness can be understood only in the context of an analysis of cultural assumptions concerning the composition and structure of the human body. Javanese medical practice is based on a highly complex notion of personhood derived from the *Sufi* mystical concept of the "perfection of man".[11] This doctrine is, in turn, founded on the virtually universal Muslim distinction between outer (*zahir*) and inner (*batin*) modes of religiosity. This opposition evolved from the pietiest tradition in early Islam which maintained a sharp distinction between internal, spiritual and external, behavioral modes of religious devotion. According to *Sufi* teachings, each individual must strike a balance between outward forms of devotion including religious law and ritual and the inner quest for purification of the soul and direct knowledge of God. The more radical forms of Sufism, which are common in Southeast Asia, maintain that the human soul is simply one of the aspects of God.[12] Religious life is seen as a struggle between the true, inner soul and the outer, animal soul (*nafs*) for control of the individual's thoughts and actions. Only by traversing the mystical path can the soul emerge victorious. This process,

---

[10]C. Geertz, "Person Time and Conduct in Bali: An Essay in Cultural Analysis," New Haven: Yale Southeast Asia Program, Cultural Report Series No. 14, 1966.

[11]On this teaching see R. Nicholson, The *Mystics of Islam: An Introduction to Sufism*. New York: Schocken Books, 1975. Traditional Javanese medical practice does not seem to be related to the Greco-Islamic "high" medical tradition of the classical period Arab Middle East. For a brief description of this system see A. Majeed, "How Islam Changed Medicine" in *British Medical Journal* vol. 331, 2005, 1486–1487

[12]See Chapter 5 and M. Woodward, *Islam in Java. Normative Piety and Mysticism in the Sultanate of Yogyakarta*, Tucson: University of Arizona Press, pp. 79–199.

often referred to as the "perfection of man", form₅ the core of many of the Javanese *Sufi* devotional traditions.[13]

The Javanese theory of anatomy employs these religious precepts to explain the structure of the human body. The Javanese terms *lahir* (Arabic *zahir*) and *batin* are employed to refer to the material and spiritual constituents of created reality. Thus, in Javanese, the distinction between, inner and outer is used in a metaphysical as well as pietistic sense. The human body is the perfect microcosm. It consists of three principle components: the physical body (*badan jasmani*), the spiritual body (*badan rohani*) and the soul (*ingsun, aku, roh suci, roh nurani* and others).

One of the common terms for soul is *roh nurani*, which means spiritual body of light. The use of this term connects the Javanese theory of personhood with the widely distributed *Sufi* teaching of *Nur Muhammad* according to which the light or spirit of Muhammad was the first thing to be created and the ultimate source of all created things.[14] The physical body forms a container (*wadah*) for the spiritual body and the soul which are referred to collectively as *isi* (content). Similarly, the physical and spiritual bodies together form a container for the soul.

The nature of the soul is constant, not being subject to change by spiritual or physical means. It is commonly believed that all human souls were created in a single moment at the beginning of time and that the remain in a state of limbo (*alam barzak*) until the preordained moment at which each descends into a physical *wadah* formed by the union of sperm and egg. The composition of the spiritual and material bodies, however, is in constant flux. Both are subject to a series of developmental processes commencing with conception which are not terminated, even by death, until the Day of Judgment. These processes may be influenced by heredity, diet, physical exercise, meditation, prayer and ritual. Together they form a causal nexus determining the health status of the individual at a point in time. The healing arts are

---

[13]This discussion is based on field work conducted in Yogyakarta in the late 1970s. At that time *Muhammadiyah* Muslims and other reformist *santri* generally did not accept the teaching of Union with God, but rather explained that one draws "close to" and develops an intuitive understanding of God. The growth of Wahhabi influenced Islamism since the late 1980s has led to heightened controversy concerning all mystically tinged understandings of Islam, including those of all but the most "Islamic" traditional healers. Islamist organizations and particularly the Front for the Defense of Islam (*Front Pembela Islam*/FPI) vociferously and often violently oppose Sufism and its cultural derivatives. In addition to bars and nightclubs they attack and ransack the clinics of traditional healers. For them the distinction between *agama* and *kebudayaan* that has developed over the past several decades is nothing more than a ruse intended to justify the continued practice of what they believe to be *bidah, kufarat*, and *shirk*. Their opposition to traditional healing practices, including those of explicitly Muslim healers, is an element of a grand strategy to transform the entire complex of religion, culture and nationality in terms of their own understandings of Islam. Their goal is hegemony, not consensus or compromise. This does not mean that they have abandoned non-medical healing. Indeed some are convinced that "western medicine" is actually Jewish medicine and as such, *haram* (prohibited). There is a growing "Prophetic" medical tradition that relies on healing techniques mentioned in the *Qur'an* and *Hadith*.

[14]I. Goldziher, *Introduction to Islamic Theology and Law,* Princeton: Princeton University Press, 1981.

understood best as attempts to manipulate the course of these processes, directing them towards and ideal state of physical and mental health and religious purity.

The physical body develops from the female egg and menstrual blood. It is comprised of four elements: heat, air, water, and earth. Each of these is associated with specific moral qualities which according to bio-medical theory are psychological, but which, according to the Javanese theory of personhood are entirely physical. Heat consists of the four varieties of passion (*nafsu*): greed, anger, moral ambiguity and the desire for perfection. The four passions are substances located in the blood, muscle, bone marrow and breath respectively. Air is the animating force or life principle. It is located in the breath and may be normal, ambiguous, evil or controlled. Water is the source of the four spiritual brothers with which every human is born. Beliefs about the four brothers vary greatly.[15] In texts and informant's statements on which the present analysis is based they are termed: *Roh Jasmani* (the spirit of the physical body), *Roh Nurani* (the spirit of the soul), *Roh Kabit* (the spirit of growth) and *Roh Hewani* (the animal spirit) which is associated with passion. Despite the use of the Arabic term *roh* (spirit), the four brothers are thought to be purely physical. They are not souls in any sense of the word and, as such, do not figure in Javanese eschatology. They guard the physical and spiritual bodies from the moment of conception until that of death, protecting them from evil spirits and magical power. They do not accompany the spiritual body and the soul to the afterlife, but decompose like the physical body. The physical body decomposes into dust while the four spiritual brothers return to water from which they were formed.

The spiritual body is comprised of sperm. It is formed prior at the physical body and remains with the soul after death. It is composed of four elements: The *tirta kamandanu* (water of life), gives life to the physical body and is the source of sense perception. *Bagaskara* is the essence or light of the sun. It forms the *roh ilafi* (spirit of light), which animates the mind and emotions. *Maruta* is wind. It gives rise to the *roh rabini* (the spirit of compassion). Unlike the four spiritual brothers, these spirits are not understood as separate entities, but rather as states of mind linking the three components of the body. The final element is *swasana* (space). It is the glue which binds the spiritual body to the physical body and the soul. As the embryo develops, the spiritual body divides into three houses or sanctuaries for the soul/God located in the brain, the heart and the genitals.[16] These are the seats of thought (*budi*), emotion (*rasa*) and passion (*nafsu*) respectively.

The physical and spiritual development of the embryo is influenced by the spiritual and physical characteristics of both parents. Since sperm and egg are colored, figuratively and literally, by passion, the balance of elements in the child's body is

---

[15] See C. Geertz, op.cit., and P. Suparlan, "The Javanese *Dukun*". *Masyarakat Indonesia,* 1978.

[16] More a more detailed exposition see Chapter 4 which explores the articulation of these concepts in the architectural symbolism of the Yogyakarta *Kraton*.

determined by those of his/her parents. A child conceived in the presence of passion will be governed by passions of lust, greed and anger. In a similar fashion, various sorts of good, evil and morally ambiguous power (*kesekten*) and knowledge (*ngilmu*) may be incorporated into the physical and spiritual bodies of the unborn child. These beliefs motivate a vast corpus of taboos and religious practices associated with sexual intercourse. Mystical texts and folk wisdom dictate that before engaging in sexual intercourse, a couple should spend an extended period in prayer, fasting and meditation.[17] This purges their bodies of passion and evil, resulting in the birth of a pure and healthy child. Popular mystical/divination manuals (*primbon*) specify precise dates and times at which sexual intercourse must be performed to product a child with a given set of physical and spiritual characteristics.[18]

The influence of the spiritual state of the parents on the child's development does not end with conception. Pregnancy is thought of as a period of meditation during which the mind and spirit, as well as the physical body of the child develop. Both parents must remain calm and refrain from impure thoughts and actions, lest the emotions (*rasa*) of the child be disturbed. Many Javanese state that pregnant women should also avoid chilies and other hot foods for similar reasons. Parents also seek to obtain the blessings of God, saints and spirits for the child through prayer, meditation and a complex series of prenatal rituals. It is also necessary to drive off any evil spirits (*setan*) who might attempt to capture the spiritual body or soul of the child.

There is an extensive body or oral tradition linking the exceptional characteristics of famous people with the devotional regimes their mothers undertook during pregnancy. Diponegara (1785–1855) the Yogyakarta prince who was the leader of the last great rebellion against the Dutch. It is often said that while she was pregnant with him she fasted regularly and told her unborn son that he must be brave and struggle against the Dutch. The mothers of many famous Kyai are believed to have devoted themselves to recitation of the *Qur'an* while they were pregnant. Abdurahman Wahid, was perhaps be most famous and highly revered Muslim scholar of the late twentieth and early twenty-first centuries. He was general chairman of *Nahdlatul Ulama* (1984–1999), played a major role in Indonesia's democratic transition of 1998 and was president between 1999 and 2001. His mother is said to have fasted for the entire 9 months that she was pregnant with him.

One of the consequences of this view of procreation is the belief that significant factors influencing the spiritual and physical potential of the child are fixed at birth. These factors determine not only the health status of the child, but also its ability to acquire knowledge and power. Among the types of knowledge and power which may be present from birth are the ability to recite the *Qur'an*, communicate with spiritual beings, and those required to become a *wali* or *dukun*.

---

[17] H. Hadiwijono, *Man in the Present Javanese Mysticism,* Baarn: Bosch & Keuning, 1967.

[18] Anonomous, *Primbon Wali Sanga*, Surakarta, 1978.

Spiritual and Physical Development

While one's potential for spiritual and physical development is fixed at birth, it can be realized only through training the physical and spiritual bodies. A common set of developmental processes govern the physiological development and growth of the child, the acquisition of religious knowledge and magical power and the quest for union with God. The degree to which an individual makes use of his innate potential determines his ultimate station in life. Advanced spiritual states, including the types of knowledge and power used in curing, may be attained only through intensive effort and discipline.

Physical development plays a major role in Javanese religious practice. It is held to be the first step on the mystical path and a prerequisite for the attainment of more advanced spiritual states. The purpose of physical training is to strengthen the *badan jasmani*, enabling it to serve as a container for the spiritual properties to be added to the *badan rohani*. This training is often referred to as *ngilmu kanurangan* (physical knowledge) or *ngilmu kanoman* (the knowledge of youth). It consists primarily of the study of martial arts and dance, fasting and other forms of asceticism. Its ultimate purpose is to enable the mind to control the physical body and the passions it contains.

The type of training a child receives greatly influences his/her subsequent spiritual development. The study of classical dance leads to the development of mystical knowledge because the child learns to control everyday movements and behavior. Dance movements are thought to be simultaneously beautiful and rigidly stylized; reflecting inward spiritual states. The control of the body developed in dance lessons contributes to control of the mind in meditation exercises undertaken later in life. Training in the martial arts (*pencat silat*) serves a different purpose. In many respects the Javanese martial arts resemble dance. In pre-colonial Java picked regiments moved into battle in dance step. As late as the 1930s, members of the Sultan's bodyguard marched in dance formations.[19] The purpose of martial arts training, however, differs fundamentally from that of the dance. Its aim is the cultivation of invulnerability and to prepare the physical body for the acquisition of the types of magical power used by warriors, healers and others who responsibilities include combating the forces of evil. Marital arts training is an important part of the curriculum in many *Pesantren*.

Fasting and other forms of asceticism establish the principle link between spiritual and physical development. During the month of Ramadan, pious Muslims refrain from eating, drinking and smoking between the hours of dawn and sunset. It is believed that Ramadan is the holiest month of the year and that strict observance of the fast "burns off" sins of the previous year. Many traditional *santri* observe additional fasts, which they maintain are the *sunnah* (practice) of Muhammad or previous Prophets. At one *pesantren* in the East Javanese city of Kudus, all of the

---

[19]Members of the Sultan's ceremonial guard are now unpaid volunteers, and do not have the time to learn these intricate maneuvers.

santri are required to fast continually for an entire year. One of the *Kyai* has fasted for more than twenty. Javanese mystics, like some other *Sufis*, are often less strict in their observance of the fasting month, but endure more extreme forms of asceticism on other occasions.[20] Many go without food for as long as 48 hours, subsist for extended periods on plain white rice or wild plants, and spend the night standing in a river or praying in a mosque.

No matter what form it takes, asceticism strengthens the physical body and cultivates the emotional tranquility required for the attainment of spiritual knowledge. Fasting is thought to purge the body of passion and sin and reduce the risk of disease. Once passion has been controlled it is possible to clear the mind (an element of the spiritual body) of conscious thought. This allows the mystic to establish contact with saints, spirits, and sources of magical power and in some cases with God.

These goals can be attained only if ascetic exercise is not injurious to the mystic's physical or mental health. Both orthodox Muslims and *Sufi* mystics believe that a fast must be broken immediately if it produces illness or psychological trauma. If it is not, the physical and spiritual bodies may suffer permanent damage or be seized by an evil spirit. Consequently, the physical body should be strengthened by less rigorous means prior to the commencement of an extensive regime of fasting or other variety of asceticism. As there is a direct relationship between the length of a fast and the benefit derived from it, an extensive period of physical training contributes significantly to the development of the spiritual body. It is for this reason that most Javanese mystical teachers require students to endure months or years of training in dance or martial arts, and in some cases manual labor, before allowing them to receive instruction in the purely spiritual aspects of mystical doctrine. One I worked with insisted that I become proficient in archery before his would discuss more than the outline of his understanding of the path leading to knowledge of and union with God. It is also for this reason that in *pesantren* the acquisition of healing and other powers is closely associated with the practice of *pencat silat* or martial arts.

Knowledge and Power: The Development of the Spiritual and Physical Bodies

The development of the spiritual body consists of the acquisition of knowledge (*ngilmu*) and magical power (*kesekten*). These two concepts are among the most complex aspects of Javanese mysticism, and the source of both the *dukun*'s healing skills and his moral ambiguity.

Ngilmu is derived from the Arabic term *ilm*. It is knowledge of the spiritual and material constituents of created reality. It differs qualitatively from *makripat* (Arabic *ma"rifa*) which is the intuitive knowledge of God acquired through mystical

---

[20]On *Ramadan* in Yogyakarta see Chapter 5. The percentage of Javanese who fast for the entire month has increased significantly since the late 1970s.

experience. *Ngilmu* may be learned, developed or acquired through conception. *Makripat* is a gift from God and is attained only by advanced mystics who have reached the state of gnosis or union with the divine essence. There are many varieties of *ngilmu*, each of which concerns a particular aspect of reality. Some are purely secular, but most concern some aspect of religious law, ritual or magic. These range from reciting the *Qur'an* to sorcery. *Ngilmu* can be acquired in several ways. It may be learned from a teacher or a book, but may also be a gift from a saint, spirit or angel. A seemingly curious feature of the Javanese theory of knowledge is that it can be transmitted physically. This led Geertz to conclude that *ngilmu* is a physical substance. It is generally believed that it is one of the attributes of the spiritual body, and is present to some extent from the moment of conception. As an element of the spiritual body it is a *halus* – refined – substance. As such it is not detectable by sense perception, but is none the less on of the elements comprising the universe. It is for this reason that *ngilmu* can be inherited. The ability to recite and memorize the *Qur'an* is, for example, thought to be transmitted in the family of the prophet Muhammad. The presence of large quantities of *ngilmu* can prolong life, even beyond the point at which one is fated to die. Consequently, old men often retire to remote caves or forest retreats to dissipate their stores of *ngilmu* when they feel that death is at hand. Young men journey to these same places to acquire the *ngilmu* as it escapes from the bodies of the old.

With the exception of those concerned with the study of religious doctrine and ritual, all *ngilmu* are morally ambiguous. While the acquisition of religious knowledge is incumbent on all Muslims, the study of magic is discouraged. Many Javanese, especially the *wong cilik* or "little people" maintain that one should acquire enough *ngilmu* to ward off evil and develop an appreciation for Islamic and Javanese ritual, doctrine and mysticism. The more esoteric varieties of *ngilmu* are potentially dangerous, even if they are not evil. Others feel that the quest for esoteric knowledge is a religious obligation.

The Javanese view of the moral propriety of esoteric knowledge is in accord with that of al-Ghazzali. Ghazzali was the great twelfth century mystic, theologian and philosopher who many have termed "the great Muslim since Muhammad".[21] Ghazzali argued that the acquisition of secular and even theological knowledge does not contribute to salvation because it distracts attention from the fundamental religious truths of Islam It is, none the less, useful.

Another factor underlying the moral ambiguity of *ngilmu* is that its possession implies not only understanding of, but also the ability to control the complex flows of matter and energy governing natural and supernatural phenomena. The possession of *ngilmu* may bring one into contact with spiritual beings and sources of power that are highly dangerous for those who have not strengthened their physical and spiritual bodies. The type of *ngilmu* used to summon spirits provides a clear example. It is used by *dukun* to cure diseases of the spiritual body. In the hands of a novice this knowledge is extremely dangerous because it is possible to summon a

---

[21] W. Watt, *The Faith and Practice of Al-Ghazzali*, London: Allen and Unwin, 1953.

spirit that can not be controlled or forced to leave. If it is angered, such a spirit may invade the spiritual or physical body causing psychological trauma, insanity or death. Many Javanese have experienced these difficulties. Among young men and adolescent boy there is a popular game called, in Indonesian, *"pangil setan,"* Combinations of charms and incantations are used to summons a *setan* who is asked to answer questions and perform tricks. Over the years I have heard many accounts of the game going wrong. Sometimes the participants are able to call the spirit but find that they are unable to make it go way. The only remedy is to call for the assistance of a *dukun,* or learned Islamic teacher who is more knowledgeable of these matters.

Healing sometimes requires *dukun* to use types of *ngilmu* which are positively evil. Foremost among these are *ngilmu telung* and *ngilmu sihr. Ngilmu telung* is black magic. It is used to enchant people and to cause objects or spirits to enter their bodies. *Ngilmu sihir* is a type of sorcery in which evil spirits (*setan*) are used to steal property or to cause illness or injury. Before a *dukun* can cure such afflictions, he must acquire virtually the same type of *ngilmu* used to cause them. This is among the primary reasons for the moral ambiguity of healing. Many Javanese believe that really powerful *dukun* are at least potentially sorcerers. *Dukun* are, consequently, both feared and respected for their knowledge of the healing arts.

Javanese are divided concerning the moral character of other types of *ngilmu.* Some state that knowledge is a gift from God. From this perspective the question at issue is not the moral quality of *ngilmu,* but the intention of the person who employs it. Some informants, and most *dukun,* maintain that even *ngilmu telung* is morally neutral because it can be used either to cause or cure affliction. This view does not, however, detract from the moral ambiguity of the *dukun.* Even if the propriety of his knowledge is granted, it is not possible to be certain of his intentions. Advanced mystics and those bent on the attainment of union with God hold that while the acquisition of *ngilmu* may be useful and at times necessary, it is never desirable because it distracts attention from more important religious concerns.

Kesekten: The Javanese Theory of Power

Anderson has called attention to the centrality of the concept of power in Javanese political and religious thought.[22] He states that power is a physical substance, that the total amount of power in the universe is constant and that it is morally ambiguous. Anderson's contention that power is morally neutral is correct in a general sense, but he errs in his assertion that it is unitary and undifferentiated. Suparlan identifies several distinct types of power each with its own disnict moral character. His list includes glorious (*pulung*), compassionate (*andaru*), evil (*teluh braja*),

---

[22]B. Anderson, "The idea of power in Javanese Culture". In: C. Holt (ed.), *Culture and Politics in Indonesia*, Ithaca: Cornell University Press, 1972.

and angry (*guntur*) power.[23] While Suparlan is generally correct, his list if far from complete. These terms do not refer to specific types of power but rather to general classes. As in the case of *ngilmu*, a complete enumeration of the types of power would be impossible.

The complexities of this problem become apparent when the uses of *pusaka* (magical heirlooms) and traditional medicines are examined. *Pusaka* are the primary means through which the power of the past is preserved. They are objects associated with particularly powerful persons in Javanese history. *Pusaka* can be used to perform magical acts requiring power greater than that which can be generated by living humans. They play a major role in Javanese dynastic theory and in popular religion. Both of the two royal courts in central Java possess hundreds of *pusaka* each of which has a particular use or uses. Some are used for military purposes, others to combat plague, drought or disease. Still others are thought to have to the power to compel conversion to Islam. *Keris*, the short swords worn by Javanese men on ceremonial occasions, are among the most important non-royal *pusaka*. Many Javanese mystics are avid *keris* collectors and believe that *keris* give them the power to control spirits and perform other magical acts. The rings worn by most Javanese men are also thought to be charged with power.

Belief in the efficiency of traditional medicines (*obat*) is also based on the theory of power. *Obat* is only roughly translatable as medicine. While many types of *obat* have medicinal uses, others are poison. The term for mosquito spray, for example, is *obat ngamuk*. The term *obat* is also used for the substances employed in sorcery. *Obat* is, therefore, any substance capable of altering the physical and/or spiritual composition of a human or other body. *Dukun* who rely on the use of *obat* explain that each medicine contains a particular type of power. The use of medicine must be governed by both an understanding of the types of power which can cause disease and of the spiritual and physical composition of the human bodies. It is for this reason that Javanese prescriptions are so complex, often consisting of twenty to thirty individual drugs. This view of the nature of medicine often leads Javanese to the conclusion that western bio-medicine is extremely crude because it consists primarily of two types of medicines – "shots and pills". This view was common in the late 1970s. As bio-medical knowledge has become more common there has been a decline in such critiques, even by *dukun*. The two modes of medical practice are increasingly seen as complimentary. While most *dukun* rely exclusively on traditional medicines some also include a variety of bio-medical drugs including antibiotics in their prescriptions. Herbal medicines are also referred to as *Jamu*. Most are infusions of herbs, spices and fruits prepared by boiling them in water. Among the most common ingredients are various types of ginger, turmeric, cloves, cinnamon, mint, fennel, cardamom, palm sugar, chilies, papaya and bananas. Some are tonics intended to preserve health, enhance beauty, sexual desire and performance. Others are curative. The Yogyakarta and Surakarta *kraton* are widely

---

[23] P. Suparlan, *The Javanese of Surinam*, Unpublished Ph.D. Thesis, Department of Anthropology, University of Illinois, Urbana-Champaign, 1976.

believed to be important repositories of this type of medical knowledge.[24] A wide variety of *jamu* are available in Javanese markets and from itinerant peddlers, most of whom are elderly women. Most *jamu* are harmless, if not beneficial. There are some, however, that contain herbs that are dangerous. Women's health groups have raised concerns that some used as vaginal lubricants endanger the health of both the mother and the child when used during pregnancy.[25] They think that the Indonesian government does not do nearly enough to regulate the *jamu* industry and that *Kraton* should stop promoting it as an aspect of *Kebudayaan Jawa*.

Holy water is also commonly used for medicinal purposes. The most efficacious and greatly valued is *zam–zam* water from the sacred well in Mecca of the same name. There are numerous Hadith according to which water from this well has curative powers and that it will sustain health and wellbeing through periods of complete fasting of up to 40 days.[26] A Saudi Arabian Sheikh whose works circulate widely in Indonesia writes:

> *Zam–Zam* water is the greatest of waters: the most beneficial, the greatest in value, the best for the body, the most expensive and the most beneficial for humanity,[27]

In the 1970s *zam–zam* water was extremely difficult to obtain. Pilgrims returning from the *hajj* carried as much as possible with them, often to the consternation of flight crews when they attempted to lift 5 l bottles into overhead baggage compartments. They usually shared the bounty with relatives, friends and neighbors. Some added a few drops to wells or springs to ensure a continuous supply, the belief being that *zam–zam* water can be almost infinitely diluted and not loose its potency or sacred qualities. Others are extremely skeptical of this practice. Now, thanks to technological innovations that have vastly increased the supply, it is far more common and can be purchased in "Islamic" shops and supermarkets world wide.[28] Some, however, express doubts about the "authenticity" of these commercial products and prefer the "genuine" article that has been hand carried from Mecca.

Many *kejawen* Muslims believe that there are locally available sources of *zam–zam* water that are equally, or almost equally, efficacious. Water from springs, wells and tanks located in the Yogyakarta and Surakarta *kraton* and in cemeteries where saints and kings are buried is commonly referred to as *zam–zam* water. There are hundreds of sources of *zama zam* water in the Yogyakarta area. Water in which

---

[24] A book published by the Yogyakarta *Kraton*, *Kraton Jogja. The History and Cultural Heritage*, Jakarta: Kraton Ngayogyakarta Hadiningrat and the Indoneisan Marketing Association, 2004, p. 249, list thirty varieties of *jamu*. In the Yogyakarta *Kraton*, *jamu* are prepared in the same kitchens and by the same female *abdidalem* who prepare both regular meals and foods used in palace *Slametan*, including the *Garebeg*. See Chapters 3 and 5.

[25] This issue was raised by at a seminar on Reproductive Health Sponsored by the Center for Women's Studies at Sunan Kalijaga State Islamic University in Yogyakarta, October 28, 2008.

[26] Here fasting refers to complete abstinence form food, not the daylight fast of Ramadan.

[27] A. Al-Jibrin, *Biar Sakit, Ibadah. Tetap Fit (If You are Sick, Pray and Certainly be Fit)*, Surakarta: PT Aqwam Media Profetika, 2008, p. 171.

[28] As part of their *Hajj* management strategy, the Saudis have greatly increased the capacity of the well. Some people say that they simply connect tank trucks to taps.

important *pusaka* have been ritually bathed is also referred to as *zam–zam* water.[29] Others, particularly those sensitive to *santri* critiques of the localization of elements of Universalist Islam often state that these waters are "almost as good" as genuine *zam–zam* water. Some *dukun* and others with similar religious orientations collect water from every holy place they visit in plastic bottles. One I met in 2008 has water from literally hundreds of different sources.

Power and Morality

While some types of power are unquestionably evil, none are entirely good. All types of power are potentially dangerous. Many Javanese claim to have become ill from handling *keris*. Truly powerful *pusaka*, which in the hands of the Sultan can prevent bubonic plague, might easily kill an ordinary person. This was explained to me by a member of the Sultan's body guard who caries an especially powerful *pusaka* in *Yogyakarta* state ceremonies. It is a spear said to have a taste for Dutch blood. He observed that while to carry it is a great honor, he is always afraid of the *pusaka*. It often tries to escape from his grasp. Were it to do so, the *pusaka* would fly through the air, killing everyone in its path especially any Dutchmen, and possibly other foreigners who happened to be present. In order to control this *pusaka* my informant stated that he must make offerings to it and fast for at least a week prior to the ceremony in which it is used.[30]

The fact that even "good" power can be dangerous is not a sufficient explanation for its moral ambiguity. There are at least two other reasons. The first is that the moral character of the use of power depends largely on the intention (*niyah*) of the person employing it. It is now very widely believed that former President Suharto was able to remain in power for so long because he had managed to acquire *pusaka* from the court of Surakarta and others from throughout Indonesia. It is also often said that he used this power for morally questionable purposes including enriching himself and his family. He is also said to have consulted with sorcerers.[31] In

---

[29]This ritual is conducted annually on the first day of the Javanese year by both *Kraton* and by private individuals. In Yogyakarta hundreds of gallons of this *zam–zam* water are distributed to people attending the bathing of the royal carriages.

[30]While most Javanese agree that some *pusaka* are genuinely powerful there are debates about *whose* these are. Both central Javanese courts claim to have the genuine ones and that those of their rivals are "*kosong*" (empty). There is a Yogyakarta legend according to which at the kingdom of Mataram was divided Sultan Hamengukuwana I and the Susuhunan of Surakarta alternated choosing *pusaka* that would become the regalia of the two new kingdoms. The Susuhunan is said, on the advise of the Dutch, to have chosen only those encrusted with precious stones, which were seemingly valuable, but entirely *kosong* while the Sultan chose those that were apparently plain, but were actually enormously powerful. The Surakarta court vehemently denies this and claims that it has the truly powerful *pusaka*.

[31]I first heard rumors concerning Suharto's acquisition of Surakarta *pusaka* in Yogyakarta in 1978. At the time I was inclined to doubt them because they occurred in the contexts of Yogyakarta anti-Surakarta polemics. Sources made public since the fall of Suharto indicate that they were well founded, A. Artha, *Dunia Spiritual Soeharto. Menelusiri Laku Ritual, Tempat-Tempat dan Guru*

another, religious, sense, any use of power is morally questionable both because it distracts one from the quest for union with God and because the entire theory of power is derived from Hindu rather than Islamic sources. The term *kesekten* is derived from the Sanskrit *sakti*. *Sakti* is the magical power associated with the Hindu gods and especially with Siva. In Saiva mythology and in some varieties of Javanese mysticism, power is generated by a type of asceticism known as *tapas*. *Sakti* is general released as heat and may be used for either constructive or destructive purposes.[32] Both Javanese mythology and the Hindu *Puranas* include accounts of ascetics whose ability to perform *tapas* was so great that they were capable of boiling the oceans and potentially of destroying the universe.

This corpus of belief is incorporated into Javanese Islam. Belief in magical power does not in any way conflict with the teachings of Islam. The *Qur'an*, Hadith and later Muslim sources all affirm the existence of magic. Two of the most frequently cited *Quranic* passages are one concerning the Prophet Solomon in which two *setan* are mentioned as having taught people witchcraft (2:102) and another concerning the contest between the between the Prophet Moses and the Pharos's magicians (20:63–66). Regarding the evil uses of power, fourteenth century Arab Muslim philosopher and historian Ibn Khaldun stated that: "It should be known that no intelligent man doubts the existence of sorcery".

The moral and ethical status of magic are, however, highly suspect. Both the *Qur'an* and Hadith associate magic with sorcery and unbelief. A Hadith recounted by the two most highly regarded authorities Bukhari and Muslim mentions the practice of magic and sorcery as being among the seven grave sins that lead to damnation.[33]

The central religious issue at stake in the evaluation of the morality of power is that of *shirk*. *Shirk* is an Arabic term meaning the association of any other beings or powers with God. Magic or miracles based on the aid and power of God is morally acceptable, while that based on any other source of power is *shirk*. *Shirk* is among the few sins for which there is no possibility of pardon. Javanese are divided concerning the morality of *kesekten*, but nearly unanimous about the fact that it does not come directly from God. Modern reformists state that any use of magical power is *shirk* and leads to damnation. Most traditional Javanese maintain that the quest for magical power is not *shirk* because it does not involve the worship of gods other than God. It is rather the investigation of a natural phenomenon and/or an aspect of Javanese culture. According to this view, the morality of power is determined

---

Spiritualnya, Yogyakarta: Galang Press, 2007, pp. 52–53, M. Shoelhi, *Rahasia Pak Harto*, Jakarta: Grafindo, 2008, pp. 34–40. Suharto is said to have "borrowed" some of the most important of the Surakarta *pusaka* early in his presidency. It is reported that many palace official wept at the loss of these heirlooms, but were powerless to prevent it because the "loan" has been authorized by the Susuhunan.

[32] W. O" Flartey, *Eroticism and Aeseticism in the Mythology of Siva,* Chicago: University of Chicago Press, 1976.

[33] For a discussion of this *Hadith* see USC-MSA Compendium of Muslim Texts accessible at http://www.usc.edu/dept/MSA/fundamentals/tawheed/abdulwahab/KT1-chap-22.html

through its application. Most Javanese mystics, however, agree that the quest for power distracts attention from more important concerns including the purification of the soul and the *Sufi* path leading to union with God. A related view is that because power is located in the spiritual body, it, like passion, prevents the soul from controlling the mind.

Kesekten is clearly inferior to power acquired directly from God. This type of power is known as *kramat*, a term which also refers to the graves and miracles of saints. This type of power cannot be used for immoral or improper purposes because it is the gift from God. *Kramat* is not, however the ultimate goal of Javanese of other formulations of the Sufi mystical path. It is only one of the stages leading to union with God. Many Javanese are of the opinion that a truly great saint who has established direct contact with God has no interest in either *kramat* or *kesekten*. Such individuals cease to have independent wills and act only as the agents of God. It is also believed that even the quest for *kramat* may be motivated by the passions of greed and egotism. It is for this reason that many mystics deny that they have any magical powers, including those which would allow them to heal. Power of either type is useful only to the extent that it may be employed to ward off evil. In this way it helps to establish the conditions required for the attainment of more advanced mystical states, but is not a goal unto itself.

The Javanese concepts of power and knowledge are linked because both involve the ability to understand and/or control the elements and forces of which the human bodies and the universe are comprised. They can be thought of as secular sciences to the extent that they do not involve the development of one's relationship with God. It is for this same reason as well as the fact that the acquisition of the wrong type of either can lead to illness or insanity, that they are dangerous and morally ambiguous. But because the alternative, direct knowledge of God is such a remote religious goal, they are the only means through which the majority of Javanese can hope to come to an understanding of and ability to control the natural and supernatural worlds. They are also the primary tools of the *dukun*.

The Etiology of Disease and Curing

Traditional Javanese medical theory holds that disease is caused by any imbalance among the elements of the physical and spiritual bodies. This may result from the accidental or intentional introduction of foreign elements into the bodies, exposure to evil or simply inappropriate types of power, the actions of spirits, passion or sorcery. It can also be caused by an unbalanced or disturbed mental condition. The most common ailments result from the presence of too great or too small a quantity of one of the elements comprising the physical body. If there is not an underlying supernatural cause, such diseases can be treated with *jamu*.

Among the most common diseases is *masuk angin*. The symptoms resemble those of the common cold. Javanese believe that it is caused by a chill or the entry of too much wind into the mouth or nasal passage. It is for this reason that it is common to encounter a group of Javanese wearing jackets huddled together in a crowded bus or train with all of the windows closed, even when the temperature is nearly 90°F. The traditional cure for *masuk agnin* is a *jamu* made from salt, lime juice and ground chili peppers, though over the counter cold tablets are increasingly popular. Other diseases of this general type include the presence of too much heat, water or earth or insufficient blood.

Dukun I interviewed stated that these diseases can be treated without appeal to supernatural agents or dangerous forms of magical power. Cures are usually attempted through some combination of traditional medicine, ritual and prayer. *Dukun* also employ a complex system of numerological divination (*petungan*) as a diagnostic technique. Calculations are based on the patient's date of birth, the date he/she became ill and the current date. *Dukun* explain that they used this system to determine exactly what the cause of the disease is which enables them to prescribe the precise combination of medicines required to cure it. Prayer, meditation and ritual are advised to secure the blessings of God, saints and spirits for the patient and to reduce anxiety. This is essential because if the patient becomes worried or upset or doubts the power of the *dukun*, the cure will be ineffective.

Most Javanese do not feel that it is necessary to consult a *dukun* about such simple ailments. Indeed, people who constantly run to *dukun* with minor complaints are ridiculed as hypochondriacs. Similarly, it is often said that *dukun* use divination, prayer and ritual to convince people that they can not cure themselves and to justify the fees they charge or their demands for gifts. Consequently, while the treatment of minor ailments does not involve a *dukun* with morally ambiguous sources of power or evil spirits, it does raise questions about his ethics and intentions. Accepting money for curing violates one of the fundamental principles of Javanese ethics. In Java social relations are structured in terms of concepts of hierarchy, obligation and mutual assistance. The social as well as mystical ideal is the "union of servant and lord" and a free flow of aid among equals (*gotong royong*). There are, of course, few circumstances in which these values are perfectly articulated. It is, however, crucial that they be fulfilled in any domain touching on religion. While it is expected that a *dukun*, as a social superior should be given homage and gifts, on appropriate occasions – most notably *Lebaran*, the holiday at the end of Ramadan – he should not charge for his services, nor should he expect to receive payment in any form. He should be *ikhlas* (have only good intentions), curing only to help those in need.[34]

These are rather exalted expectations and almost no *dukun* live up to them despite the fact that many claim to. This, however, raises serious questions about the intentions of healers, and owing to the types of power and knowledge they control, is cause for fear and concern. For while *dukun* can cure, they are conceptually and socially associated with sorcery. Thus while any Javanese feel that it is not proper to

---

[34]With the exception of midwives there are very few female *dukun*. Other female *dukun* are regarded with extreme suspicion. They are widely believed to specialize in the preparation of "love charms" that make their clients irresistible. Sex workers of both genders often seek out the services of such *dukun*.

pay a *dukun*, few would refuse his demand or even suggestion. Patients, other than friends and relatives, generally give healers "gifts" to express their appreciation for his services. These may be in either cash or kind and can range from a chicken or basket of fruit to luxury cars and houses. Healers who have wealthy, politically powerful, clients are often themselves very well to do. Former President Suharto's relationships with *paranormals* provide examples of the complexities of the financial relationships between *dukun* and their clients. Suharto consulted *paranormals* on a regular basis. In some cases he asked advice when there were difficult decisions to be made and in others about what pilgrimages and spiritual exercises he should undertake to advance his quest for power.[35] Ki Agen Selo, one of the paranormals Suharto consulted, claimed that he never received more than twenty pieces of fruit for his advice.[36] Ki Ageng Pamungkas, another nationally known *paranormal*, later commented that this is in keeping with the tradition according to which *paranormals* are "actually not oriented towards the material".[37] But at the same time Romo Diyat, another of Suharto's spiritual guides, lived lavishly and owned an enormous house enclosed by fortress like walls.[38] Suharto had a well deserved reputation for rewarding loyalty. Given his own enormous wealth such gifts were not particularly extravagant. I doubt that the gift of a house was as much of a financial sacrifice for Suharto as that of a pair of chickens is to my friends who live in Yogyakarta *kampung*.

While these factors come into play in the evaluation of *dukun* concerned with physical ailments, they are more fully articulated in cases of spiritual or inward (*batin*) disease. There is a marked tendency for *dukun* to discover spiritual causes for all but the simplest ailments. Most chronic, degenerative and psychological disorders are thought to stem from spiritual causes. The attribution of underlying spiritual causes also enables *dukun* to justify their failures. *Dukun* often explain that while they can temporarily relieve the symptoms of chronic diseases, a lasting cure is possible only if the patient strengthens and purifies the spiritual body.

Diseases of the spiritual body may have any number of causes. Among the most common is the loss of one of the four spiritual brothers. Since there is an innate connection between the spiritual body and those of the four brothers, losing one of them is extremely dangerous. A lost brother may fall under the influence of an evil spirit or be captured by a sorcerer. In either case it serves as a conduit through which foreign elements and power, or the spirit itself, may enter the physical body. This

---

[35] Rumors about Suharto's involvement with the "supernatural" have circulated for many years. I began to hear them almost as soon as I arrived in Yogyakarta for the first time. They did not begin to appear in print until after his resignation on May 21, 1998. They began to appear almost immediately after he announced that he would "*Lengser Kaprabon*" (renounce the throne) and more than a decade later remain enormously popular.

[36] *Bernas*, June 2, 1998.

[37] K. Pamungkas, *Rahasia Supranatural Soeharto*, Yogyakarta: Penerbit Narasi, 2007, p. 23, Artha, op. cit., p. 157.

[38] Artha, *op. cit.* pg. 160.

can cause severe illness, insanity or death. In less extreme cases, where the spiritual brother is simply lost, the individual becomes ill or confused. The reason for this is that the spiritual brothers" primary function is to maintain a balance among the elements of the two bodies.

Other diseases of the spiritual body are caused by offending one of the numerous types of spiritual beings in which Javanese believe. There are four major types of spirits:[39] *Jinn* are morally ambiguous. Islamic *jinn* are generally benevolent, while non believing *inn* are mischievous, if not evil. *Jinn* are composed entirely of the element air and have only spiritual bodies. They do not have souls. *Demit* are place spirits. They tend to inhabit abandoned buildings, peculiar trees and geological formations and territories not occupied by humans. They are morally neutral and cause trouble for humans only when disturbed. *Setan* are evil. They are subject to *Iblis* (the Devil), have bodies of fire and are governed by the passion of anger. They are easily offended and a major source of spiritual illness. The fourth type are the spirits of the dead. The moral character of these spirits depends on the exact composition of the spiritual body. The purified spirits of saints may be of great aid to humans, while those of evil people or those who accumulated a great load of passion are perilous. Others are morally ambiguous and are dangerous if approached in the wrong manner. This can be true even of saints.

The spirit of Sultan Agung provides a telling example. Sultan Agung, who reigned between 1613 and 1645, was among the great kings of Mataram and figures prominently in the state cults and popular religion in central Java. He was a great military leader and is thought to have acquired the power of invulnerability. He was also a mystic and patron of Islamic scholarship. Consequently, he has the ability to bestow great boons. But his power is so great that it can easily overcome those who have not sufficiently strengthened themselves. He will not aid, and may harm supplicants who have impious desires. Sultan Agung's grave is located at *Imogiri*, a hill top cemetery south of Yogyakarta. The grave is guarded by a powerful *jinn* who sometimes appears to pilgrims in the form of a white tiger.[40] The *jinn* assess the nature of every pilgrim's intentions. If he/she is devout and free from the passions of greed and anger, the Sultan will often grant requests. But if the pilgrim has evil intentions, the *jinn* will, at the Sultan's direction, deny access to the grave and frighten the pilgrim so severely that illness or death may result.

---

[39] For a more detailed account of the variety of spiritual beings Javanese recognize see Geertz, op. cit.

[40] Throughout Indonesia and much of insular and mainland Southeast Asia tigers are believed to be the forest counterparts of humans and to have the ability to acquire great stores of magical power. Javanese often describe forested areas, including those on other Indonesian islands, as being *gawat*; powerful, but dangerous and as being populated by "tigers and snakes". Tigers are now critically endangered if not extinct in Java. Some *dukun* display snake skins and skulls and those of other jungle animals in their homes and claim to have traveled to remote areas, especially Kalimantan, in a quest for power.

A second, and more extreme, example of the dangers and moral ambiguity of spirits is provided by Gusti Kangeng Ratu Kidul, the queen of the southern ocean and of all the spirits of central Java. Ratu Kidul is believed to have been the wife of the kings of the Mataram dynasty and to be among the major sources of the Sultan's power.[41] She is the focus of numerous state ceremonies and is thought to advise the Sultan on all manner of political and military affairs. But at the same time she is exceedingly dangerous. She commands an army of spirits who cause havoc along the southern coast and in areas surrounding the palaces of Yogyakarta and Surakarta. While she is visiting the Sultan, these spirits run wild through the *kampung* surrounding the *kraton*, occasionally seizing the spiritual bodies of people they find attractive. These individuals invariably die, and join Ratu Kidul as servants in her palace in the middle of the ocean. The same is true of those foolish enough to enter the ocean at Parangtritis of the coast to the south of Yogyakarta which is the gateway to her domain. She is also capable of causing plague if she becomes angry with the Sultan.

Beliefs concerning Ratu Kidul present Javanese with a major paradox. On one hand, it is only with her help that the Sultan is able to control the other spirits inhabiting his realm. This is among his most important duties and is vital for the prosperity and health of his subjects. On the other hand, she is extremely dangerous and potentially life threatening for those who lack the power to control her. Other spirits, usually *setan* or the spiritual bodies of humans, who have died prematurely, may attempt to capture the physical and/or spiritual bodies of the living. It is often said that *setan* envy humans because they have physical bodies and sense perception. Consequently, they attempt to displace the spiritual bodies and/or souls of their victims. The spirits of humans who die prematurely must wander the earth until the time at which God fixed for their deaths. They often attempt to find physical bodies in which to live out the remainder of their "lives". These are thought to be among the major causes of mental illness and degenerative disease. Possession by *setan* is particularly dangerous. When a *setan* takes control of a physical body, the mind is dominated by the passions of anger and greed of which the spirit is comprised. The victim becomes violent, irrational and extremely dangerous. The power of the *setan* greatly enhances the strength of the physical body. A possessed person may acquire the strength of many men, the ability to appear in two or more places simultaneously, to fly through the air, to assume the form of a tiger, pig or other animal or the power to kill without touching the intended victim. Others become raving lunatics prone to seizures resembling epilepsy. In the most extreme cases, the *setan* may alter the form of the physical body to match its own spiritual qualities. The body is slowly and

---

[41] Pakubuwana X–XIII of Surakarta are exceptions. They are known as the adopted spiritual sons of Ratu Kidul. There is a Surakarta *Kraton* tradition that when the future Pakubuwana X was an infant his nurse dropped him. Ratu Kidul appeared and swept him into her arms before he could hit the floor. She exclaimed: "Oh my son!" The precipitous decline of the Surakarta court in the post-colonial era is sometimes attributed to the fact that she is no longer married to the Susuhunan (the Surakarta royal title.)

painfully transformed into that of a half human, half demonic creature known as a *Raksasha*.

Other, less powerful spirits, cause illness only if they are offended. *Demit* are an example. These are place spirits often found in ruined buildings, trees and unusual geological features. In general the same rule of politeness and propriety which govern social relations among humans apply to spirits as well. This can cause difficulties because spirits can not be seen. It is quite easy to accidentally bump into, sit on or step over a spirit. If the spirit is offended it will use its power to bring on mental confusion or physical illness. For the victim is to recover, offerings must be made to the offended spirit. While these are generally simple and inexpensive, it may be quite difficult to discover which spirit has been offended and where it lives. Offerings are placed at locations known to be inhabited by *demit* on a regular basis. Many Javanese say *"Bismillah"* (In the name of God) when approaching places though to be inhabited by them. *jimat* (amulets) are thought to have powers that frighten them off. Unlike more powerful spirits *demit* are most often simply a nuisance.

Diseases of the spiritual body may also be caused by sorcery. Javanese are so frightened of sorcery that they seldom mention it by name (*ngilmu sihir*). It is almost always referred to as "an illness caused by a person" (*sakit dipun damel*) or some other similarly indirect term. I have never encountered a Javanese who claimed to be a sorcerer or who would admit having employed one. Many, however, claim to be the victims of sorcery or to know of cases in which it has been used by others. Sorcery is most commonly used against relatives, neighbors or business partners. It can also be used to acquire riches or in cases of unrequited love, divorce or fraud. In some instances accusations of sorcery arise in remarkably trivial disputes. In one I encountered in 1978 two brothers quarreled over the profits from a cigarette stand they operated. The dispute involved only a few thousand Rupiah, which at that time was valued at 325 to the US Dollar. It was widely believed in the *kampung* that one sought out the services of a sorcerer to make his niece go blind. He was severely beaten and banished from the *kampung*.

Accusations of sorcery also figure significantly in contemporary politics. As is also true in South Africa, local authorities are sometimes criticized for refusing to prosecute suspected sorcerers and their clients.[42] Siegel has shown that accusations of sorcery were especially common during the turbulent period of the late 1990s. In some parts of Java there were virtual epidemics of accusations and reprisal killings not unlike those that occurred during the European Witch Craze of the seventeenth century.[43] It is widely believed that these accusations, many of which were directed against prominent *Kyai*, were instigated by supporters of the Suharto government in an attempt to discredit opposition forces.

With the advent of contested elections accusations of sorcery by electoral campaigns have become common. The Jakarta gubernatorial elections of 2007 provide

---

[42] A. Ashcroft, Witchcraft, *Violence and Democracy in South Africa*, Chicago, University of Chicago Press, 2005.

[43] J. Siegel, *Naming the Witch*, Stanford: Stanford University Press, 2006.

and intriguing example. The election was contested by two candidates, one from the Islamist *Partai Keadilan Sejahtera* (The Justice and Prosperity Party, or PKS), and the other from a coalition of nineteen parties who put aside their differences to ensure that the PKS candidate did not win. In what was perhaps the strangest statement of the closely contested campaign Prijanto, the coalition candidate for Deputy Governor, accused PKS of using sorcery to influence the election. At a religious gathering celebrating the Prophet Muhammad's journey to heaven he stated: "This is not made up slander. What is being used is hypnotism, witchcraft and shamanism". He then asked a group of tradionalist Muslim clerics to pray to stop the effects of "voodoo and black magic rites and spells".[44] The PKS candidate did not win the election. The Javanese logic of sorcery would suggest that in this case prayers triumphed over spells.[45]

Sorcery is practiced by *dukun* who control evil spirits and sources of power. It is widely believed that many *dukun* will practice sorcery if the price is right. To bring about the death or illness of an enemy it is customary to seek out a *dukun* living in a remote area known to be inhabited by evil spirits or a least one far from home. There are both religious and social reasons for this practice. A *dukun* in one's own community might resort to extortion to obtain a higher fee, gossip, or worse still harm the client instead of the intended victim. It is also thought that evil powers and spirits are concentrated in remote areas far from towns and centers of beneficial magical power. Many believe that it is impossible to practice sorcery in the city of Yogyakarta because of the spiritual power of the Sultan. Yogyakarta residents feel that to find a powerful sorcerer it is necessary to journey to one of the mountainous regions on the borders of the kingdom or to sections of the south coast controlled by Ratu Kidul's spirit legions.

The sorcerer often requests some of the victim's hair or nail clippings and if possible his or her umbilical cord. In simple cases, the goal of which is to cause physical or mental illness, the *dukun* combines these bodily products with a mixture of traditional medicines and recites a spell. Connections between these bodily products and the spiritual and physical bodies of the intended victim enable evil power or spirits to displace either one of the four spiritual brothers or one of the elements of her or his spiritual body. The *dukun* may also attempt to steal one of the spiritual brothers, forcing it to serve as a conduit through which evil power can be introduced into the victim's bodies at will. In more extreme cases the *dukun* uses his power to send a *keris* through the air to harm the intended victim or gives his client one or more amulets to place in the victim's house or place of business. The most virulent types of sorcery, which, if left untreated, cause a slow painful death, involve sending one or more spirits to invade the victim's spiritual body. The spirits are often accompanied by pieces of wire, nails, glass and other objects which are deposited at

---

[44] *Kompas*, August 1, 2007.

[45] On the role of religion in this election see M. Woodward, "Indonesia's Religious Political Parties: Democratic Consolidation and Security in Post-New Order Indonesia," *Asian Security*, vol. 4, no. 1, 2008, pp. 41–60.

various places in the physical body. To ensure success and frustrate efforts to cure the victim, the *dukun* may send hundreds of invading spirits, all of which must be exorcised if the illness is to be cured.

Dukun acquire the ability to practice sorcery by meditating for long periods in dangerous (*gawat* or *angker*) places. The power generated by this meditation enables them to control *setan* and other evil spirits. It is perilous even to attempt to become a sorcerer because if one's power is not sufficient to control the spirits, they will be enraged, destroying both the physical and spiritual bodies. Sorcerers are also believed to be grave robbers. Robbing graves serves two purposes; it allows the sorcerer to capture the spirits of the dead, which are forced to perform evil acts and it provides them with materials, chiefly bones and burial shrouds, used in the preparation of satanic medicines. The bones and skins of snakes, tigers, apes and other jungle animals are also used for this purpose. The fact that these materials are available in many public markets speaks for the prevalence of sorcery.

To diagnose diseases of the spiritual body *dukun* must be familiar with the types of spirits and magical power which cause them. Here it is important to recall that in Javanese cosmology knowledge of a class of phenomena implies the ability to control it. This means that a *dukun* specializing in treatment of diseases of the spiritual body is the mirror image of a sorcerer and could, if he wished, become one. The cure of a disease caused by sorcery is often thought of as a personal struggle between the sorcerer and a *dukun*. A *dukun* involved in such a struggle may use magical power and/or spirits to attack the sorcerer directly as well as to control the proximate causes of illness. He may also choose to attack the sorcerer's client. In each of these cases the medicines, sources of magical power and spirits used to cure diseases of the spiritual body are closely related to those which cause them. Consequently, the practice of spiritual medicine is both difficult and potentially dangerous. If the *dukun* looses the battle he, as well as his patient, may die.

Even if the sorcerer and his spiritual agents are vanquished, the spirits and/or objects placed in the victim's body must be disposed of properly. A *dukun* must have a great store of power and/or the aid of powerful spirits to control these evil objects and beings. If left unattended they could easily harm others, including the *dukun*, his family and neighbors. Usually these objects (and spirits) are taken to a remote *gawat* area such as the crater of a volcano or are dumped into a river or the ocean. Few *dukun* believe that they have the power to destroy evil. Most feel that it is in principle impossible to destroy any type of magical power and that their task is simply to remove it from the geographical and social domains occupied by humans. The *dukun*'s primary function may, therefore, be understood as on of establishing and maintaining a partition of the universe into areas which are dangerous and powerful (*gawat*) and holy (*kramat*). The moral ambiguity of the *dukun* is rooted in the fact that he must use potentially dangerous and/or evil sources of power to maintain this partition.

All of this suggests that *dukun* specializing in the treatment of diseases of the spiritual body and especially those caused by sorcery are extremely dangerous people. The line between sorcery and curing is established only by intention. As was stated previously, the fact that many *dukun* expect payment or gifts for their services raises questions concerning the nature of their intentions. Moreover, any use of magical power is morally ambiguous, and curing involves *dukun* with some of the most dangerous sources of power. Similarly a *dukun* may harm one or more persons in order to cure another, especially in cases of sorcery.

Javanese distrust of *dukun* is based not only on the fear of sorcery, but also on its eschatological consequences. Sorcerers are believed to suffer horrible deaths and torment in the grave in direct proportion to the amount of suffering they caused in life. This view is based on the common Islamic doctrine that the souls of the dead remain in the grave until the Day of Judgment where they receive a taste of either the rewards of heaven or the punishment of hell.[46] In the most extreme cases the sorcerer does not die until the Day of Judgment, but is slowly and painfully transformed into a snake or demonic creature. While many Javanese, like some other *Sufis*, do not accept the normative Muslim doctrine of hell or at least interpret it in an allegorical sense, others maintain that a special place in the flame is reserved for sorcerers. The sorcerer's client is thought to suffer in precisely the same manner: hence the reluctance of Javanese to mention sorcery by name the near universal denial of any association with it.

Religious Cures and the Religious Strategies of *Dukun*

To avoid accusations of sorcery and reduce the religious risks it entails, *dukun* make systematic, through rarely successful attempts to present themselves as saints or at least as holy men. *Wali*, Kyai, mystics and other holy men and *dukun* are all thought to have the ability cure diseases of the physical and spiritual bodies. The difference between these modes of medical practice is that saints, mystics and other holy men do not rely on magical power or spirits. Their cures are based entirely on the ability to communicate directly with God and to intercede with him on the behalf of patients. While most Javanese believe this type of cure to be possible, it is difficult to obtain. Most mystics have claim to have neither the ability nor the desire to cure. Even those mystics who feel they can cure are reluctant to do so. This reluctance is based on the example of Muhammad, who taught that holy men should avoid public display of miraculous powers. Muslim leaders and mystics will often pray for the sick, reciting sections from the *Qur'an* or religious formula (*dihkr*) over them, but generally decline to perform more specific curing rites or to prescribe medications. One Yogyakarta mystic explained that he often prayed for the sick, asking God to cure them, but did not wish to be known as a *dukun*. He continued that curing distracts attention from more important religious activities and that the temptation to become *dukun* was a sign of passion. In general mystics will serve as curers only when the strength of kinship or other social bonds overpowers purely religious considerations.

---

[46]On Islamic views of the afterlife see J. Smith and Y. Haddad, The *Islamic Understanding of Death and Resurrection*, Albany: State University of New York Press, 1981.

Most *dukun* are fully aware of their ambiguous moral and social positions and the dangers that curing exposes them to. Consequently, many attempt to present themselves as mystics or Muslim saints. They boast of wildly exaggerated – from a Javanese perspective – religious attainments including direct communication with God, angels and other unambiguously holy spiritual beings. Others claim that God has granted them explicit authority to use specific types of esoteric knowledge and power and that they have a religious duty to cure. *Habib* and *tabib* seek to establish their religious legitimacy through appeal to their Arabic ancestry and often by claims to be descendents of the Prophet Muhammad. They generally make extensive use of *Qur'an* recitation and Arabic *jimat* (amulets) which are generally verses from the *Qur'an*. Some claim that the *jamu* they recommend are *hallal* (permissible) and/or that they are imported from Arabia.[47] Those who have "clinics" often display signs in Arabic as well as in Indonesian. Many explain that they acquired healing powers while on pilgrimage to Mecca.

The relationships between these modes of medical practice and the largely unsuccessful attempts of *dukun* to present themselves as saints or holy men are apparent in each of the following cases. These examples have been chosen because they illustrate the range of treatment styles and legitimation strategies employed by Yogyakarta *dukun*. One of the three *dukun* described relies primarily on Muslim spirits of Arabic origin, a second on his supposed appointment by God, and the third on a complex spirit cult rooted in, but opposed to, the Yogyakarta theory of kingship. To varying degrees all are examples of the ways in which concepts of ethnicity, nationality and religion are intertwined in daily life in Yogyakarta.[48]

Pak Mustafhim: A *Santri Dukun*

Pak Mustafhim is what Geertz refers to as a *santri dukun*. He is a conservative, traditional Muslim who studied theology, mysticism and ritual in a *pesantren* as a young man. He is what Schimmel and other Islamicists refer to as a *Shari"ah* minded mystic.[49] He attends Friday services at the local mosque, prays five times per day, fasts during Ramadan and plans to make the pilgrimage to Mecca. His devotional activities center on *doa* (the nonobligatory form of prayer) and fasting. Pak Mustafhim summarized his religious beliefs as follows: "Religion without fasting, fasting without prayer, neither is correct". He uses prayer and fasting to control passion and to establish contact with God, saints and angles. Pak Mustafhim claimed to have developed a personal relationship with the angel Jibrail (Gabriel) by fasting for 100 days and by praying until the early hours of the morning. This is an extremely

---

[47] The claim that *jamu* are *hallal* is entirely symbolic because all vegetable products are *hallal* by definition.

[48] All of these men are now deceased. My use of the present tense reflects an ethnographic present of the late 1970s.

[49] See A. Schimmel, *Mystical Dimensions of Islam*. University of North Carolina Press, Chapel Hill, 1975.

exalted claim because Jibrail was the spiritual guide of the prophet Muhammad, the vehicle though which the *Qur'an* was revealed and who will announce the Day of Judgment at the end of the world.[50] Pak Mustafhim claims that Jibrail helps him with the curing and a wide variety of daily tasks, including finding empty seats on crowded buses. To diagnose diseases of the spiritual body he combines meditation, in which he asks for the angel's aid, with a complex form of divination based on Western, Islamic, Javanese and Chinese calandrical systems. His cures usually involve a combination of prayer, meditation and traditional medicines.

On the surface it would appear that Pak Mustafhim is an orthodox Muslim medical practitioner similar to those found in the Middle East and South Asia with a bit of Chinese numerology thrown in for good measure.[51] However, the types of medicines he uses link him directly to the dangerous (*gawat*) side of the Javanese theory of power. Pak Mustafhim imports most of his medicines from Kalimantan (Indonesian Borneo). A sign outside his house proclaims that he is a specialist in traditional Kalimantan medicine as well as an Islamic scholar. His medicines include various types of oil, plants and the bones of snakes and apes.

There is a clear and direct link between these substances and what Javanese hold to be the evil power of the jungle and other uncivilized regions. It is believed that jungles are inhabited by dangerous spirits and that nature is basically evil. It is civilized only the intrusion of *kramat* and other beneficial types of magical power in the hands of kings and saints. Kalimantan is thought to be among the most *gawat* regions of Indonesia. The apes of the jungle and the Dyak tribesmen are thought to control many dangerous spirits, which, because they are not native to Java, are almost impossible to control. The Dyak are particularly feared because many in Yogyakarta know that they were formerly head hunters. For many in Yogyakarta, Kalimantan and other "outer islands" are Indonesian, and yet not really civilized, i.e., not Javanese. Pak Mustafhim claims that it is necessary to use these medicines because of the great power of the virulently anti-Muslim spirits left in Java by the ancient Hindu-Buddhist dynasties. He told me that he had been sent to Kalimantan by Jibrail who had granted him the authority to tap these sources power. Consequently, his use of dangerous sources of power is balanced by extreme claims to religious legitimacy. While his claims to control potent sources of power are generally accepted by members of the community, his claims to religious legitimacy are open to serious question. While some of Pak Mustafhim's neighbors and patients think of him as a holy man, others told me that he was deeply involved with sorcery and used Kalimantan spirits to enchant unsuspecting patients.

Pak Hario: Mysticism and Spirits

Pak Hario was a retired military officer who, prior to his death in 1979, was a minor official in the Yogyakarta *Kraton*. Unlike Pak Mustafhim, he was not an observant Muslim. Like most Javanese mystics, Pak Hario accepted the validity of the five

---

[50]See M. Watt, *Muhammad, Prophet and Statesman.* Oxford University Press, Oxford. 1961
[51]On Islamic folk medicine in South Asia see G. Herklots and J. Shariff *Islam in India.* Oxford University Press, Oxford, 1921.

pillars of Islam, but was convinced that they are only a preliminary step on the mystical path. Like other *Sufis*, he believed that emphasis should be placed on the inward, spiritual aspects of religion rather than on outward ritual and devotion. He practiced a type of meditation focusing on contemplation of the names and attributes of God.

Pak Hario became a *dukun* during the Indonesian revolution when there was a critical shortage of bio-medical doctors and medicines. He explained that one day after a battle he prayed over a group of gravely wounded solders. Much to this surprise, they recovered completely. His friends and comrades began to think of him as a *dukun*, though Pak Hario claimed that he was not. He explained his ability as a *wahyu* or divine appointment, which gave him both the power and the duty to cure the sick and wounded. When I met him, Pak Hario was among the leading *dukun* in Yogyakarta and specialized in the treatment of children. According to several of his patients parents, Pak Hario was particularly adept at recovering spiritual brothers who had been lost or captured by evil spirits.

Pak Hario claimed that his cures were based entirely on his ability to communicate directly with God. When a sick child was brought to him he held it in his arms and meditated for several minutes tying to empty his mind of all conscious thought. Then a message would come from God telling him what was wrong with the child and what combination of prayer, pilgrimage and medication was required to cure the disease. Pak Hario's medicines and the amulets displayed in his house indicate that he relied on many types of power as well as meditation and divine intercession or at least that he wished his patients to believe that he did. Most of the medicines he used were aromatic herbs, flowers, rice straw and other standard Javanese remedies. However, he also prescribed unusual combinations of ground coral and sea shells which indicated to many of his clients that he had some connection with Ratu Kidul. His house was filled with *batik* paintings, Balinese *wayang* (Shadow Theater) puppets and carvings of Hindu gods and demons. This suggests that Pak Hario relied on essentially the same types of magical power as Pak Mustafhim. But in this case the spirits were thought to be those of the Hindu-Javanese period rather than the native spirits of Kalimantan. Many Javanese Muslims believe that the Balinese form of Hinduism was the "original" religion of Java. Hinduism is often interpreted as a cult devoted to the worship of evil spirits, which though extremely powerful, are hostile to Javanese Islam. The root of this hostility is the fact that while Islam recognizes the existence of a wide variety of spirits, worshipping them is *shirk*. According to many Javanese informants Balinese Hindu spirits are angry because they are no longer worshipped in Java.[52]

It is true that some aspects of Hindu-Javanese *kesekten* are preserved in the Javanese courts and that the ever popular Javanese *wayang* is based on the Hindu epics *Mahabharata* and *Ramayana*. But the Hindu power preserved in royal *puska* has been tamed and islamicized. In the Javanese *wayang* the Hindu gods are transformed into humans. They are linked by exceedingly complex genealogies to both

---

[52]The extent of these beliefs was made clear to me when I told my neighbors of my plans to visit Bali. Many warned me of the dangerous spirits that inhabit the island and admonished me about bringing any of them back with me. One gave me a ring that he said had the power to protect me from them.

the Muslim prophets and the Javanese kings. At least some of the principle figures in the *wayang* are thought to have been converted to Islam. The power and spirits which escaped to Bali at the time of the Islamicization of Java were not converted and are seen as both dangerous and hostile. It is, in this respect, significant that all of the *wayang* puppets and statues Pak Hario displayed in his home were from Bali. Many of his patients thought that Pak Hario had made a secret trip to Bali to capture "Hindu" spirits. None of them believed that his powers were derived exclusively from Islamic meditation.

The extent of this belief became clear when Pak Hario died. His funeral was attended by several hundred friends, relatives, neighbors, patients and their families. The crowd was so large that the prayers were broadcast over loudspeakers. Immediately after the *modin* (Muslim ritual officiant) finished the required recitations, two of Pak Hario's daughters began screaming, tearing at their clothes and clawing the mourners. The *modin* concluded that the girls had been possessed by spirits and attempted to exorcise them with *Qur'an* recitation. This only increased the girls' hysteria. The screams were carried through the neighborhood by the loudspeakers, attracting a crowd of over a thousand. At this point Pak Hario's widow sent for a *dukun*. The *dukun* brought a *keris* which he said had been made during the Hindu-Javanese period, with which he extracted two of Pak Hario's "Hindu" spirits from the girls" bodies. This he said was possible because the spirits were attracted to the "Hindu power" of the *keris*. He later told me that because Pak Hario had died suddenly, he had not been able to dispose of the spirits. He continued that the spirits were from Bali and that they did not wish to remain in a foreign, and particularly a Muslim, country. As it was impractical to take them back to Bali the *dukun* escorted the spirits to the south coast and entrusted them to Ratu Kidul.[53]

This case is interesting both because of its specific reference to non-Muslim and non-Javanese spirits and because it is illustrative of the view most Javanese have of *dukun*'s claims to mystical attainments. Pak Hario never told anyone that he had captured Hindu spirits. His clients, and seemingly even his daughters, inferred this from the types of amulets and paintings he kept in the house. Pak Hario told me that he had acquired these objects because other people thought that they were sources of power and would not believe in him if he did not display the outward signs of being a *dukun*. While Pak Hario insisted that all of his power came directly from God, it is clear that not even his family believed him. They continued to bring their

---

[53] A similar issue arose concerning the *pusaka* that Suharto had "borrowed" from the Surakata *Kraton* after his resignation in 1998. According to some sources they were returned by his daughter Siti Hardiyanti Rukmana (more commonly known as Tutut). The fact that the former president suffered a stroke shortly after resigning is sometimes mentioned as evidence that they had been returned and that Suharto had lost the power that had maintained him for so long. Surakarta *Kraton* sources claim that they have not been returned, Shoelhi, op. cit., p. 37. Some attribute this failure to Tutut's political ambitions. There are rumors in both Yogyakarta and Surakarta that they will eventually be returned, but not to the *kraton*. It is said that they will be placed in a museum, either in Surakarta or Jakarta and that they will be considered as national property, not that of the Surakarta *Kraton*. The affair of the "missing *pusaka*" is a clear example of the ways in which ethnic Javanese concepts of power and authority have shaped the course of Indonesian national history.

children to him for the simple reason that he had a reputation for curing diseases that baffled other *dukun* and bio-medical doctors. The fact that Pak Hario's spirits attempted to harm his daughters so shortly after his death speaks for the danger of relying on such potent and *gawat* sources of power.

Pak Mulyono: Curing and the Yogyakarta State Court

The last of the three *dukun*, Pak Mulyono, is perhaps the most interesting and certainly the most extreme about his claims to religious legitimacy. Unlike Pak Mustafhim and Pak Hario, he specializes in the cure of diseases of the spiritual body caused by sorcery. With the aid of some of the most power spirits in Java he performs "spiritual operations" (*operasi batin*) during which he extracts long pieces of wire, nails, broken bottles and other objects from patients" bodies. The operations were the central foci of a highly developed quasi-messianic spirit cult and were attended by as many as 350 people.

The cult was based on a complex combination of meditation, ritual, saint veneration and spirit possession. While it grew out of Pak Mulyono's medical practice, the social organization, mythology and ritual program of the cult reflected those of the Yogyakarta state cult. This points to strong similarities between theories of curing, kingship and political organization.

The origin myth of the cult is as follows:

> Once when Pak Mulyono was meditating at *Imogiri* the spirit of Sultan Agung appeared and informed him that he would become a *pitulung* (helper) to guard people against the acts of evil sorcerers and spirits who plague the world during periods of moral and religious decline. Sultan Agung stated that Pak Mulyono had been granted a *wahyu* by God. He was then told to travel to a remote mountainous region to search for the grave of a saint who would help him with his duties. Pak Mulyono and three friends fasted for several days and then went to search for the grave, which they discovered was that of one of the sons of the last Hindu-Javanese king. The saint's name is Prabu Lingasari. He was converted to Islam after destroying his physical body through intense meditation. He then came to know Ratu Kidul, Sultan Agung and his grandfather Panembahan Senopati. Lingasari taught Pak Mulyono and his friends a series of *mantra* enabling them to call on these and other spirits. Now when he meditates Pak Mulyono asks Prabu Lingasari to help him or to send an appropriate spirit, which enters the body of one of his friends to perform the operation.

Pak Mulyono also uses an extensive array of traditional medicines. His prescriptions are extremely complex, often including as many as fifty distinct substances. Both the prescription and quality of the ingredients were checked by Prabu Lingasari or some other powerful spirit.

The operations are extremely complex. Several days in advance Pak Mulyono sends written invitations to his followers, explaining the nature of the illness to be treated and the names of the most important of the spirits to be consulted. The invitations are in Javanese and are written in a Latin script stylistically similar to Javanese script.

Prior to the beginning of the ritual the patient bathes, is wrapped in a burial shroud and placed on a cot in the middle of a large room. Pak Mulyono sometimes uses the front room of his own home and if a particularly large audience is expected rents a room from the near bye primary school. The operations often involve as many as 1,000 spirits, usually drawn from Ratu Kidul's legions. The are contained in white cotton bundles approximate one inch in diameter attached to bamboo sticks They are used to isolate and surround the evil spirits or substances in the patient's bodies driving them to a point in the patient's chest from where they can be extracted. The process takes as long as an hour. Pak Mulyono directs their movements and assistants repeated strike the patient's body with the bundled spirit legions. Once they are surrounded and captured the invading evil spirits and foreign objects are removed by the possessed medium with a *keris* and a large pair of bolt cutters which he inserts into the shroud. This is also a protracted process that can take as long as an hour. Once removed the evil spirits and associated objects are removed they aresealed in a container and immediately sent to the coast by courier for disposal. The patient emerges from the shroud and is liberally coated with a special *jamu* to heal the spiritual wounds resulting from the operation. When I asked Pak Mulyono why there was never any blood on the patient's body he replied that because the operations were purely spiritual, that they did not leave physical signs. Patients were also required to undertake extensive programs of prayer, meditation and pilgrimage to strengthen the spiritual body and to ward off future attacks. They are also invited to subsequent operations and other rituals staged by the cult.

Pak Mulyono hosts other rituals on Muslim holy days and during Soro, the first month of the Javanese year that do not involve *operasi*. They were referred to as *lengahan* (visitations). In a general sense they resemble *slametan*. They are rituals meals at which Islamic prayers are recited, and saints, ancestors and other spirits invoked. The critical difference between an ordinary *slametan* and a *lengahan* is that in the later case the sprits, including those of Prabu Lingasari, Ratu Kidul and Sultan Agung, are physically present and speak directly to cult members through the possessed medium. Cult members offer food to and receive blessings from the spirits. Pak Mulyono allows his followers to speak to them about all sorts of medical, personal and religious problems. For many of those in attendance this greatly enhances the spiritual quality and efficacy of the ritual because this type of communication is normally only possible for extremely advanced mystics and in the case of Ratu Kidul is the exclusive prerogative of the Sultan.

This aspect of the cult is based on widely held messianic beliefs that in times of spiritual and political decline the powerful spirits intervene directly in the lives of ordinary people.[54] Pak Mulyono's claim to religious legitimacy is based on the presumption that the traditional system of royal control of and intercession with the spirit world has broken down. His followers believe that God has selected him as the spiritual guide whose primary task is to protect the people of Yogyakarta during the ensuing interregnum. In 1979 many of them believed that Pak Mulyono

---

[54]On Javanese messianic movements see: J. van der Kroef "Javanese Messianic Expectations: Their Origin and Cultural Context". *Comparative Studies in Society and History,* vol. 2, pp. 229, 1959.

would soon announce the arrival of a *Ratu Adil* (just king) who would restore the Muslim traditions and political power of the Sultanate and install a new dynasty. This element of the cult may well have been based on the commonly held belief that kingdoms fall in years ending 00. The field work on which this analysis is based was conducted in the Islamic year 1400 when messianic expectations were heightened. It is very clear that Pak Mulyono did not accept the Yogyakarta dynasty's claims to religious legitimacy. He made this particularly clear when I spoke with him in 1991 after the death of Sultan Hamengkubuwana IX and the coronation of his son. He explained that the new Sultan had "merely risen in rank" and that he had neither *wahyu* nor *kesekten*.

The culmination of the cult's ritual cycle is a pilgrimage to Prabu Lingasari's grave. Pak Mulyono rents as many as ten mini-vans for this trip. He sends formal invitations written in an archaic form of Javanese used only in the royal palace, with an accompanying Indonesian translation, to all cult members. The pilgrimage is usually conducted during the month of Sawal. This month follows the fasting month of *Ramadan* and is the traditional time for visiting and repairing the graves. The trip lasts 4–5 days and includes several *Lengahan* conducted at the grave site and in the cave said to have been used by Prabu Lingasari as a meditation cell. It is believed that this cave is linked to Ratu Kidul's palace in the southern ocean by an underground passageway and that she too can attend the *Lengahan*.

Pak Mulyono's claims are extremely daring. His role in the cult of Lingasari resembled that of the Sultan in the traditional Javanese state. He and the Sultan claim to control many of the same spirits, including Ratu Kidul, and to direct the flow of power and blessing in their respective domains. The origin myths of the Sultanate and the cult are remarkably similar. In both a spiritual being informs the king/cult leader that he has been appointed by God and explains his duties. In both instances the leader is taught a *mantra* enabling him to call on powerful spirits at will, although in the case of the royal myth Senopati, the founder of the Mataram dynasty, receives the *mantra* from Ratu Kidul. The spirit of Prabu Lingasari is the only unique element in Pak Mulyono's pantheon. It served to legitimize the claim that Pak Mulyono is the successor of the Mataram dynasty and the agent through which the *wahyu* of God is activated. Prabu Lingasari's position in Pak Mulyono's cult resembles that of Ratu Kidul in the state cult in that he provides access to other major figures in the spirit world. The Sultan claims to control the spirit world through his relationship with Ratu Kidul, while Pak Mulyono claims to control Ratu Kidul and other spirits through Prabu Lingasari.

The rites of the cult of Lingasari, like those of the state cult, serve to establish and maintain the flow of blessing and mercy from God. Both are intended to purge society of evil. The difference is that while state ceremonies operate at the macro, societal level, those of the cult benefit only its members. While the rites of the state cult are more inclusive, those of the cult of Prabu Lingasari provide members with direct, personal access to the most powerful saints and spirits of the royal cult. Princes and court officials I asked about the cult, maintained that only the Sultan can control such potent sources of blessing and power and that one of his principle duties is to mediate between his subjects and the spirit world. Cult members argued that this was true in the past, but that the political and economic decline of the dynasty in the postcolonial era is proof that the *wahyu* has departed and that others must now fulfill this mediating role. Many believe that when the *Ratu Adil* arrives he will assume this role, but until that time the cult provides the only sure access to vital sources of blessing, protection and power. The persoanlistic and ritual aspects of the cult help to insulate Pak Mulyono from charges of fraud and deceit. His followers genuinely believe that participation in these rituals allows them to speak directly with some of the most powerful inhabitants of the spirit world who would not tolerate fraud on such a massive scale.

Many Javanese feel that it is easier to lie about one's relationship with God than to control spirits. To be sure, God punishes hypocrites and fraudulent mystics, but only in the afterlife. The wrath of Ratu Kidul would fall swiftly and violently on a *dukun* who falsely claimed to control her. Several informants were surprised and puzzled by the nature of Pak Mulyono's claims, but found them difficult to reject out of hand because of their certainty concerning the power of Ratu Kidul. Consequently, by making the most daring possible claims, Pak Mulyono dispels doubt about his intentions more convincingly than *dukun* basing their claims to legitimacy on putative relationships with God.

The fact that Pak Mulyono can treat psychological and psychosomatic illnesses with a fair measure of success also contributes to his reputation. Many of his clients are firmly convinced that they are victims of sorcery and exhibit a wide variety of physical and emotional symptoms. Pak Mulyono's operations provide visible evidence, in the form of wires and nails, that the root cause of the disease has been destroyed. The spirit performing the operation also instructs the patient to develop a calm state of mind and to make peace with his/her enemies. By appealing to deeply rooted cultural notions of the causes of health and illness, Pak Mulyono is able to cure patients who bio-medical doctors can not help. On several occasions I observed rituals in which patients suffering seizures and other disorders recovered with remarkable speed. This is a clear example of what Tambiah refers to as the "performative efficacy" of healing rites.[55] As Kleinman observes, healing rites cure through a transformation of culturally defined symbols of illness in the context of a native explanatory model. He argues further that, in the case of traditional Chinese medicine, ritual constitutes a "potentially important therapeutic mechanism" not included in or explainable in terms of the Western bio-medical model.[56] Pak Mulyono's successful treatment of illnesses which baffled bio-medical doctors (and similar cures performed by other *dukun*) indicate that in Java there is a class of ailments which are perhaps treated best in the traditional context.

The Javanese distrust of *dukun* and their reluctance to believe that they can cure all diseases has provided an important avenue for the development of a health care system employing both Javanese and bio-medical practitioners. Many *dukun*, Pak

---

[55] S. Tambiah, "The Cosmological and Performative Significance of a Thai Cult of Healing through Meditation". *Culture, Medicine and Psychiatry*, vol. 1, 1977, 97.

[56] op. cit.

Mulyono among them, are aware of limitations on their ability to cure. Pak Mulyono often refers patients with infectious diseases to hospitals. He also makes a clear distinction between diseases caused by sorcery and those sent by God at the end of one's allotted life span. He explained that in the later case nothing can be done to cure the disease and the only suitable treatment is a program of prayer and meditation to prepare the soul for death. He will not treat patients suffering from cancer or tuberculosis in any other manner, nor will he perform operations on those he considers to be terminally ill. His followers are impressed with his honesty because, they explain; many *dukun* and bio-medical doctors claim to be able to cure any disease. It also prevents failures. Pak Mulyono's operations are performed by spirits of such great power that, from a Javanese perspective, failure is almost impossible. If they were to fail on anything close to a regular basis, very grave questions would arise concerning the validity of Pak Mulyono's claim that he controls them.

Pak Mulyono's Cult of Lingasari is entirely Javanese in origin and in the nature of the religious claims it makes. It can exist only within an Indonesian context. From a Yogyakarta *kraton* perspective it is clearly heresy. On several occasions I discussed it with *kraton* officials, all of whom found Pak Mulyono's claims to be absurd. Those who did not see him as a charlatan questioned his sanity. There can be little doubt that in the political context of a Javanese state, the cult would have been outlawed. Pak Mulyono might well have been executed. Pak Mulyono died soon after I last spoke with him in 1991. The Cult of Lingasari was so dependent on his personal charisma that it did not survive him. It was located in a particular point in the history of both Indonesia and Yogyakarta when the New Order was at its apex and the Sultanate at its political nadir. I have often wondered how Pak Mulyono would have interpreted the collapse of the New Order and the reemergence of the Sultanate on the national political stage. In 1979 and even in 1991 his claim that the *kraton* was an impotent anachronism was at least plausible. Subsequent events considered in Chapter 7 demonstrate that it is far more resilient than he imagined.

Medical Knowledge, Cosmological Knowledge and Political Contexts

This analysis of the Javanese *dukun* began with the observation that many Javanese have serious doubts about the morality and intentions of traditional medical practitioners. It has been shown that in their attempts to cure diseases of the spiritual and physical bodies, *dukun* are forced to rely on dangerous and morally ambiguous types of knowledge and magical power. Concepts of health and illness are defined in terms of a Muslim theory of personhood. Curing is the consequence of a partition of the universe into "good" and "evil" domains.

This section clarifies relationships between cosmological and medical knowledge in Javanese culture, and in a more general sense, the manner in which curing reinforces traditional beliefs concerning the nature of the human body, health, illness and the cosmos. Javanese cosmology has traditionally been viewed as a homeostatic system in which every unit mirrors the structure of the cosmos as a whole.[57] In the ultimate sense notions of both good and evil are of little significance because both were created by God. According to this view, the purpose of kings, *dukun* and other powerful figures is to maintain the cosmos in a constant state of balance and harmony. This is the basis of tranquility, social harmony, prosperity and health.

The difficulty with this position is that it is based on the most esoteric formulation of Javanese/Islamic mystical theory which is derived from the *Sufi* doctrine of the unity of being which holds that there is no clear distinction between creator and created and nothing but God can be said to exist in the ultimate sense. According to this theory all humans are equal because all share in the divine essence. Most scholars have failed to consider the fact that this is an extremely esoteric doctrine intended only for the most advanced students of mysticism. The public teaching of this doctrine is believed to lead to disregard for the essential proximate distinction between good and evil and religious obligations to God and humanity. Prior to the nineteenth century the public teaching of this doctrine was punishable by death.[58]

In a more general sense emphasis on the macrocosm, microcosm equation has led scholars to ignore the fact that Javanese cosmology is hierarchically ordered and that this hierarchy is based in part on the partition of the cosmos into *gawat* and *kramat* elements. Thus while all microcosms, including the human body, share a common set of structural principles, they are not identical. The distinction between saints and ordinary humans provides a particularly cogent example. All humans possess spiritual and physical bodies composed of varying combinations of fundamental elements. Among these are the passions which lead to sin, anger and greed as well as spiritual factors and types of knowledge directing the mind towards religious attainments. The difference between saints and normal people is determined by the degree to which holy, evil and morally ambiguous components of the bodies influence mental processes and social behavior. While in one sense all humans are perfect microcosms, they can be ordered with respect to their relative proximity to the divine ideal. This state of perfection is attained only by saints who have acquired an intuitive, experiential understanding of God and the unity of being. It is only at this point that homeostasis is operative. This state is rarely, if ever, obtained by living human beings. Individuals at lower levels of spiritual attainment are forced to view religious life as a struggle between the forces of good and those of evil. It is for this reason that Javanese mystics often refer to life as a holy war (*perang sabil* or *jihad*) between faith and passion. The Sultan, *wali*, *dukun*, physical and mental training all share a common purpose which is to establish and maintain a partition between these forces in their respective domains.

This principle finds expression in beliefs concerning the structure of the human body and that of the traditional Javanese state. In both cases a *wadah* (boundary) is established within which the state of *kramat* can be cultivated. This is possible

---

[57] S. Moertono, *State and Statecraft in Old Java: A Study of the Later Mataram Period, 16th to 19th Centuries*, Ithaca: Cornell University Modern Indonesia Project, 1968.

[58] For a discussion of this aspect of Javanese religion see M. Woodward, *Islam in Java ... op. cit.*

only if the boundaries of the system are strong enough to resist the intrusion of evil objects, beings and power. The physical and mental training of children and the programs of prayer, meditation and ritual recommended by *dukun* and religious teachers strengthen the defenses of the body. Similarly one of the primary functions of the Sultan is to establish a territory in which evil cannot function. A link between the power of the state and the health of the people is established by the fact that sorcery cannot, in principle, be practiced within the boundaries of the Yogyakarta. The result of this is that evil is forced into areas outside of Muslim civilization; the jungles, mountains and outer islands which are considered to be *gawat*. *Dukun* who rely to the *gawat*, bringing it into the domain of civilization are inherently suspect.

In the absence of perfect saints the partition is imperfect and the boundary permeable. The Sultan at the level of the state and the *dukun* at the level of the individual struggle to maintain and repair the boundary. They must rely on varieties of magical power and knowledge which are at least potentially *gawat*, but which are temporarily governed by the will of God (*wahyu*) to purge their respective domains of evil. It is through this process that the well being of the state and the health of the individual are maintained. The moral ambiguity of the *dukun* arises as the consequence of his use of magical power and his knowledge of evil. These are the only means available to him, but fall far short of the religious ideal. The same is true of those aspects of the state cult based on the theory of power. The Sultan is exempt from moral criticism only because of the strength of his *wahyu*. He is revered and worthy of the respect due to both a religious teacher and a secular lord because he is thought to approach the mystical ideal. But if the *wahyu* is lost or withdrawn by God, he becomes a dangerous figure, possessed of great magical power but devoid of divine guidance. In such a case his position is strictly analogous to that of the *dukun*. This is how many Javanese explain the political turmoil of the late 1990s. Until the economic collapse of 1997 many in Yogyakarta accepted the view that Indonesia's President Suharto was God's choice to rule Indonesia. In the mid 1980s Yogyakarta mystic explained the Indonesia's first president, Soekarno had been chosen to regain the nation's independence, that Suharto had been chosen for economic development and that perhaps God would choose a future president to establish democracy. The *Reformasi* (reformation) movement that brought Suharto's "New Order" regime to an end was motivated in part by conviction that time had come.[59]

Dukun are aware of their ambiguous moral status and attempt to present themselves in the best possible light. With the exception of a small number of particularly daring individuals such as Pak Mulyono, few succeed. Most remain distinctively liminal figures caught between religious doctrines denouncing the use of magical power and the lack of alternative means to prevent the intrusion of evil into the human bodies. They are also faced with the practical necessity of restoring this partition to cure disease. *Dukun* are confronted with the dilemma that they must employ potentially evil forces to prevent the further spread of evil.

---

[59] See Chapter 7 for an analysis of the role of Sultan Hamengkubuwana X and the Yogyakarta *Kraton* in the democratic transition of 1998.

Given the religious basis of Javanese theories of health and illness, medical knowledge can not be considered as a distinct domain in Javanese culture. The patterns of belief that Kleinman describes as central features of health care systems are but a single articulation of higher order principles of Javanese cultural knowledge. Curing is understood simultaneously as medical practice and ritual. Its goals are both medical and mystical. These relationships are understood best in terms of Keesing's theory of cultural knowledge. Keesing argues that culture is a hierarchically organized system of knowledge:

> including specific routines and understandings appropriate to particular contexts and more general assumptions about the social and natural world.[60]

The relationship between these 'specific routines" and "general assumptions" is more precisely stated in Schulte Nordholt's analysis of the political and kinship systems of the Atoni of Timor. He argues that:

> certain structural principles which are present in a society and which are firmly rooted in, among other things, man's structures of thinking[61]

are used to generate a diversity of distinct surface structures and to regulate social behavior. In Javanese culture many of these structural principles are derived from *Sufi* theories of cosmology and the mystical path. But this does not imply that all Javanese see every aspect of social and natural reality in overtly theological terms. Similarly, the historical and causal primacy of religion in Javanese cultural knowledge does not justify the claim that every aspect of social discourse can be interpreted as a religious act. Buying a chicken in the local market is not a religious act even though the code of politeness employed in this transaction id derived from religious principles. Rather, aspects of religion have been used in the construction of abstract principles which govern or structure a multiplicity of surface domains. Only those social acts which establish alter or maintain the individual's relationship with God and other spiritual beings can be considered religious. Curing is both religion and medicine because Javanese theories of anatomy, health and illness are explicitly defined in terms of religious beliefs concerning the divine origins and ultimate fates of souls and bodies.

This framework also allows for the explanation of the Javanese view if relations between bio-medical and traditional models of health and illness. Because the duties of *dukun* are based on proximate rather than ultimate notions of religious truth, the two systems need not be mutually exclusive. As was observed previously, *dukun* can often treat ailments which baffle bio-medical doctors. Similarly, most Javanese and many *dukun* believe that some illnesses are treated most effectively by bio-medical practitioners. I observed several cases in which *dukun* referred patients to hospitals and it is not uncommon for Javanese bio-medical doctors to believe in the powers of *dukun*. Indeed, there were several medical doctors in the cult of Prabu Lingasari.

---

[60]op. cit.

[61]H. Schulte Nordholt, *The Political System of the Atoni of Timor*. Martinus Nijoff, The Hague, 1971

When I questioned them concerning the seeming conflict between bio-medical and traditional curing techniques, the generally replied that Javanese occasionally contract disorders which bio-medical theory can neither explain nor cure. Most bio-medical doctors doubt *dukun*'s ability to cure physiologically based disorders, but recognize that many psychosomatic and mental disorders have supernatural causes which can be treated by *dukun*, *wali* and other traditional healers.

The knowledge on which bio-medicine is based is referred to as *ngilmu kedoktoran*, the *ngilmu* of doctors. This is significant. Since bio-medical knowledge is seen as a variety of *ngilmu*, and as such subordinate to *makripat* (the intuitive knowledge of God acquired through the mystical path) it can be readily assimilated into Javanese cultural knowledge. Similarly, antibiotics and other western medicines are commonly understood as varieties of *obat*. Consequently many Javanese, including many with Western educations, do not recognize a fundamental distinction between "Western" and "Javanese" science. Both are held to be useful, and indeed vital, but are at the same time subordinate to *makripat* and other forms of religious knowledge. This suggests that in Java bio-medical and traditional modes of medical practice are interpreted as elements of a single health care system.

It is also clear that the ways in which these abstract principles take concrete form is simultaneously shaped and constrained by social and political contexts. All of the *dukun* discussed here root their practices in Javanese Muslim cosmological principles. At the same time, the complex process of *bricolage* that produces unique styles and claims to legitimacy incorporates non-Javanese Indonesian components. Pak Mulyono's Cult of Lingasari is imaginable only in a post-colonial Indonesian context in which the state does not prosecute Javanese heretics and the Yogyakarta *Kraton* ignores and/or dismissed those who would question its" legitimacy. Pak Mustafim's stated reliance on Muslim prayer and devotions was profoundly shaped by his experience during the darkest days of the Indonesian Revolution. Both he and Pak Hario attempted to incorporate elements of Indonesia, spirits and power form Bali and Kalimantan, into Javanese medical practice.

Thirty Years Later

Developments in Javanese understandings of health, illness and health care over the 30 years since the initial fieldwork on which this chapter is based reflect broader trends in the globalization of knowledge and the increasing professionalization of Indonesian society. Access to bio-medical healthcare has improved dramatically, at least until the economic crisis of 1997 made it unaffordable for many. There is now an "international standard" hospital in Yogyakarta. But as one friend put it, "It also has international standard prices". And yet, there has been no corresponding decline in the popularity and believability of traditional medicine. Given the state of the Indonesian economy Javanese are, if anything, more dependent on *dukun* than they were a quarter of a century ago. Even in cases where care is heavily subsidized the cost of medicines is prohibitive for many. Mahoney's recent study of *dukun* in East Java confirms not only that traditional healing remains an important element of Javanese culture and that, as she points out, beliefs concerning the religious basis of disease and healing have not changed greatly since Geertz conducted his fieldwork in the early 1950s and I conducted my initial studies in the late 1970s.[62] Fieldwork conducted in Yogyakarta in 2007 and 2008 confirms this conclusion subject to the caveat that a continuing process of *bricolage* has adapted traditional healing practices to changing social political and religious conditions.

Javanese traditional medicine continues to adapt to changing social and technological environments and equally importantly to developments in bio-medical knowledge and practice. Today healers often refer to themselves as *paranormal* and to see themselves as participants in a global discourse concerning psychic powers, alternative medicine and metaphysics. These terms are frequently used in English. The variety of ailments for which they offer treatments has also expanded. Increasingly *dukun* offer treatments for weight loss, sexual dysfunction, which are sometimes compared with Viagra, infertility, strokes, cancer and HIV/Aids. Some attempt to place themselves in national and trans-nation contexts. In November of 2008 one stated in an advertisement in *Post-Mo*, that he had received the "Best Indonesian Professional Para-normal" and "Best ASEAN Professional Para-normal" awards in 2007.

Sociological developments are equally significant. In some instances the practice of traditional medicine has become increasingly rationalized. Some *dukun* advertise their services in tabloid newspapers. This practice dates to the early nineteenth century, but has become increasingly common and socially acceptable. Some appear on talk shows or advertise on Yogya TV and other local television stations. Many have opened clinics. Some of these resemble western medical practices. Others rely heavily on collective religious performance including prayer and mediation. In their advertisements medical/religious entrepreneurs typically list the types of ailments they are prepared to treat, their office hours and the fees they charge.[63] This is a major departure from tradition as are the books published by Ki Ageng Pamungkas and other nationally know *paranormals*. There are also for profit schools offering courses such as "The Quick Path to Becoming a Paranormal".[64] Some religious healers have Websites. Many more advertise that they are available for consultation by mobile phone text messages. The Barzakh Foundation, headquartered in Jakarta is a Sufi movement dedicated to treating HIV/Aids on line. It maintains a Website in English as well as Indonesian.[65] The fact that in most cases these materials are published in Indonesian indicates that the arena in which Javanese healers operate has shifted. The Javanese healing arts are now a national as well as an ethnic tradition

---

[62]I. Mahony, "The Role of Dukun in Contemporary East Java a case study of Banyuwangi Dukun". www.murdoch.edu.au/acicis/hi/field_topics/inez.doc. accessed October 24, 2006

[63]Consultations cost anywhere from 25,000 to 100,000 Rupiah or USD 2.50–10.00.This is far beyond the means of the poor many of whom make USD 2.00 per day or less.

[64]*Meteor*, July 25th, 2005, p. 4. This 1 day course was offered for a fee of 300,000 Rupiah or approximately USD 30. For most Javanese this is a substantial sum.

[65]http://www.all-natural.com/sufi.html accessed October, 2008.

and are of political as well as personal importance as former President Suharto's reliance on paranormals and spiritual guides suggests.

Increasingly Javanese turn to transitional healers for hospice care, in part because prolonged hospitalization is beyond the financial reach of all but the wealthiest Indonesians. Many realize the value of modern bio-medical practice but are simply unable to afford it. Others feel that when death is inevitable that traditional medical practices are the best form of palliative care.

The preparation of *jamu* and other traditional medicines has become increasingly commercialized. There are now more than a thousand firms that produce traditional medicines on a commercial basis. Some commercial *jamu* are sold as packets of dried herbs with instructions for preparing them. There are also more fully processes varieties, some of which are sold in soft drink cans but in other respects resemble those sold by street vendors. The Indonesian government has taken steps to regulate the industry because there are some cases in which dangerous chemicals have been added to herbal medicines. Public Health laws passed in 1992 allow for penalties of up to five years imprisonment and fines of more that USD 10,000 for serious violations.[66]

Some *jamu*, especially those intended to promote health, rather than cure disease, are now marketed internationally as "spa products". Some of these resemble the medicines the Pak Mulyono used to heal the spiritual wounds of the operations he performed. The processes of globalization are such that the wealth international clientele of exclusive spas receive beauty treatments similar to those used by Javanese *dukun* to combat sorcery!

Dukun have learned to operate within functionally rational systems in a wide variety of ways. Some *dukun* have claimed to have the ability to recover lost or stolen property for many decades. Some now work with the Indonesian police. When I was staying in a small Yogyakarta hotel in June of 2007, my room was burglarized and my cameras and laptop computer stolen. I immediately reported the theft to the hotel management who called the police, who sent out a team of investigators who photographed the crime scene and dusted it for finger prints. I spent the next several hours at the police station answering questions and filing out forms. The officers were polite, courteous, apologetic and promised to do all they could, but told me not to hold out much hope. When their investigation failed to turn up any leads, the hotel manager contacted the leader of the local *preman* (organized crime) groups in the vicinity offering a reward for the return of the "misplaced" items. When this effort failed he contacted his insurance company and a *paranormal*. The *paranormal* informed the insurance company that the items had indeed been stolen and could not be recovered because they had been sent to Jakarta to be sold on the black market. The insurance company accepted his judgment and came to a very reasonable settlement. This speaks to the degree to which "modern" firms rely on the judgments of traditional practitioners.

---

[66] *The Jakarta Post*, December 6, 2006.

Pengobatan Nabi – Prophetic Healing and Islamism

The democratic transition of the late 1990s led to the emergence of a wide variety of Islamist political parties and social movements. Many of these are based on the political and theological works of Hasan al-Bana, Sayid Qtb and others associated with the Egyptian Muslim Brotherhood (*Ikwhan al-Muslim*) and on the religious practices of Saudi Arabian Wahhabis. While the term, is used much more broadly to refer to a wide variety of Islam practices they often refer to themselves, and are often described in the literature on Political Islam, as *Salafis* or *Salafiyah*.[67] They reject anything that they understand as being a compromise between religion and culture. They seek to remake Javanese and other Indonesian cultures on the basis of models of what they believe to be the religious and social practice of the Prophet Muhammad and his immediate companions.

They are best known for their political activities and in some cases for violent *jihad* campaigns.[68] They have also redefined other aspects of Javanese culture, including traditional medicine. Many Javanese and other Indonesian Islamists acknowledge the powers of *dukun* and other traditional healers but consider them to be sorcerers who generally cause disease rather than heal it. One I interviewed in 2008 explained that a *dukun* may actually cure one ailment, but will often use a combination of "black magic" and evil spirits (*setan*) to cause an even more serous one, and that they are "bent on the destruction of Islam and the Muslim community".[69] Many are as critical of *habib* and *tabib* as they are of other

---

[67] The term *Salafi* refers to those who practice what they believe to be the Islam of the Prophet Muhammad and his close companions. The term "companions" can refer to either those Muslims who actually knew the Prophet or to as many as four generations of their descendants. Muslim extremists have attempted to appropriate the term *Salafi* in much the same way that American Evangelical extremists have appropriated the term "Christian". Almost *all* Sunni Muslims use the term to refer to their own understandings of Islamic faith and practice. Shiah generally do not use it because their understanding of Islam is based on the assumption that, in addition to the Prophet Muhammad, a series of divinely guided Imams were religious authorities. The term has been, and currently is, used by groups including Western oriented educational reformers, Sufi mystics and Wahhabis, who actually are puritanical and exclusivist. To describe "*salafis*" as puritanical is to mirror the theological views of the most radical among them. It has much the same effect as denouncing "Islam" or "The Muslims". It plays into the hands of extremists. By far the largest "*salafi*" movement, with over forty million members and many more supporters, is the Indonesian *Nahdlatul Ulama* (Renaissance of the Muslim Scholars). Its understanding and practice of Islam includes Sufi theology and devotionalism and the veneration of saints, practices that self proclaimed Islamist *Salafis* denounce as "unbelief". Politically it strongly supports pluralism, freedom of religion, democracy and human rights.

[68] On religious violence in Post-New Order Indonesia see, A. Azra, *Indonesia, Islam and Democracy, Dynamics in a Global Context*, Jakarta: Solstice Publishing, 2006, N. Hasan, *Laskar Jihad: Islam, Militancy and the Quest for Identity in Post-New Order Indonesia*, Ithaca: Cornell University Southeast Asia Publications, 2006 and M. Woodward, Religious Conflict and the Globalization of Knowledge: Indonesia 1978–2004, In: L. Cady and S. Simon (eds.), *Religion and Conflict in South and Southeast Asia. Disruption Violence*, London: Routledge 2006

[69] This is a common theme in Islamist discourse. Indonesian Islamists frequently accuse their cultural and political opponents of this intent.

healers, because the Islam in which these healers rely is rooted in Sufi devotional practices.

Despite their opposition to almost the entire range of Javanese healing practices many Islamists maintain a keen interest in and commitment to what they consider to be properly *Islamic* healing. Some go so far as to denounce "chemical" (bio-medical) medicines as being "Jewish" and therefore *haram* (forbidden). Most, however, seek to combine what they consider to be Islamic healing practices with modern bio-medical practice, in much the same way that other Javanese healers do. Some practitioners of *Pengobatan Nabi* are specialists in traditional herbal medicine who have added Islamist practices to the repertoire of healing techniques. Others are deeply committed to the use of Universalist Muslim scriptures as medical textbooks. They often rely on selections from the *Qur'an* and *Hadith* concerning illness and healing and on medical manuals written by Arab Wahhabi scholars.

Syaikh Al-Jibrin's *Biar Sakit, Ibabah, Tetap Fit* (*If You are Sick, Pray and Certainly be Fit*), is an example.[70] Substantial portions of this texts concern the ways in which the sick should conduct obligatory rituals including the five daily prayers. Others extol the virtues of *Zam–Zam* water, herbal remedies said to have been used and recommended by the Prophet Muhammad who is described as a practitioner of *Pengobatan Alternatif.*[71] Some ailments especially mental illness, are attributed to spirit possession or the nefarious acts of *dukun*. Prayer and *Qur'an* recitation are recommended for treatment of these and other ailments.

Mas Budhi: Traditional Healing in the New Century

I close this chapter with an account of a self described twenty-first century Javanese healer. Mas Budhi is now in his mid fifties. I have known him since the day I first arrived in Yogyakarta. He has lived in one of the *kampung* inside the Yogyakarta *Kraton* walls all of his life.[72] His family has lived in the same *kampung* for generations and prior to the Second World War were *kraton* servants. Mas Budhi was the first in his family to attend school. He is proud of the fact that he can read and write and considers himself to be a "modern Javanese". He speaks some English and for years made a living on the margins of the tourist industry. For a time he made and sold batik paintings and later offered instruction in the art to foreign tourists. In the 1980s he described himself as a "young Javanese philosopher". When the tourist industry collapsed amid the turmoil of the late 1990s he and

---

[70]op. cit., There are also Websites devoted to Prophetic Medicine. See, for example, http://www.nursyifa.net/pengobatan/info_penyakit

[71]op. cit., p. 174.

[72]Mas is a respectful Javanese term of address that translates literary "older brother" Mas Budhi and I have both used this honorific with each other for the entire 30 years we have known each other.

his wife started a small noodle shop catering primarily to college and university students.

When I first met him in 1978 Mas Budhi was definitely not a *dukun* 30 years later he still does not consider himself to be one. Some of his neighbors do not agree. Mas Budhi is in most respects a *kejawen* Muslim. When I first met him he was concerned with the mystical interpretation of *wayang*, meditation and pilgrimage to holy graves. He often told me that all religions are basically the same and that it is possible to come to know God through any of them. He found *dukun* somewhat frightening because he shared the common Javanese view that they are capable of using their powers for evil and well and beneficent purposes. He found Pak Mulyono to be particularly frightening because of the dramatic character of his "operations". When one of his assistants was unintentionally possessed by the spirit of a tiger at a *lengahan* he attended with me Buhdi very nearly panicked and insisted that we leave immediately.

Over the years Mas Budhi has become increasing involved in the ritual life of the *kampung* mosque which is located only a few yards from his home. He explained that the shift in his religious orientation was motivated in part by the aid he had received from the mosque community when he faced economic difficulties including paying the fees for his children to attend Muhammadiyah schools. He still does not perform all of the five daily prayers, but does attend the Friday congregational prayer on a regular basis. When I first met him Budhi fasted only 2 or 3 days at the beginning of Ramadan and two or three more at the end of the month. He now fasts for the entire month. This reflects a more general trend for *kejawen* Muslims to become increasingly observant.

Mas Budhi's increasing commitment to orthoprax Islam has done nothing to diminish his involvement with mysticism. He does not visit holy graves as often as he did as a young man in part because of his family obligations, but continues to meditate on a regular basis. In the late 1980s he began to notice that he had the ability to sense things that "rationally" he had no way to know. He refers to this ability by the English acronym ESP, though he did not know what it stood for until I explained it to him. With this ability came the power to do many of the things that are normally done by *dukun*. He now says that he can prevent it from raining at weddings and funerals, recover lost or stolen property and help people with physical and mental problems. He is most proud of the fact that he was able to help people find possessions that they lost in the 2007 Yogyakarta earthquake and that his prayers helped them to overcome what he correctly diagnosed as "trauma". And yet, he insists that he is not a *dukun*. He explained that he is a rational modern person and that he does not "use ritual, but the power of the mind". Clearly his modernist orientation has led him to seek to obtain traditional goals with what he is convinced are modern scientific methods. He considers people who take courses to become *paranormals* or place ads in tabloids to be unethical at best, and probably frauds. His view is that the healing arts can not be learned. One simply receives the gift.

Conclusions

All of these developments are examples of the ways in which cultural systems develop through *bricolage* and how this process contributes to the emergence of cultural hybridities. Levi Strauss uses the concept of *bricolage* in a collective sense to explain the development of widely shared cultural patters. In the case of the Javanese *dukun* it operates at the individual level. *Dukun*, and other healers, uses it to construct a unique identity and structure of religious legitimacy. In this chapter it has been argued that Javanese healing is based on a broadly shared set of religious concepts, but that individuals develop idiosyncratic strategies to distinguish themselves from potential rivals and from the public at large. These strategies are shaped by prevailing social conditions. Pak Hario, for example, drew on his experience of the most desperate days of the Indonesian revolution, which in the late 1970s still resonated strongly with those of other survivors, their children and to a lesser extent grandchildren. At that time those days were only three decades in the past, and still figured significantly in collective memory. An additional three decades have passed and the memories have faded. While they are memorialized, there are now few in Yogyakarta who experienced them directly. For many, those days are now three generations in the past. For most Javanese the frame of reference within which traditional healing is located is the New Order in which "development" replaced "revolution" as the dominant theme in Indonesian nationalist discourse. It was also an era in which concept of "Indonesia" assumed a larger role in personal and collective identities, except among the most diehard Yogyakarta traditionalists. This may account for the growing tendency for healers to define themselves as "*paranormal*" or practitioners of "*pengobatan alternative*" both of which assume western rationality as a reference point, and for them to adopt organizational structures including that of the "*klinik*" linked to them. Beginning in the late 1980s concepts of the "global Muslim community" rooted exclusively in Universalist Islam, and it struggle against the "Secular-Christian-Zionist" West have captured the imagination of a small, but significant section of Javanese society. *Pengobatan Nabi* locates traditional healing in these contexts.

These changes parallel those in Javanese society as a whole. They have kept traditional healing "up to date" and in sync with increasing levels of functional rationality, bio-medical developments and with the increasingly global and Muslim contexts in which Indonesia, Java and Yogyakarta are located. But these changes have not, in any sense, led to the "disenchantment" of the world, Indonesia, Java or Yogyakarta. Illness and misfortune are attributed to religious causes today as frequently as they were three decades ago. People continue to place their trust in religious healers, however defined, particularly when the seek relief from problems for which bio-medical practitioners can offer no relief. In this sense, Yogyakarta is as enchanted as ever, and not likely to change all that much in the *next* 30 years.

Photos

Commercially produced jamu

Women selling traditional jamu

Chapter 3
The *Slametan*: Textual Knowledge and Ritual Performance in Yogyakarta

This chapter concerns the *slametan*, a ritual meal at which Arabic prayers are recited and food is offered to the Prophet Muhammad, saints, and ancestors, who are implored to shower blessings on the community.[1] In a larger sense it concerns relationships between textual Islam and popular Muslim piety in Yogyakarta.[2] Geertz identifies the *slametan* as: (1) the "core ritual" of Javanese culture; (2) an animistic rite the purpose of which to reinforce social solidarity and (3) as being primarily a village ritual.[3] On point one he was entirely correct; on the others he could not have been more wrong.

This chapter presents an alternative interpretation. It is argued that the *Slametan* is a locally defined Muslim rite and that: (1) the criteria Geertz employs to distinguish Islam from animism are misleading; (2) the *slametan* is an example of a ritual complex that links blessing (A., *barakah*) and food and extends from Arabia to Southeast Asia; (3) that it is not primarily a village ritual; (4) that its religious and social goals are defined in terms of Islamic mystical teachings; (5) most of the modes of ritual action it employs are rooted in universalist texts including the *Qur'an* and Hadith; and (6) that elements of the *slametan* derived from pre-Islamic traditions are interpreted in Islamic terms.

The portrait of Javanese religion emerging from this analysis suggests that mystical interpretations of Islam have served as paradigms for devotionalism, social order, and social life. This, in turn, suggests that contemporary Javanese religion must be understood in light of fields of meaning established by the larger Muslim tradition and raises questions concerning the style of cultural analysis on which Geertz's account is based. It is, at the same time, an illustration of the

---

[1] I would like to thank Bianca Smith for observations, in print, B. Smith, "*Kejawen* Islam as Gendered Praxis in Javanese Village Religiosity," In: S. Blackburn, B. Smith and S. Syamsiyatun (eds.), *Indonesian Islam in a New Era*, Clayton, Monash University Press, 2008 and in person, concerning the role of women in the *slametan* and its role in the religious lives of women in Yogyakarta.

[2] Malay informants were interviewed in North Sumatra, Malaysia and Singapore. Pakistani, and Turkish informants were interviewed at the Islamic Cultural Center, Tempe, Arizona. "U". denotes Urdu

[3] C. Geertz, *The Religion of Java*, Glencoe, Ill.: The Free Press, 1960, pp. 10–15.

M. Woodward, *Java, Indonesia and Islam*, Muslims in Global Societies Series 3, DOI 10.1007/978-94-007-0056-7_3, © Springer Science+Business Media B.V. 2011

way in which local variants of trans-cultural religions emerge from the process of *bricolage*.

Ritual Meals in Muslim Cultures

Geertz's analysis of the *slametan* assumes that ritual meals are characteristic of animism but foreign to Islam. This is not true, unless one wishes to define a substantial portion of Universalist Islam as animism.[4] The Hadith include numerous descriptions of ritual meals and the distribution of blessed food. For present purposes the following is significant because it outlines the structure of a meal at which Muhammad officiated.

> I asked the Holy Prophet's permission to go home and said to my wife: I have seen the Holy Prophet in a condition that I am unable to endure. Have you anything in the house? She said: I have some barley and a lamb. I slaughtered the lamb and ground down the barley and we put the meat in the cooking pot. Then I went to the Holy Prophet. In the mean time the flour had been kneaded and the meat in the pot was nearly cooked. I said to the Holy Prophet: I have some food Messenger of God, will you come with one or two? He asked: How many should there be? I told him. He said: Many would be good. Tell your wife not to take the pot off the fire nor the bread from the oven till I arrive. Then he said to the Emigrants and the helpers: Let us go. They all stood up. I went to my wife and said: Bless you the Holy Prophet, the Emigrants, the Helpers and the whole company are coming over. She said: Did he ask you? I said yes. The Holy Prophet said to his companions: Enter, but do not crowd in. Then he started breaking up the bread and putting meat on it. He would take from the pot and from the oven, then cover them up and approach his companions and hand it over to them. He would go back and uncover the pot and the oven. He continued to break up the bread and putting meat on it till all had eaten their fill and some was left over. Then he said to my wife: Eat of it, and send it as a present, for people have been afflicted with hunger.[5]

The performative structure of the *slametan* parallels the narrative structure of this Hadith. A man invites a group of others, including a religious leader, to his home for a meal; his wife prepares food which is distributed to the assembly and the remainder among the poor. Feeding the poor is charity (A., *sadaqah*) and yields blessing for both donor and recipient. The *Qur'an* and Hadith define charity very broadly. It includes almost any act of benevolence toward one's fellow humans, and even animals.[6] The distribution of food to the poor, neighbors, and kin are among the examples of charity mentioned in the *Qur'an* and Hadith.[7] One Hadith

---

[4]The term "animism" has become increasingly problematical, but Geertz can not be held to task for using terminology that was generally accepted at the time he wrote.

[5]M. Kahn, *Gardens of the Righteous. Riyadh as-Salihin of Imam Nawawi*. London: Curzon Press, 1975, p.111, RS 523. Throughout this chapter Hadith will be referred to by the number they appear in the collection as well as by page number in the English translation.

[6]See M. Ali, *The Religion of Islam*, Lahore, 1944, pp. 458–60

[7]See *Qur'an*, 2:177, 262–65;76: 8; and esp., 107:1–7: "Hast thou seen him who cries to the doom? That is he who repulses the orphan and urges not the feeding of the needy. So woe to those that pray and are headless of their prayers, to those who make display and refuse charity". Also, see Kahn, op. cit., p. 66, RS 267, 268, 270, 271.

mentions feeding the poor as an example of the "best Islam".[8] Even when they cannot be considered charity, gifts of food are meritorious and recommended by Hadith.[9]

Javanese of all theological orientations believe that feeding the poor is a religious obligation and a source of blessing. Sermons in mosques often mention charity as one of the basic duties of Islam. While alms are particularly important on Muslim holy days, *santri* believe that they should be given throughout the year. *Kejawen* Muslims take pains to invite poor people to *slametan* or, at least, to send them some of the food. Many also donate uncooked rice and other foods to augment the small amounts of sacred food distributed at the ritual.[10]

Some *kejawen* Muslims feel that the food distributed in the *slametan* is of greater importance than the *zakat* (the alms tax mandated by *Shari'ah*). It is often stated that the *zakat* is a legal duty, not a pure gift in Javanese (or Maussian sense.)[11] Conversely, *slametan* food is referred to as a "gift from the heart" stemming from a deep desire to help one's fellow humans with no expectation of rturn. This conforms with the more general *kejawen* belief that spontaneous piety is of greater value than that required by the *Shari'ah*. Thus, even though many do not pay *zakat*, *kejawen* Muslims are aware of the importance of, and actively embrace, the Islamic concern with charity.

The textual notion of charity, and particularly the distribution of food, inform ritual practice in many Muslim societies and is associated with the veneration of saints and Prophet Muhammad. These are examples of Islamicate cultural patterns that transcend ethnic distinctions. Burton observed that it was customary to offer feasts at the Prophet's tomb and that these meals were understood as both alms and a source of blessing.[12] Snouck-Hurgronje reports that on their return, Meccan pilgrims held a feast at which food was distributed to neighbors and the poor.[13] This custom is still observed. Von Grunebaum observes that since at least the thirteenth century, Muslim Sultans, Emirs and Caliphs have long incorporated the distribution of food into

---

[8]Ibid., p. 117, RS 553

[9]Ibid., p. 72, RS 306.

[10]One *kejawen* informant explained that he usually sent poor neighbors five kilos of uncooked rice and powered milk formula for their children. He stated that it was his obligation to give poor people what they need and that the small amount of *slametan* food they received was not sufficient. Generally speaking, close neighbors are among those invited to *slametan*. Given the fact that in traditional neighborhoods there is not a strong correlation between residence and socio-economic class, inviting one's neighbors usually ensures that poor people are included among the guests.

[11]A "pure gift" is one in which there is no expectation of return, H. Mauss, *The Gift. Forms and Functions of Exchange in Archaic Societies*. London: Cohen and West, 1966. The Javanese equivalent is a gift, which is give in the spirit of *ikhlas*, again, one in which there is not expectation of return.

[12]R. Burton, *Personal Narrative of a Pilgrimage to El-Medinah and Meccah*, vol. 2:97 London: Longmans, Brown, Green and Longmans, 1855–56. This observation was made prior to the Wahhabi conquest of Mecca and Medina.

[13]C. Snouck-Hurgronje, *Mekka in the Latter Part of the Nineteenth century* Leiden: E. J. Brill, 1931, p. 121.

imperial *mawlid* (celebration of the birth of the Prophet) performances.[14] In contemporary Egyptian Sufi orders the distribution of food is among the means through which the *sheiykh's* blessing is conveyed to disciples. It is of such importance that officials are appointed to supervise its preparation and distribution.[15]

While ritual meals are known throughout the Muslim world, the *slametan* is most closely related to the Indo-Persian *kanduri* (J. *kenduren*, Malay *kenduri*, Acehnese *kanduri*, U. *kanduri*). In Java this term is used primarily by *Santri*. The etymology of *kanduri* is complex. It is a Persian term, the literal meaning of which is tablecloth, used in *Shafiite* legal texts to refer to feasts held in honor of the Prophet Muhammad, saints, and souls of the dead.[16] In Malay its literal meaning is a table for feasts and by extension the feast itself. It is derived from the Persian *kundur* (incense), which almost always accompanies food offerings.[17]

With the exception of rites required by the *Shari'ah* the *kanduri* is the most common ritual in Malay, Achenese, and South Indian Islam. In all these societies the *kanduri* is remarkably uniform. Like the *slametan* it includes recitation of portions of the *Qur'an*, the distribution of blessed food, and prayers for saints and the local community. The wide distribution of this ritual complex and particularly its centrality in South Indian Islam suggest that the modes of ritual action that make up the *slametan* are neither animistic nor native to Southeast Asia.[18] Indeed, Snouck-Hurgronje offers these parallel ritual systems as support for his theory concerning the South Indian origin of Southeast Asian Islam.[19]

In South India *kanduri* are held to celebrate the *Mawlid al-Nabi*, in honor of saints, for Muslim dead, at funerals, for the sick, and other calendrical and life-crisis ceremonies.[20] The food is thought to be a source of blessing and may be taken to a tomb or simply distributed to friends, relatives, and the poor. Herklots also mentions that "silly women" believe that the dead "eat" the food presented to them.[21] This is similar to the *lejawen* notion that saints and ancestors consume the *halus* (subtle) essence of *slametan* food. Cuisener describes the Malay *kenduri* as being both a distinct rite and a component of other rituals. She observes, "The *kenduri* may be a ceremony in itself: to place a little rice on a grave, or to prepare with pious intent a meal that will be shared with the poor, is to perform *kenduri*".[22] Malay informants state that the *kenduri* secures the blessing of God and the saints and that it may be

---

[14]G. von Grunebaum, *Muhammaden Festivals*, London: Abelard Schuman, 1951, pp. 73–76. See also Chapter 5.

[15]See M. Gilsenan, *Saint and Sufi in Modern Egypt*, London: Cruzon, 1973, p. 50.

[16]See H. Federspiel, *Persatuan Islam: Islamic Reform in Twentieth-century Indonesia*, Ithaca: Cornell University Modern Indonesia Project, 1969, p. 204.

[17]J. Cusinier, *Danses Magiques de Kelantan*, New Haven, Conn.: Human Relations area files, 1963, p. 15–E–5.

[18]See G. Herklots, *Islam in India or the Qanun-i-Islam: The Customs of the Musalams of India Comprising a Full and Exact Account of the Various Rites and Ceremonies from the Moment of Birth to the Hour of Death*, London: Cruzon, 1921, pp. 118, 201.

[19]C. Snoudk-Hurgronje, *The Achenese*, Leiden: E.J. Brill, 1906, p. 204.

[20]On the *Mawlid al-Nabi* in Yogyakarta see Chapter 5.

[21]Herklots, op. cit., p. 207.

[22]Cuisiner, op. cit., p. 15–E–5.

performed for the dead as well as the living. Achenese *kanduri* resemble those of Malaya. In Ache the *kenduri* is of such general significance that the term together with the name of the principle food offering is used to designate months of the Islamic year.[23]

The wide distribution of this ritual complex and the association of the distribution of food with saint veneration and blessing and, in the case of royal ritual, with political authority, indicate that while the *slametan*, as a totality, is a "local" Muslim ritual, it is also an example of a larger, trans-cultural tradition that parallels that of the *Shari'ah*. This suggests that other local Islams, as well as Muslim texts, contributed to the development of Islam in Java.

The Distribution of *Slametan* in Javanese Society

Geertz describes the *slametan* as a village ritual that loses much of its force in urban environments.[24] The association of the *slametan* with village life and animism lies at the heart of his theory that Javanese culture has resisted Indic and Islamic influence. My experience in Yogyakarta does not support this interpretation. The *slametan* is not exclusively, or even primarily, a village ritual. Nor is it limited to the *kejawen* community. *Slametan* are performed in mosques, at *pesantren*, at the graves of saints, and in the homes of traditional *santri*. *Santri slametan* make more extensive use of *Qur'an* recitation and less of local *kejawen* saints. Similarly, *santri* often state that prayers are the most important part of the ritual while *kejawen* Muslims stress food and blessing. Some *santri* also refer to it as *sedakah* (charity) and emphasize the distribution of alms.

Most royal rituals are elaborate *slametan*. *Slametan* are held in conjunction with royal life crisis ceremonies (birth, weddings, circumcision, funerals, etc.). State ceremonies are *slametan* performed on a massive, imperial scale. These are discussed in Chapter 5. The *haul* conducted at the tombs of major saints to commemorate the anniversaries of their deaths are also *slametan* some of which are attended by tens of thousands of people. Most are traditional *santri*. At the annual *haul* for Sunan Kudus (one of the legendary Nine Wali) meat from as many as fourteen water buffalo and numerous goats and literally tons of cooked and uncooked rice are distributed.

The Concept of Slamet

As Mulder observes, the purpose of the *slametan* is to establish the condition of *slamet* in the local community and the hearts of its members.[25] Most scholars have defined *slamet* in negative, psychological terms. Koentjarangingrat describes it as "a state in which events will run their course and nothing untoward will happen to

---

[23] Snouck-Hurgronje, op. cit., pp. 210–16.

[24] Geertz, op. cit., pp. 11–15.

[25] N. Mulder, *Mysticism and Everyday Life in Java*, Yogyakarta: Gadjah Mada University Press, 1979, p. 202.

anyone".[26] Geertz refers to it as "that peculiarly negative state of bodily and mental equanimity".[27] Zoetmulder's characterization of *slamet* as psychological and social "homeostasis" is perhaps the best, but he, like others, errs in attributing it to Javanese animism.[28] Javanese generally refer to both the social and psychological dimensions of *slamet* when asked to define it. In social discourse it refers to both mental states and social conditions. The individual is *slamet* when her or his mind is at rest, untroubled by worldly concerns or supernatural fears. This state does not suggest withdrawal from the world but, rather, the absence of strong emotions and acceptance of one's position in the social hierarchy. The community (however defined) is *slamet* when there is an adequate level of material prosperity together with an absence of social or political conflict. Javanese often state that two modalities of *slamet* are interdependent because psychological tranquility is possible only in well-ordered social contexts, while social harmony is possible only when the emotions of individuals are stilled.

But *slamet* is more than homeostasis. It is a religious and mystical term derived from the Quranic term *salam*. In the *Qur'an*, *salam* is used in a general sense for tranquility in this life and in the world to come. *Al-salam* (the peaceful one) is one of the names of God, while *Dar al-salam* (abode of peace) is among the terms used for paradise.[29] *Salam* is used as a salutation for humans, spiritual beings, saints, and angels in many social and ritual contexts. The phrase "*al-salam alaykum*" (peace be upon you) is a request that God bless the person addressed. The response "*wa- alaykun wa-rahmat Allah wa-barakatuhu*" (On you be the peace, blessing, and mercy of God) is motivated by the Quranic injunction that when a person is saluted he must return a better salute and by the notion that conferring a benediction on someone is a source of blessing for both.[30] Among the relevant passages from the *Qur'an* are:

> When ye are greeted with a greeting, greet ye with a better one than it or return it. Lo! God taketh count of all things" (4:86).

> But when ye enter houses, salute one another with a greeting from God, blessed and sweet [the *salam* greeting] (24:61).

> When those who believe in Quranic revelations come unto thee say: Peace be unto you! (6:54).

Nawawi lists 26 Hadith describing the ways in which *salam* is bestowed on and by prophets, angels, Muslims, and others.[31] For present purposes the most significant of these are:

---

[26] Koentjaraningrat, "The Javanese of South Central Java," In: G. Murdock (ed.), *Social Structure in Southeast Asia*, Chicago: Quadrangle Press, 1960, pp. 88–115.

[27] Geertz, op. cit., p. 13.

[28] P. Zoetulder, *The Cultural Background of Indonesian Politics* Columbia: University of South Carolina Press, 1967.

[29] See A. Jeffery, *A Reader on Islam. Passages from Standard Arabic Writings Illustrative of the Beliefs and Practices of Muslims*, The Hague: Gravenhage, 1962, p. 553.

[30] E. Lane, *Manners and Customs of the Modern Egyptians* London: Arden Library, 1908, p. 203.

[31] Kahn, op. cit., pp. 164–67, RS 848–7

Bara'a ibn 'Azib relates: The Holy Prophet enjoined the following seven on us: Visiting the sick, following a funeral, calling down the mercy of God on one who sneezes, supporting the weak, helping the oppressed, multiplying the greeting of peace, and fulfilling vows.[32] Abdullah ibn Salam relates that he heard the Holy Prophet say: O ye people, multiply the greeting of peace, feed people, strengthen ties of kinship and be in prayer when others are asleep, you will enter Paradise in peace.[33]

In texts and religious discourse, *salam* is bestowed at every mention of a prophet and frequently in the case of angels, saints, and other esteemed religious figures. Muhammad is said to have used the *salam* as a salutation for the prophets who proceeded him and for martyrs and other Muslim dead.[34] Hadith concerning Muhammad's salutations of the dead are among the sources of Islamic eschatology and, in part, motivate the customs of visiting graves and offering prayers for the dead. One example is:

Buraidah relates that the Holy Prophet taught that any of them visiting a cemetery should say: Peace be on you dwellers of this home of believers and Muslims, and we, if God so wills, shall join you. I supplicate for peace for you and ourselves.[35]

In South India and Java, Muslim funeral rites include seven ceremonies in which prayers are said for and offerings presented to the deceased.[36] In *kejawen* memorial ceremonies the prayers include a *dihkr*, which may last for several hours. Javanese informants explained that the purpose of these *slametan* is to ease the transition between life and death and to ensure the tranquility of the dead person and his or her survivors. *kejawen* and traditional *santri* custom requires that family members visit graves at the beginning and end of *Ramadan*, at which times they are cleaned, and that *slametan* be held at the cemetery or at home. Traditional *santri* and many *kejawen* Muslims recite portions, usually *Surah Yasin*, or all of the *Qur'an* on these occasions.[37]

Saluting and calling down blessing on the Prophet Muhammad is required of all Muslims. The *Qur'an* states that:

God and his Angels shower blessings on the Prophet. O ye who believe! Ask blessings on him and salute him with a worthy salutation (36:54).

Among the Hadith concerning the salutation of Muhammad are:

Abdullah ibn Amr ibn As relates that he heard the Prophet say: He who calls down blessing on me, God sends down blessing on him ten times.[38]

---

[32] Ibid., p. 164, RS 850.

[33] Ibid., pp. 164–65, RS 852.

[34] C. van Arendock, "*Salam*," In: H. Gibb and J. Krammers (eds.), *The Shorter Encyclopaedia of Islam*, Leiden: E.J. Brill, 1953, p. 490.

[35] Kahn, op. cit., pp. 123, RS 585.

[36] For South India, see Herklots, op. cit., pp. 104–8.

[37] *Surah Yasin* is almost always among the passages recited.

[38] Kahn, op. cit., p. 234, RS 1402.

Ibn Mas'ud relates that the Holy Prophet said: The closest to me on the day of judgement will be those who call down blessings on me the most.[39]

In Java and elsewhere in the Muslim world, Muhammad's birthday is celebrated with readings of his biography (A., *Mawlid*; J., *Malud*). *Kejawen* Muslims maintain that holding a *slametan* on this day is the defining mark of being a Muslim. It is also the occasion of the largest imperial ceremony, the *Garebeg Malud*.

During the *shalat* prayer the worshiper must "*salam*" Muhammad, his fellow worshipers, and all of God's servants.[40] Many *santri* believe that the use of the *salam* formula in the communal Friday prayer reinforces the theological position that Islam is based on the notion of community and that each Muslim must pray for the community to receive the blessing of God. It is largely for this reason that communal prayer is said to yield a greater blessing than that performed in solitude. In Java, Islam is commonly understood as including two sets of obligation: one to God and another to one's fellow humans. The *salam*, while numbered among the duties owed to humans, is thought to be pleasing to God and a source of blessing.

In the late 1970s *salam* was rarely used in ordinary social discourse in Yogyakarta. Even *Shari'ah*-minded *santri* used *slamet* except in ritual contexts.[41] *Slamet* is used as a greeting by Javanese of all religious orientations. It expresses a wish that a temporal-period activity be marked by psychological, social, and spiritual tranquility. The salutation "*slamet* x" is returned with "*slamet* y," conveying a similar wish. The use of the *salam* greeting in social discourse and especially in public discourse, such as the opening of speeches has become increasingly common. By the turn of twenty-first century it had become very nearly universal in public contexts, except among Christians and other religious minorities. It has also been politicized. Some Muslims, and especially Islamists, strongly believe that non-Muslims should not use it.

All but the most ardent reformists believe that *slamet* and *salam* are equivalent. This point is illustrated by a controversy I observed at a reformist mosque in Yogyakarta in the late 1970s. A visiting Sumatran *ulama* delivered a sermon condemning the *slamet* greeting as non-Muslim. The Javanese audience was not impressed. One of the elders of the mosque later explained that *slamet* is an Indonesian and Javanese way of saying *salam* and that it has the same effect. He continued that he too was a pious Muslim; that he could read and speak Arabic — but that he found no reason to substitute it for Javanese in ordinary discourse. Over the course of the past three decades use of the Arabic greeting has become much

---

[39] Ibid., p. 234, RS 1403.

[40] Ali, op. cit., p. 416.

[41] As M. Nakamura, *The Crescent Arises over the Banyan Tree*, Yogyakarta: Gadjah Mada University Press, 1983, p. 165, observes, the *salam* greeting is used in sermons and other ritual contexts. When I was first in Java, it was rarely employed in ordinary social discourse. Nor is the *slamet* greeting always used. It is also common to greet someone by asking "where are going to/coming from?"

more common. It is now almost obligatory on public occasions and is even used in recorded messages

The concept of *slamet* is also linked to Javanese formulations of the Sufi mystical path. Like *salam* it is used as a *dihkr*. It is associated with the mystical state *mutmainah* (A., *mutma'innah*). In the *Qur'an* and Hadith, *mutma'innah* refers to the peaceful or tranquil soul.[42] In Egyptian mystical texts it is defined as "tranquility, liberality, trust, gentleness, adoration, gratitude, contentment with fate, and patience under calamities".[43] In Javanese Sufism, *mutmainah* is associated with intuitive knowledge of God and is the condition to which those who have attained mystical union return. It is characterized by tranquility, security, and equanimity. It is also the interior (J. and A., *batin*) aspect of the exterior (A., *zahir*; J., *lahir*) state of *slamet*. While *slamet* is attained through prayer and blessing, *mutmainah* arises from purification of the soul. One informant stated that those who have attained *mutmainah* do not need to perform *slametan* because, for them, blessing and tranquility are "automatic" consequences of mystical attainment. But, he continued, they should continue to host *slametan* to share the fruits of their accomplishments with others.

As a whole, etymological evidence and local exegesis suggest that *slamet* is a social and psychological transformation of Sufi (and more general Muslim) notions of peace, blessing, and tranquility. It is a collective, social manifestation of a crucial stage on the mystic's path to God as well as an internal psychological state influenced by the Quranic notion of tranquility. A *kejawen* informant, when questioned about this relationship, explained that what the mystical path does for the soul, the *slametan* does for the community. The difference, he said, is that meditation is more effective and far more difficult.

Slametan Ritual Forms

The *slametan* includes three principle components, an invocation (J., *ujub*), an Arabic prayer (J., *donga*) and the meal. Inviting guests and preparing food are also integral components of the ritual. In every case, ritual symbols and modes of action constitute an instrumental use of textual and mystical Islamic concepts and are illustrative of the deep penetration of Sufism in the fabric of Javanese culture.

Slametan Participation and the Notion of Community

Muslims often observe that Islam does not distinguish between the social and the religious. Consequently, the notion of community (A., *umah*; J., *umat*) is both social and religious. The selection of guests for *slametan* is based on a social/religious notion of community and more specifically on obligations toward the poor, kin, and neighbors set forth in the *Qur'an* and Hadith.

---

[42] See T. Burckhardt, *An Introduction to Sufi Doctrine*, Lahore: Ashraf, 1959, p. 151.

[43] J. Trimingham, *The Sufi Orders in Islam*. Oxford: Clarendon, 1971, p. 156.

While in a grand, utopian and never realized sense, Islam forms a single community, the *Qur'an* and Hadith specify neighbors, kin and the poor as people to whom one owes special obligations. The *Qur'an* states:

> Show kindness unto parents, and unto near kindred, and orphans, and the needy, and unto the neighbor who is of kin and the neighbor who is not of kin, and the fellow traveler and the wayfarer and whom your right hand possess [slaves] (4:36).

These themes are elaborated in Hadith requiring Muslims to honor their parents and recommending sending gifts of food to neighbors:

> Ayesha relates that she asked the Holy Prophet: I have two neighbors; to which of them shall I send a present? He said: to the one whose door is nearer to yours.[44]

> Abu Hurairah relates that the Holy Prophet said: O Muslim women, disdain not doing a kindness to a neighbor, even if it were sending a lamb's shank.[45]

> Abu Hurairah relates that the Holy Prophet said: He who exerts himself on the behalf of widows and the indigent is like one who strives in the cause of God.[46]

These concerns are echoed in the problems Javanese have in selecting guests for *slametan*. Ideally, one should invite neighbors, kin, poor people, and the others with whom one has significant social relationships. Often this is not possible because of the cost involved. Men generally consult their wives before inviting guests, asking how many and often, whom they should ask.[47] Jay observes that in villages, geographic proximity is the dominant factor determining *slametan* attendance. This is also true in urban settings.[48] Given the economic heterogeneity of Javanese neighborhoods this ensures that poor people will be invited. In the neighborhood in which I lived in Yogyakarta the selection of guests is a complex affair. The guests at minor *slametan* were usually neighbors, in part because it would be prohibitively expensive to invite all of one's friends, relatives and neighbors to every ritual. However, kin, business associates, and others with whom the host has important social relationships are invited to the large ceremonies held for rites of passage, particularly weddings, circumcisions, and funerals.

Often some of the guests find it impossible to attend. In such cases participation is restricted to accepting parcels of food. Sharing *slametan* food is understood as a means of distributing blessing beyond the small group of men who actually attend. Accepting food serves the same ends as attending a *slametan* and draws women and children (who do not often attend) into the circle of blessing.

In Yogyakarta nobles, and other high-status individuals, generally do not attend the *slametan* of their poor neighbors, and while the poor often help with those of the rich, they are reluctant to attend.[49] The usual reason given for this is that both

---

[44] Khan, op. cit., pp. 72–72, RS 312.

[45] Ibid., p. 72, RS 308.

[46] Ibid., p. 66, RS 267.

[47] Ibid., pp. 111–12, RS 523.

[48] Jay, op. cit., pp. 206–13.

[49] Funerals are an exception. Everyone in the neighborhood, regardless of status, must attend.

the host and the guest would feel uncomfortable and that this would prevent them from attaining the state of *slamet*. Sending food to neighbors of higher or lower social status ensures their participation and, for high-status individuals, resolves the contradiction between the duty of charity and the tension that might result from ritual interaction with social inferiors.[50]

Slametan **Food**

In many Muslim cultures, certain foods are thought to be appropriate for ritual use and to convey special types of blessing.[51] Some of these are linked to Hadith. Burton cites Hadith stating that dates were Muhammad's favorite food and that he always broke a fast with them.[52] Consequently, many Muslims eat dates during Ramadan and offer them to the spirit of the Prophet. Those from a grove near his tomb in Medina are sold to pilgrims for outrageous prices. Turkish informants state that bread is so sacred that it can never be thrown away. In Pakistan *biryani*, a rice dish prepared with ghee and saffron is the primary food used in ceremonies commemorating the deaths of Sufi saints. Informants describe this dish as having been one of Muhammad's favorites.

At *kejawen slametan* incense, flowers and other *sajen* usually accompany trays of food. *Sajen* are the most basic Javanese offerings. They may be as simple as a few flower petals, or enormously elaborate, including numerous foods and drinks, cigarettes and other items considered appropriate for the occasion. They are offered at places known to be inhabited by spirits, at graves and to *pusaka*. Both the Yogyakarta and Surakarta *Kraton* prepare hundreds every day. Many *santri* do not include incense, flowers or other *sajen* in their *slametan*. In Kudus in East Java this distinction is institutionalized. *Santri* who live in the *Kauman*, the *kampung* surrounding the grave of Sunan Kudus, do not include *sajen* in *slametan*. *Santri* and *kejawen* Muslims living in other parts of the city do.

Nowhere is the association of food and blessing stronger than in Java. Many *santri* feel that dates should be used to bread a fast. Dates, coffee, and other food items from Arabia are considered sacred. As Geertz observes, there are

---

[50]In Java adult men rarely eat together because of possible status conflicts. The higher status person should eat first. Because there are numerous sources of status (rank, wealth, religious learning, age, etc.) it is often difficult to determine whose status is higher. At a *slametan* everyone eats at the same time. While the temporary elimination of status distinctions is among the goals of the ritual, it is difficult to accept in the case of extreme status differences. This problem is particularly vexing in Yogyakarta where it is not uncommon for princes and poverty stricken migrants from villages to be neighbors. Nobles and the wealthy feel that to attend the *slametan* of the poor would place an extra burden on them because they would spend more than they could afford. The poor are afraid of making social or linguistic mistakes in the presence of nobles.

[51]Herklots, op. cit., p. 118, 184, 201; and R. Provincher, "Orality as a Pattern of Symbolism in Malay Psychiatry," In: A. Becker and A. Yengoyan (eds.), *The Imagination of Reality:Essays in Southeast Asian Coherence Systems*, Norwood, N.J: Albex Press., 1979), pp. 43–53.

[52]Burton, op. cit., 2:201.

hundreds of *slametan* foods.[53] Of these, two merit special consideration. *Apem*, rice flour cakes, are illustrative of the South Asian influence on the *slametan*, and rice cones (*tumpeng*) demonstrate the Islamic interpretation of ancient Javanese symbolism.

Apem (Sinhalese, *appa*; Mappila, *appam*; Malay, *appam*; Indian English, *hoppers*) are popular snacks in South India and Malaya and are offered to the dead in many Asian Muslim cultures.[54] In Java they are almost exclusively ritual food. They are included in many *slametan* and are distributed at traditionalist mosques prior to the feast of *Ramadan*, when graves are repaired and offerings made to the dead, who, like the living, must "fast". A giant *apem* is prepared by the Yogyakarta palace to honor the royal dead. The association of *apem* with death is so strong that many Javanese, particularly the elderly, refuse to eat them. Consequently, what is in much of South and Southeast Asia a common snack, is, in central Java, primarily a sacred food. This suggests that it was introduced as an element of Muslim mortuary ritual. There is an alternative explanation from Jatinom, a village in central Java where *apem* are iconic of the local saint. Ki Ageng Gribig. The saint is said to have been instrumental in the propagation of Islam in the area. Legend has it that he brought *apem* with him as gifts for his grandchildren and others in the village when returning from the *hajj*. Because there were not enough his wife cooked more and distributed them to all of the people in the village. For at least the last century the distribution of *apem* has played a central role in the *haul* commemorating the anniversary of the saint's death. This festival attracts as many as 50,000 people from all parts of Indonesia. Following the Friday noon prayer, tens of thousands are thrown to crowds from towers located approximately 100 m from the mosque. They are also given to pilgrims visiting his tomb. In 2009 approximately ten thousand pounds of *apem* were distributed.

Yellow rice cones are included in almost all *slametan*. In state ceremonies they are replaced by bamboo *Gunungan* (J., mountain) adorned with rice and other foods. While there are oblique references in the Hadith to "mountains of blessing,"[55] Mountain symbolism dates to Hindu/Buddhist and, perhaps, animistic periods in Javanese history.[56] Mount Meru, the Buddhist cosmic mountain, figures prominently in Old Javanese texts and in Balinese symbolism, which is influenced by Old Javanese textual traditions.[57] But *slametan* Rice Mountains are also linked to Muslim tradition. They are made from *sekul wuduk*, rice cooked in coconut milk, which, according to some *santri* informants is a substitute for a dish of rice and

---

[53] Geertz, op. cit., p. 13.

[54] R. Miller, *Mappila Muslims of Kerala,* Bombay: Orient Longmans, 1976, p. 245.

[55] See Khan, op. cit., p. 118, RS 564. The term *gunungan* is used in Indonesian Hadith translations (see H. Bahreisy, *Himpunan Hadits Pilihan Hadits Shahih Bukhari,* Surabaya 1980, p. 234).

[56] See H. Quaritch-Wales, *The Universe around Them: Cosmology and Cosmic Renewal in Indianized Southeast Asia,* London: Probsthain, 1977, pp. 1–24.

[57] See ibid., pp. 84–111; and I. Mabbett, "The Symbolism of Mount Meru", *History of Religions,* vol. 23, 198, pp., 64–83.

oil said to have been one of the Prophet's favorites.[58] They are important because blessing descends into the cone and from there to surrounding dishes. This concept parallels what Martin and Wensinck mention as a basic principle of Quranic cosmology, that is, that revelation, beings, objects, and blessing descend downward from heaven while prayers and supplications move upward.[59] This belief finds expression in commonly held Sufi theories concerning the descent and ascent of the perfect man as well as in the spatial orientation of prayer.[60] Muslims pray toward the *Kabah* in Mecca, which is located on a cosmic axis directly beneath the throne of God. In this sense prayer moves toward the center and upward while blessing moves downward and toward the periphery. The *slametan* replicates this pattern on a local level in that prayers move upward and blessing descends into the rice cone and from there to the local community. *Slametan* food, therefore, defines a local model of the Islamic cosmos and is among the means through which blessing is attained and distributed.

The *Ujub*

A *slametan* begins with an *ujub* or statement of intent. The *ujub* is a welcoming speech given by the host. Its purpose is to welcome the guests, to explain the purpose of the *slametan*, and to mention the saints and spirits who have been invited and the dish that is dedicated to each of them. It is delivered in the most polite language possible, though the hose apologizes for his lack of eloquence and the inadequacy of the food. The general tone of the speech resembles the style of religious discourse described in Hadith in which Muhammad is invited to share a simple meal.[61] In both cases the host apologizes for the inadequacy of the food and expresses the desire that the Prophet Muhammad and his companions partake of it.

The *ujub* is not, however, simply a polite speech. It has at least five religiously motivated purposes: (1) to link and elaborate feast with the simple ritual meals at which Muhammad officiated; (2) to define the community to whom blessing will be imparted; (3) to specify saints and other beings to whom food and prayers are dedicated; (4) to establish the good intentions of the host; and (5) to establish his humility.

Statements concerning the inadequacy of the food are in keeping with the spirit of Hadith describing ritual meals at which Muhammad officiated and other Hadith

---

[58]This dish, which is colored with tumeric, resembles Indian Muslim *biryani*. *Biryani* is prepared with rice, gee (clarified butter), curds, saffron, and other spices. Dairy products are rare in Java, in part because of a high incidence of lactose intolerance. Coconut milk is a substitute for both butter fat (ghee) and curds. In Java and Pakistan yellow rice dishes are associated with the veneration of the Prophet and saints. In Yogyakarta large quanities of *sekul wuduk* are sold at the *Garebeg Malud*, which commemorates the birth and death of the prophet.

[59]R. Martin, *Islam: A Cultural Perspective*, Englewood Cliffs.: Prentice Hall, 1982, pp. 90–94; and A. Wensinck, "Kaba," in Gibb and Krammers, eds., op. cit., pp. 191–98.

[60]See R. Nicholson, *The Mystics of Islam: An Introduction to Sufism*, London: Routledge and Paul, 1975, pp. 120–48.

[61]Khan, op. cit., p. 111, RS 523.

according to which his diet was simple to the point of malnourishment. Many Hadith mention the excellence of hunger.[62] Among them are:

> The Holy Prophet never at off a tablecloth, nor did he ever eat bread made of fine flour throughout his life. He never even saw a whole roast lamb,[63]

> The Holy Prophet said: The food of two suffices for three and the food of three suffices for four".[64]

Slametan usually include a number of elaborate dishes. However, statements to the contrary and the fact that each person eats only a small amount (the host eats nothing) establish a symbolic link between a feast and dietary customs attributed to Muhammad. This concern with dietary simplicity is not restricted to ritual contexts. *Kejawen* and *santri* informants agree that holy people limit their intake of food and often state that small amounts of blessed food are as filling as a normal meal. Similarly, many villagers believe that if a small amount of the food distributed at state *slametan* is placed in the rice bin there will always be an adequate supply of food.[65]

While the community shares in the blessing generated by the *slametan*, it is performed for a particular individual or social group. This can be the host, a member of his family, or a collectivity, in the case of calendrical *slametan* such as those commemorating the harvest of the annual cleansing of the village. This declaration is in keeping with the Muslim notion that prayers can be offered for others.

It is also necessary to dedicate offerings and prayers to each of the saints and spirits and to welcome them to the ritual. This practice would appear to be based on the Islamic concept of salutation and requires them to return a blessing. One *kejawen* informant explained that if they are not mentioned by name, they will not know that they have been invited. He next explained that this is exactly the same as inviting people to attend. The spirits must also be informed of which of the many types of food are intended for them so that they will not be confused. This is particularly important in light of the fact that a large number of "spirits", ranging from that of the Prophet Muhammad to local guardians, may be invited. The host generally mentions as many saints and spirits as he can remember in order to identify as many sources of blessing as possible. While the Prophet Muhammad is always included, lists vary greatly. Among the most common are the nine *wali*s who are said to have brought Islam to Java, as well as the spirits of the ancestors, Javanese kings, and local guardian spirits (who are most commonly the souls of local historical figures). *Santri* generally invite more Arabic saints, while those invited to *kejawen slametan* often include Hindu-Javanese kings, many of who are said to have been converted to Islam after death.

---

[62] See ibid., pp. 106–13, RS 494–523.

[63] Ibid., p. 107, RS 497.

[64] Ibid., p. 119, RS 568.

[65] See Chapter 5.

The *ujub* and the expressions of humility it includes are also congruent with the textual concept of intention (A., *niyah*; J., *niyat*) and the belief that prayer is submission to God. A common Muslim view is that intention, rather than the precise detail of ritual form, determines the efficacy of a ritual performance. This is clearly expressed in the statement of intent required for those performing the liturgical prayer (*shalat*).

> I have purposed to offer up to God only with a sincere heart this morning (or as the case may be) with my face Qiblah-wards two (or as many as the case may be) *rak'ah* (sets of) prayers.[66]

Similar statements are required before setting out on the *hajj* (pilgrimage to Mecca) or performing other important ritual acts. This notion of intent is so thoroughly ingrained in Islam that according to some accounts God grants salvation to those who honestly intend to avoid things that hinder obedience to divine commands even if they fail to fulfill the requirements of the law. Wensinck summarizes the doctrine of intention as follows:

> It constitutes a religious and moral criterion superior to that of the law. The value of an *ibada* [ritual act] even if performed in complete accordance with the law, depends on the intention of the performer, and if his intentions should be sinful, the work would be valueless.[67]

The *ujub* adds to the classical formulation of intent only the notion that the intrinsic worth of the host and the value of his offerings are inadequate. This is in keeping with the Javanese view that self-denigration is the utmost form of politeness and the Muslim view that religion is submission to God. It also expresses a fundamental ritual concern also found in the *shalat* prayers. Humility, like good intention is a precondition for God's acceptance of prayer. The *Qur'an* states:

> Successful indeed are the believers who are humble in their prayers (23:1–2).

> And the slaves of the Beneficent are they who walk on the earth modestly, and when the foolish ones address them answer: Peace (25:63).

Humility and modesty are also among the virtues attributed to the Prophet Muhammad, who is described in Hadith as "more modest than a virgin behind her veil".[68] Humility is among the cornerstones of Sufi mystical practice. The terms Sufi is derived from *suf* (wool), which refers to the coarse garment worn by early Muslim mystics. Humiliation plays a central role in the initiation rites of historical and contemporary Sufi orders. Nicholson observes that a novice must be like a corpse in the hands of the washer and must "regard all, without exception, as being better than himself".[69]

---

[66] T. Hughes, *Dictionary of Islam: Being a Cyclopedia of Doctrines, Rites, Ceremonies and Customs, Together with the Technical and Theological Terms of the Muhammadan Religion*, Clifton: Reference Books Publishers, 1965, p. 434.

[67] A. Wensinck, "*Niyat*," In: Gibb and Krammers, (eds.), op. cit., p. 449.

[68] Kahn, op. cit., p. 138, RS 687.

[69] Nicholson, op. cit., p. 33.

Javanese mystics and *santri* teachers require similar levels of obedience and take great pains to cultivate a sense of humility. Mystics frequently live on diets of wild plants to cultivate humility. Even learned Muslim scholars apologize for their lack of knowledge and preface complex theological discussions with "If I am not mistaken". Concern with humility extends to the highest levels of the royal and *santri* hierarchies. Even in secular contexts, Javanese social discourse is punctuated by expressions of humility and modesty. The elaborate codes of politeness so characteristic of Javanese society involve presenting one's self in the most humble light possible. This concern is manifest in a mode of social interaction known as *andop asor* (J.) in which individuals attempt to present themselves as inferior, regardless of their actual social positions. This mode of interaction is frequently employed when people eat or drink together: each requesting at great length that the other begin first. While it is a basic pattern in Javanese culture, this mode of interaction is also present in the biographies of Sufi saints. Nicholson describes an episode in which two Sufi masters sit conversing on the floor because neither wishes to be the first to sit in a chair.[70]

While it is not manifestly drawn from Arabic textual sources, the *ujub* is motivated by Islamic religious concerns. It specifies the beneficiary of the prayers, conveys a salutation on the assembled community including the saints and spirits, is a declaration of intent, and establishes the humility of the host. It serves much the same purpose as the statements of intention required for rituals prescribed by the *Shari'ah*. The standardization of this speech is illustrative of the deep penetration of Islam in Javanese culture, even for those (the majority) who are unaware of the textual origins of their traditions. For the *kejawen* majority, Islam is not primarily a textual corpus but a living component of cultural and religious knowledge. Most are unaware that in hosting a *slametan* they are re-contextualizing Hadith. But then, one of the purposes of Hadith collection was to establish Islam as the basis for social and ritual behavior. For *kejawen* believers Muslim ritual action speaks louder than the lack of Arabic words.

After completing the *ujub* the host seats himself in the circle of guests and remains silent for the remainder of the ritual. He should clear his mind and focus his concentration on God. This concept is most fully developed in state *slametan* where the Sultan is thought to attain mystical union. In another sense the host's behavior mirrors that described in the Hadith in which the host invites the Prophet but does not participate in the distribution of food.[71]

The *Donga*

The *ujub* is followed immediately by a *donga* (A., *dua*). This is an Arabic prayer, ideally, it should be recited by a mosque official, but in his absence anyone who

---

[70] Ibid., p. 43.

[71] Kahn, op. cit., p. 111, RS 523.

knows Arabic will suffice. The *donga* is preceded by the Quranic formula "*Bismillah al-rahma al-rahim*" (in the name of God the compassionate, the merciful). This phrase, which occurs at the beginning of all but one of the chapters of the *Qur'an*, is said to contain the essence of Islam and is widely used as a supplication.[72] Some Hadith state that it can drive off evil spirits (A., *shayta*n; J., *setan*).[73] The "*Bismillah*" is recited by *santri* and *kujawen* Muslims to ward of evil and to promote the conditions of *slamet*. It is also used in exorcisms. In written form (in Arabic) it is included, along with rose petals and incense, in the *Sajen* packet that hangs above the door of *kejawen* and traditional *santri* houses. Its purpose is to protect the house from evil. This is congruent with the general Javanese belief that evil beings cannot abide the sound or presence of the *Qur'an*.

The *donga* is drawn largely from the *Qur'an*. Passages suitable to the occasion are often selected, but the *Fatihah* is essential. The *Fatihah* is the first chapter of the *Qur'an* and the most common prayer in the Muslim world.

> Praise be to God, Lord of the worlds! The Beneficent, the Merciful! Owner of the Day of Judgment! Thee we worship and Thee we ask for help! Show us the straight path, the path of those whom Thou hast favored; not (the path) of those who earn Thine anger nor of those who go astray. [1:1–7].

The *Fatihah* is mentioned in a subsequent chapter as "the seven verses which ought to be constant recited" (15:87) and is included in the *shalat* prayer. Throughout the Middle East and Muslim Asia it is used to heal the sick, to intercede for the souls of the dead, and to sanctify food distributed in the name of saints.[74] In Java it is used as a mystical formula (A. and J. *dihkr*).

The *Fatihah* is followed by one or more other selections from the *Qur'an*. This is in accordance with the Muslim principle that certain chapters of the text yield special types of blessing. There is an extensive Hadith literature on this topic, specifying uses for a number of popular chapters.[75] *Surah Ya Sin* (Chapter 35) is always recited at death *slametan*, while *al-Ikhas* (Chapter 112) or *Qaf* (Chapter 50) are often recited at exorcisms and *slametan* intended to restore tranquility.

The *donga* is not restricted to *slametan*. *Donga* is a Javanese gloss for the Arabic term *dua*. It is a prayer of supplication that may be included in *shalat*. Muslim prayer manuals from the Middle East and from South and Southeast Asia include *dua* for hundreds of occasions.[76] In Java they are recited at saint shrines and by *santri* in night prayers held at the mosque. Many *kejawen* Muslims use Javanese *donga* when visiting tombs, but there are occasions when Arabic is essential. In addition to *slametan*, Arabic *donga* are required at royal cemeteries and in state ceremonies. When Arabic is necessary the supplicant informs the *santri* ritual specialist of his/her needs to enable him to select appropriate Quranic verses. During

---

[72] Jeffery, op. cit., pp. 556–57.

[73] Ibid., p. 558.

[74] See Hughes, op. cit., p. 123; Herklots, op. cit., p. 200; and Lane, op. cit., p. 383.

[75] See Kahn, op. cit., pp. 187–89, RS 1013–26.

[76] See C. Padwick, *Muslim Devotions,* London: SPCK, 1961.

the recitation non-Arabic speakers intone "*ingih*" ("yes"), while those who know Arabic at all join in the recitation.

During the *donga* the guests and host hold their palms facing upward greeting each pause with a loud *amin*. This posture is used as a gesture of supplication in the *shalat* rite and at the tombs of saints. Geertz states that the participants appear to expect a gift from God.[77] Not only in the *slametan* but also at tombs and at the conclusion of the *shalat* rite, *kejawen* Muslims and traditional *Santri* rub their faces to absorb the blessing descending from heaven. An English speaking informant referred to the blessing as "a present from God". The practice is not, however uniquely Javanese. It is a common devotional practice in the Middle East and Muslim Asia and is derived from a posture used in *shalat*. At the end of the *shalat* the worshiper cups and raises his hands imploring God for blessing. Hughes mentions the following Hadith concerning this posture; "Verily your Lord is ashamed of his servants when they raise up their hands to Him in supplication to return them empty".[78]

According to *Shafiite* law the expression of assent, *amin*, must be said at the conclusion of the *Fatihah*.[79] It is spoken by the congregation in the *shalat* prayer after the *imam's* (prayerleader's) recitation. The use of this assent transforms an individual recitation into a collective prayer. By saying *amin*, a Javanese who does not understand a single word of Arabic receives the same benefits as the reciter. It is believed that it is better to yell *amin* than to say it in a soft voice.[80] In Javanese mosque the *Fatihah* is greeted by a thunderous chorus of *amins*. Similarly, *Kejawen* Muslims feel that yelling *amin* at *slametan* enables the saints and spirits to hear it and share in the benefits of the recitation.

At death *slametan* and those of *santri*, the *donga* is followed by a *dihkr* that may last for several hours. The host and all of the guests recite the confession of faith – "There is no God but God and Muhammad is Prophet" – in either Arabic or Javanese but more frequently in Arabic. This recitation is intended to benefit both the community and the souls of the dead.

The Distribution of Food

With the chorus of *amin*, the food is sacralized. One of the guests jumps into the center of the circle and begins to distribute food. This individual, rather than the host, performs the function attributed to Muhammad.[81] The food is served on banana leaves, distributed, and eaten with the right hand. Nawawi lists several Hadith describing the ways in which food should be handled and eaten that parallel the performative structure of the *slametan*. Among these are:

---

[77] Geertz, op. cit., p. 13.

[78] Hughes, op. cit., p. 469.

[79] Ibid., p. 125.

[80] Ali, op. cit., p. 243.

[81] See Kahn, op. cit., p. 111, RS 523.

Eat together and pronounce the name of God over your food. It will be blessed for you. Blessing descends upon food in its middle, so eat from the sides of the vessel and do not eat from its middle.[82]

Kejawen Muslims often state that blessing descends into the center of the rice cone and, and, consequently, that the foods surrounding it should be distributed first. After the food has been distributed each person eats a few bites. Some informants state that it is important not to stay too long because the host might be shamed if all the food was eaten, and there would not be enough to send to others. Such statements are, again, in keeping with the Hadith quoted at the beginning of this chapter according to which there were quantities of food remaining after Muhammad officiated at a meal and others that state that staying so long that the host exhausts his means of hospitality is sinful.[83]

Many *keuawen* Muslims feel that the distribution of food is the most significant element of the *slametan*. During this brief period links are forged between God, the saints, and the local community. Commensality defines the socio-mystical community and more than any other element of the ritual establishes the state of *slamet*. In the case of life crisis and other personal *slametan*, it multiplies the blessing accruing to the host or the individual he designates. By participating in the *slametan* the community contributes to the resolution of the individual crises and/or ensures a smooth transition between life stages. In communal *slametan* the distribution of blessed food serves as the basis for social harmony. It ensures and even distribution of the types of blessing requires for a tranquil society in which individuals can attain material prosperity and spiritual development.

The *Slametan* as a Social/Mystical Rite

In Yogyakarta, *slametan* are performed on the occasion of, and often replace, rites required by the *Shari'ah*. In many respects the meanings of the *slametan* parallel those of liturgical prayer. Differences are based on a distinction between *Shari'ah*-centric and mystical notions of community. While they share the Islamic concern with community, *Santri* and *kejawen* Muslims define it in different ways, which influences their interpretations of the *slametan* and the *Shari'ah*. For *santri*, the public rituals required by the *Shari'ah* define a community – be it a village or an urban mosque, a *pesantren*, or, in an extended sense, all those who participate in the *hajj*, in the feast of sacrifice, and so on. For traditional *santri* participation in the *haul* of major saints serves a similar purpose. Participation in the public *Id* services is of great importance because it constitutes a supra-local Muslim community. Sermons often express the hope that relationships within this community will extend beyond ritual and urge people to make the mosque and *Shari'ah*-centric Islam the focus of social, economic, and political life.

---

[82] Ibid., p. 151, RS 746–47.
[83] Ibid., p. 144, RS 710.

Kejawen ritual transforms a preexisting group of people into a religious community. This may be a geographic area – a neighborhood, village, urban ward, or, at the level of state ceremonies, the entire kingdom; a kin group; or, in contemporary context, a government office or a private firm. The *slametan* links these individuals to common sources of blessing, thus sacralizing an existing entity that is not inherently religious. While traditional *santri* consider the *Slametan* to be important, they understand it as a supplementary source of blessing. For *kejawen* Muslims the reverse is true. The *Slametan* is essential, and *Shari'ah*-centric piety is supplemental.

The public rituals of *Shari'ah*-centric and *kejawen* Islam are both understood temporarily to abrogate hierarchical structures on which Javanese social organization and social and linguistic discourse is based. While there are multiple, and often conflicting sources of status – age, court rank, wealth, education, religious attainment, teacher/student links, and so on – *santri* and *kejawen* Javanese share a concern with social hierarchy. These concerns are expressed in the traditional political system and even in the complex system of speech levels in the Javanese language. In most instances Javanese interact and speak on the basis of assumptions concerning the relative status of social actors. Ritual is among the few exceptions to this rule.

Santri informants state that, in the Friday prayer, status distinctions are dissolved and that the individuals stand before God on an equal footing. This is a clear example of Victor Turner calls *communitas*.[84] Among the most common topics in sermons are the community of Islam and the theory that Islam is "democratic" because it does not recognize religiously based social distinctions. One informant explained that prayer is submission to God and that the differences between God and Humankind are so great that in this context, distinctions among humans are not important. This does not mean that *santri* are anti-hierarchical in other contexts. It is often stated that God will not bless anyone who is disrespectful to his religious teacher and that blessing flows to the student only through the teacher.

Many Sufis understand submission to God in terms of the theory of mystical union. Sufi communities in the Middle East and in South Asia are dominated by *turuq* (mystical brotherhoods). Social relations are characterized by a strict hierarchy based on saint / disciple or student / teacher relationships. Submission to religious superiors facilitates the attainment of higher mystical states leading to union with God. In this state, known in Java as the union of servant and lord, the interests, thoughts, and emotions of the disciple are merged with those of the saint. In classical Sufi formulations of the mystical path, this relationship involves a single disciple and his mystical guide. In Java it is also used as the basis for a mystically defined notion of community that supplements that defined by the law and liturgical prayer. The union of servant and lord is a social as well as mystical state that should, ideally, characterize all hierarchical relations including those on which the state is founded. It is often used to describe relationships between the Sultan and his subjects.

When describing the effects of the *slametan* Javanese often say that everyone is equal and that they do not wish to split up. This suggested that the *slametan* can

---

[84]See Chapter 5 for a more detailed discussion.

be understood a ritual means for obtaining the psycho-social state Victor Turner described as communitas.[85] This equality and unity the *slametan* strives to establish extends beyond the human community including the deceased saints as well. This state of equality is obtained as the consequence of a state of spiritual union with the saints, the result of which is that human status distinctions are obliterated. *Kejawen* informants frequently observe that in the *slametan* the hosts, guests and saints attain a state of tranquility approaching that of mystical union. Like union with God, this state is momentary. When guests leave, the resume their normal positions in the social hierarchy. But the ritual is thought to establish the social condition of union of servant and lord, which is believed to be essential if individuals and the community are to be truly *slamet*. Thus the purpose of the ritual is not to destroy hierarchy but to ensure its proper articulation. *Slamet* is, therefore, not the social equivalent of *fana'* (mystical union), but of *baqa*, the state of tranquility to which the mystic returns.

From this we may conclude that in Yogyakarta, the functions of *slametan* parallel those of liturgical prayer but in a socio-religious context dominated by Sufi notions of mystical union. Herein lies the unique quality of the *slametan*. Many of its components are drawn from non-Javanese Islamic textual and ritual traditions. But as a totality it exemplifies the use of esoteric Sufi concepts as a social as well as religious ideal.

The *Slametan* and Local Islam

In this chapter it has been argued that the *Slametan*, which Geertz has identified as the core ritual of *kejawen* Islam, is, in historical and comparative perspectives Islamic, not animistic as is commonly assumed. These arguments have implications for the understanding of both the Islamicization of Java and the nature of Local Islam in general. They require us to abandon the view that Java is trivially Muslim. The question the *slametan* raises is that of how the Javanese were so thoroughly converted to a version of Islam that combines elements of Middle Eastern and South Asian popular piety with esoteric mystical theory. This issue is explored in more detail in Chapter 5.

Myths concerning the origin of the *slametan* connect it with saints and Muslim kings believed to have established Islam as the official religion of central Java. They also speak of the relationship between royal and popular variants of *kejawen* Islam and the Islamicization of older religious concerns. There are two myths: one emphasizes the religious responsibilities of Javanese kings, the other conversion to Islam:

> The kings of Majapahit [the last Hindu-Javanese kingdom] used to have rituals at which offerings of food were presented to the people. At the time of Demak [one of the first Islamic states] this practice was discontinued and as a result crops were poor and many people went hungry. The Sultan of Demak asked Sunan Kalijaga [one of the nine *wali*] what he should do about this. Sunan Kalijaga replied that even though he was a Muslim he had a duty to provide for the well being of his people and to teach them Islam. He then

---

[85] See Turner, op. cit.

instructed the Sultan on how to perform the *Slametan* in ways which did not violate the tradition of the Prophet and told him to teach it to his subjects.

This myth speaks of the importance of state ceremonies, ritual meals, and the continuity of Hinduism and Islam. It focuses on the social interpretation of the concept of the union of servant and lord and on the political/religious theory that state ceremonies contribute to prosperity and tranquility. Informants state that one of the purposes of the *Garebeg Malud*, which is the subject of Chapter 5, is to ensure agricultural fertility. This indicates a connection between veneration of the prophet and fertility, preserving an ancient theme in Javanese religion, but casting it in Muslim garb. The myth also refers to the processes through which pre-Islamic religious concerns may be retained in local Islams. What remains are culturally specified goals of ritual performance, which are accomplished by Muslim means.

The second myth, which also concerns the *Garebeg Malud*, is more directly concerned with the court/village axis in the Islamic era.

To celebrate the *malud* regional lords and palace officials were called to the court. Officials of the religious department performed *dihkr* in the mosque while giving explanations about religion and the confession of faith to people thronging to the mosque to see and hear *gamelan* [Javanese orchestra]. As a means of attracting people to the mosque a large *gamelan* was played as it was carried to the mosque after the evening prayer. In the courtyard of the mosque, two large matching *gamelan* were placed in buildings on the right and left and played constantly in the afternoon and evening except during the hours of prayer. Many people were attracted to the sound of the *gamelan* and came to the mosque. There, while waiting to receive portions of food which had been made ready for them, they received instruction concerning the ritual duties of Islam and the biography of the prophet. They received *sedekah* [charity, in this case food] over which a *donga* had been recited and [they] ate together. Those who were attracted to Islam were then instructed to recite the confession of faith in order to enter the Islamic religion. This was done every day for 7 days. The last day was the climax of the festival. Beginning in the morning Sultan Syah Alam Akbar, as Kalifah of the Muslim community, sat in front of officials, regional lords and important functionaries. *Gunungan* were carried from the palace to the mosque for a *Slametan* organized by the king for the people. At the time of the evening prayer the sultan, followed by the officials came down from the palace and walked to the mosque. There the sultan served as *imam* for the prayer. After the prayer, the *pengulu* recited a *donga*, then the Sultan ate the *slametan* food together with the people.

This myth speaks of the *slametan* as a conversion ritual. *Kraton* tradition maintains that during the early Muslim era circumcisions were performed at the *malud* and that many people became Muslims so that they could receive the Sultan's blessing.

Conjointly, the two myths provide a basis for understanding the origins of Javanese state ceremonies and their influence on popular ritual. They suggest a strong conceptual link between court and village formulations of *kejawen* Islam and that the *santri* hierarchy played a vital role in the formulation and dissemination of *kejawen* Islam. Given the centrality of the *slametan* in the Javanese imperial cult, it cannot be interpreted as an element of an archaic village religion. Its wide distribution suggests that the relationship between court and village religion is similar to that described by Tambiah for the Theravada Buddhist cultures of mainland Southeast Asia where royal cults are models for village ritual.[86]

If the history of the *slametan* is understood as that of a state ceremony that spread to the general population rather than an animistic response to a foreign religion, the process of Islamicization can be viewed as one in which Islamic states strove to redefine an existing court-village axis in Islamic terms. The links among Islamic texts, royal, and popular *slametan* suggest that non-Javanese texts and modes of ritual action served as a model for the formulation of a Sufi imperial cult in central Java and that this served, in turn, as a model for popular piety and ritual performance.

Conclusions

The *slametan* provides an example of the complexity of local Islams. Questions concerning the degree to which it is "Islamic" can be phrased either in the context of anthropological theory or Islamic theology. Clearly it includes elements, especially varieties of food and spirits which are unique to Java. But they are unique to Javanese *Islam*. The ritual can be understood as the product of *bricolage* through which concepts derived from various Muslim textual and ritual traditions and elements of Islamicate culture that transcend locality are fused with things specifically Javanese.[87] It is reasonable to suggest that other local Islams are equally complex. If we are to understand them it is essential that more attention be paid to both the ways

---

[86] S. Tambiah, *World Conqueror and World Renoucer: A Study of Buddhism and Polity in Thailand against a Historical Background*, Cambridge: Cambridge University Press, 1974.

[87] Beatty's analysis of the *slametan* in Banyuwangi in extreme eastern Java is exemplary of the ways in which the process of *bricolage* can be shaped by the social and political context in which it occurs. A. Beatty, "Adam and Eve and Vishnu: Syncreticism in the Javanese Slametan," *Journal of the Royal Anthropological Institute*, (N.S.) vol. 2, 271–288. In most respects Beatty's analysis is congruent with that presented here. However, as he observes Banyuwangi was among the last areas of Java to become Islamic. Here, conversion to Islam was encouraged by the Dutch who, when the conquered the region in the late eighteenth century completely destroyed the "high culture" of the kingdom of Blambangan. In the 1960s Banyuwangi was one of the strongholds of the Indonesian Communist Party. The massacres of communists and their supporters in 1965 and 1966, in which Muslim organizations played major roles, led many in the region to "reconvert" to Hinduism. Beatty reports that in some instances Muslims and Hindus continue to participate in *Slametan*, though often with prayers appropriate for their respective communities, and that they share a common concern with social order and harmony. Unfortunately his otherwise penetrating analysis is limited by failure to appreciate the Islamic roots of Javanese mysticism (see Chapters 2 and 4) and his characterization of traditional *santri* Islam as unreflective and being based on "old-fashioned rural seminaries where village boys memorized the *Qur'an* and magical formula for healing" – p. 276. This is simply not the case. Many of the *pesantren* (Islamic Boarding Schools) to which he refers are, in fact, Islamic theological academies of the first rank. More careful consideration of the complexities of the textual foundations of all varieties of Javanese Islam would have greatly enriched his analysis. I cannot speak to his statement that in Banyuwangi the *slametan* is not referred to as an Islamic ritual. This may reflect either regional differences or the fact that by the early 1990s, during which his field work was conducted, the shift from *agama* to *kebudayaan* as a term of reference for *kejawen* ritual practice was well underway.

in which received Islams are interpreted in local context and to the historical, economic political and religious factors influencing the communication of texts, rituals,
and ideas within the larger Muslim world. When the question is phrased theologically it is necessary to acknowledge that Javanese Muslims have multiple voices.
There is not one Javanese Local Islam. There are many. Some consider the *slametan*
to be an essential component of Islam, others believe it to be *bidah, kufarat* and
shirk: unlawful religious innovation, unbelief and polytheism. Still others maintain
that it is an element of Javanese culture, but not actually Islamic. Others describe
is as an element of Muslim culture (*Kebudayaan Muslim*), in contrast to Islam,
defined as formal acts of submission to God. In the late 1970s the *slametan* was
often referred to it as being an element of *Islam Jawa* or *Agama Jawa*. There has
been a gradual shift towards referring to it as *Kebudayaan*. This has not, however,
diminished its' significance in the religious lives of Javanese even among many who
do not call it "religion".

Photos

Slametan

Slametan at Yogyakarta Mosque

Boys as well as adult men
participate in slametan

Sajen are the most basic Javanese offerings
and are almost always included in slametan

Simple sajen

Sajen at Kraton Surakarta

Chapter 4
Order and Meaning in the Yogyakarta *Kraton*

In his classic article *Order in the Atoni House*, Clark Cunningham described the ways in which the Atoni of Timor construct dwelling space as a representation of social and cosmological order.[1] His major thesis was that the analysis of architectural symbolism can be used to discern the basic structural principles that frame social life and discourse. In a more general sense his analysis of the symbolism of the Atoni house resembles those of Heine-Geldern and Eliade who have argued that there is a global tendency for domestic architecture to reflect cosmological structures.[2] This chapter will examine the architectural, political and religious symbolism of the Yogyakarta *kraton*. The *kraton* is a Javanese house, but a very special one. It is the house of the Sultan who is understood as being Allah's representative on earth and as the "perfect man" of classical Sufism. Like that of the Atoni house, the architecture of *kraton* is an earthly representation of cosmic order. It is also an *axis mundi* through which God's blessing and mercy flow into the world and a stage for ritual performances which define the Sultanate as a Muslim community.

Heine-Geldern observed that the architecture and iconography of Southeast Asian palaces constitutes a symbolic representation of the cosmos and that by creating the palace and the state as cosmic models, the kings establishes their religious legitimacy. This theme echoes through most subsequent studies of kingship and religion in the "Indianized states" of Southeast Asia. In general, the religious and political significance of the Javanese *kraton* resembles that of the royal palaces of the Indianized states of mainland Southeast Asia and pre-Islamic Java and is expressive of what Eliade refers to as "the symbolism of the center."[3] But unlike either the Hindu and Buddhist palaces of Southeast Asia or the Ancient Middle Eastern examples cited by Eliade, the Javanese *kraton* is not a replica of a cosmic mountain. Nor is it arranged as a *mandala* or set of concentric circles. Its architectural and

---

[1] C. Cunningham, "Order in the Atoni House," *Bijdragen tot de Taal-, Land- en Volkenkunde*, vol. 70, 1964, pp. 34–68.

[2] R. Heine-Geldern, "Conceptions of State and Kingship in Southeast Asia," Far Eastern Quarterly, 2, 1942. M. Eliade, *The Myth of the Eternal Return or, Cosmos and History*. Princeton: Princeton University Press, 1954.

[3] Op. cit., pp. 12–20.

M. Woodward, *Java, Indonesia and Islam*, Muslims in Global Societies Series 3,   137
DOI 10.1007/978-94-007-0056-7_4, © Springer Science+Business Media B.V. 2011

geometric form is linear, comprising a series of gates and passages oriented on a north-south axis. The cosmic structure depicted in the Yogyakarta *kraton* is that of a Javanese variant of Islamic mysticism. The iconography, symbolism and architecture of the palace depict the structure of the Muslim cosmos, relationships between Sufism and the *Shari'ah* (Islamic law), introspective and cosmological formulations of the mystical path, the descent and ascent of the perfect man.[4]

The *kraton* is said to have been designed by Sultan Hamengkubuwana I. Palace documents state that it was completed in 1756. There have, however, been numerous additions and modification, a practice which continues to the present day. Court officials explain that most of these changes involved the construction of larger and more elaborate structures in place of older ones and that the basic design and meaning of the various elements of the palace have not changed in nearly two and a half centuries. The *kraton* encompasses an area of approximately 14,000 square meters, including hundreds courtyards and trees, buildings, open pavilions, walls, gates, courtyards and trees, each of which has one or more religious meanings. It is a complex, polysemic symbolic system weaving the diverse threads of Javanese religious and political thought together into a single coherent system focusing on the person of the Sultan. The *kraton* can, therefore, be understood as a text and the doctrinal statements it contains compared with those of Javanese literature and informants. This understanding of the religious meanings of the *kraton* is shared by many Yogyakarta Javanese and by the court itself. In the introduction to Brongtodiningrat's guide to the *kraton* Hadiatmaja explains:

> Every part of the *kraton*, every tree within it, every decoration, every chronogram, every building and gate will speak to you. However you must understand its language, which is the language of culture, religion and mysticism.

----

[4]The lineal structure of the Javanese *kraton* differs fundamentally from those of the Hindu and Buddhist palaces of mainland Southeast Asia and of pre-Muslim Java. Hindu and Buddhist palaces replicate the structure of the cosmos, forming a mandala or series of concentric circles. The Buddhist palaces of Thailand, Burma and Buddhist Java are structural replicas of Mount Meru, the cosmic mountain at the center of the Buddhist universe. The Javanese *kraton* is, therefore, a clear departure for the Indianized traditions of pre-Muslim Java. The analysis of the Yogyakarta *kraton* has major implications for the more general study of Javanese religion. The thesis that the architectural symbolism of houses, palaces and temples reflects that of the cosmos as a whole is one of the central axioms of Southeast Asian cultural studies. This is, in large measure, the reason why Clark Cunningham's *Order in the Atoni House* is such a classic. It is also the reason while the earlier version of this chapter included in *Islam in Java: Normative Piety and Mysticism in the Sultanate of Yogyakarta* proved to be extremely controversial. Indonesianists committed to the Islamaphobic Orientalism of Dutch colonial and missionary scholarship were outraged at the suggestion that anything as obviously sacred as the *kraton* could possibly be Islamic. M. C. Ricklefs, *Journal of the Asian Studies Association of Australia*, vol. 14(3), 1991, resorted to combination of *ad hominem* remarks directed as important officials of the Yogyakarta court as well as myself and what appear to be intentional failures to note references to readily available Javanese texts in an attempt to dismiss this analysis as "unhelpful." Mitsuo Nakamura, who is well known for his Islam affirming studies of Javanese culture, was more positive. He wrote: "This is an astonishing discovery." M. Nakamura, Review of "Islam in Java" in: *Journal of Asian Studies*, 1990:718.

The discussion of the religious meanings of the Yogyakarta *kraton* presented in this paper is based on a series of descriptive texts written by palace officials and on interviews conducted in Yogyakarta between 1978 and 2009. The most important of these texts in Brongtodiningrat's *Arti Kraton Yogyakarta* (The Meaning of the Yogyakarta *Kraton*), the publication of which was authorized by the late Sultan Hamengkubuwana IX, and which palace officials consider to be authoritive. The text is, however, extremely dense and difficult to interpret because it presumes an understanding of the complexities of Javanese/Islamic mystical thought. I discussed it at length with numerous palace officials and used it as a guide on many journeys through the *kraton* over three decades.[5]

The *kraton* is a text, but it is more than a text. It is the sacred precinct defining the state and society. In this respect it is the analog of the *Ka'ba* at Mecca which is the center and *axis mundi* of the Muslim world as a whole. Just as the *Ka'ba* defines the Muslim community as a totality, the Yogyakarta palace defines the Sultanate as a local Muslim community, with the Sultan, who is also known as *Kalifutallah* (the Caliph or representative of God) as its head. The *kraton* is the mystical center and spiritual body of the Sultanate, serving as a container (J. *wadah*) for the manifestation of the divine essence (J. *Dat*) represented by the Sultan. It is a stage for the performance of royal rituals through which the spiritual power of the dynasty and the blessing of God are infused into the population and territory of the kingdom. It is thought that by moving from one section of the *kraton* to another the Sultan controls the flows of blessing, and power into, through and out of the sacred precinct and that depending on his exact position, he represents either the transcendent or immanent characteristics of God.

The *Kraton*, the Ka'ba and the Perfect Man

Eliade has argued that the replication of celestial or cosmological archetypes in temples, palaces and in ritual is among the most common features of pre-modern religious thought.[6] At first glance Islam might appear to provide an important exception to his thesis. Unlike those of Christianity, Buddhism and most other pre-modern religious traditions, the central texts of Islam have relatively little to say about cosmology or cosmogonic mythology. While the *Qur'an* often touches on cosmological themes, it is more explicitly concerned with the nature of God and his relationship

---

[5] Behrend presents an alternative interpretation of central Javanese *kraton* in which he argues that the symbolism of Mount Meru, rather than the Sufi Perfect Man is the celestial archetype on which palace architecture is based. T. Behrend, "*Kraton* and Cosmos in Traditional Java," *Archipel*, 37, 1989, pp. 173–187. Unfortunately, Behrend relies largely on pre-Islamic sources and the assumption that one can use such sources to explain contemporary Javanese religion and symbolism. He does not appear to have encountered the contemporary texts discussed here. This is peculiar, at least, because they are available, at nominal cost, at the entrance to the Yogyakarta *Kraton*, and the old royal cemetery at Kota Gede, and have been continuously since 1975.

[6] Op. cit., passim.

or covenant with humanity.[7] The *Qur'an* is not a chronologically ordered universal history, nor does it include a detailed, explicit cosmogonic mythology.

This does not, however, mean that cosmology has not been among the central concerns of Muslim scholars, but only that textual locus of Islamic cosmology and cosmogony is, for the most part, external to the *Qur'an*. Cosmogonic myths, cosmologies and universal histories are found in works on *tafsir* or Quranic exegesis, astronomy, philosophy and mysticism rather than in the *Qur'an*.[8] The fact that cosmology is not among the central themes of the *Qur'an* has contributed to the great diversity of cosmological thought in the later Muslim tradition. Nasr has argued that there is a strong tendency of Islamic cosmologies to employ the concept of the unity of God (A. *Tawhid*) as a starting point for cosmological speculation about the natural world, the mystical path leading to union with God, planetary astronomy and the human mind. The result is a rich and highly varied corpus of cosmological texts and doctrines.

The diversity of Islamic cosmological thought has significant implications for the study of cosmological symbolism in Islamic Southeast Asia. One can not look to a single text or closely related body of texts to find the celestial archetypes which are replicated in Southeast Asian (and other) Islamic architectures and sacred geographies.[9] Because there is not a single Universalist cosmology, or even a limited range of cosmological beliefs and doctrines, the ethnographer or historian of religions encounters a vast and sometime perplexing array of cosmologies. To make sense of this variety it is necessary to look not for a precise correspondence between texts on the one hand and ritual and architectural symbolism on the other, but rather to the ways in which sets of more general cosmological concepts are used in the construction of particular cosmologies.

In this chapter it will be argued that the Yogyakarta *Kraton* can be read as a cosmological text which builds on four cosmological principles common in the

---

[7] For a thematic analysis of the *Qur'an* see F. Rahman, *Major Themes of the Qur'an* Minneapolis: Bibliotheca Islamica, 1980.

[8] For an overview of Islamic cosmological and cosmogonic thought from the classical period see A. Wensinck, *The Ideas of the Western Semites Concerning the Navel of the Earth*. Amsterdam: Johannes Muller, 1916 and Nasr, S. Hossein, *An Introduction to Islamic Cosmological Doctrines*. Boulder: Shambhala, 1978.

[9] In this respect of study of cosmology, symbolism and sacred architecture in Islamic Southeast Asia is more challenging than it is on the Theravada Buddhist Mainland. On cosmology and sacred geography in Buddhist Thailand see S. J. Tambiah, *World Conqueror and World Renouncer. A Study of Buddhism and Polity in Thailand Against a Historical Background*. Cambridge: Cambridge University Press, 1976. The Javanese cosmological text most closely resembling the *kraton* cosmology is the nineteenth century *Serat Wirid* by the Surakarta court poet Roggowarsito which Hadiwijono describes as "an example of the Javanese attempt to create unity in the variegated streams of Javanese mysticism," H. Hadiwijono, *Man in the Present Javanese Mysticism*. Baarn: Bosch and Keuning, 1967, p. 12. It is, however, clear that the *kraton* is not based on *Serat Wirid* or probably on any other textual model, but rather that its meanings draw on a wide range of similar mystical traditions. It is not a physical representation of a text or group of texts but is rather an architectural product of the same process of *bricolage* from which literary and ritual texts emerged.

Javanese and other Islamic textual traditions. These are the Quranic notion that the *Ka'ba* is the house or sanctuary of God, the Sufi concept of the perfect man, the idea that the human body is a microcosm, and as Nasr puts it "the symbol of Universal existence," and the simultaneous immanence and transcendence of God.[10] The interaction of these themes results in a distinction between cosmologies centered on the notion to ascent of an *axis mundi* moving towards a transcendent God, and others centered on the notion of a journey into the self, moving towards an immanent God. Both themes are expressed in the iconography and architecture of the Yogyakarta *kraton*.[11]

Sufism is the mystical tradition of Islam. While modernist and fundamentalist Muslims are often critical of mysticism, at times denouncing it as "unbelief", it was for centuries a major force in Islamic religious thought and popular devotion. At the time Islam came to Southeast Asia, and until the rise of modernist movements such as Muhammadiyah in the early twentieth century, it is safe to say that there were few, if any, Javanese Muslims who were not also Sufis. Two seemingly abstract and difficult Sufi theories provide the key to understanding the architecture and symbolism of the Yogyakarta *kraton*: that of the "perfect man" who has full knowledge of the Divine Will and Essence and the view that the true *Ka'ba* is located in the human heart rather than at Mecca.

The doctrine of the perfect man is plays a central role in the teachings of the great Sufi master Ibn al-'Arabi (1165–1240) whose works profoundly influenced the development of Islam in South and Southeast Asia. Nicholson describes the perfect man as the saint who: "fully realized his essential oneness with the Divine Being and who, Bodhisattva like, guides his disciples along the path he has trodden."[12] Chittick describes the relationship between the perfect man and divine perfection in the following terms:

> In the case of perfect man, spiritual realization has open up the imagination to the actual vision of the embodiment of God when He discloses Himself in theophany. He does not know how God Discloses Himself, but he sees Him doing so. He understands the truth of God's similarity with all things through a God-given vision.[13]

The descent of the perfect man from the Absolute and his return to it are among the central themes of Ibn al-'Arabi's thought. Chittick describes this mystical journey as follows:

> As an existent thing who lives at once on every level of the cosmos, perfect man embraces in himself every hierarchy. But as a human individual who has come into existence and

---

[10]Op. cit., p. 234

[11] This distinction is among the basic themes of Ibn al-Arabi's understanding of God which has had a profound influence on Javanese religious thought. See W. Chittick, *The Sufi Path of Pnowledge: Ibn al-Arabi's Metaphysics of Imagination*. Albany: State University of New York Press, 1989, p. 9.

[12]R. Nicholson, *Studies in Islamic Mysticism*. Cambridge: Cambridge University Press, 1921, p. 78.

[13]Op. cit., p. 29.

then returned to his Creator, he has tied together the Origin and Return. He lives fully and consciously on all the levels of descent through which light becomes separate from Light and on all the levels of the ascent through which light retraces its steps and human intelligence rejoins divine knowledge.[14]

The equation of the *Ka'ba* and the heart is another important theme in Sufi thought. Chittick summarizes Ibn al-Arabi's understanding of the equation of the *Ka'ba* and the heart as follows:

Ibn al-Arabi compares the heart to the *ka'ba*, making it the "noblest house in the man of faith" (III 250.24) He also declares that it is the throne of God (*al-'arsh*) in the microcosm, alluding here to the oft-quoted *hadith qudsi*, [revelation external to the *Qur'an*] "My earth and My heaven embrace me not, but the heart of My believing servant does embrace Me."[15]

The relationship between the soul, the body and God is often explained by reference to the symbolism of the *Ka'ba* and the rites of the *hajj* (pilgrimage to Mecca). The *Ka'ba* is an irregular cubical structure located near the center of the great mosque in Mecca. It is the chief object of the *hajj* and the *qiblah* (A. direction of prayer) towards which all mosques are oriented. The *Ka'aba* also figures prominently in Islamic cosmology and creation mythology. According to these traditions it is the earthly representation of the throne of God and the sanctuary of Adam, the perfect man. It is also described as the "house of God" and the center of the universe.

One of the most common Islamic cosmologies includes seven heavens, the earth and seven under worlds. At the center of each of these cosmic levels is a sanctuary. That of the highest heaven is the throne of God, while the *Ka'aba* is that of the earth which is the central layer standing between the heavens and the under worlds. A vertical axis runs through each of these sanctuaries so that if the throne of God were to fall to earth it would land directly on top of the *Ka'ba* which is then not only the center of this world, but of the entire universe. Of these sanctuaries only the *Ka'ba* and the *Bait al-Ma'mur* (frequented house) are mentioned in the *Qur'an*. The *Bait al-Ma'mur* was originally located in the Garden of Eden in the seventh heaven and is described as a ruby red tent in which Adam lived prior to the fall. It was brought to earth when Adam complained that he could no longer hear the songs of the angels surrounding the throne of God. God instructed Adam to circumambulate the tent, just as the angels walk around the throne. He also promised Adam that all future prophets would congregate at the *Ka'ba* and that it would be center of their respective cults. The tent remained at Mecca until the time of Noah when it was removed to the first heaven. It will return to the Garden of Eden on the Day of Judgment. The present *Kab'a* is thought to have been constructed by Abraham with the aid of the angel Gabriel. The black stone which pilgrims attempt to kiss is said to be a relic of the *Bait al- Ma'mur which* swallowed the covenant made between God and the children of Adam.[16]

---

[14]Op. cit., p. 30.

[15]Op. cit. p. 107.

[16]See A. Wensinck, "Ka'ba" in H Gibb and J. Kramers, *The Sorter Encyclopedia of Islam*. Leiden: E.J. Brill, 1953, pp. 191–198.

The spot on which the *Ka'ba* is constructed is believed to be the first part of the world to be created and the highest point on the earth, having emerged from the primeval ocean 2000 years before the creation of the world.[17] It is the *axis mundi* of the Muslim cosmos being the location at which communication with the upper and lower realms is possible. The religious and mystical import of the *hajj* is determined by the fact that prayer at the *Ka'ba* is held to be the same as that performed by the angels in the presence of God. It is perhaps for this reason that some of the Sufis who reject the law and other aspects of normative Islamic piety place such great importance on the *hajj*. The *hajj* is believed to be a source of mystical inspiration and prayer at the *Ka'ba* a means of attaining union with God.[18] But according to many Sufis the true *Ka'ba* is not the stone structure located at Mecca, but the house of God found in the human heart. Nicholson observes that:

> They have invested these rites and ceremonies with a new meaning; they have allegorized them, but they have not abandoned them. Take the pilgrimage, for example. In the eyes of the genuine Sufi it is null and void unless each of the successive religious acts which it involves is accompanied by corresponding movements of the heart.[19]

Classical Sufism uses the equation of the *Ka'ba* and the heart in a metaphoric sense to demonstrate the primacy of mysticism over normative piety, and to establish the centrality of mystical practice in religious life. The Turkish mystic Yunus Emre, for example, states that: "When you seek God, seek Him in your heart – He is not in Jerusalem, nor in Mecca nor in the *hajj*"[20].

Muhammad bin al-Fadl explains the link between mystic contemplation of God and pilgrimage to the *Ka'ba* as follows:

> I wonder at those who seek the House of God in this world; why do they not seek to contemplate him in their hearts? For sometimes they find the House, sometimes they fail to find it, and contemplation they might always find. If it is incumbent on them to visit a stone, where they may behold Him, once a year, surely there is a greater obligation to visit the heart, where He may be contemplated hundreds of times each day. For the true sanctuary is the place where contemplation is.[21]

Many Javanese mystics understand the equation of the *Ka'ba* and the heart is quite literally. The nineteenth century Surakarta text *Serat Wirid* states that the *Ka'ba*, which is referred to as *Betal Mukaram*[22] (the holy house), the *Betal Makmur*

[17] 1. The most readily available classical source on the creation of the *Kab'ah* is F. Rosenthal, *The History of al-Tabari Volume I General Introduction and From the Creation to the Flood*. Albany: State University of New York Press, 1989.

[18] A. Schimmel, *The Mystical Dimens of Islam*. Chapel Hill: University of North Carolina Press, 1975, pp. 191–198.

[19] R. Nicholoson, *The Mystics of Islam. An Introduction to Sufism*. New York: Schocken Books, 1975, pp. 91–92.

[20] Schimmel, op. cit., p. 106.

[21] Quoted in.J. Smith and Y. Haddad, *The Islamic Understanding of Death and Resurrection*. Albany: State University of New York Press, 1978, p. 212.

[22] 1.From Arabic *Bait al-Mu'haram*, which has the same meaning and can be used to refer to the *Ka'ba*.

(A. *Bait al- Ma'mur*) and Solomon's temple at Jerusalem (J. *Betal Mukadas*, A. *Bait al-Makdis*) are located in the head, the chest and the genitals respectively. Mind (J. *budi*), the soul (J. *suksmo*), passion (J. *nepsu*), feeling (J.*rasa*) and the divine essence are located in the head and the chest, while feeling, the divine essence and creative power are located in the genitals.[23] This section of *Serat Wirid* is a description of the spiritual and physical characteristics of the perfect man. The doctrine it presents has exerted a profound influence on contemporary Javanese mysticism and the Yogyakarta royal cult. The teaching of the perfection of man serves as the basis of Javanese theories of anatomy and medical practice and as a model for the interaction of passion, faith, the mind and the soul in the human body as is discussed in Chapter 2. The architecture and symbolism of the Yogyakarta *Kraton* are based on a similar understanding of the heart, the *Ka'ba* and the descent and ascent of the perfect man. These are among the most esoteric of Sufi teachings. They are important in Java in part because of their mystical significance, but also because they are the basis of the Javanese/Islamic theory of kingship. As Milner observes, through out the Islamic world of Southeast Asia, the teaching of the perfect man was strongly associated with sacral kingship. Sultans have claimed to be both God's representative on earth and the perfect man of Ibn al-'Arabi's understanding of Sufism.[24]

The *Kraton* and the Mystical Path

The *kraton* is a model of the body of the perfect man and the paths leading to perfection. While the architecture of the *kraton* subsumes and includes a representation of the *axis mundi*, this is made possible by the fact that the heart of the perfect man is equated with the pillar of the universe and the *Ka'ba*. The *kraton* has nine gates which represent the openings in the human body which according to *Serat Wirid* must be closed in meditation as well as in Muslim mortuary ritual.[25] It is divided into three principal segments, each of which includes a throne which is a representation of one of the divine sanctuaries in the human body.

The representation of the human body in the architecture and symbolism of the *kraton* is illustrative of the influence of Sufi understandings of relationships between humanity and divinity in Javanese religious thought. For Ibn al-Arabi and other Sufis the human body is the perfect microcosm. Chittick describes this relationship as follows:

---

[23] Hadiwijono op. cit., pp. 108–109 None of the information on the religious meanings of sections of the *kraton* are included in the Dutch literature. According to K.P.H. Poerwokoesoemo, the reason is that the Javanese chose to keep them in ignorance.

[24] A. Milner, "Islam and the Muslim State," *Islam in South-East Asia.* (Ed.), M. Hooker. Leiden: E.J. Brill, 1983, pp. 23-49.

[25] The association of the *kraton* gates and the openings in the body is well known in Yogyakarta, however, I have been unable to discover which gate is linked with any particular bodily orifice. I was told by several princes that there was not a precise correspondence and by others that this knowledge had been lost during either the Java War or the Japanese occupation.

The microcosm reflects the macrocosm in two ways which are of particular significance for Ibn al-Arabi's teachings: as a hierarcy of existence and as a divine form, a theomorphic entity. The three basic worlds of the macrocosm – the spiritual, imaginal, and the corporeal – are represented in man by the spirit (*ruh*), soul (*nafs*) and body (*jism*). [26]

In Ibn al-Arabi's theological anthropology the spirit is the spirit of God, the corporeal body is the clay from which Adam was created. The soul stands between the two on a hierarchy of being. The divine names and attributes are all concentrated in the microcosm of the human body. The journey of the soul is one from darkness to light, in which it seeks harmony with the spirit of God. The southern third of the *kraton* depicts the descent of the perfect man from the divine essence and the birth of a royal infant. It may be read only from south to north. The northern third of the palace is a model of introspective and cosmological formulations of the mystical path. Read from south to north it depicts the path leading to momentary union with God, while from north to south it depicts the cosmological and eschatological paths leading to lasting union. Viewed from the south, the central segment of the *kraton* is the administrative center of the kingdom in which the concepts of loyalty and duty are of primary importance. This is equated with normative piety and devotion to God. Viewed from the north, passage to the center of the palace is equated with ascent of the *axis mundi*, entry into heaven and the attainment of permanent union with God. From this perspective the Sultan is the analog of the transcendent deity and his court of the angels who surround the throne of God.

The symbolism of the *kraton* and the Javanese symbolism in general make extensive use of word play and pseudo-etymologies.[27] This variety of symbolic thought is based on the proposition that the existence of a common set of phonetic features implies both an historical relationship and the intersection of the semantic fields of any pair of phonetically related terms. A similar process is used to establish semantic intersections through the comparison of the physical characteristics of objects nominally assigned to distinct semantic classes. Moreover, if either member of such a pair is a religious or mystical state or being, the other acquires a nearly identical set of religious meanings by virtue of the postulated intersection. This mode of symbolic thought is extremely productive in the sense that it may be used to generate a virtually unlimited number of symbol systems to express a relatively small set of meanings. It is used both as a mode of argument to establish connections between seemingly unrelated phenomena and as a way to construct metaphoric statements about aspects of mystical knowledge which can not be discussed openly.

---

[26] Op. cit., p. 17.

[27] Folk etymologies are one of the most common means through which Javanese attempt to unite diverse elements of mysticism and history. Any phonetic similarity is held to be sufficient grounds for positing an historical and mystical relationship between two terms, be they Arabic, Javanese, Sanskrit or even Indonesian. As Ricklefs observes many of the "folk etymologies" on which the symbolism of the *kraton* relies are wildly inaccurate when viewed from the perspective of historical linguistics. Ricklefs missed the point. From a Javanese perspective it is phonetics and not historical linguistics which is important. The critique of the analysis presented in this paper which he bases on supposedly incorrect etymologies is insignificant.

The symbolism of the *kraton*, and particularly that of the southern segment which concerns the processes of conception and birth relies extensively on this variety of symbolic thought. Many of the symbols of this section of the *kraton* are trees and other mundane objects which are linked to the Sufi doctrine of the descent of the perfect man by means of pseudo-etymologies.

The southern third of the *kraton* is divided into seven segments, each representing one of the steps in the descent of the perfect man. These states do not correspond exactly with those of *Serat Wirid* perhaps in part because they describe the birth of a royal infant (J.*Sang Anak*) rather than the descent of the proto-type of humanity. The first stage is represented by the villages of Krapyak and Mijen. Krapyak is located seven kilometers to the south of the *kraton*. It takes its name from a small two-story brick building located on the southern edge of the village which Hamengkubuwana I used for a hunting lodge. The literal meaning of the term *krapyak* is "fenced hunting preserve" It is used to refer to the *alam barzak* (J. from A. *al-barzak*) that is the abode of the soul after its separation from the divine essence but prior to its descent into an embryo.[28] According to court traditions the two concepts are associated because the Sultan kept deer in an enclosed area in exactly the same manner that God holds pre-created souls until the proper moment for them to descend into the world.

The village of Mijen is located immediately to the north of Krapyak. The term *Mijen* is held to be similar to *wiji* (J. sperm), which may be either male or female.[29] Male sperm is white and is the source of the spiritual body. Female sperm is red and is the source of passion and the material body. According to the Javanese theory of conception both are present in the body from the moment of birth and, like the soul, are held in reserve until needed and should be purified through prayer and meditation. The first stage in the development of the child is therefore the potential for human life which exists in heaven and the bodies of all humans.

The second stage is represented by the road leading from Mijen to the southern gate of the *kraton*. It is lined with *Asem* (J. tamarind) and *Tanjung* (J. a large tree with small white flowers) trees. *Asem* resembles *nengsemaken* (J. attractive) while *tanjung* is linked to the phrase *disanjung sanjung* (J. flattery). Together they symbolize the life of a child who is spoiled by his/her parents. It also refers to the childlike innocence of adults who have temporarily renounced sexuality for the sake

---

[28] In the most general sense the term *barzak* means barrier. In Muslim eschatology it is the state in which souls exist between death and judgement. Sufis have used it to refer to the border between the material and spiritual worlds. The view that the souls of unborn children as well as those of the dead abide in *barzak* is a logical outgrowth of the doctrine that souls were created from the *Nur Muhammad* (A. light of Muhammad) prior to the creation of the heavens and earth. This belief is common in Sufi theories of creation Massignon, op. cit., p. 452.

[29] Ricklefs questions this identification stating that Mijen is derived from *piji* meaning set aside. The English version of Brongtodiningrat!s text op. cit., p. 9, states: "This word comes from '*wiji*,' which means seed." The Indonesian version, op. cit., p. 13, states: "*Mijen, berasal dari perkataan Wiji (Benih).*" The literal translation of this is: "*Mijen*, which originates from the expression *Wiji* (semen)."

of purification. The *Nirbaya* gate (J. without difficulty) marks the onset of puberty. Trees symbolizing female and male puberty rites are planted at the gate. The fuzzy leaves of tamarind trees are referred to as *sinom* (J.) meaning young, and which is also used to refer to the short, fine hairs on a girl's forehead that are considered a mark of beauty. A pair of *Beringin* (*banyan*) trees named *Wok* is male puberty symbols. The term wok is derived from *brewok* (J. whiskers). The gate is associated with the *siraman* (J. bathing) ritual conducted for males at the time of circumcision and for females immediately prior to marriage. A related meaning for this gate is the awakening of sexual desire.

The third stage is the southern *Alon Alon* (J. square in front of a *kraton*). It is a representation of mature sexuality. The square is surrounded by two varieties of mango trees: *Pakel* and *Kuweni*. *Pakel* is associated with *akil baligh* (J.) the literal meaning of which is adult. *Kuweni* resembles *wani* (J. brave or to dare). In the center of the *Alon Alon* there is a pair of banyan trees from which the crowns have been pruned named *Supit Urang* (J. circumcision shrimp). Each tree is surrounded by a brick wall. The symbolism of these trees is complex. The term *Supit Urang* is said to refer to the penis (*supit*) and the clitoris (*urang*). The shape of the trees, the tops of which have been removed, is a reference to circumcision. The pair of trees represents the testicles while the walls are an expression of the fact that genitals must be covered or concealed.[30] Five roads crossing in front of the trees represent sensual desire and the five senses (J. *panca indriya*) while the empty space between the roads and the *kraton* represents unfulfilled desire. Taken as a whole, the southern *Alon Alon* symbolizes sexual desire and at a more esoteric level the longing for mystical union with God

The fourth stage is *Tratak Siti Inggil* a pavilion at the southern end of the *kraton*. It is surrounded by *Gayam* trees the shade and sweet smell of which is thought to calm the mind and emotions. It symbolizes the feelings of a pair of young lovers. The fifth is the *Siti Inggil* (J. high place). It is the site of one of the thrones, a symbol of sexual intercourse and the location of the sanctuary *betal muchadas*, which according to *Serat Wirid* is located in the genitals.

At audiences conducted at the southern *Siti Inggil* males and females were allowed to sit together. This symbolizes the closeness of a pair of young lovers. The pavilion is surrounded by red and white hibiscus plants the flowers of which intermingle. This symbolizes the mixture of male and female sperm in sexual intercourse. The entire complex is enclosed by walls and a pair of roads forming square open on the south named *Pamengkang* which is derived from *mekangkang* (J. to hold the legs wide apart). This structure represents a woman in the act of sexual intercourse. To the east and west of *Siti Inggil* there are tanks for bathing which represent the normative Muslim purification rites which must be performed after sexual contact.

---

[30]This interpretation was supplied by a Yogyakarta prince. He continued that the walls surrounding the two trees serve the same purpose as a *sarong* and observed that in Islam it is essential that the genitals be covered at all times.

The sixth stage in the development of the child in the *Kemandungan* courtyard located to the north of *Siti Inggil*. The term *kemandungan* is derived from *ngandung* (J. pregnant and to wait). The yard is planted with *Pelem* and *Kepel* trees (two varieties of mango) and *Cengkir Gading* (J. a small coconut palm). *Pelem* is associated with *gelem* which can mean either mutual understanding or sexual desire. *Kepel* is linked to *kempel* the meaning of which is to bring together. *Cengkir Gading* is a coconut used in the *tinkeban* ritual performed during the 7th month of pregnancy. Two doors on either side of the *Kemandungan* yard represent the passion and other evil influences endangering the unborn child.

The final stage in the development of the child is the *Kemagangan* courtyard and the *Gandungmlati* gate through which it is entered. *Gandungmlati* is the name of a light green color which, when observed in meditation, is thought to be the essence of God. Here, however, the term means birth and the narrow passage through this gate represents the birth process. The *Kemagangan* courtyard represents the state of early infancy and the potential of the child. It is derived from the term *magang* (J. apprentice). This is a reference to the Javanese belief that an infant is not fully human and that its potential for good or evil can not be determined. Two kitchens located on the east and west sides of the *Kemagangan* represent the care the child receives from its parents. The roads leading to them represent the negative and positive paths that the child may follow in life. The ideal course of life is that leading through the *Kemagangan* gate to the *Kedaton* (J. main section of the palace). passage through this gate is interpreted as entry into a life of service to both the Sultan and God.

These seven stages explain the birth of a child by describing the ultimate sources of the spiritual and physical bodies and the soul and then by tracing the development of the sexuality of its parents. This configuration differs somewhat from that of *Serat Wirid* and the cycle of prenatal rituals. It is reasonable to suggest that one of the reasons for this is that the system is designed to place the southern *Siti Inggil* at the *Betal Mukadas*. This is necessary because of the equation of the Sultan and the divine essence. For if the *kraton* is to be a model of the body of the perfect man, as well of his descent and ascent, the divine sanctuary must be occupied by the God as represented by the enthroned king. When applied to non-royal infants the southern third of the palace forms a cycle in that passing through the *Kamagangan* gate is representative of entry into the social world of the *Kedaton* and entering the cycle of development at Mijen. As soon as it is born the child begins to undergo the series of transformations described in this path which ultimately produces the next generation. If the southern section of the *kraton* is seen as a model of the birth and development of the total population of the kingdom, the final stages define each individual as a subject (J. *kuwala*) and the Sultan as lord (J. *gusti*). Service rendered to the Sultan is equated with devotion to God. A related interpretation supplied by a Yogyakarta prince is that loyalty to the Sultan is the same as devotion to God because the essence of God located in the genitals is also the same as the soul of the Sultan when he sits at the southern *Siti Inggil*. Carrying the logic of this equation one step further he observed the people of Yogyakarta are devoted to the Sultan because his spirit guided their conception and prenatal development.[31]

The remaining sections of the *kraton* are concerned with the mystical and religious paths followed by the Sultan and the manner in which he establishes union with God while serving as a saint (J. *wali*) for his subjects. The northern segment of the *kraton* is an audience hall that is used as a stage for the performance of the *Garebeg* rituals. These rites are conducted in celebration of the three major Islamic holy days: *Id al-fitr* (A.) at the conclusion of the fasting month of *Ramadan* (J. *Garebeg Sawal*), *Id al-adha* (A.) the feast of sacrifice held in connection with the *hajj* (J. *Garebeg Besar*) and the *Mawlid* (A.) the birthday of the prophet Muhammad (J. *Garebeg Malud*). On these occasions the Sultan proceeds from the *Kadaton* to the northern *Siti Inggil* while offerings charged with blessing are conveyed to the state

---

[31] Ricklefs, Op. Cit., reserved his most virulent criticism of the thesis that the architecture of the Yogyakarta *Kraton* is based on the Javanese/Islamic doctrine of the Perfect Man for this portion of the exegesis of the southern segment of the *kraton*. He states: "Nor should a serious scholar of Islam accept an interpretation supplied by a Yogyakarta Prince" that "the essence of God [is] located in the genitals (p. 205) whether by this is meant mankind's genitals or the even more bizarre idea that God is endowed with genitalia." This statement combines an apparent disregard for the religious views of Yogyakarta princes and perhaps of other Javanese as well, with an extremely limited knowledge of Islam and other religions and/or deliberate obfuscation. Anthropomorphic conceptions of divinities, including endowing them with genitalia, are extremely common. Christianity provides an obvious example, unless one is prepared to entertain the heretical view that Christ was somehow less than fully human. The eminent Tubingen Islamicist Josef van Ess (1988) has shown that debates between advocates of anthropomorphism and those of a transcendent understanding of God figured significantly in the formative period of Islamic theological discourse and that both positions can be upheld on the basis of close readings and exegesis of the *Qur'an*. Professor Ricklefs would appear to be unfamiliar with this facet of Islamic theology. It is, however, extremely unlikely that, a specialist in Javanese history and literature, he would be unfamiliar with the anthropomorphism of *Serat Wirid*, although he seems not to have read Brongtodiningrat's works. While such errors, and perhaps even the deliberate misrepresentation of fact, can be excused in a highly polemical review, the orientalist dismissal of indigenous opinion and exegesis can not. Javanese Princes are at least as well qualified to speculate about the nature of God as professors at Australian Universities. Professor Ricklefs seems inclined to view his own musing about the nature of God as somehow superior to those of Javanese religious thinkers. It is indeed unfortunate that my informant is no longer able to reply to Professor Ricklefs' (apparently) Protestant Christian polemic. For reasons of his own my informant, on this and many other matters related to the Yogyakarta palace, wished to remain anonymous for the remainder of his earthly life, but gave me explicit permission to use his name once he had joined his ancestors. He was the noted Javanese lawyer, journalist, author and from 1947 until 1966, mayor of Yogyakarta, Kangjen Pangeran Hario Poerwokoesoemo. Pak Poerwo, as he was affectionately known in his later years, was a trusted advisor of Sultan Hamengukuwana IX and regarded by many in Yogyakarta as one who, by virtue of his combination of learning, wisdom and experience, was well qualified to speculate about the nature of God. Unfortunately, Pak Poerwo left this world, or as is commonly said in Indonesian "returned to the mercy of God," prior to the publication of Professor Ricklefs' comments. I have no doubt that he could have formulated a more theologically sophisticated reply to Professor Ricklefs than I.

mosque on the northern *Alon Alon*.[32] The enthroned Sultan is believed to attain union with God and with his assembled subjects, assuming the mediating role of a Sufi saint.

The route from the *Kedaton* to *Siti Inggil* consists of seven steps and is a model of the introspective formulation of the mystical path. It beings at the *Danaprata* gate, which is a symbol of the Muslim virtue of alms giving and of Sufi meditation. The term *Danapratapa* is derived from two Sanskrit words: *dana* meaning gift and *tapa*, asceticism as the Sultan focuses his attention on the gifts to be distributed at the mosque and the religious benefits which, according to the *Shari'ah*, are acquired by both the donor and recipient of charity.[33]

Passing through the *Sri Manganti* gate the Sultan observes the *Bangsal Pancaniti*. This is a small building in which gamelans are stored. *Panca* (J. five) refers to the *panca indriya* (J. the five senses). *Niti* (J.) means to investigate. The building is a symbol of the stage on the mystical path at which the novice begins to investigate and attempts to control sense perception.

The third stage is represented by the northern *Kemandungan* courtyard within which *Bangsal Pancaniti* is located. The meaning of the northern *Kemandungan* is quite different from that of its southern counterpart. Here the term *Kemandungan* is linked to *mandung* (J.) the meaning of which is to collect. Like the southern *Kemandungan* the courtyard is filled with *Kepel* and *Cengkir Gading* trees. *Kepel* is again linked to *kempel* (J.) which in this context means to solidify. Here the color of the *Cengkir Gading* palm provides the key to its interpretation. The leaves and fruit of this tree are light yellowish green. Yellow is the traditional color of royalty. It is also held to be the color of complete submission to the will of God. The total meaning conveyed by the northern *Kemandungan* is therefore that the mystic (the Sultan) must unify the five senses to that he may humble himself totally before God.

The fourth stage in the path is represented by the *Brajanala* gate. *Braja* (J.) means weapon while *nala* (J.) is a literary term for heart, thus the meaning weapon of the heart. This gate refers to the holy war (A. *Jihad*) waged between passion and faith.

The Sultan then reaches a stone wall called *Renteng Mentog Baturana*. *Renteng* (J.) means doubt, *mentog* (J.) because, *batu* (J.) stone and *rana* (J.) a screen for blocking an open door. The term refers to the barrier of doubt which must be overcome by the mystic. The Sultan does not cross, but rather walks around the barrier, which some informants refer to as the veil between God and man.[34] This act is

---

[32]During the colonial period regional officials were required to present themselves on the *Alon Alon* on the morning of the *Garebeg*. Failure to appear was treason.

[33]On the Muslim theory of alms see Weir, in Gibb and Kramers, (eds.) op. cit., pp. 483–484.

[34]According to some Sufi teachings God is separated from the human soul by as many as seventy thousand veils. The purpose of Sufism is to remove these veils. This imagery is also present in a ritual performed by the Sultan at the state mosque on the occasion of the *Garebeg Malud Dal* (a larger, more complicated version of the *Garebeg Malud* staged only in the year *Dal* of the 8 year Javanese *windu*). At this time the Sultan kicks down a brick wall while leaving the mosque. This is said to represent the destruction of the veils separating him from the divine essence.

symbolic of the Sultan's confidence that he will become the tool of God and dispense divine justice to his subjects.

At the sixth stage the Sultan ascends the stairs leading to *Siti Inggil*. Here there are *Jambu Tlampok Harum* (J. guava) trees which are said to be especially fragrant. The Javanese term *Harum* is linked to the Arabic *haram* (sacred or forbidden) is a term used to describe the holy cities of Mecca and Medina. Concentrating his attention on these trees the Sultan comes to understand that his words must always be just and fragrant so that the smell of his purity and holiness will be noticed throughout the world. *Siti Inggil* is both a place of meditation and a throne room. It combines the symbols of royalty with those of the Sufi mystical path, and is a representation of the divine sanctuary *Bektal Makmur* located in the head of the perfect man. Entering *Siti Inggil*, the Sultan observes four *Kemunin* (yellow flowering) trees. *Kemuning* is associated with *hening* (J.) which means "pure" or "clean." These trees symbolize the purity of mind required to attain union with God. To the north of these trees is the *Bangsal Witana* within which is the *Bangsal Mangunturntangkil*. *Witana* is a Kawi (old Javanese) term meaning "seat in heaven," but is associated with the modern Javanese *wiwit* (to begin). It symbolizes the purification of the mind and the beginning of meditation. During the *Garebeg*, the *Bangsal Witana* and the *Siti Inggil* grounds are occupied by members of the court, each in a distinctive costume, members of the Sultan's body guard, and during the colonial period representatives of the Dutch Government. The *ampilan* (J. state regalia) and some of the most important *pusaka* (J. Sacred heirlooms) are placed behind, to the left and right of the throne. The members of the court and the *ampilan* serve as objects of meditation while the purpose of the *pusaka* is to prevent evil forces from interfering with the ritual. The Sultan wears a *pusaka* coat named *Kyahi Gantro Kusumo*. This is a patchwork frock which belonged to the first Sultan and is said to have been the property of the prophet Muhammad. While the coat is extremely elaborate it is based on the patchwork cloaks of Sufi mendicants and it is a symbol of mystical attainment and humility.[35]

The throne or "seat of gold" (J. *Dampar Kencana*) is placed in the *Bangsal Mangunturtangkil*. The location of this building within *Bangsal Witana* is a symbolic expression of the doctrine that the divine essence is located within the physical body. *Manguntur* means "raised seat" while *tangkil* (J.) means "royal audience" The combined symbolism of the assembled court, the throne and the buildings is that the Sultan receives homage from his subjects while giving it to the divine essence which forms his own soul. The Sultan is thought to attain mystical union as the offerings to the people are carried to the mosque and as a *gamelan* tune, the purpose of which is to purify the heart, purging it of passion (A. *nafs*), is played.

At this time the Sultan's attention should turn to the northern most sections of the *kraton*, the symbolism of which concerns social and mystical dimensions of the

---

[35] Prior to 1945 the *Penghulu* and other officials of the state mosque wore similar coats. This same design is used in *batik* patterns which form a sampler of the most common designs. This pattern could be worn only by the *Sultan* and the *Penghulu*.

doctrine of the unity of servant and lord. Immediately to the north of the throne at the head of the stairs leading down to the *Alon Alon* is the *Tarub Hagung* (J. great pavilion). It is a small square pavilion from which low ranking officials and commoners may address the Sultan. Its meaning is explained as follows:

> One who is devoted to the practice of meditation and submits to the will of God is perpetually in the heavenly realm.

Here *Hagung* is equated with the greatness of God. Viewed from the perspective of the throne, this building symbolizes the quest for union with God, while from that of a petitioner it is a statement about the godlike qualities of the Sultan. Combining these two perspectives, submission to the Sultan is equated with submission to God. The image of the enthroned Sultan seated on a raised "golden" throne, mentioned as being a heavenly seat surrounded by the nobles of the court dispensing blessing and mercy recalls the image of the early Islamic anthropomorphic descriptions of God seated on a throne surrounded by angels. While most contemporary Muslim do not accept this understanding of God, it is rooted in the famous "throne verse" (2:255) of the *Qur'an* which states:

> God! There is no god but He. The living, The self-subsisting, Supporter of all. No slumber can seize Him nor Sleep. His are all things in the heavens and on the earth. Who is thee can intercede in His presence except as he permitteth? He knoweth what (appeareth to His creatures) before or after or behind them. Nor shall they compass aught of His knowledge except as He willeth. His throne doth extend over the heavens and the earth and He feeleth No fatigue in guarding and preserving them for He is the Most High, the Supreme.

The Sultan is, of course, not God. One of his titles is *Ngabdulrachman* which means "servant of the Merciful" which is often glossed "Servant of God" because "The Merciful" is one of the names of God. However, given the fact that the perfect man is said to partake of divine knowledge and the attributes of God is not difficult for Javanese to establish symbolic connections between the imagery of the enthroned Sultan and that of the Throne Verse of the *Qur'an*. It is perhaps for this reason that modernist Muslims are often critical of more traditional Javanese for treating the Sultan with "god like" reverence.

At the base of the stairs leading to the *Tarub Hagung* is the *Pagelaran*. This was traditionally the main audience hall of the *kraton*. Regional nobles and other officials whose rank did not allow them to accompany the Sultan to *Siti Inggil* were required to present themselves here on the morning of the *Garebegs* and on other state occasions. Here they paid homage to and received instruction from the Sultan. In part because taxes and land rents were paid on the morning of the *Garebeg Malud*, failure to appear was tantamount to treason. The mystical meaning of the *Pagelaran* is that everything is clear to the meditator because he receives instruction directly from God. The term *Pagelaran* is derived from *gelar* (J.). The meaning of this term is complex. It is simultaneously (court) "title" and "to spread out" or "spread before." Both meanings would seem to contribute to that of the *Pagelaran*, as nobles of all ranks are arrayed in the Sultan's presence. Here, the Sultan assumes the position of God vis-à-vis the nobility, but because is his concentration is focused on the symbolism of the assembled nobility and the nature of his own position in the court system; he receives instruction directly from God.

The northern *Alon Alon* is the place at which the general public assembles for the *Garebeg*. Its symbolism is entirely different from that of its southern counterpart. It represents the shoreless ocean seen by the mind in meditation which, in turn, is a common image for the infinity of God.[36] A pair of banyan trees (J. *Kyai Dewadaru* and *Kyai Jagadaru*) located at the center of the Alon Alon depict the identity of microcosm and macrocosm. *Kyai Dewadaru* represents the union of the Sultan and God, Kyai *Jagadaru* the unity of the Sultan and his subject. Together they represent the two aspects of the doctrine of the unity of servant and lord. Just as nobles common to the *Pagelaran* to petition the Sultan, commoners may perform a rite known as *pepe* between the two trees, if they wish to bring an injustice to his attention. In this rite the petitioner dresses in white (a symbol of purity of intention), makes small offerings (J. *Sajen*) to each of the trees and sits motionless until he/she comes to the attention of the Sultan who is required to decide the case without regard to the status or social position of the petitioner. The four sides of the fences surrounding the trees represent the four stages of the Sufi mystical path: *Shari'ah* (law), *Tari'qah* (mystical practice), *Ma'rifah* (knowledge of God) and *Hak'ikah* (union with God).

While the *Alon Alon* is primarily a symbol of mystical knowledge and the infinity of God, it is surrounded by sixty-two *waringin* trees which represent the age of the prophet Muhammad. It is also the place where *salat* (A. liturgical prayer) is performed on the morning of the *Garebeg Syawal* which is held on *Idl Fitri* the day immediately following the conclusion of the fasting month of Ramadan. As a whole the doctrine it presents is that of the *Dewa Ruci Lakon*.[37] The boundless ocean of mystical knowledge is enclosed by the symbols of normative piety (Muhammad), while at the center the mystic realizes the essential unity of creator and created.

---

[36] The symbolism of the *Alon Alon* resembles that of the *Dewa Ruci* story from the Javanese *wayang* literature, in which Bhima discovers Dewa Ruci in the middle of the ocean. The names of the two trees are said to be derived from a conjunction of Sanskrit based Javanese terms for gods (*dewa*) and the world (*jaga*) and the Arabic term (*dar al*) for domain. They mean domain of the *dewa* and domain of the world respectively. Ricklefs suggests an alternative etymology according to which *daru* is a Javanese term for "fire ball." While this is possible many *kraton* Yogyanese mention the combination of Arabic and Sanskrit terms mentioned here. In either case the significance of the trees is that the represent the identity of microcosm and macrocosm, a concept shared by Sufi and Hindu Javanese cosmologies. Yet another interpretation included in *Keterangan Tentang Museum SitiHinggil-Pagelaran Kraton Yogyakarta* is that *Kyai Dewadaru* was brought to Yogyakarta from the east Javanese Hindu/Buddhist kingdom of Majapahit and the *Kyai Wijayadaru,* as it refers to the tree on the eastern side, was brought from the west Javanese Hindu/Buddhist kingdom of Pajajaran. According to this text the meaning of the two trees is that the world (*dunia*) is inherently dualistic being characterized by opposite pairs of attributes (*sifat*). The text does not offer any further explanation. This is however a common theme in Javanese religious thought.

[37] The *Dewa Ruci lakon* is considered to be among the most esoteric tales in the Javanese *wayang* tradition. The hero, Bima, dives into the ocean searching for the essence of life. He encounters a miniature of himself, referred to as *Dewa Ruci*. He enters Dewa Ruci's body and is surprised to discover that it contains the entirety of creation.

The social dimension of this doctrine is expressed by the fact that commoners come here to pay respect to, petition are receive blessing from the Sultan. The groups of people assembled in the *Alon Alon*, *Pagelaran* and *Siti Inggil* represent the totality of Javanese society. Social hierarchy is graphically depicted by relative proximity to the Sultan and is equated with position on the mystical path because the Sultan is equated with God. Unity, in both the social and mystical senses of the term, is articulated in the symbolism of the two *banyan* trees in the center of the *Alon Alon* and by the fact that commoners as well as nobles are entitled to petition the Sultan. In a religious sense this is an expression of the fundamental Islamic doctrine that all humans are equal in the eyes of God.

The *Alon Alon* does not, however, represent the goal of the mystical path. It is symbolic of the knowledge of unification, not of unification itself. The road through the center of the *Alon Alon*, which according to court protocol may be used only by the Sultan or his representatives, represents the straight path leading to mystical union. A crossroad at the northern end of the *Alon Alon* represents the temptations which can distract the mystic's attention. The most dangerous of these are the market and the *Patihan* (residence of the prime minister). The market represents the distracting influence of wealth, sensual pleasure and social discord. K.P.H. Poerwokoesoemo explained the mystical dangers of the market as follows:

> You can buy anything you want there, clothing, food, drink, radios – anything. Even seeing these things causes passion to flare up in the form of greed. Some people are poor and others are rich. Having many material goods causes rich people to think that they are superior so they ignore God. Poor people worry because they cannot afford all of the things that they see in the market. They become angry with the rich and forget their duty to God because of the passion of anger.

The *Patihan* can be equally dangerous because it emphasizes the worldly aspects of government and power. K.P.H. Poerwokoesoemo explained that:

> The *Patihan* is a very dangerous place because political decisions involve the use of magical power and lead people to think that because they have power and rank that they are like God. If political and magical power is not used correctly it leads to the separation of the Sultan from the people. People who work in the *Patihan* are subject to the passion of pride and must always remember that they are nothing more than the tools of the Sultan and of God.

The *Tugu* (J. needle), a brick monument 15 m tall, located 2.5 km to the north of the *kraton*, symbolizes attainment of the mystical and social goals of the union of servant and lord. According to court traditions it was constructed as a guide post for subjects coming to pay homage to the Sultan. Brongtodiningrat explains the significance of the *Tugu* as follows:

> Now we have arrived at the end of our journey, the *Tugu*, the symbol of the light of God in the heart, the union of servant and Lord, the union of the self and God that gives rise to a feeling of absolute confidence that everything that happens is the consequence of the will of God. There is no power other than that of God the all powerful.

A similar statement is found in the conclusion of the English (but not the Indonesian) version of the text where it is explained that the *kraton*, taken as a totality represents the twenty attributes (A. *Sifat*) of God. Here it is explained that:

The numbers one till twenty symbolize the twenty adherent characters of God, to strengthen our belief in Him and adoring Him. He only is almighty, all Powerful and All Merciful. So it is clear that what lives and moves in the world is shaped by God. As so it is also clear that we must have implicit faith in the Prophet and his divine message too. This is in brief the explaining of the profound meaning of the lay-out of the Yogya royal palace or *kraton*. Only God is Omniscient.

During the *Garebeg* it is at the moment when the Sultan's attention is focused on the *Tugu* that gives a sign that the *gunungan* ("mountains" of rice) for his subjects should be taken to the mosque, where after an Arabic prayer (A. *do'a*) for the welfare of the Sultan, the kingdom and the population is recited, they are distributed to the waiting crowd. While the Sultan's meditation on the *Tugu* speaks of an immanent God, the prayer appeals to a transcendent divinity. What follows is an English translation of a Javanese version of the prayer recited on the occasion of the *Garebeg Malud* in the mid 1920s.[38]

Remember that these prayers and praises belong to God the almighty who rules over everything. Remember that God's blessing and our well-being at all times are the result of the exalted position of His messenger, our lord the Prophet Muhammad and also that they belong to the Prophet's followers at all times. God, please help your servant, the Sultan of Yogyakarta to conquer his enemies and to be invincible with your help. And God, please give him a long and glorious life. And may, God, you grant greatness to the palace. And please, God, grant to our Sultan a generous hand. And please grant God, that the Sultan's justice is superlatively just. And may You, God, take good care of our Sultan's state and all of the people in it. And please, God, rain down your mercy and blessing upon our king and grant him an extensive domain.

This prayer establishes a clear connection between the institution of kingship, prosperity and Islam. God is asked to shower blessings on the Sultan "in the same manner that they have been given to the Prophet and his family", to establish good relations between the Sultan, his family, the *ulama*, nobles and peasants. It is also asked that he be generous, just and fair with all of his subjects and that he be spared the punishments of the grave. But there is also a mystical element to this prayer. The Sultan is referred to as the *kawula* (servant) of God and of the Prophet, but as the lord (*Pangeran*) of the kingdom. God is also asked to destroy the evil in the hearts of all of the Sultan's subjects and unite their hearts in a sense of oneness. This last request refers state of *slamet* in which individuals are spiritually united because of their common submission to God and the saints.

Taken together these statements and ritual acts reveal a great deal about the theological underpinnings Javanese concepts of authority They combine Asharite understandings of the absolute authority and power of God and divine determinism, with Ibn al-Arabi's view of the identity of the essence of God and the human spirit.[39]

---

[38] K.P.H. Poerwokoesoemo supplied me with the text of the prayer.

[39] Questions concerning free will and determinism played a central role in the development of Islamic theology. Javanese and other Southeast Asian Muslims have long been associated with the Asharite position which maintains the teaching of determinism. For a discussion of these concepts in the Arabic tradition see Montgomery Watt, *The Formative Period of Islamic Thought*. Edinburgh,

It suggests that royal power is (in theory) absolute because the Sultan has submitted to the power and authority of God who is at once transcendent and immanent.

The concept of divine determinism has played a central role in Islamic political thought since the days of the Prophet Muhammad. Goldziher has suggested that the development of a deterministic understanding of the relationship between divine authority and human agency can be observed within the text of the *Qur'an*.[40] He suggest that the *Surah* revealed during the Meccan period of Muhammad's prophecy tended to emphasize the efficacy of moral choice, while those revealed at Medina take a strong deterministic position. This points to a positive correlation between theological determinism and the growth of religio/political authority. During the Meccan community the Muslim community was small and often found itself in a precarious position. After the establishment of Muhammad's political as well as religious authority in Medina following the *hijra* in 622 C.E. (1 A.H.) determinism appears to have formed at least part of the basis for the religious legitimation of political and military authority. This tendency continued during the Umayyd period. The Umayyds were the first dynasty in Islamic history. They were regarded by many as usurpers and as being the murderers of the family of the prophet. They used the doctrine of divine determinism to legitimize their authority arguing that even the most brutal aspects of their rule were "foreordained in God's inalterable decree." Throughout the history of Islam despotic rulers have found the political appeal of *takdir* almost irresistible.

The doctrine of *takdir* has figured prominently in Javanese religious and political thought from the time that Islam was established as the religion of Java. Pre-colonial Indonesian, and especially, Javanese Islamic states were, at least in theory, absolutist polities centered on Sultans who claimed to be the Perfect man of classical Sufism and the *Kaliputuallah*, God's representative on earth. Javanese social structure was, and to some degree still is, characterized by enormously complex social, linguistic and political hierarchies. The doctrine of *takdir* played a significant role in establishing the legitimacy of the state and of the social system on which it was based. The section of *Babad Tanah Jawi* concerning the establishment of the kingdom of Mataram states that it is *takdir* that Penembahan Senopati will be the ruler of all of Java. Perhaps the clearest example of the influence of the doctrine of divine determinism of human events is the frequently cited metaphor in which God is described as a *dalang* (puppeteer in the Javanese shadow play), and humans as the puppets the *dalang* moves and speaks for. A clear example can be found in the Javanese *suluk* materials translated by Zoetmulder:

> The meaning of this teaching, my brother, is this: the most High God is the exalted *dalang*. He creates us all. Before we were born of our mothers He already fixed everything immutably: good and bad fortune, long or short life, failure of success, all was already apportioned when we were still in the abode of secrecy, enveloped by veils and invisible.

Edinburgh University Press, 1973 and R. Martin, M. Woodward and D. Atmaja, *Defenders of Reason in Islam. Mu'tazilism from Medieval School to Modern Symbol.* Oxford: One World, 1997.
[40] I. Goldziher, *Introduction to Islamic Theology and Law.* Princeton: Princeton University Press, 1981, p. 81.

The most high is the exalted *dalang*. The external appearance and classification of material being and the manifestation of that which exists: these are the puppets on the screen. It is the *dalang* who governs their doings. The true *dalang* is also the king who governs the doings of all that lives. To him it is given by the Most High to receive the revelation of predestination (*takdir*), of the nature and character of mankind. The king is therefore the veil of the Most High. He follows his disposition (*takdir*) which is already written down on the well preserved tablet. The king himself has no power there over, but merely approves the course of things.

This passage is an example of the ways in which Javanese Islam combined the use of *takdir* in the legitimation of imperial authority with a more general formulation of a determinist understanding of the relationship between divine authority and human agency. As Zoetmulder notes, similar imagery and symbolism can be found in the mystical writings of Ibn al-Arabi and other Arabic and Persian Sufis.[41] The *suluk* literature includes a heavily Javanized presentation of Islamic doctrine formulated in court literary circles. It is therefore not surprising that it presents an interpretation of *takdir* suited to the interests of an authoritarian state. This section of the palace, as a whole, serves to establish the Sultan's position as a saint-king and can be understood as an iconographic representation of the teachings of the *suluk* literature.

While the southern approach to the *kraton* concerns the descent of the soul and the origin of the perfect man, the northern approach articulates relationships between God, a Sufi saint and his devotees. The population of the Sultanate reaps the fruits of the Sultan's mystical attainment, but does not, in this context, practice mysticism independently. The political and social formulations of the doctrine of the union of servant and lord can be understood best as representing the Sufi doctrine of absorption or passing away in the saint who leads the devotee to God and serves as a source of spiritual blessing.[42] They can, however, partake of the saint's (the Sultan's) blessing only through conformity with the demands of normative piety. Participants in the *Garebeg ritual* recite the confession of faith (There is no God but God and Muhammad is the Messenger of God) and perform normative purification rites before entering the compound of the state mosque. According to court tradition, this ritual was also among the means through which conversion to Islam was achieved, as male subjects were required to be circumcised before they could receive a portion of the offerings presented to the populace by the early Muslim rulers.

This coupling of the notions of sainthood and kingship is among the most striking examples of the imperialization of Sufism in central Java. The northern approach to the palace does not simply make claims about the religious attainments and legitimacy of the Sultan. It also employs the relationships between a saint and his devotees and the structure of the mystical path as a model of social and political organization. The purpose of the *Garebeg* is to establish both the loyalty and

---

[41] P. Zoetmulder, *Pantheism and Monism in Javanese Suluk Literature. Islamic and Indian Mysticism in an Indonesian Setting.* (Translated by M. Ricklefs) Leiden: KITLV Press, 1995, pp. 220–225.

[42] Schimmel, op. cit., pp. 205–207.

prosperity of the population and to draw it into a religio-political system of dependency in which the Sultan is simultaneously a secular lord and an object of religious devotion.

The *Garebeg* also define the Sultanate as an Islamic community (A. *umma*). The concept of the community of believers is among the most important sociological principles of Islam. An *umma* is a community of religious believers who are part of God's plan for salvation. An *umma* is a united community, guided by a prophet who establishes social and ritual orders in accordance with the will of God. Islamic tradition holds that social and religious discord are the consequence of humanity's rejection of God's messages and messengers. Because the *Qur'an* teaches that there is an intrinsic link between social conduct and salvation, unity and harmony are among the most basic religious concerns of Islam. It is stated in the *Qur'an* that:

> And verily this *Ummah* of yours is single *ummah* (community) and I am your Lord and Cherisher: Therefore fear Me and no other. But people have cut off their affair of unity. Between them, into sects; Each party rejoices in that which is with itself. But leave them in their confused ignorance for a time.
> The Believers are but a single Brotherhood: So make peace and reconciliation between your two brothers; And fear God, that ye may receive Mercy. (49:10)

Together these passages suggest that brotherhood and unity are necessary conditions for a community to enjoy the blessing and mercy of God. In Java this state of unity is often referred to as *slamet*, a social and spiritual condition characterized by psychological tranquility and social harmony.[43] The *Garebeg* are state *slametan*, a Javanese Islamic ritual involving Arabic prayer and the distribution of blessed food the purpose of which is to produce this state of social and spiritual harmony.[44] *Slametan* establish a geographically defined territory as a *umma*. It is essential that all of ones neighbors be invited and considered highly inappropriate not to attend. In the case of the *Garebeg* representatives of all social classes gather on the northern *Alon Alon* and in the mosque where prayers are said for the prosperity and tranquility of the Sultan and the state and blessed food distributed to the assembled community. The understanding of the concept of *umma* expressed in the *Alon Alon* differs from that in the *Qur'an* in one significant way. In the Quranic usage of the concept only the Prophet serves as an intermediary between the community and God. While the trees which surround the *Alon Alon* represent the Prophet Muhammad and are said to serve as reminder guidance, the community is defined not by prophecy, but by Sultan/saint as an intermediary between God and the community. This distinction is expressed in comments about the *Alon Alon* included in *Keterangan Tentang Museum Sitihinggil-Pagelaran Kraton Yogyakarta*. The text mentions the *Alon Alon* as the place where *Bupati* were required to assemble for state ceremonies, as the location of *slametan* held by court officials during the month of *Ramadan* and as a place where people could come seeking justice, as well as being the site of

---

[43] See Chapter 3 for a more detailed discussion of this concept
[44] See Chapter 5.

tournaments and military exercises. Its role in the public life of the Sultanate is summarized as follows:

> The northern *Alon Alon* is an integral part of the *kraton* complex. The *Alon Alon* is a very important part of the *kraton* complex because it is here that the *Raja* can establish direct connections with his subjects *kawulonya*.

The *Kraton* and the Afterlife

Read from north to south, the northern section of the *kraton* is a model of the eschatological path and the quest for lasting union with God. It is based on the belief expressed in *Serat Cabolek* and in popular eschatological theory that lasting union with God is only possible for the dead.[45] It also provides the key to the mystical and cosmological significance of the *Kedaton* or central part of the *kraton*. Again, the Sultan's passage through the *kraton* in the *Garebeg* ritual is of primary importance. This portion of the ritual is known as *Jengkar Dalem* (J. return to the eternal realm). It is equated with death and ascent of the axis mundi. Leaving *Siti Inggil* the Sultan observes the *Keben* trees of the *Kemandungan* courtyard. *Keben* is linked to *tangkeben* (J. to close). The meaning of these trees is that the openings in the body should be closed and sense perception blocked as the moment of death approaches.

Passing through the *Sri Manganti* gate, the Sultan rests with his wives and children in the *Bangsal Sri Manganti*. This represents the period between death and the final judgement during which the purified soul enjoys a taste of the pleasures of heaven in *alam Barzak* (J. from A. *al-Barzak*). Cool drinks are brought to *Bangsal Sri Manganti* by two high ranking officials who represent the angels Munkar and Nakir who question the soul in the grave concerning the *Qu'ran*, the prophet Muhammad and the direction of prayer.

Leaving *Bangsal Sri Manganti*, the Sultan encounters *Bangsal Traju Mas* (J. Building of the Golden Scales). The term *Traju Mas* refers to the scales to be used by God to weigh good and evil on the day of judgement. By observing this building the Sultan should realize the transient nature of worldly desire (represented by his family) and come to appreciate the importance of distinguishing good from evil in all of his actions.

Next, his attention is drawn to the *Gedong Purwaretna* (J. Tower of the First Diamond). This is a three story building which straddles the wall between the *Sri Manganti* court and the *Kedaton*. The literal meaning of *purwa* is "first." Here the term is associated with the notion of origin and the doctrine that the ultimate goal of the mystical path is the return of the physical and spiritual bodies and the soul to their respective origins. The literal meaning of *retna* is "diamond," but here it is associated with light (J. *nur* or *cahaya*) through which the divine essence is manifest in the created world. This building is a model of the Islamic cosmos, the body of the perfect man and the mystical path. The three floors represent the divine sanctuaries.

---

[45]On Javanese understandings of death and the afterlife see M. Woodward, 1989: 172–176.

Four windows in the upper floor represent the *Shar'ah* (Muslim law), *Tarikah* (A. the discipline of the path), *Hakekah* (A. knowledge of the truth of God) and *Ma'rifah* (A. union with God) as well as the four elements comprising the physical body: earth, wind, fire and water.

The reason for the location of this building between the *Sri Manganti* court and the *Kedaton* is not entirely clear. Most princes refused to discuss this building at all, saying that its meaning was known only to the Sultan. Others said that it represents a human at the moment of death, being between this world (*Sri Manganti*) and heaven (the *Kedaton*).

Next, the Sultan passes through the *Danapratapa* gate and enters the *Kedatan*. The four pillars supporting the gate are another representation of the four stages in the development of mystical knowledge. The two eastern pillars are joined, representing the combination of *Shari'ah* and *Tarekah*, the meaning of which is "action," while the two western pillars represent the combination of *Hakekah* and *Ma'rifah* as an expression of the truth of God. Two *raksasa* (demons) on either side of the gate represent the varieties of passion leading to evil and those promoting moral action.

It was observed previously that from the perspective of the southern *Alon Alon*, the *Kedaton* represents the social and political life of the state. The southern approach to the *kraton* depicts the descent of the soul from *alam Barzak*. Similarly, the Sultan passes outward through the *Danapratapa* gate as an earthly king/saint bent on the attainment of momentary.union with the divine essence. His return combines the symbolism of the eschatological path with that of Muhammad's journey to heaven. Viewed from the perspective of the *Sri Manganti* court (which is the entrance normally used by visitors to the *kraton*) passage through the gate constitutes ascent of the *axis mundi*, from *alam Barzak* while the *Kedaton* is simultaneously the *Ka'ba*, the sanctuary of the heart and the site of the divine throne. This duality is possible because the *Kedaton* contains two fundamentally different types of buildings. One set consists of administrative offices, residences for princes and servants, a library, storage sheds and other mundane structures. The other includes only the throne hall and the Sultan's-private quarters. These structures, which will be discussed below, are highly charged with mystical and cosmological significance.

Upon entering the *Kedaton*, the Sultan proceeds directly to the *Bangsal Kencana* (J. Golden Building). This building is a representation of the union of servant and lord and the ritual center of the *kraton*. In this context the color gold represents the unity of all of the lights through which the divine essence is manifest.[46]

After the completion of the ceremonies at the State Mosque, the throne and the *pusaka* are brought to *Bangsal Kencana*. Here the Sultan conducts a ritual known as *Ngepeli*, the literal meaning of which is "to make a ball of something with the fist." He sits on the throne surrounded by all of the *pusaka*, the *ampilan* and the members of the court. Rice is prepared in a pot which is said to have belonged to the *wali*

---

[46]Gold is also the color of royalty. Only the Sultan is allowed to use a gold umbrella (J. *payang*).

Sunan Kaliiaga[47]. The *Pengulu* (chief official of the state mosque) is ordered to pray for the welfare of the state and the Sultan, after which the Sultan personally distributes cooked rice to the members of the court. It is significant that this ritual is the only occasion at which the velvet covers are removed from the *pusaka*. This is possible only because of the mystical strength of the Sultan and the members of the court and because of the sanctity of the *Kadaten*. The uncovered *pusaka* represents the attributes of God and are virtually all said to have been the property of either one of the nine *wali*, one of the early kings of Mataram or the Prophet Muhammad.[48]

This ritual is an internal *kraton* affair equivalent of those conducted earlier at the state mosque. Only those members of the court who were present with the Sultan at *Siti Inggil* are allowed to attend. This rite is, however, of much greater mystical significance. One of the participants explained that when the Sultan sits on the throne in *Bangsal Kenca* he is the direct representative of and acts as God. *Bangsal Kencana* is simultaneously the sanctuary of the heart, the *Ka'ba* and the site of the throne of God in the highest heaven. The members of the court are analogues of the angels who surround the divine throne. *Bangsal Kencana* is, therefore, the center of the universe, and is appropriately located on a direct line between the northern and southern *Siti Inggil*.

Regardless of its position as the central point of the palace and of the cosmos, *Bangsal Kencana* is not the most sacred part of the *Kedaton*. Immediately behind *Bangsal Kencana* is *Bangsal Prabayeksa*. *Prabayeksa* means "flash of light." It is the representation of the divine essence, which, unlike the throne of God does not have a physical form. *Bangsal Prabayeksa* is a large hall which no one other than the Sultan and the highest ranking members of the court may enter. It is used to store and honor the most sacred *pusaka*. At the very center of *Bangsal Prabayeksa* is a lamp by the name of *Kyai Wiji*, the flame of which is never allowed to go out. Significantly the meaning of *wiji* is sperm, the source of the spiritual and physical bodies. But in this context it is used to refer to the divine essence which is the ultimate source of both bodies and the soul. The light of this lamp, unlike the trees of the *kraton* courtyards, is not held to be a symbolic representation of a mystical state. Rather it is thought to be an actual manifestation of the divine essence. The symbolism of *Kyai Wiji* is significant for three reasons. It is a representation of the Javanese/Islamic view that divine appointment (J. *wahyu*) is manifest as light. It also recalls the architecture of the *Ka'ba*, the interior of which is empty except for lamps hanging from the roof. The third and probably most important is that it is a representation of the concept of God found in the "Light Verse" of the *Qur'an*

---

[47]Sunan Kalijaga is the mythical Javanese Islamic saint who is believed to have instructed the founder of the Mataram dynasty on the conduct of state ceremonies. He is widely regarded as the patron saint of Javanese mysticism. See Woodward, op. cit., *p. 96–98*.

[48]Two of the holiest *pusaka* are *Kangjeng Kyai Ageng Plered*, a spear which is said to have originally belonged to Seh Maulono Maghribi, one of the nine *wali* and later to have been used by Senopati in the founding of Mataram, and *Kangjeng Kyai Tunggul Wulung,* a black flag which is said to have been made from the cloth used to cover the grave of the prophet Muhammad.

(2:35–36) upon which Javanese and other Sufi doctrines concerning the "light of God" are based.[49] The Light Verse describes God as follows:

> God is the Light of the Heavens and the Earth. The parable of His Light is as if there were a Niche and within it a Lamp: The Lamp enclosed in Glass. The glass as it were a brilliant star. Lit from a blessed tree, an olive neither of the east nor of the west, whose oil is well-nigh luminous, though fire scarce touched it. Light upon Light! God doth guide whom He will to His Light God doth set forth parables for men and God doth know all things. Lit is such a Light in houses which God hath permitted to be raised to honour; for the celebration, in them of His name; In them he is glorified in the mornings and in the evenings. (24:35)

In his commentary on these verses Yusuf Ali explains that the Quranic to "houses which God hath permitted to be raised in his honour" is often understood to refer to "special mosques such as the *Ka'ba* and those at Medina and Jerusalem." The symbolism of *Prabayeksa* and *Kyai Wiji* suggest that in Yogyakarta, the *kraton* is understood as being among the houses raised for the celebration of the name of God.

After the completion of the *Ngepeli* ritual the Sultan, accompanied only by the select group of princes, whose task it is to care for the most sacred *pusaka*, enters *Bangsal Prabayeksa* prior to returning to his own quarters. This act depicts, in visual form, the highest stage of Sufi meditation and the goal of the cosmological formulation of the mystical path.

Other buildings in the *Kedaton* depict the normative Muslim view of the after-life. *Gedong Kuning* (J. yellow tower) are the Sultan's private apartments. Yellow represents the attributes of *God*. *Gedong Kuning* is a representation of the eternity of paradise and the soul that is clear, pure, and clean. The *Kaputren* (J. women's quarters) represents the passion of lust, excessive indulgence in which leads to Hell, which is represented by a small building used to house a *pusaka* axe formerly used for executions. The name of this building is *Bangsal Abang* (red building) which is also associated with the passion of anger. The depiction of passion in the *Kedaton* and at the *Siti Inggil* is necessary because of the Javanese belief that passion as well as the divine essence is present in each of the three sanctuaries. The *Kedaton* is both the throne of God and the heart of the perfect man and as such must include a representation of the Passions (*nafsu*) which cling to the soul, distracting those who undertaken the path leading to union with God.

The *Kraton* and the Javanese Islamic State

Geertz has argued that the Hindu-Javanese kingdom of Majapahit was used as a model for the establishment of Mataram and those central Javanese courts and kingdoms are only marginally and perhaps trivially Islamic.[50] In the introduction to this volume it is argued that Geertz's understanding of Javanese religion builds on an Islam denying Orientalism that was an integral part of the Dutch colonial strategy

---

[49] For a discussing of the role of light in Islamic theology and mysticism see Massignon, op. cit., pp. 451–452.

[50] C. Geertz, *Islam Observed*. Chicago: University of Chicago Press, 1968, p. 40

to dominate and domesticate the Javanese elite combined with a marked tendency to confuse modernist Muslim theological polemics with historical and cultural analysis. The analysis of the symbolism of the Yogyakarta *Kraton* and of its use as a stage for the performance of Islamic ritual suggest a very different understanding of the roles of Islam in Mataram and its successors Yogyakarta and Surakarta. What Javanese states retained from the Hindu (and Buddhist) past was the general notion that palaces and states should be constructed as symbolic representations of cosmic order. As Cunningham argues this concept occupies a central position in Southeast Asian cultures, not just those of the Indianized States of the mainland and pre-Islamic Indonesia and Malaysia. In a broader sense Eliade's *Myth of Eternal Return* suggest that this concept is among the universal elements of religious thought. It is, therefore, not surprising the founders of a Javanese Islamic state should attempt to represent the cosmos in the architecture of the palace and the performative structure of imperial ceremonies. The difference between Yogyakarta, the Hindu and Buddhist states of other times and places in Southeast Asia and the Atoni and other tribal people are simply that it is an Islamic cosmos which finds expression in the architecture and ceremonies of the palace. The analysis of the symbolism of the Javanese *kraton* presented here suggests that Mataram and subsequent central Javanese kingdoms should be understood not as "consciously modeling itself, despite its supposed Islamism, upon Majapahit,"[51] as Geertz puts it, but rather, as self consciously Islamic states, modeling themselves on cosmological and mystical doctrines drawn from the larger Islamic tradition

Changing Spaces: The *Kraton* in Colonial and Post-Colonial Contexts

If the *kraton* can be read as a text, it is a living text to which new materials are appended, others deleted and still others written over. When it was first constructed the *kraton* was simultaneously residential, political, military and ritual space. The balance between these organizational principles has shifted, with the political fortunes of the Sultanate. The *kraton* was constructed at a time when Yogyakarta was a significant military power. In the late eighteenth century most of the city's population was lived inside the walls, which were, at that time formidable defensive structures. Chinese, Europeans and other non-Muslims were prohibited from living inside the walls. The Dutch fort, located to the north of the palace is considerably less impressive. The northern *Alon Alon* was used not only for ceremonial purposes but as a field for conducting military training exercises. *Bangsal Pemandengan*, located in the *Pagelaran* was used as a "war room" where the Sultan met with his commanders to plan military strategy. He received reports from the commander in chief in Bangsal *Pengapit* located at the southern end of *Bangsal Pagelaran*. *Bangsal Pengrawit*, located in the southeast corner of *Bangsal Pagelaran*, was used for the

---

[51] Ibid.

installation of the *Patih* (prime minister). These buildings and others including sta-
bles and store houses do not figure at all in the religious symbolism of the palace.
They were intended to be used as the administrative, political and military offices of
the palace. Placing them in such close proximity to the ritual space which is used to
define the spiritual links between the Sultan and his subjects indirectly associates the
administrative and military functions of government with the religious, charismatic
authority of the Sultan.

The demise of the political authority and armed might of the *kraton* in the
nineteenth century led its original military functions to be redefined as ritual.[52]
Battalions of infantry (*prajurit*) were maintained but only as ornately uniformed
honor guards who fired salutes with blank cartridges. Sultans held the honorary
rank of major general in the Netherlands Indies army. The political contracts signed
at the beginning of each reign gradually reduced the authority of the Sultan to the
extent that in the late 1930s he was, like those of colonial India, a "king without a
kingdom." At least two buildings were added that reflected the colonial condition.
Bangsal Manis (Sweet Building) is a western style banquet hall used to entertain
Dutch officials, while Bangsal *Mandalasana* is a gazebo with stained glass panels
depicting western musical instruments. There are numerous European style furnish-
ings, oil paintings and other works of art. From a Dutch perspective they represent
the domestication of the Javanese state and with it Javanese Islam. Taken as a whole
this set of indexical symbols defined the *kraton*, the Sultan and the Sultanate as an
integral components of the colonial state.

The *kraton* underwent a second and equally dramatic transformation following
the Indonesian revolution. It was, for a time, almost the only territory controlled by
the Indonesian republic. It was then *the* political space of Indonesian nationalism.
While the current Sultan, Hamengkubuwana X and his father have both been significant political functions the palace functions as ceremonial but not political space.
The governor's office and the provincial legislature are, however, located on the
grounds of what was formerly the *Patihan*. An entirely new set of indexical symbols
define the palace and the Sultanate as integral, and according to many Yogyanese,
central, elements of the Indonesian state. Today the *kraton* is simultaneously and
profoundly Indonesian and well as Javanese space. It has been redefined as *public*
cultural space.

Sultan Hamengkubuwana IX began this process which has been continued by his
successor. HB IX eliminated the office of *Patih* and moved his own offices out of the
palace, first to the *Patihan* and when the revolutionary struggle was brought to a conclusion, to Jakarta where he played an active role in the political life of Independent
Indonesia. The Sultan's absence from the *kraton,* and his very public presence
outside of it were of great symbolic significance. For generations the Sultans of
Yogyakarta had been virtually prisoners in the *kraton.* They rarely ventured outside

---

[52]Artillery and cavalry units were disbanded and have never been reestablished. Even these ceremonial units were disbanded and their firearms confiscated by the Japanese in 1942. They were
re-established in 1970. Horses and elephants were re-introduced in small numbers in the 1980s.

the walls, except on ceremonial occasions. Contact with the Javanese masses was extremely limited. Hamengkubuwana IX changed all of this. Throughout the revolution he was a highly visible public figure. He drove his own jeep, was active in political and military affairs and to the amazement of his subjects even ate in road side *warung* (food stalls). He is widely believed to have traveled *in cognito* in Dutch occupied territory to better understand the sufferings of his people. The Sultan's public profile symbolized the egalitarian ethos of Indonesian nationalism. He was often referred to as Bung Sultan (Brother Sultan). In a real sense he reversed the emphasis of the traditional theory of the union of servant and lord. While in the past this doctrine had been used to emphasize the hierarchical character of the state, Hamengkubuwana IX was often described as a "democratic Sultan" who used his power and authority on behalf of his subjects. The lord became the servant of the servants – an ideological shift captured by the title of a volume published in honor of his seventieth birthday titled *Tahta Untuk Rakyat* (To Reign for the People).

The *kraton* played a central role in Hamengkubuwana IX's redefinition of the Javanese concept of kingship. The Sultan greatly reduced the scale of state ceremonies and allowed Gadjah Mada University to use the northern *Siti Inggil* and the *Pagelaran* as a "temporary campus" for 25 years, beginning in 1949. There were symbolic as well as practical considerations involved in this decision. The Sultan was a strong proponent of modern education and did much to rationalize the administration of Yogyakarta. Allowing ordinary people (students and teachers) to enter the sacred areas of the *Siti Inggil* was a radical departure from *kraton* tradition, which limited access to these areas, and which required anyone entering them to abide by strict, and complex sumptuary regulations. What had been private Javanese space became public Indonesian space. He also opened portions of the *kraton* complex to Indonesian and foreign tourists. Before the Indonesian revolution, ordinary people were not allowed to enter the *kraton* other than as employees or servants. Today tens of thousands of people per month pay the nominal fee and are shown through the outer sections of the palace by guides dressed in traditional court costumes. They explain something of the history and mystical significance of the buildings, always stressing the importance and power of the Sultan and the role of Yogyakarta in Indonesian history. Most foreign tourists regard the *kraton* as one more stop on the "road" leading from the beaches of Bali to Chiengmai in northern Thailand. But for many Javanese the line between tourism and pilgrimage is a very fine one. Many come seeking the blessing and spiritual power they believe it to preserve.

Today the *kraton* is described as a museum. There are portrait galleries, displays of antique European furniture and decorative items. In the late 1980s a series of relief carvings depicting crucial events in the lives of Sultans Hamengkubuwana the first and the ninth were installed on the northern wall of the *Pagelaran*. They depict the founding of Yogyakarta and the struggles of its two greatest Sultans against the Dutch. They are simultaneously Yogyakarta and Indonesian nationalism. There are also daily shadow puppet play (*wayang*), dance and percussion orchestra (*gamelan*) performances for Javanese, Indonesian and international visitors. The *kraton* offers lessons in gamelan performance and classical dance free of charge.

Recent additions include a museum exhibiting antique *batik* cloth, an upscale restaurant and coffee shop and a branch of a major Jakarta based department story that sells all manner of Javanese, and other Indonesian handicrafts. Probably the most remarkable aspect of the *Kraton* Museum is a series of displays chronicling the life and career of Hamengkubuwana IX. Some of the artifacts displayed, include examples of the traditional Javanese clothing he wore in his youth are Javanese. Others, including his Boy Scout uniform, cameras and cooking gear are Indonesian. The Office he used during the Indonesian has been preserved. A copy of his biography, *To Reign for the People,* is prominently displayed on his desk. The table at which the Dutch signed the transfer of power documents has also been preserved. This is *bricolage.* It is *bricolage* with a purpose. It simultaneously Indonesianizes Java and Javanizes Indonesia. It makes powerful claims about Yogyakarta as the symbolic center, and cultural, if not political or commercial capitol of Indonesia.

Certainly the most ironic of the modern elements of *Kraton* symbolism is the reformation and transformation of the Dutch Fort. When I was first in Yogyakarta is was in decrepit condition. The walls were crumbling and the roofs on many of the buildings had collapsed. It was littered with all manner of garbage. It has since been meticulously restored as a museum of the Indonesian revolution. There are displays of Indonesian and Japanese weaponry and uniforms and artifacts. Of these probably the most significant are uniforms and belonging of General Soedirman, the revolutionary leader who was in charge of guerilla forces in the Yogyakarta area. Perhaps the most important of these is the bed in which he died on January 29th, 1950. The walls of many of the barracks display large paintings of key events in the Indonesian nationalist movement and revolution. Both are viewed from a clearly Yogyakarta perspective. The founding of Muhammadiyah and Taman Siswa, the uprising of March 1, 1949 and the Sultan's participation in the revolutionary struggle all figure prominently in this visual narrative. What was originally a symbol of Dutch colonialism as well as a fortress is now one of the hybridity of Indonesian and Yogyakarta struggle and nationalism.

My most recent visit to the *kraton* was in April of 2010. I spent an afternoon revisiting familiar places and sitting drinking tea with the *abdi dalem* (servants/tour guides) some of whom I have known for many years and others of who I met for the first time. When I asked about the "modern" additions to the *kraton* one of them explained that especially because of all the changes that Indonesia has experienced in the last decade that it is very important to work to preserve *Kebudayan Jawa* and that even though he is a Roman Catholic rather than a Muslim he feels honored to play a part in these efforts. Sultan Hamengkubuwana X expressed similar sentiments when he wrote:

> The current dynasty (reign) is the latest phase of laying down the foundation and defining the *Kraton's* role in the community and the nation. The next generation will continue building on this foundation helping to build the New Indonesia we all ideally desire.[53]

---

[53]Hamengkubuwana X, Introduction, S. Alimin, (ed.) *Kraton Yogyakarta: The History and Cultural Heritage.* Yogyakarta: Indonesian National Marketing Association, 2002

Chapter 7 is the story of how the *kraton* re-emerged as Javanese and Indonesia political space during the final days of the New Order.

Photos

Kraton Yogyakarta

Pagelaran   **Regol Srimanganti**

The Grand Mosque

Frontal view with Kraton coat of arms   **Interior View**

Chapter 5
The *Garebeg Malud*: Veneration of the Prophet as Imperial Ritual

This chapter examines the way in which the Yogyakarta *Kraton* celebrates one of the most important Muslim holy days, *Mawlid al-Nabi*, which commemorates the birth of the prophet Muhammad. The central component of the *Mawlid* is the recitation of texts expressing respect and love for the Prophet Muhammad and his family. The *Mawlid* is celebrated throughout the Islamic world but is also closely linked to local modes of Muslim piety. Consequently, the meanings of the rite may extend far beyond its stated purpose of venerating the Prophet. Von Grunebaum, Kaptein and Schimmel have shown that Muslim monarchs have used elaborate *Mawlid* performances to demonstrate their piety and power and in so doing to establish their Islamic legitimacy for many centuries.[1] Today the *Mawlid* is a public holiday in most Muslim countries, with the notable exception of Saudi Arabia, where the Wahhabi establishment considers it to be an unlawful innovation (*bid'ah*).[2] In many Muslim societies it is also among the most important components of popular piety and, as Denny observes, links local religious concerns, including agricultural fertility and prosperity with Universalist and Essentialist Islam.[3]

The *Mawlid* is as controversial as it is popular. For most Muslims, in Java and elsewhere, celebrating the birth of the Prophet Muhammad is among the defining marks of be being Muslim. For a powerful and vocal minority, it is an anathema and the object of vituperative critiques. Javanese and other Indonesian interpretations of the *Mawlid* mirror those of the global Muslim community. *Kejawen* Muslims and those linked to *Nahdlatul Ulama* consider the celebration of the *Mawlid* to be an essential, and for some an obligatory (*wajib*) part of Islam. On the morning of the 2010 *Malud* loudspeakers on the northern *Alon-Alon* repeatedly broadcast the message that it is a tradition of great "historical, religious and cultural value" and that it

---

[1] G. von Grunebaum, *Muhanmadan Festivals*. New York: Henry Schumann, 1952, pp. 73–76, N. Kaptein, *Muhammad's Birthday Festival: Early history in the Central Muslim Lands and Development in the Muslim West until the 10th/16th Century*. Leiden: Brill, 1993 and A. Schimmel, *Mystical Dimensions of Islam*. Chapel Hill: University of North Carolina Press, pp. 146–147.

[2] Despite the fact that it is officially condemned as unbelief by the Saudi government and public *Mawlid* celebrations banned, many Saudi Muslims observe it in private.

[3] F. Denny, "Islamic Ritual: Perspectives and Theories." in R. Martin (ed.) *Approaches to Islam in Religious Studies*. Tucson: University of Arizona Press, 1985, pp. 63–77.

M. Woodward, *Java, Indonesia and Islam*, Muslims in Global Societies Series 3, DOI 10.1007/978-94-007-0056-7_5, © Springer Science+Business Media B.V. 2011

is "celebrated to fulfill the Sultan's Islamic obligation (*kewajiban*) to promote Islam in the territory of the Sultanate of Yogyakarta." NU scholars, like those in other historical and contemporary Muslim societies, are fully aware that the *Mawlid* is an innovation, that is not mentioned in the *Qur'an* and that it was not observed during the lifetime of the Prophet. Like most other Muslim scholars they distinguish between religious innovations that are reprehensible and those which are praiseworthy (*hasanah*) and are based on general themes in the *Qur'an* and Hadith instead of specific behavioral injunctions. The *Mawlid* is among the most commonly mentioned examples of praiseworthy innovation. This view is shared even by some of the most strident opponents of most other modalities of popular Islam. Ibn Taymiyyah (1263–1328), the Kurdish reformer who most Indonesian and other Islamists take as their spiritual ancestor and mentor, was subdued in his critique of the *Mawlid*. His position was that those who performed it with pious intent and out of love for the Prophet Muhammad would be rewarded for their actions, and forgiven any sin from *bid'ah* that they might incur.[4] *Wahhabi* and other contemporary condemnations of the *Mawlid* are based on extremely narrow readings of Universalist Islamic texts, according to which *any* innovation is necessarily evil. Among the most prominent proponents of this position was the late Mufti of Saudi Arabia Sheikh Abdul Aziz bin Baaz (1909–1999), who condemned those who celebrate the *Mawlid* as unbelievers destined for hell. At least in this case Saudi attempts to promote their own Local Islam as being Universalist Islam have meet with little success[5]. In the days leading up to the *Mawlid* in March 2009 there were hundreds of *fatwa* (legal opinions) countering bin Baaz's views posted on the internet in Arabic, English, Indonesian and other languages.[6] Some Javanese and other Indonesian Islamists have opinions similar to, and in many cases derivative of, that of bin Baaz. One with whom I spoke on the day of the *Malud* in 2009 stated that it is "100% *bid'ah* and people who participate are definitely going to hell." Most would not go so far. *Muhammadiyah* tolerates the Yogyakarta *Malud* and justifies it continued performance by defining it as *kebudayaan* instead of *agama*. An elderly *Muhammadiyah* woman who ran a food stand at the 2009 Malud explained that: "*Agama* descends from God, and so of course we can not change it. But this is *kebudayaan* and it is not perfect like Islam and we change it every year to make it better." Some NU

---

[4]M. Memon, *Ibn Tamya's Struggle Against Popular Religion with an Annotated Translation of his Kitab Iqtida as-sirat al Mustaquim Mukhalafat a Shab al Jahim (Book of the Necessity of the Straight Path Against the People of Hell.)* The Hague, Mouton, 1976 and S. ul-Islam, "Ibn Taymiyyah on the Mawlid" http://www.thenoblequran.com/sps/sp.cfm?subsecID=BDH06&articleID=BDH060002&articlePages=1

[5]On questions concerning the status of the *Mawlid* in Islamic law see: A. Schussman, "The Legitimacy and Nature of Mawid al-Nabi: (Analysis of a Fatwa)". *Islamic Law and Society*, vol. 5(2), 1998, pp. 214–234.

[6]See for example, *The Permissibility of Celebrating the Meelad un Nabi (saw) in Refutation to the Fatwa of Sheikh Abdul Aziz bin Baaz of Saudi Arabia,* Compiled by the Imam Raza Academy of South Africa, http://www.sunnah.org/publication/salafi/mawlid_refute.htm In Dubai, bin Baaz's writings are banned, in part because of his condemnation of the *Mawlid.* http://www.sunnah.org/ibadaat/mawlid_dubai.htm

scholars hold similar views of the *Garebeg*. Others have opinions similar to those of Ibn Taymiyyah concerning its specifically Javanese elements.[7] In Yogyakarta it is impossible for *Muhammadiyah* to condemn the *Malud*, because the Grand Mosque of the Sultanate is also the "Mother Mosque" of *Muhammadiyah*. In 2009, Dr. Din Syamsul Din, the General Chairman of *Muhammadiyah* and other of the organizations' leaders, endorsed it as a means of uniting the Indonesian Muslim community and as an opportunity for *Muhammadiyah* Muslims to demonstrate their love and respect for the Prophet Muhammad.[8] Some others share the view that it is *kufarat* and should not be celebrated. The difference of opinion reflects a deep divide in the reformist movement between those willing to accommodate *agama* and *kebudayaan* and those with more puritan inclinations.

In this Chapter 1 will be concerned with the history, religious meanings, and performative structure of this ritual complex, known locally as the *Garebeg Malud*, in Yogyakarta. The *Malud* is among the most important, and today certainly the most popular of the Yogyakarta state ceremonies.[9] The *Garebeg* was performed annually from the time of Hamengkubuwana I until the Japanese invasion of 1942. The first postwar performance was in 1970.[10] In addition to its stated purpose of celebrating

---

[7] T. Hanim, *Pesantren dan Tradisi Mawlid: Telaah Atas Kritik Terhadap Tradisi Membaca Kitab Mawlid di Pesantren*, 2009, http://www.sunnah.or g/ibadaat/tradisi_mawlid.htm

[8] http://musadiqmarhaban.wordpress.com/2008/03/21/muhammadiyah-pun-merayakan-maulid-nabi-saw/ A. Adham, "Maulid Nabi di Mu'allimaat Muhammadiyah Yogyakarta", *Kabar Indonesia,* March 31, 2008, http://www.kabarindonesia.com/berita.php?pil=13&jd=Maulid+Nabi+di+Mu%92allimaat+Muhammadiyah+Yogyakarta&dn=20080331192835   It   is clear that all parties to this debate can find support for their positions in the textual corpus of universalist Islam. They differ on questions of hermeneutics, or how these texts should be interpreted and acted upon.

[9] Others include the *Garebeg Syawal* and *Besar* which celebrate *Idul Fitri*, the feast at the conclusion of the fasting month of Ramdan and *Idul Adha*, the Feast of Sacrifice, held in conjunction with the *Hajj* or pilgrimage to Mecca; the *Labuhan*, which celebrates the Sultan's birthday and which offerings are made to the guardian spirits of the four directions; *Siraman Pusaka* conducted of the 1st day of the Javanese year in which *kraton pusaka* are ritually bathed and blssed water distributed. For a comprehensive account of these rituals, see, Sayumi, *Upacara Ritual di Kraton Yogyakarta. Refleksi Mithologi dalam Budaya Jawa.* Yogyakarta: Kepel Press, 2008.

[10] The reasons why it was renewed at this time is not clear. Some say that it was simply because "the time was right" others that it was an attempt to restore social and religious harmony in the Sultanate in the wake of the violence of 1965–1966. The violence was not nearly as intense in Yogyakarta as it was in other parts of Java, including Surakarta. According to many, this was because the Sultan worked to prevent it both politically and by putting his spiritual powers to use. Even so an unknown number of actual and suspected Communists were killed. The anti-communist campaign was based in the *Kauman*. Many of the victims were from other *kampung* in the central part of the city, some of them from areas located within the *kraton* walls. Many understand the *Garebeg Malud* of this era as *slametan* intended to heal the trauma of 1965 and particular to rebuild ties between the *kejawen* and *santri* populations. The fact that the Sultanate also undertook a program of mosque construction the stated purpose of which was to rehabilitate former "Communists" so that it "would not be necessary to kill them" at this time supports this interpretation. Some compare the period between 1942 and 1970 when there were no public *Malud* celebrations with the mythological account of the Majapahit-Demak inter-regnum during which state ceremonies were abandoned discussed later in this chapter. Others say that the reestablishment of the *Garebeg*

the birth of the Prophet Muhammad, the Yogyakarta *Garebeg Malud* serves four basic purposes: (1) it makes symbolic statements about the Islamic legitimacy of Javanese kingship; (2) it establishes a chain of blessing linking the state and its people with the Sultan, local saints, Muhammad, and God; (3) it links Javanese mysticism with Essentialist Islam and; (4) it mediates between a religiously inspired theory of kingship and changing political and economic conditions. Comparison of *Malud* performances of 1979, 1989, 2008 and 2009 with those of the colonial past will allow us to isolate a stable set of core performative units and equally meaningful, though variable, sets of indexical symbols through which the ritual and Javanese notions of kingship are recontextualized.

Conventional and Emergent Meanings: Patterns of Ritual Change

Studies of ritual by Schieffelin and Tambiah have emphasize the concept of emergent meanings, that is, those which are created, as opposed to expressed, in ritual performance.[11] While this approach has heightened awareness of the creative dimension of ritual, it presents a number of theoretical problems. Chief among these is the fact that, while some aspects of ritual are subject to frequent, and often dramatic, change, others are relatively constant. The question of which parts of the Yogyakarta *Malud* complex are held constant and which are subject to change is complicated by the imbrication of Universalsist and Local Islams that are legitimized by links to the past with elements of *kebudayaan* which are in principle, constantly changing. Some of the "traditional" components of the *Malud* complex link the post colonial present to the colonial and pre-colonial pasts preserve, or are said to preserve, parts of the ritual praxis of pre-colonial Muslim and pre-Muslim states. These historical and mythological connections figure significantly in the legitimization of the post-colonial Yogyakarta monarchy. At the same time an ideological commitment to constantly updating other aspects of the ritual is an important theme in the history of the ritual and is among the strategies the Sultanate employs

Tambiah's use of the Piercian concept of duplex structures provides a basis for explaining the interplay of continuity and change in ritual performance. He argues

---

was what is now referred to as "public diplomacy" because the Queen of the Netherlands attended. Viewed from Yogyakarta this was a state visit which redefined relationships between the Sultanate and the former colonial power, because for the first, and only, time Dutch and Javanese monarchs shared a ceremonial stage as equals. It is possible that all of these interpretations are correct. It is significant to note that I did not encounter suggestions of connections between the reestablishment of the *Malud* and the mass killings of 1965 and 1966 until after the fall of the New Order in 1998. Still others are of the opinion that state ceremonies were reinstituted to attract foreign and domestic tourists.

[11] E. Schieffelin, "Performance and the Cultural Construction of Reality," *American Ethnologist*, vol. 12(4), pp. 707–724, S. Tambiah, *Culture, Thought, and Social Action: An Anthropological Perspective*. Cambridge: Harvard University Press, 1985.

that indexical symbols, that is, signs that may be interpreted simultaneously as religious symbols and as indexes in "existential pragmatic relationship" with the objects they represent, link religious and social dimensions of ritual. The symbolic half of an indexical symbol conveys abstract meaning. Its indexical half links that meaning with a particular person, group, or social role. Ritual modulates the interplay of systems of belief, that is, intellectual systems concerned with cosmic ultimates, with pragmatic dimensions of social life. Ritual is liminal in that it defines the religious meaning of novel social phenomena and at the same time renders metaphysics socially relevant.

Indexical symbols are among the sources of emergent meaning and among the means through which *bricolage* is accomplished. Following Tambiah, we can think of a ritual as a conventional core structure to which indexical symbols may be attached. Typically, the meanings of indexical symbols are distinct from those of the religious core of the ritual, but upon incorporation into its performative structure those meanings suggest new interpretations linking elements of the ritual core to the person (or other kind of being) place or object to which an index refers. As Tambiah observes, increasing the scale and expense of a ritual may serve to create an indexical symbol.[12] Here the message to be inferred is that the more elaborate the ritual, the greater its transformative or constitutive power. This power in turn validates the relations of inequality that make ritual elaboration possible. There are other aspects of indexical symbolism Tambiah does not consider. Among these is the fact that, because they are distinct from the symbolic and performative core of the ritual, the meanings of indexical symbols are never entirely predictable. Rather, they must be inferred or computed.[13] Consequently they may "misfire," that is, assume meanings quite different from those intended by the sponsor of the ritual or of those who attempt to enhance their own status by attaching indexical symbols to widely celebrated rituals.[14] Secondly, the simplification of ritual may also be understood as an act of indexical symbolizing. The significance of simplification

---

[12]Op. cit., pp. 123–168.

[13]Tambiah states that the meanings of indexical symbols are inferred by the observer. The notion of inference links semiotics with the cognitive approach to symbolism advocated by Sperber (D. Sperber, *Rethinking Symbolism*. Cambridge: Cambridge University Press, 1975) and Lehman (F.K. Lehman,"Cognition and Computation: On Being Sufficiently Abstract." *Directions in Cognitive Anthropology*. Ed. J. Dougherty. Urbana: University of Illinois Press, 1986.) Lehman has written that symbolic thought is based on the computation of meaning by interpreting individuals. Ritual and other symbolic systems do not communicate anything other than a set of "objects" which motivate observers to create meaning for them. The distinction between symbol, index, and icon turns on the degree of similarity between two objects. An iconic relationship is one in which two objects are physically isomorphic, an indexical relationship one in which they share salient pragmatic characteristics, and a true symbolic (in the Piercian sense) relationship is one based on the interaction of abstract properties. The notion of computation of meaning is essential to the analysis of the *Garebeg Malud* because many of the exact, literal meanings of objects used in the ritual depend on the types of meanings computed by thousands of observers.

[14]See Chapter 6 for an example of how Islamist attempts to attach indexical symbols to the fasting of month of Ramadan in 2008 misfired.

may go beyond that of merely refraining from using certain symbols. It can also have positive, not entirely predictable meanings. In this chapter it is argued that the history of the *Garebeg Malud* can be understood in terms of these three principles: incorporation (through which a popular Muslim rite is linked to Javanese notions of kingship), elaboration of royal symbolism together with the inclusion of indexical symbols of colonialism in the nineteenth and early twentieth centuries, and simplification, de-colonialization and the incorporation of indexical symbols of Indonesian Nationalism and Islamic resurgence during the New Order and depoliticization and increased emphasis on *kebudayaan* following the democratic transition of 1998.

Kingship and Ritual in Yogyakarta

The Sultanate of Yogyakarta is an Islamic state, though not in the sense that the term is now generally used. The *Garebeg Malud is* predicated upon a complex set of cultural and religious presuppositions concerning the nature of kingship. These include the equation of kingship and sainthood, the theory of power (*kesekten*), and dynastic myths linking Yogyakarta with older Javanese states, Muslim prophets, and the Indian epics *Mahabharata* and *Ramayana.* The equation of kingship and sainthood is based on local interpretations of Islamic concepts of revelation and miracles, both of which are viewed from the perspective of the Sufi theory of the "Perfect Man."[15] Kings, and in post-colonial Indonesia, presidents, are thought by many to be chosen by God and to be endowed with *wahyu* (A., *wahy*), "revelation."[16] *Wahy* is revelation and the means through which God communicates with his prophets and, according to some Sufi traditions, with saints. Javanese understand *wahyu* as a flash or beam of light that confers a divine appointment on an individual assigning him or her a particular task. While there are many types of *wahyu,* that of kingship is the most important for understanding the *Malud* and other elements of the Yogyakarta *Kraton* ritual system. It provides the basis for the most important royal title *Kalipatulah* ("the representative of God").[17] Informants explain that

---

[15]The theory of the "Perfect Man" *(al-insan al-kamil) is* closely associated with the great medieval Spanish mystic philospher Ibn al 'Arabi (1165–1240). See Schimmel op. cit., pp. 263–286). 'Abd al-Karim al-Jili (d. ca. 1408) who wrote in the tradition of Ibn 'Arabi, produced the classic work on the Perfect Man, which is studied in Javanese *pesantren* and exists in an interlinear Arabic/Javanese edition. A thorough analysis of al-Jili's *Al-Insan al-Kamil is* found in R. Nicholson, *Studies in Islamic Mysticism.* Cambridge: Cambridge University Press, 1921, pp. 77–142.

[16]See Chapter 7 for a discussion of the role of this concept in New Order legitimation strategies.

[17]The idea of the *Kalifah* (Caliph) and the Caliphate as a governmental institution have long been among the most intensely contested concepts in Islamic political thought. For general discussions see of the Caliphate see: M. Ayoob, *The Many Faces of Political Islam.* Ann Arbor: University of Michigan Press, 2008; A. Black, *The History of Islamic Political Thought.* New York: Routledge, 2001; H. Bodman, "Caliphate" in M. Eliade (ed) *The Encyclopedia of Religion.* New York: Macmillan, vol. 3, pp. 21–24. In *God's Caliph: Religious Authority in the First Centuries of Islam.* Cambridge: Cambridge University Press, 1986, Patricia Crone and Marin Hinds have shown there is a fundamental tension between personalistic and textual authority in the Islamic tradition which dates to the period immediately following the death of the Prophet Muhammad.

a king who has *wahyu* glows with an inner light and that he cannot be defeated.[18] Nor is he subject to sin or error. Consequently, many Javanese feel that to oppose the Sultan is to oppose the will of God.

Kings are also believed to have the ability to attain union with God and to be the Perfect Man. [19] While others may also attain union, it is of special significance when coupled with kingship. Union may be attained only for an instant and is referred to

---

The Caliphs who followed Muhammad as leaders of the Muslim community claimed to the "representative of Allah on earth," and as such to be legitimate sources of Islamic law and social norms in much the same way the Prophet Muhammad was. While the authority of first four "Rightly Guided" (*Rahidun*) Caliph is accepted by most Sunni scholars, that of subsequent Caliphs is disputed. Some *ulama* have maintained that no legal authority was vested in later Caliphs and that the text of the *Qur'an* and *Hadith* – as interpreted by the *ulama* – are the only legitimate sources of religious and legal guidance for contemporary Muslims. In *"Quis Custodiet Custodes:* Some Reflections on the Persian Theory of Government, *Studia Islamica*, 5, pp. 125–148, 1956, Anne Lambton argues that all varieties of traditional Islamic political thought are theocratic, but that the Caliphal and text centered traditions developed in relative isolation from one another, and that in the early centuries of Islam juridical theory became increasingly removed from political reality. By the fifth century A.H. the theory that all rulers were "shadows of Allah on earth," directly appointed by him and responsible to him alone, was common throughout the Muslim world. The Caliphal tradition provides the basis for Islamic theories of kingship, including that of Java where rulers adopted titles including *Kalifutallah* (J. The Caliph of Allah) and *Sunan* – a Javanese variant of the Arabic term *sunnah* referring to the religious and social practice of a legitimate Islamic authority – among whom are numbered all of Allah's Prophets and Caliphs, including those of Java. It was not until the rise of the *Wahhabi* movement in the eighteenth century and modernist reformism in the nineteenth that the *shari'ah* centered discourse of the *ulama* regained a central position in Islamic political discourse. Javanese Muslims associated with *Nahdlatul Ulama* accept the authority of the *Rashidun* Caliphs as legally binding. *Muhammadiyah* and other modernist organizations consider only the religious practice of the Prophet Muhammad to be authoritive. The *Kalifah* concept does not figure significantly in Indonesian or Yogyakarta nationalism, but is an important element of contemporary Indonesian Islamist discourse. The last generally recognized claimants to the title *Kalifah* were the Ottoman Sultans. The office was abolished by the republican regime of the "Young Turks" in 1924. Some utopian Islamist organizations look to the re-establishment of the Caliphate as the key to solving all of the problems of the Muslim world. Of these Hizbut Tahrir Indonesia (HTI) is among the most vocal. HTI is the Indonesian branch of Hizb al Tahrir al-Islami (Islamic Liberation Party) which was founded in Jerusalem in 1953 by Taqi al Din al Nabhani (1909–1977). Al Nabhani studied at al Azhar in Cairo and was subsequently a religious teacher and judge in Palestine. He founded the organization when he and a group of associates split from the Muslim Brotherhood. Their primary goal was to restore what they considered to be an authentic Islamic way of life to the Muslim community and to purge it of the vestiges of colonialism, westernization and secularism. They hoped to achieve these goals and to restore the glory of Islam by the re-establishment of the universal Caliphate. Hizb al Tahrir is now a global organization headquartered in London. It maintains web sites in numerous European and Islamic languages. It is increasing visible and active in Indonesia, one of the few Muslim countries in which it operates legally. Hizb al Tahrir web sites can be located at http://www.hizb-ut-tahrir.org/

[18] See Chapter 7 for a discussion of the ways in which this aspect of royal authority is problematized in the context of democracy.

[19] At least until the fall of the New Order in 1998 these concepts were also applied to the Indonesian presidency. Both Soekarno and Suharto are widely believed to have to have come to power through the grace of God and to have ruled until their moral failings led him to withdraw

as *djumbuhing kawula gusti,* "the Union of Servant and Lord"[20] A person who has
attained this state has full understanding of the inner (*batin*) and outer (*lahir*) aspects
of reality and works for the salvation and worldly good of others.[21] In the case of
the Sultan this means that blessing is distributed to all of his subjects. Many believe
this to be the primary source of the tranquility and prosperity of the state and of
agricultural fertility on which it depends.

The Sultan is also described as the teacher or mystical guide of the state. Subjects
should submit to his will in the same sense that he submits to God's will.[22] This
state, like mystical union, is called the "Union of Servant and Lord." The Sultan
is the servant of God and the Lord of the state. As servant he serves as a link to
God for the state and its people, with respect to whom he is Lord.[23] These relationships are expressed in two royal titles: *Ngabdurahman* ("servant of the merciful")
and *Hamengkubuwana* ("he who holds the world on his lap"). In his capacity as
Panatagama ("regulator of religion") the Sultan must defend the *Shari'ah* (Islamic
law), support the *ulama,* and prohibit heresy. This aspect of kingship is clearly stated
in the eighteenth century text *Serat Cabolek*:

> "Do not repudiate the Law for this is treason against the king; truly the king has the
> authority to punish, since he is the representative of the greatest man on earth [the Prophet
> Muhammad]"[24] The text continues, "For it is the duty of the king to protect the tradition
> of the Prophet. If a king disregards the body of tradition of the Prophet, the grace of his
> countenance will vanish [and] he will defile his realm."[25] Later it is stated: "The king's
> order continues as follows: 'Let no one discuss (or) desire to study esoteric knowledge, or
> within the realm to teach the Science of Reality apart from that [derived from] the Law

---

the mandate. The extent to which this grafting of traditional concepts of authority onto "modern" political offices still applies in an era where presidents are democratically elected remains
unclear.

[20]"Servant/ Lord" terminology dates at least to the sixteenth century. See G. Drewes, *The
Admonitions of Seh Bari: A Sixteenth Century Javanese Text Attributed to the Saint of Bonan.*
The Hague: Martinus Nijhoff, 1969, p. 57. It is common in eighteenth and nineteenth century texts
and contemporary religious discourse. The core meaning of *kawula is* "servant" or "subject" of
the king. It is reasonable to suggest that the use of *gusti* for both "lord" in the sense of the Sultan
and in the sense of God is a product of a theory of kingship based on mystical union and that the
double meaning of the phrase "Union of Servant and Lord" is an example of manipulation of the
multivocal, evocative power of symbols.

[21]Union is momentary because *nafsu* ("Javanese from Arabic *nafs,* passions") are material elements of the body and cannot be destroyed. Permanent union may be attained only after death.
Contemporary Javanese mystics state that momentary union has important social consequences.
One who has attained this state is eternally tranquil. Such a person is detached from the world, yet
continues to live in it, serving as a source of blessing (*berkat*) and tranquility (*slamet*) for others.

[22]With respect to the state the Sultan occupies a role very similar to that of the *qutb* (*"pole"*), a
God-appointed human who is at the pinnacle of the hierarchy of saints and reigns as guardian and
spiritual director of the world. See Schimmel, op. cit., p. 200.

[23]On the social and political dimensions of the theory of the Union of Servant and Lord see
S. Moertono, *State and Statecraft in Old Java: A Study of the Later Mataram Period, 16th to
19th Centuries.* Monograph Series, Modern Indonesia Project. Ithaca: Cornell University, p. 26.

[24]S. Soebardi, *The Book of Cabolek.* The Hague: Martinus Nijhoff, 1975, pp. 67–68.

[25]Ibid., p

which may be taught within the realm. If anyone violates my command I will execute the death sentence."[26]

The Sultan's judicial authority was eroded during the colonial era, to the point where only the territory within the *kraton* wall was subject to even limited royal jurisdiction and eliminated with the establishment of the Indonesian republic. The last two Sultans have been revered as a proponents of Muslim piety. Many Muslim reformers consider them both to be supporters of, if not participant in, their cause in part because of close relationships between the palace and *Muhammadiyah* which is charged with the care and administration of the Grand Mosque of the Sultanate. In the late 1970s *santri* and *kejawen* mystics often said that Hamengkubuwana IX used his spiritual powers to travel to Mecca for the Friday prayer and that he appeared simultaneously in numerous Yogyakarta mosques at the same time. I have not heard this said of his son.

The Javanese theory of power (*kesekten*) is also an important component of the theory of kingship.[27] The term *kesekten is* derived from Sanskrit *sakti* and is the power associated with Hindu gods, particularly Siva. But in Muslim Java it is thought of as one of the forces of nature. It is acquired through a combination of *tapabrata* ("severe asceticism") and *semedi* ("concentration"). Power may be used for either good or evil purposes, but is usually destructive in nature. In the hands of the Sultan it is used to defeat enemies and evil spirits, stop epidemics and prevent pests from harming the rice crop. But in the hands of a sorcerer it may cause illness and even death.[28]

The religious significance of a Sultan does not end with death. Sultans of the past are revered as saints and sources of blessing. Their graves are sacred (*kramat)* and are among the most popular pilgrimage sites in the Sultanate. Pilgrims include Muslims, not just from Yogyakarta and Surakarta, but from all over Indonesia. They royal graves are especially popular among politicians. Access to these shrines and to the blessing obtainable at them is regulated by the *kraton*. State ceremonies conducted at the royal cemeteries seek the blessing of kings of the past for the current Sultan and the state. One of the purposes of the *Garebeg Malud is* to distribute this blessing as well as that derived from the current Sultan's mystical attainments to regional officials and the general public.

The court also attempts to monopolize power. Objects associated with great men of the past (*pusaka)* are imbued with *kesekten* and are *kraton* heirlooms. *Pusaka* may be *kramat* (holy), *sekti* (powerful), or both. While the two concepts are distinct, there is often uncertainty concerning which is responsible for extraordinary phenomena attributed to a particular *pusaka*. Consequently, even objects associated with the prophet Muhammad may be sources of power (*kesekten*). Because power is dangerous, it must be carefully controlled. The power of some *pusaka* is believed to be so great that it could cause floods, earthquakes, and other natural disasters. One

---

[26] Ibid., pp. 99–100.

[27] See Chapter 1 for a more detailed discussion of this concept.

[28] See Chapter 2. In this respect the powers of the Sultan resemble those of *dukun*.

of the duties of the Sultan is to determine how much of what type of power should be released at what time. This is accomplished through the public display of *pusaka* at the *Garebeg Malud* and other state ceremonies.

There are also complex genealogical myths connecting Yogyakarta with earlier Islamic and pre-Islamic states, the Hindu gods, and Islamic prophets. According to these myths the *dewa* ("Hindu gods") were humans. They, and through them, the kings of Majapahit, are the descendants of one of the two sons of Adam. The other son is the ancestor of the Muslim prophets. The two branches are joined in the house of Mataram. This myth serves several purposes. First, it allows a Muslim state to retain symbolic connections with its pre-Islamic roots. Secondly, it transforms the nature of Hindu gods. They are no longer divine but are numbered among the sainted ancestors for whom prayers may be offered and from whom blessing may be sought.[29]

The theory of kingship is sufficiently inclusive to allow individuals with divergent views of Islamic and pre-Islamic aspects of Javanese religion and culture to identify closely with one or more of its legitimation strategies. Because it draws on the totality of the theory of kingship, the *Garebeg Malud is* capable of establishing meaningful connections between the imperial cult and virtually every segment of Javanese society other than those Islamic modernists and Islamists who opposed it in principle.

The *Garebeg Malud in* Myth and History

Javanese texts and oral tradition state that the *Garebeg Malud* dates from the fifteenth century, the time of the first Islamic states. Questions arising from these traditions include those of the Islamic ritual patterns informing the early *Maluds* and the nature of the transformations involved in the imperialization and localization of a trans-cultural Muslim ritual. Stripped of local symbolism the *Mawlid al-Nabi* consists of a recitation of the biography of the prophet Muhammad, a prayer (*doa*) calling down blessing on him, and the distribution of gifts and alms. In India, which is among the probable sources of Javanese Islam, the *Mawlid is* celebrated with ritual meals and offerings of food to the spirit of the Prophet Muhammad.[30] The association of prayer, food, and veneration of the Prophet is fundamental to local formulations of Islamic piety in Java and elsewhere in the Malay world of Southeast Asia. In Java ritual meals *(slametan)* are held on major Islamic holidays, during rites of passage, and at times of personal or social crisis. As was argued in Chapter 3, hierarchical relations are temporarily abrogated in the context of this ritual. But for many Javanese, *slamet* implies more than the abrogation of hierarchy. It is the spiritual union of humans, saints, and ancestors. Many Javanese describe *slamet* as the

---

[29] It is also believed that many of the *dewa* were converted to Islam either before or after death.

[30] Schimmel, op. cit., pp. 186–187

social analog of mystical union and say that it has the same consequences for the community that meditation has for the individual. The ritual abrogation of hierarchy in the *slametan is* thought to define non-ritual social relations in terms of the "Union of Servant and Lord" ideal. This is not the abrogation of hierarchy. Rather it reinforces it by defining relationships of inequality in religious terms. The ritual ideal is not the social ideal, but makes its attainment possible. The *Garebeg Malud is* a series of *slametan* at which the Sultan offers food to his subjects. It is thought to transform social relations in the Sultanate in the same way that *slametan* transform local communities. When asked if the *Garebeg Malud* is a *slametan,* one court official replied, "Yes, but it is one that only the Sultan can give because he is like a father to everyone."

In rural Java the *Mawlid is* celebrated with a *slametan* called *Maludan.* The *Maludan* and the *Garebeg Malud* have much in common. At both offerings of rice cooked in coconut milk are presented to the spirit of the Prophet Muhammad. Some *santri* informants explained that this takes the place of the dish of rice and oil believed to have been the Prophet's favorite. Eating it on the day of the *Malud is* understood as a sign that one is a true Muslim. It is also a source of blessing and is sold at many food stands on *Alon-Alon Utara* on the morning of the *Malud* and at the month long night market that precedes it. Both rituals include prayers calling down blessing on the Prophet and recitation of his biography. Seen from the *kraton,* the *Slametan Maludan* is the *Garebeg Malud* stripped of its royal indexical symbols. Seen from the village, the *Garebeg Malud* is a *Maludan* with royal indexical symbols attached. In post-New Order Java, some villages have begun to use *Gunungan* in collective *Maludan* observances. Often these are carried in These structural similarities provide few clues about the history of either ritual. These are, however, data suggesting that the *Garebeg Malud/Slametan Maludan* pattern derives from the state cult of Demak and that state ceremonies were instrumental in the conversion to Islam of rural Java.

Two myths connect the *Garebeg Malud* with Demak. The first explains the continuity of the state ceremonies of Demak and Majapahit and hence that of Hinduism and Islam. The second explains some of the duties of Muslim kings and the historical role of the *Garebeg Malud* as a conversion ritual. Jointly, they provide a basis for understanding the ritual forms and conventional meanings of the *Garebeg Malud* in Yogyakarta.[31] The Majapahit/Demak myth is as follows:

> The kings of Majapahit [the last Hindu-Javanese kingdom] used to have rituals at which offerings of food were presented to the people. At the time of Demak [the first Islamic kingdom] this practice was discontinued and as a result crops were poor and many people went hungry. The Sultan of Demak asked Sunan Kalijaga [one of the nine *wali*] what he should do about this. Sunan Kalijaga replied that even though he was a Muslim he had a duty to provide for the well being of his people and to teach them Islam. He then instructed

---

[31] These same myths explain the origin of the *slametan.* They were also quoted in Chapter 2. They are repeated here because they are equally essential to the argument presented in this chapter.

the Sultan on how to perform the *Slametan* in ways which did not violate the tradition of the Prophet and told him to teach it to his subjects.[32]

This myth speaks in general of the importance of state ceremonies and in particular of the continuity of Demak and Majapahit. It focuses on the social dimension of the "Union of Servant and Lord" and more specifically on relationships between state ceremonies, prosperity, and social harmony. It links Islam and agricultural fertility, preserving an ancient Javanese religious theme but casting it in Muslim garb. It also describes the processes through which pre-Islamic custom may be brought into and structurally dominated by Islam. Hindu kings, we are told, used ritual to provide for the well being of the populace. Muslim kings must do the same but through ritual performance based on Islamic tradition. The second myth is more directly connected with the *Garebeg Malud*.

> For the kingdom of Demak the holidays which had to be celebrated were Idul *Fitri, Idul Adha* and the *Malud* of the prophet Muhammad, the last being the most important. To celebrate the day of the *Malud,* seven days beforehand all of the regional nobles and court officials were called to the palace. The purpose was to give devotion to the king. The officials of the religious department were ordered to perform *dhikr* in the mosque while giving explanations about religion to the public and give guidance in the confession of faith to people thronging to the mosque to see and hear *gamelan.* As a means of attracting people to the mosque, a large *gamelan* normally kept in the palace was played as it was carried to the mosque after the evening prayer. In the courtyard of the mosque, two large matching *gamelan* were placed in buildings on the right and left and played constantly in the afternoon and evening except during the hours of prayer. Many people were attracted to the sound of the *gamelan* and came to the mosque. There, while waiting to receive portions of food which had been made ready for them, they received instruction concerning the ritual duties of Islam and the biography of the prophet. They received *sedekahan* (Javanese from Arabic, charity-in this case, food), over which a *donga* had been recited and then ate together. Those who were attracted to Islam were then instructed to recite the confession of faith in order to enter the Islamic religion. This was done every day for seven days. The last day was the

---

[32] Sunan Kalijaga was one of the legendary *Wali Sanga*, (nine saints) believed to have played central roles in the establishment of Islam as the religion of Java. He is associated with the construction of the Grand Mosque of Demak, which is the architectural model for that of Yogyakarta. Myths concerning the construction of the Demak mosque mention Sunana Kalijaga as having fixed the *kiblat* or direction of prayer and by so doing oriented Java towards Mecca and Islam. It is said that after the mosque was constructed it refused to orient itself towards Mecca and spun in circles. Sunan Kaligaga, is said to have fixed the direction of the *kiblat* by holding one hand to the canter pillar of the mosque and by reaching out with the other and touching the Kabah in Mecca. This myth bends Java towards Mecca and Universalist Islam While Sunan Kalijaga used the *wayang* and other elements of *Kebudayaan Jawa* as tools for *Dakwah* he is also said to have played a central role in the wars that led to the conquest and destruction of Majapahit, the last of the Hindu Javanese states. Geertz, describes Sunan Kalijaga as exemplifying the syncretic "classical style" of Javanese Islam. He seriously understates the importance of Universalist and Essentialist Islam in legends concerning Sunan Kalijaga and the other *wali*. See C. Geertz, *Islam Observed: Religious Development in Morocco and Indonesia*. New Haven: Yale University Press, 1968 and Woodward, 1989, op. cit., for a critique of this view. On the *Wali Songo* see also, A, Bashah, *Wali Songo dengan Perkembanngan Islam di Nusantara* (The Nine Saints and the Spread of Islam in Indonesia). Selangor Malaysia: Pustaka Al Hijaz, 1993 and D. Rinkes, *Nine Saints of Java*. Kuala Lumpur Malaysia: Malaysia Sociological Research Institute, 1996.

climax of the festival. Beginning in the morning Sultan Syah Alam Akbar, as Kalifah of the Muslim community sat in the *sila*[33] position in front of officials, regional lords, and important functionaries. *gunungan* (mountains) of rice and accompaniments were carried from the palace to the mosque for a *Slametan* organized by the king for the people. At the time of the evening prayer the Sultan, followed by all of the regional lords and officials, came down from the palace and walked to the mosque. There the Sultan served as *imam* for the prayer. After the prayer the *Penghulu* (chief official of the state mosque) recited a *donga*, then the Sultan ate the *slametan* food together with the people.

The narrative structure of this myth parallels the performative structure of the Yogyakarta *Garebeg Malud*. The *Garebeg* employs elaborate *slametan*, recitation of the prophet's biography, and a procession from the palace to the mosque to ensure the well-being of the state. Wellbeing has two dimensions. In a material sense it means peace, prosperity and agricultural fertility. These themes are articulated in the Majapahit/Demak myth. In a religious sense well-being means conversion to Islam. The Demak myth stresses this theme. The use of *gamelan is* justified by the fact that it attracts non-Muslims to the mosque. According to palace tradition circumcision rites were performed at the *Garebeg Malud* during the Demak period. It is said to have been among the primary means through which rural Java was converted. Significantly, many contemporary Javanese maintain that holding the *Slametan Maludan is* the minimal criterion for distinguishing Muslims from nonbelievers. This suggests that conversion-oriented state *slametan* served as models for Muslim piety among the newly converted.

Three themes: continuity with the pre-Muslim past, prosperity, and conversion distinguish the *Garebeg Malud* from the *Mawlids* of other Muslim societies. Javanese myth implies that in the transition from Hinduism to Islam, ritual meanings were incorporated into the *Mawlid* as indexical symbols to establish the cultural (i.e., continuity), political (i.e., material prosperity), and religious (i.e., sponsoring conversion) legitimacy of the Islamic state of Demak. It speaks to both the Islamicization of Javanese culture (in both senses) and the Javanization of Islam.

Performative Structure of the Yogyakarta *Malud*

The Demak myth describes five ritual complexes: (1) *gamelan* performances at the state mosque; (2) a royal audience in which the Sultan assumes the posture of a mystic, (3) a procession to the mosque; (4) the recitation of the prophet's biography; and (5) *Slametan* for nobles, court officials, and the general public. The Yogyakarta *Malud* deviates only slightly from this pattern. The order of performance is altered to draw a sharper distinction between components of the ritual dominated by elite political concerns and those intended for the general population. Additional symbols of historical continuity, chiefly sacred heirlooms, have been added to connect

---

[33] *Sila is* to sit with folded legs, a position commonly used for meditation.

Yogyakarta with earlier states.[34] The *Malud* includes two basic ritual complexes: *Sekaten,* a series of rituals held at the state mosque and the *Garebeg,* a procession from the *Kraton* to the mosque.

Sekaten

Sekaten is a combined fair, night market, and religious observance. The night market, at which there are a wide variety of popular entertainment events, runs for an entire month. *Sekaten* itself lasts for 7 days, culminating in the Sultan's visit to the Grand Mosque the evening prior to the *Garebeg.*

Elite components of *Sekaten* include a religious observance and ritual meal attended by the Sultan, court officials, and *ulama.* Public components combine the distribution of alms, "conversion," and entertainment. *Sekaten* retains the conversion symbols attributed to the Demak *Malud.* On the first night two *gamelan* are carried from the palace to the mosque. One is said to have belonged to the first Sultan of Demak. The other is a copy made at the time of the partition of Mataram when the *pusaka* were divided between the Yogyakarta and Surakarta *Kraton.* They are thought to have the power to attract people to the mosque, and to compel conversion to Islam. They are played continuously except during hours of prayer. The melodies are slower and deeper than normal and represent the weeping of the Prophet's daughter Fatimah when she heard of the death of her son Husain at the battle of Karbala.[35] Court and mosque officials also explained that these melodies are a Javanese version of the *azan,* the Arabic call to prayer, but in a symbolic medium that Javanese can better appreciate. Spectators are required to perform purification rites and to recite the confession of faith before entering the mosque compound.

In 1978 and 1998 a large banner with the confession of faith in Arabic script, transliterated Arabic and Indonesian translation was hung at the top of the gate leading to the mosque. When asked why these conversion rites have been continued, informants replied that was tradition. Some *santri* added that Javanese still needed to be attracted to the mosque. In 2009 there were banners on food stalls in the court yard of the mosque urging people to seek assistance only from God – a

---

[34]The following account is based on the comparison of the colonial *Garebeg Malud* and the performances I witnessed in 1979, 1989, 2008 and 2009. *Graebeg* of the colonial era are described in I. Groneman, *De Garebegs te Ngajogjakarta.* The Hague: Martinus Nijhoff, 1895 and S. Tirtokoesoemo, *The Garebegs in the Sultanaat Jogjakarta.* Jogjakarta: H. Bunning., 1935.

[35]While this motif is characteristic of Shia'h Islam, there is no evidence that Shi'ah thinking has played a significant role in the development of Javanese Islam. The traditional of venerating the family of the Prophet Muhammad is shared by Sunni and Shi'ah Muslims. What differentiate the two is the Shi'ah belief in a series of divinely guided Imam among whom Ali, the cousin and son-in-law of the prophet was the first. Javanese and other Indonesians of Arabic descent (*Habib*) are particularly devoted to Ali, from whom many claim descent, but clearly distinguish themselves from Shi'ah. They are particularly insistent about rejecting the Shi'ah theory of divinely inspired Imam.

common theme in *Muhammadiyah* discourse that is implicitly critical of the cult of saint veneration that is characteristic of other variants of Javanese Islam.

Like the Sultan in the Demak myth, those of Yogyakarta use the *Malud* to make public statements about their commitment to Islam and the Islamic foundations of the state. On the final evening of *Sekaten* there is a procession from the palace to the state mosque. The Sultan, or a designated substitute, is accompanied by members of the court and by troops of *prajurit*. He distributes coins and flowers at the palace gate, in front of the *gamelan,* and in the mosque. Enormous crowds gather, hoping to catch a glimpse of the Sultan and, if possible, to obtain some of the alms. It is believed that those lucky enough to grab one of the coins the Sultan throws to the crowd will prosper in the coming year. Farmers bury them in their rice fields with the expectation of increased yields. While these practices originally established links between the Sultanate and its rural population, many urban Javanese now participate, for very similar economic reasons. Those who are not lucky enough to obtain one of the coins, and even many of those who are eat *nasi gurih* (rice cooked in coconut milk served with chicken, peanuts, beans and other accompaniments), which has the same result. Many non-Muslims, especially Chinese, share these beliefs.

Throughout the fair women chew betel nut mixed with tobacco (*kinang*) which is said to preserve youth and strengthen teeth. In the late 1970s many Javanese women, though almost no men, chewed betel, but the practice is now extremely rare. Over time chewing betel turns your teeth red. This is one of the reason the reasons why few young people indulge in it on a regular basis. Many young women who try it during *Sekaten* do so only because it is "tradition" and find the taste disgusting. Some say that it makes them sick. Many people also purchase boiled eggs that have been dyed purple that are also said to be charged with blessing. Men purchase whips used to herd cattle and other livestock and agricultural tools said to enhance the fertility of crops and livestock.

Sekaten is also a night market and provides a wide variety of popular entertainments. This aspect of the ritual is subject to almost constant change. It is said to have originated as a competition between dance troops of the regional nobility. During the colonial period gambling was common, while in the eighteenth and early nineteenth centuries there were fights between tigers, buffaloes, and other animals and tests of martial skills.[36] Movies were introduced in the 1930s. Currently classical dance, drama, carnival rides, Indonesian and Western music, and patriotic and religious speeches are included. There are many food and beverage stalls and merchants selling goods ranging form agricultural tools to clothing, cooking utensils, toys and souvenirs. If there is a general rule concerning this component of *Sekaten*, it is that whatever form of entertainment is currently popular is included. Another generalization is that culturally conservative Javanese bemoan the changes.

The elite component of *Sekaten* consists of a *Malud* celebration at the state mosque attended by the Sultan, court officials, regional officials, and *ulama*. Today

---

[36]Gambling is now illegal, but still occurs.

Indonesian government officials are also included. The Sultan serves as *imam* for the prayer, after which the biography of the prophet is recited, a sermon delivered, and a prayer *(donga)* said for the welfare of the Sultan and the state. There are also *Qur'an* recitations and prior to the Second World War there were *dhikr* with drum and tambourine performances. These have been discontinued as part of a compromise with *Muhammadiyah*, by whom they are seen as *bid'ah* (religious innovation) but continue to play important roles in *malud* and other celebrations in other mosques controlled by the *kraton*. Finally, there is an elaborate *slametan*. The Sultan sits on a golden throne surrounded by officials holding the most cherished and powerful *pusaka*. Rice is cooked in a pot from which Sunan Kalijaga is said have fed vast throngs of people with a small quantity of rice. The Sultan presses a small amount of rice into his hand of each of the guests. This is called *ngepeli* (from Javanese, *ngepel*). Subsisting on this amount of food is a common form of *tarekat* (Javanese, asceticism). The rice is charged with blessing and is valued by nobles and *ulama* in the same way peasants value alms distributed by the Sultan. When the *slametan is* finished, the Sultan pays his respects to descendants of the prophet Muhammad gathered in front of the mosque.[37] He leaves through a side gate and once in every 8 years kicks down a brick wall representing the 70,000 veils separating humanity from God. The bricks, like the alms he distributes, are thought to be highly charged with blessing.

Sekaten can be interpreted in at least two ways: first, as a conversion ritual in which the rural agricultural population is encouraged to embrace Islam and receive the Sultan's blessing, and second, as an elite ritual uniting the palace officials, regional lords, and the *ulama* as the political and religious servants of the Sultan. The Sultan is depicted as a Sufi saint and a source of blessing which is, in turn, the source of his political authority and the wellbeing of the Sultanate. All of these concerns are expressed in the *donga* recited by the *Penghulu*. God is asked to:

> .....defeat the enemies of the state, grant the Sultan a long life, secure the glory of the palace, the Sultan's justice, and generosity, protect the state, bestow blessing on the Sultan, ensure prosperity, save the Sultan from sin and hell, make him a just and righteous protector of subjects and officials, prevent him from becoming cruel, make his reign righteous and grant him the rewards of heaven, protect the royal family, the *patih* (chief minister) the *ulama* and other subjects, unite the hearts of the entire kingdom, banish feelings of ill will and bestow blessing on the prophet Muhammad, his family and companions.[38]

This prayer illustrates the transitive character of the "Union of Servant and Lord." God is referred to as the "lord of the universe" and is asked to bless, protect, and

---

[37] *Sayyid*, here this means Arab descendents of the Prophet Muhammad. Many Javanese, including those of the Mataram dynasty and many *Kyai* families claim descent from the Prophet through his grandson Hasan. Most *Habib* claim descent from his other grandson Hussein. Because Javanese kinship is bilateral, many will recognizes descent from the Prophet through genealogical links of either gender. *Habib*, like other Arabs, recognize only patrilineal descent. It is for this reason that they strongly disapprove of their daughters marrying outside the community, because the children of such unions are not, by their reckoning *Sayyid*.

[38] I would like to thank K.P.H. Poerwokoesoemo for sharing it with me.

show mercy towards the Sultan. Here the Sultan is clearly the servant. But God is also asked to make the Sultan the spiritual guide and protector of the state. Here he is lord. It is also asked that the hearts of all people be united and purged of ill will. This is the essence of the state of *slamet*. Taken as a whole, the prayer asks God to make the Sultan a proper servant of the divine and a proper lord for his subjects, thus ensuring the prosperity and wellbeing of all. This text is from the 1930s. In 2009 a young Javanese man expressed these sentiments more precisely: "The Sultan submits to God, we submit the Sultan and everything is good."

The Garebeg

The *Garebeg* is an enormous *slametan* held on the day of the *Malud*. While the *Sekaten slametan* is for the elite, the *Garebeg is* for the general public. It is an icon of relationships between God, the Sultan, and his subjects. Its purpose is to provide blessing to the common people and to establish the ideal of "Union of Servant and Lord" as social reality. Like *Sekaten* the *Garebeg* is a procession.[39] The Sultan walks from the center of the palace to a raised throne hall at the northern end. He is accompanied by princes and officials of the highest rank. Immediately below him are seats for regional nobles and foreign ambassadors. Today these have been replaced by reviewing stands. "Invitations" are available for a small price. Tens of thousands of other people jam the northern *alon-alon*. The Sultan is surrounded by regalia (*ampilan*), representing the qualities of a saint who has attained mystical union.[40] After he is seated, rice mountains and other offerings are carried to the state mosque where they are distributed by the *Penghulu*. They are escorted by *prajurit kraton* carrying important *pusaka* and court officials.

The *gunungan* are gifts from the Sultan to his subjects. There are several types; *Gunungan Kakang* is the most important. It is a cone made from bamboo, sticky rice, long green bean pods and other types of food. It is a massive version of the rice cone (*tumpeng*) used in ordinary *slametan*.[41] The *gunungan* are assembled by

---

[39] For a more detailed discussion of this procession see Chapter 3

[40] These are golden figures of a goose, the white feathers of which represent purity; a deer representing quickness; a cock representing bravery; a peacock representing the Sultan's function as cleanser of souls; a gunpowder box representing benevolence; and a lantern symbolizing the belief that the Sultan gives light to his subjects in times of darkness. Several informants stated that these regalia were not *pusaka,* but rather a form of visual *dhikr* to aid the Sultan in his quest for mystical union.

[41] *Gunungan* are also carried from government offices to mosques in other parts of Java to celebrate the *Malud* and in *haul* which commemorate the deaths of saints. Some Javanese Muslims describe the *Garebeg Malud* as a *haul* for the Prophet Muhammad. Since the collapse of the New Order in 1998 the use of *Gunungan* in *Malud* celebrations in rural Java has increased significantly. These *gunungan* resemble those constructed by the Yogyakarta and Surakarta *kraton* in a general sense. They usually include local agricultural products that are not used in *kraton gunnungan* including cabbages and carrots. Because this is a new, and still developing, ritual tradition the composition varies considerably from year to year.

male *abdi dalem* the day before the *Malud*. Preparation of the food begins at least a month in advance and is done by female *abdi dalem* who also are specialists in the preparation of *jamu*.[42] On top there is a crown made from balls of rice flour, some of which are in the shape of fish. There are three other *gunungan* constructed in the shape of umbrellas[43] and one which is a metal tray containing parcels of food. In the year *Dal* of the 8 year Javanese *windu* cylce an additional *gunnungan* called *Bromo*, after an immense volcano is east Java is added.[44] All of the *gunungan* are thought to contain both blessing and power. While the distribution of alms to the public is a secondary feature of *Sekaten,* it is the principal purpose of the *Garebeg.* Food offerings are given to mosque officials and other *abdi dalem* and, in theory, each of the Sultan's subjects should receive a portion of the *gunungan.*

In post-colonial Yogyakarta the *Gunungan* and *prajurit* are historical symbols linking modern Yogyakarta with the pre-colonial past. The *Gunungan* and the uniforms worn by the *prajurit* have changed very little over the course of time. Photographs of the *Gunungan* included in Groneman's account of the *Garebeg Malud* of 1895 indicate that they have changed little, if at all, in the last century. Illustrations in a *kraton* manuscript dating to 1804 indicates that the uniforms worn by the *Prajurit Kraton*, their flags and weapons are similarly unchanged.[45] Despite and indeed because of this historical continuity there meanings have changed. In 1804, the ceremonial guards were the parade troops of a formidable military force. The uniforms were hybridities combing Javanese batik and the latest European fashion, including top hats. After the Java War (1825–1830) the were little more than ceremonial guards. Today, these seeming anachronisms are symbols of historical continuity and of *Kebudayaan Yogyakarta*. They are symbolically important not because they are "up to date" as they were in 1804, but because of their anachronism. There is no shortage of men willing to serve in these units, despite the fact that they are paid only 2000 *Rupiah* (approximately 20 US cents) per month. Wood and plastic replicas are sold, primarily to domestic tourists, throughout the city and can be found at grave sites and other shrines controlled by the *kraton* and in the homes of many traditionalist Yogyakarta Javanese.

The Sultan is believed to attain mystical union as the *gunungan* are carried to the mosque. This, according to court informants, is the most important moment of

---

[42] See Chapter 3.

[43] On the *gunungan* see Tirtokoesoemo op. cit., pp. 76–23. The group of *gunungan* are analogous with offerings presented at ordinary *slametan. gunungan kakang* resembles the yellow rice cone which is the most important offering. The trays take the place of the small offerings which surround it. The umbrella shaped *gunungan* are appropriate for a royal *slametan* because umbrellas are important regalia and status markers.

[44] Unlike the others, *Gunnungan Bromo* is returned to the *kraton* intact after it is carried to the mosque on the morning of the *Garebeg Malud*. It is then presented to *abdi dalem* who scramble to grab pieces as it is torn to shreds in exactly the same way that the others are in the courtyard of the Grand Mosque.

[45] *Buku Gambar Prajurit Kraton Ngayogyakarta Adiningrat* Yogyakarta *Kraton* Manuscript D39 YMK/W-363. Reproduced in D. Marihandono and H. Juwono, *Sultan Hamengku Buwono II. Pembel Tradisi dan Kekuasaan Jawa.* Yogyakarta: Banjar Aji Production, 2008, pp. 241–257.

the *Garebeg Malud.* It is the source of the blessing distributed through the *gunun-gan* and allows him to channel and control the power released into society by the *pusaka.* The combination of mystical union and the *Garebeg slametan* are thought to establish the prosperity, social and spiritual tranquility of the state and to define social relationships in terms of the "Union of Servant and Lord" ideal.

Indexical Symbols and Ritual Change

Viewed from the perspective of the pan-Islamic *Mawlid al-Nabi, gamelan, gunun-gan,* and the Sultan's attainment of mystical union can be understood as indexical symbols localizing a trans-cultural Muslim ritual and linking it with kingship and pre-Islamic religious concepts of authority and power. Viewed from Yogyakarta, they are the performative core of the *Garebeg Malud.* Descriptions of these aspects of the ritual by Groneman (1895) and Tirkoesoemo (1935) indicate that they have changed little in the past century and even less in the past three decades. Contemporary court informants explained that the ritual could not be performed without them.

While this ritual core corresponds closely with the narrative structures of the Demak and Majapahit myths, the indexical symbols attached to it have changed dramatically. Changes include the addition and subsequent deletion of indexical symbols of imperial grandeur and colonialism, the incorporation of symbols of Indonesian nationalism, "democracy;" and reformist Islam. The scale and complex-ity of the two processions to the mosque are illustrative of the ways in which the *Garebeg Malud* has changed. In the eighteenth and early nineteenth centuries, the participation of imperial troops was a clear symbol of the Sultan's military power. Participation in the ritual was an act of political submission as well as an expres-sion of Muslim piety. Those who refused to attend could be executed for treason.[46] The ritual forms of the traditional imperial system were retained and even elabo-rated during the colonial period. Stripped of its military might, Yogyakarta became what Geertz calls a "theater state"[47] Sultans rode in elegant carriages resembling those of European monarchs. They were accompanied to the mosque by thousands of retainers, including palace officials, regional lords, female officials carrying the regalia, a company of mentally and/or physically disabled people (as symbols of royal mercy) and a group of *hajji.* Horses and elephants bowed as the *gunungan*

---

[46]Ricklefs, op. cit., pp. 133, 146–147, 274, 335) has shown that the *Garebeg* of the eighteenth century were also arenas for elite political competition precisely because all of the contending factions were required to appear at court. The Sultan's troops were, at that time, more than symbols. They provided security and posed a clear threat to real and potential rebels and to the Dutch. Given the size of the crowds security is still a concern. It is provided by the Yogyakarta provincial police force. In the late 1970s the police were clearly Indonesian. Today this is far less clear. There is still a police presence, but there are also *kraton* security guards. They are assisted by students from *Muhammadiyah* secondary schools who lock arms to hold back the often surging crowds.

[47]C. Geertz, *Negara The Theatre Stare in Nineteenth-Century Bali.* Princeton: Princeton University Press, 1980.

were carried to the mosque, and a salute was fired from the Dutch fort. On the day of the *Malud* nobles and Dutch officials were seated in an audience hall, and watched while as many as thirty *gunungan* were carried to the mosque.[48] After a large *slametan* they were divided and distributed to provincial officials and village head men.

In modern Indonesia the Sultanate does not have the funds, or the desire, to conduct ritual drama on such a vast scale. The *Sekaten* procession is limited to members of the Sultan's family, *prajurit* and *kraton* official. Anyone able to pay a small fee may sit in the audience hall on the day of the *Garebeg*. Only one set of *gunungan is* constructed. They are not given to officials but placed in the courtyard in front of the Grand Mosque, where crowds tear them to shreds. Many informants believe that Sultan Hamenkubuwana IX was "democratic" and that, by reducing the scale of the *Garebeg Malud*, he eliminated barriers between himself and his subjects. Numerous village and urban informants commented that the new system is better than the old because the Sultan gives gifts to the people directly rather than passing them through a complex administrative system. This directness is interpreted as a sign that he is the protector and benefactor of the common people. From this claim we may conclude that the political meanings of contemporary *Malud* processions are strikingly different from those of the past. Contemporary ones garner popular support rather than controlling regional elites. Indexical symbols of colonialism have been eliminated and replaced with those of democracy. During the colonial period the Sultan, dressed in the uniform of a Dutch general, presided over a review of Dutch and "native" troops. He was accompanied to the mosque and the throne hall by the Dutch governor. The Dutch national anthem was played and a toast drunk to the king or queen of Holland. In official discourse the governor was referred to as the Sultan's elder brother. He was also presented with a *gunungan*.

This set of indexical symbols was subject to contradictory interpretations. According to palace informants, the Dutch sought to "modernize" state ceremonies by introducing European customs and wished to present themselves as the benefactors and older brothers of the Javanese. The court saw things differently. At best the Dutch were viewed as guests. They were offered the chance to submit to the Sultan and to embrace Islam but chose to drink wine while the Sultan prayed. Numerous informants stated that such an act was a clear statement of Dutch disdain for Islam and Javanese culture.[49]

---

[48]Tirtokoesoemo, op. cit., p. 58.

[49]This is a clear example of the way in which indexical symbols may misfire. In the eighteenth century Yogyakarta's contempt for the Dutch was stated very clearly. In 1783 a Dutch captain was stabbed by a Javanese officer. The resident was tricked into formally requesting clemency for the offender. The Sultan complied and as a token of "friendship" invited the resident to a fight between a tiger and a buffalo. As Ricklefs (1974:275) points out, the buffalo is a symbol of Java and the tiger represents the Dutch. Buffaloes always kill tigers in these contests.

Other changes reflect the reformist orientation of the *santri* community in Yogyakarta.[50] Many overtly Sufi elements of the rite have been eliminated, including tambourine performances and *dhikr.*[51] Even clothing styles have changed. Before the second world war the Sultan and the *Penghulu* wore patched coats associated with Sufi orders. These have been replaced by white for the *Penghulu* and pale green for the Sultan. White is associated with purity, "Arab" custom, and Universalist Islam. Pale green is a more subtle reference to Javanese Sufism, because it is the color said to appear as the mystic attains union with God.[52] Perhaps the most significant change is that the *slametan* for nobles and officials has been moved from the mosque to the palace. It is now held on the day of the *Garebeg* after the distribution of the *gunungan.* A high ranking official explained that this change was necessary because the *Penghulu* does not approve of *slametan* and would be unhappy if *pusaka* to be brought into the mosque because he is a *Muhammadiyah* member, He continued that the purpose of the Sultan's visit to the mosque was to honor the Prophet, the *Penghulu* and the *santri* community and that the ritual must, therefore, fit with the spirit of the times. This theme was echoed in a sermon delivered at *Sekaten* in 1979. The speaker was a prominent Muhammadiyah theologian. He explained that *gamelan,* the Javanese shadow theater, and the *Garebeg Malud* are permissible because they are expressions of Javanese culture (*kebudayaan*) and that they heighten awareness of an important Muslim holiday, but that unspecified non-Islamic customs should be eliminated. The speaker took great pains to emphasize both the purity of the reformist community and the religious acceptability of customs many consider to be *bid'ah.*

Muhammadiyah interpretations of the changes vary but fall into two basic categories. Some see them as signs that the Sultan supports the movement. Others see them as an attempt to circumvent the reformist program by employing a simpler, though still unacceptable, Javanese ritual performance. Despite these uncertainties,

---

[50]*Muhammadiyah,* was founded within the palace walls in Yogyakarta in 1912. Most of the *ulama* affiliated with the *kraton,* including the present *Penghulu,* are members of this organization. When I asked him about his role in the *Garebeg Malud,* the *Penghulu* stated that it a duty assigned by the Sultan and a part of Javanese culture. He continued by saying that such celebrations were not part of the "true Islam."

[51]While they are not included in the *Garebeg, shalawatan* performances (recitations or Arabic texts praising the Prophet Muhammad) are now sponsored by and held in the *kraton.* In May of 2010 a performance that featured both Arabic and traditional Javanese variants was held in the *pagelaran* to commemorate the 263rd anniversary of the construction of the *kraton* (on the Islamic calendar), It featured the wildly popular Hadrami-Javanese performer Habib Syech Assegaf and attracted thousands of devoted fans, most of them young people. These performances are widely understood as efforts to "bring Islam back to the *kraton*" and to forge ties between conservative Muslims from the *pesantren* tradition, the Indonesian Arab community and the palace. This is the most remarkable development in Javanese Islam that I have witnessed in 30 years.

[52]Green is also, of course, the sacred color of Islam, closely associated with the Holy Prophet, with whom all Sufi spiritual lineages begin.

Muhammadiyah have attached indexical symbols of its own to the *Sekaten* fair. *Qur'an* recitations and sermons are broadcast over loudspeakers. There are also banners and information booths describing the social, educational, and religious programs of *Muhammadiyah* and other Muslim organizations.

The second set of indexical symbols attached to the *Garebeg Malud* are those of Indonesian nationalism. In one sense these symbols resemble those of colonialism in that they link Yogyakarta with a higher level, non-Javanese political system. It is, however, significant that Indonesian symbols have not replaced those of colonialism. The Sultan is not, for example accompanied to the throne by an Indonesian official and does not wear an Indonesian military uniform on ritual occasions. Indonesian indexical symbols have been added to *Sekaten* but not to the *Garebeg*. This can be interpreted as an indexical symbol of Yogyakarta nationalism, because the *kraton* has taken clear steps to establish itself as an independent ritual entity.

In the 1970s films about the Indonesian Revolution were shown on the *Alon Aon*. At that time television was not common and films were a popular form of entertainment, but one that many Javanese could not afford. Televisions are now common place and the scale of broadcasting has expanded enormously. Classical and popular music performances and carnival rides are now the most popular forms of entertainment at *Sekaten*. There are also displays of what can only be described as nationalist *pusaka,* including a briefcase owned by the late president Sukarno. Many Javanese believe that these objects contain magical power in exactly the same manner as those dating to the pre-colonial era. There are also tours of the palace and displays of *pusaka* both of which would have been unthinkable during the colonial period. Vendors sell a wide variety of mundane goods, kitchen utensils, house and garden plants, clothing and many other items. Some sell posters, figurines and other items representing both Islam and Javanese culture. One I encountered in 2010 offered posters spanning the continuum from Universal to local Islam and symbolizing Indonesian and Yogyakarta nationalism. Images included: *Ayat Kursi* of the *Qur'an*, The Rightly guided Caliphs revered by Sunni Muslims, Sunan Kalijaga, Indonesia's first president Soekarno and Sultans Hamengkubuwana IX and X.

Conclusions

The *Garebeg Malud* links veneration of the prophet Muhammad with Javanese notions of kingship. The Sultan controls potent sources of blessing and power. The *Malud* distributes blessing and power, establishing the peace and prosperity (including agricultural fertility) of the kingdom. From a Javanese perspective the *Garebeg Malud is* a constitutive rite. Its performance does not mirror cosmic realities; it defines them, establishing the state as a Sufi order headed by a saint/king who, by virtue of his mystical attainments, is linked directly to God. It establishes a bond of blessing linking the Sultan with nobles, the *ulama,* and villagers. The symbolism of conversion, veneration of the prophet, and other aspects of Essentialist Islam are essential parts of this process, because only Muslims may be subjects/devotees of a king/saint.[53]

The religious core of the *Garebeg Malud* dates from the time of the first Javanese Islamic states. Indexical symbols have been added and deleted to contextualize the religious core in shifting social and political environments. But *Garebeg Malud* defines as well as mirrors reality. Originally (according to myth and tradition), it was a conversion ritual which established an Islamic court/village axis and linked the new state of Demak to the pre-Islamic past. During the eighteenth century it was used to define Yogyakarta as a legitimate state. At that time Yogyakarta was struggling to establish itself in a religious and political context which included both the Dutch and the older Javanese Islamic kingdom of Surakarta. Given the Javanese theory of kingship, elite and popular participation in the state ceremonies of the new kingdom were as essential as economic and military resources. With the establishment of Dutch power in the nineteenth century, Yogyakarta became a theatre state. Ritual and the arts were the primary means through which the Sultanate could retain its position at the center of Javanese life and culture. The Sultan could offer blessing to nobles and villagers but did not have recourse to military power. The *Garebeg Malud* was also a means of accommodating, and at the same time making subtle derogatory statements about, colonial power.

The modern *Garebeg Malud* links the Sultan directly to his subjects. The meta message of the modern indexical symbols is that the Sultanate remains politically and religiously viable despite its incorporation into the Indonesian republic. The fact that hundreds of thousands of villagers attend the ceremonies indicates that they have not dramatically changed their views of either the ritual or the Sultan. In modern Indonesia this show of support has significant political implications, particularly at a time when the future of the monarchy is in question. Sultan Hamengkubuwana IX was an old man when I first witnessed the *Garebeg Malud*. He had reigned for nearly half a century and it was clear that he would not live much longer. In 1979 it was not certain that his son would be allowed to succeed him or that the special status of the Sultanate would be retained after his death. At that time many in Yogyakarta believed that the *Garebeg Malud* had been reintroduced to show the national government that the Sultan's subjects remained royalists at heart. The fact that Prince Mangkubumi, the Sultan's son and heir apparent, was given highly visible roles in the *Garebeg Malud is* further evidence for this position. By simplifying the *Malud*, the Yogyakarta court has redefined the very nature of kingship in ways which *may* allow it to continue beyond the reign of the current Sultan Hamengkubuwana X. The Sultan is now presented as a benefactor and source of blessing but not as a remote, authoritarian political authority. The modern *Garebeg Malud* emphasizes his close relationship with the common people. Moreover, by going directly to the people, he avoids the implication that the *Garebeg Malud is* an

---

[53]Officially, non-Muslims may not live within the old city of Yogyakarta, i.e., the area within the palace walls. I was able to live there in 1979 only with the explicit permission of Sultan Hamengkubuwana!X

attempt to impose royal control on Indonesian officials. From this perspective the entire modern ritual is an indexical symbol. It defines the Sultanate in terms of personal links between the saint/king and his subjects rather than a hierarchy of blessing and power. This definition can be understood as an attempt to preserve religious and cultural components of kingship in the context of the modern Indonesian state. Only time will tell if the *Garebeg Malud* retains the constitutive power to define society as a cosmic reality.

Epilogue

The preceding analysis is based primarily on field work conducted in 1979 though I have been unable to resist the temptation to update it. I attended the *Malud* for the second time in 1989 and found that, while the ritual core had not changed, the indexical symbols attached to it had changed significantly. The Indonesian nationalist elements of *Sekaten* were reduced and those of Essentialist Islam enhanced. A new complex of symbols emphasizing the historical continuity of kingship and its links to the development orientation of the Indonesian government were introduced. These changes provide a clear example of how indexical symbols are used to link the cosmologically defined transformative core of ritual to changing theological, social and political contexts.

Sultan Hamengkubuwana IX died on October 3, 1988, a few weeks prior to the *Malud*. The ritual was performed but poorly attended. For much of the coming year the attention of the court and of Yogyakarta focused on the elaborate series of funerary rites and on a complex succession crisis in which two of the Sultan's sons claimed the throne. After a period of negotiation with the central government Pangeran Mangkubumi was crowned Hamengkubuwana X on March 7, 1989. The 1989 *Malud* was considered by many as a test of the new Sultan's popularity and legitimacy. As many as a million people lined the road while an antique horse-drawn hearse carried Hamengkubuwana IX from the *kraton* to the royal cemetery at Imogiri. While this turn-out spoke strongly for the regard in which he was held by his subjects, it was not clear that the son had inherited the charisma as well as the crown.

In the 1989 *Malud* indexical symbols linking Hamengkubuwana IX and the Indonesian revolution were replaced with a set focusing on the new Sultan, his succession to the throne, and his role in Indonesia's development. A huge portrait of Hamengkubuwana X was installed at the entrance to the *Alon Alon*. He was depicted standing with his arm outstretched and his head bowed in a typical Javanese gesture of welcome; the *kraton,* the Grand mosque, and royal cemetery were in the background. His clothing was not the ornate brocade associated with royalty but the rough, hand-woven fabric of the lowest ranking court servants. This style has become his trade-mark. A legend at the bottom of the portrait stated, "Welcome to the *Garebeg Malud* 1989-Sultan Hamengkubuwana X".

The Sultan's attire and constant references to economic development in speeches and interviews indicated that the new Sultan wished to be seen as the servant of the people. The fact that he moved his family into the *kraton* was taken by many as a sign that he considered Yogyakarta and its people to be more important than national politics.[54] There were no displays of nationalist *pusaka* at the 1989 *Malud*. Unlike his father the new Sultan was not a major national-level political figure.[55] Hamengkubuwana IX was revered as a revolutionary hero. The incorporation of revolutionary symbols in the *Malud* established a symbolic connection between kingship and nationalism. The current Sultan was born in 1946. While he held several political positions at the time of his coronation, it seemed unlikely that he would acquire anything like his father's status. His legitimacy depended very much on his appeal to Yogyanese. Moreover, development had replaced revolution as the central component of Indonesian ideology. Hamengkubuwana IX was portrayed as a revolutionary hero of national significance, whereas his son was presented as Sultan and servant of the people of Yogyakarta. Shifts in the indexical symbolism of the *Malud* reflected both the changed reigns and these ideological developments.

The new Sultan continued to draw on his father's legitimacy. Hamengkubuwana IX's presence was strongly felt at the 1989 *Malud*. His portrait and inexpensive prints of photographs of his funeral were sold at the Grand Mosque and by vendors throughout the city. Many of the same vendors sold photographs of the new Sultan's coronation and a large assortment of t-shirts, bumper stickers, paintings, and plaques adorned with the royal coat of arms. A portrait made at the time of Hamengkubuwana IX's coronation was placed in front of the throne. On the left side were large photos of his funeral. On the right side were photos of the new Sultan's coronation and a large guest book in which visitors were asked to describe their impressions of the *kraton* and the *Malud*. The 1989 *Garebeg Malud* can be understood both as a memorial to the old Sultan and as a symbolic statement about dynastic continuity.

Among the most striking changes was the introduction of a new set of indexical symbols linking the *kraton* with Universalist Islam. In the 1980s Java underwent a major Islamic renewal. Many new mosques were constructed. Crowds at Friday prayer services began to spill into the streets. Many Javanese who had previously been suspicious of Essentialist Islam adopted more outwardly Islamic forms of behavior and dress. But this renewal had pietistic as well as fundamentalist dimensions. Sufism and Sufi orders figured significantly in this distinctively Javanese Islamic resurgence, as did the theologically conservative organization *Nahdhatul Ulama* ("renaissance of the religious scholars"), or NU, as it is usually called.[56] Resurgent Islam presents itself as a modernizing force. NU's vision of modernity

---

[54]Hamengkubuwana IX spent far more time in Jakarta than in Yogyakarta. He was sometimes criticized for paying more attention to national politics than local affairs.

[55]This was to change dramatically in the coming decade as is explained in Chapter 7. I have left this section of this chapter unchanged to better reflect the dramatic nature of this change.

[56]On the roles of Sufi movements in the Indonesian Islamic revival of the 1980s see J. Howell, "Sufism and the Indonesian Islamic Revival," *The Journal of Asian Studies*, vol. 60, 2001, pp. 701–729 and on more recent developments her subsequent article, "Repackaging Sufism in Urban Indonesia," ISIM Review, vol. 19, 2007, pp. 22–23

differs fundamentally from that of such reformist organizations as *Muhammadiyah*. Like *Muhammadiyah*, NU rejects the concept of an Islamic state, arguing that Islam, as a religion, places greater emphasis on piety than politics.[57] While it advocates democracy and modernity NU maintains an emphasis of traditional Sufi piety closely related to that of the Yogyakarta *kraton*. With the exception of the Grand Mosque, all of the *kraton* mosques endorse modes of ritual practice associated with NU. Conservative Muslim scholars have argued that mystical experience is built into the *Qur'an* and that it can help to resolve the tensions of modern urban life. In the 1980s rural religious schools *(pesantren)* began teaching secular as well as religious subjects and became active in economic development projects.[58]

The Islamic renewal was clearly reflected in the symbolism of the *1989 Garebeg Malud*. One of the *pusaka* displayed in the *Kraton* was a *Qur'an* said to have belonged to one of the Sultans of Demak. The Demak myth of the origins of the ritual was told almost constantly over loud speakers. After the myth was recounted, it was explained that the *Malud* was a Javanese form of *Dakwah*. By appropriating the term, the *Kraton* made an implicit claim that Islamic renewal need not imply a fundamentalist, *Shari'ah* centered theological orientation.

The ministry of religion erected a large pavilion on the *Alon Alon* in which both *Muhammadiyah* and NU had booths selling books, bumper stickers, and other religious items. NU displayed a large poster in which *pesantren* were depicted as drug addiction and juvenile delinquency treatment centers and as preparatory schools for

---

[57]On NU's understanding of religion-state relations focusing on the views of former president Abudrrahman Wahid see M. Woodward, " Islam, Pluralism and Democracy by Abdurrahman Wahid", COMPOS Journal, ASU Consortium for Strategic Communications 2007 http://www.comops.org/article/113.pdf

[58]This assessment of the Javanese Indonesia Islamic revival of the 1980s was written in 1990 and was clearly overly optimistic. It is now clear that only the iron fist of the New Order security forces limited the growth of Islamist movements. They began to appear almost as soon as the New Order collapsed in 1998 and today (2010) figure significantly in electoral and cultural politics. On the changing role of the *Pesantren* in Indonesian education see R. Lukens-Bull, *A Peaceful Jihad. Negotiating Identity and Modernity in Muslim Java.* New York: Palgrave Macmillan, 2005. There is now a substantial literature on Islamist politics in contemporary Indonesia to which I have made modest contributions. Detailed discussion of these movements in beyond the scope of this volume. See M. Van Bruinessen, "Genealogies of Islamic Radicalism in post-Suharto Indonesia," *South East Asia Research,* vol. 10(2), 2002, pp. 117–154 for a general overview and Z. Abuza, *Militant Islam in Southeast Asia: Crucible of Terror.* Boulder: Lynne Rienner Publishers, 2003; G. Barton, *Jemaah Islamiyah: Radical Islam in Indonesia.* Singapore: Singapore University Press, 2005; N. Hassan, "September 11 and Islamic Militancy in Post New Order Indonesia" in: K. Nathan and M. Kamali (eds.), *Islam in Southeast Asia: Political, Social and Strategic Challenges for the 21st Century.* Singapore: ISEAS, 2005, pp. 301–324; M. Lim, *Islamic Radicalism and Anti-Americanism in Indonesia: The Role of the Internet.* Washington: East-West Center, 2005 and M. Woodward, M. Woodward, "Indonesia's Religious Political Parties: Democratic Consolidation and Security in Post-New Order Indonesia," *Asian Security,* vol. 4(1), 2008, pp. 41–60 and "Contesting Wahhabi Colonialism in Yogyakarta," *COMOPS Journal: Analysis, Commentary and News from the World of Strategic Communications,* November, 2008 http://comops.org/journal/2008/11/06/resisting-wahhabi-colonialism-in-yogyakarta/

village youth hoping to acquire university educations. In a nod toward Javanese culture, Essentialist Islam, and modernity, young women dressed in Middle Eastern style costumes performed dances combining traditional Javanese and modern western styles. In 2009 political Islam and Islamic political parties were noticeably absent for the *Malud* festivities. At a time when political posters and banners were almost everywhere in Yogyakarta, there were none on the *Alon Alon*. There were two common interpretations. The first that the *kraton* wanted to emphasize the unity of the Muslim community. The second was that because the promotion of *Kebudayaan Jawa* is a central component of his own political strategy, that the Sultan would not allow rivals to claim the *Malud* as their own, by attaching political indexical symbols to it.

Clearly, the *kraton* endorsed the Islamic revival but also sought to draw it into the orbit of *kebudayaan Jawa*. There were two indexical symbols that indicate that it claimed to be among its sponsors. A huge minaret was erected in the middle of the *Alon Alon*.[59] The Indonesian flag flew from the top. An Islamicized version of the royal coat of arms was painted on the four sides of the minaret. The coat of arms is a gold crown, *Garuda* wings, and the letters "HB" (in Javanese script) on a red background.[60] Here the background was green, the sacred color of Universalist Islam. Similarly, new green and white banners with the royal coat of arms against the traditional red background were placed in front of the *Kraton*. Very similar indexical symbols were included in the 2009 and 2010 *Malud*. This indicates that they have now become "tradition."

Post-colonial changes, and those following the installation of Hamengkubuwana X, in the indexical symbolism of the *Garebeg Malud* indicate that the rite retains its power to link religious aspects of the theory of kingship with shifting social and political contexts. For many Javanese the ritual retains its power to define society as a cosmic reality. The 1989 *Malud* associated the new Sultan with Indonesia's development ideology, Islamic renewal, as well as with his father's charisma. Official estimates placed the crowds at the *Malud* at more than one hundred thousand. On the last evening of *Sekaten* there were so many people on the *Alon Alon* that it was nearly impossible to walk from the display of *pusaka* at the *kraton* to the *gamelan* performance at the Grand Mosque. If, as many informants stated, the 1989 *Garebeg Malud* was a test for the new Sultan, he passed with. This spoke not so much for his personal qualifications as for the faith his subjects have in the charisma of the throne, the concept of the saint/king and their hope that the flow of blessing will continue.

This very tentative assessment of Sultan Hamengkubuwana X's potential proved to be more than somewhat less than accurate. I was simply wrong. I have left this passage almost unchanged because it accurately reflects my assessment of the state

---

[59] The Grand Mosque does not have a minaret.

[60] The Garuda is the golden sun bird of Hindu mythology and the steed of the god Visnu. The Garuda motif is very common in traditional Javanese and contemporary Indonesian iconography, in the puppet theater (*wayang*), and classical dance on the national coat of arms, and as the name and symbol of Indonesia's national airline.

of Indonesian politics at the time it was written. The fact of human agency and the unpredictability of political and economic events makes the use of ethnographic crystal balls a dangerous enterprise. Hamengkubuwana X's role in the political turmoil that led to the end of the New Order are discussed in Chapter 7.

Photos

Sekaten – PasarMalam

Carnival rides

Nasi Gurih. Eaten for good
fortune in the coming year

continued

Selling Kinang at the Grand Mosque

Sajen for Gamelan Sekaten

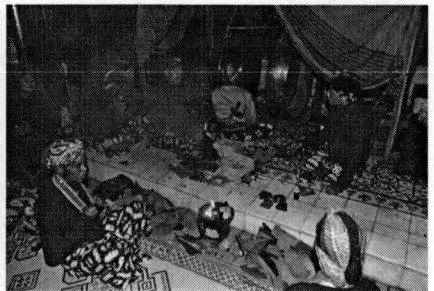

Gamelan Sekaten

At the Grand Mosque 2008   **In the Kraton 2009**

Procession from the Kraton to the
Grand Mosque

Descent from Siti Ingill

Escort – Prajurit Dhahneng

On the Alon   **Prajurit Lombok Abang**

Gifts from the Sultan to his subjects

. After Doa for the Sultan and
the people of Yogyakarta

. A minute later

Students from Sunan Kalijaga State Islamic University with pieces of
Gunungan. They returned to their villages immediately to share the blessing
with families, friends and neighbors

Chapter 6
The Fast of Ramadan in Yogyakarta

> *Abu Hurairah relates that the Holy Prophet said: When*
> *Ramadan arrives the gates of Paradise are opened and the gates*
> *of hell locked up and the setan are put in chains (Bukhari and*
> *Muslim).*

This chapter examines the place of the fasting month of Ramadan in Islamic discourse, religious practice and experience in Yogyakarta. In a more general sense, I will be concerned with the way in which the interpretation of Arabic textual materials and the performance of orthoprax Muslim ritual contribute to the development of what Marshall Hodgson referred to as Islamicate cultures and the interplay of trans-cultural and a-historical religious texts and historically and culturally situated Local tradition in the religious life of Muslim communities.[1] The central thesis of this chapter is that the distinction between the Local and the trans-cultural is never absolute when it is viewed from the perspective of Islam as lived experience. Even those social groups and individuals who place the greatest emphasis on the Universal Islam necessarily experience Ramadan and other elements of Muslim piety in local cultural context. At the same time Local Islams, and the elements of belief and ritual they include, make use of concepts abstracted from the larger tradition to provide

---

[1] M. Hodgson, *The Venture of* Islam (3 volumes). Chicago: University of Chicago Press, 1977. Viewed from the perspective of the early Muslim tradition the *Qur'an*, Hadith and other elements of Universalist Islam can be understood as historically and culturally situated. However, from the perspective of contemporary Muslim communities they are scriptural constants which are not subject to growth, development and change in the same way that locally defined modes of religious belief and practice are. Given the fact that Muslim communities understand the scriptural tradition as a "given," the historical contexts of its development is of relatively little consequence for understanding the faith and practice of contemporary communities. While conservative Indonesian Muslim scholars are concerned with the context of revelation, in the case of the *Qur'an*, and the contexts in which the Prophet Muhammad spoke or acted in the case of the Hadith, as well as with the context of transmission, historical criticism of the Quranic text meets with fierce resistance. Modernists and Islamist tend to reject even the limited historicization of the Quranic text, though they are quick to reject Hadith the content of which they disapprove on theological grounds as "inauthentic" or "questionable." Feminist scholars are the most likely to employ modernist and post-modernist hermeneutics.

answers to questions that the scriptural tradition does not address directly. The result is a dynamic tension between the two poles of Islamic life and experience.

Theoretical Perspectives

The month of Ramadan and the various modes of discourse and ritual practice associated with it provide clear examples are of the tension between the Local and the universal in the lives of Muslim communities and the creativity this tension engenders. Nurcholish Madjid and Marjo Buitelaar have argued that every Muslim society has a particular set of customs concerning the observance of the fasting month.[2] Buitelaar shows that while Moroccan interpretations of the fast are informed by universal Islamic values, the articulation of these values in social and religion action is also shaped by Moroccan culture and history. She stresses the fact that participation in the fast serves as a highly important symbolic marker which distinguishes between Muslims and non-Muslims. This is also true in Indonesia where bars and discos and other establishments that sell alcohol frequented by non-Muslims (and some Muslims) are required to close for the month in many parts of the country.

I will be concerned not only with the ways in which the fast is observed and celebrated in Yogyakarta, but also with the ways in which it serves as a symbolic marker of differentiation within the Javanese Muslim community. Ramadan is of great importance in the religious lives of almost all Javanese Muslims. Madjid has suggested that Ramadan and the feast of *Id al-Fitr* at the end of the month are held in greater regard in Indonesia than in most other parts of the Islamic world.[3] It is certainly true that Javanese and other Indonesians consider *Id al-Fitr* to be the most important Muslim holy day, despite the fact that it is technically speaking, the lesser of the two Id celebrations.[4] Despite the fact that there is very nearly unanimity

---

[2]N. Madjid, "*Penghayatan Makna Ibadah Puasa Sebagai Pendidikan Tentang Kesucian serta Tanggung Jawab Pribadi dan Kemasyarakatan.*" in Budhy Munawar-Rachman (ed) *Kontekstualisasi Doktrin Islam Dalam Sejarah.* Jakarta, Yayasan Wakaf Paramadina, 1994, pp. 411–422. M. Buitelaar, *Fasting and Feasting in Morocco. Women's Participation in* Ramadan. Oxford: Berg, 1993.

[3]Madjid mentions an Arabic source, *Hikmat al-Tasyri' wa Falsafatuhu* by Syeikh 'Ali Ahmad al-Jurhawi, Beirut, Dar alFikr, n.d., pp. 233–234 as support for this position. Buitelaar makes similar observations concerning the importance of the fast of Ramadan in Morocco. She argues that Moroccan Muslims are particularly concerned with the fast and it role in the global Muslim community because of their location on the western edge of the Islamic world. She suggests a connection between the geo-political location of Morocco on the borders of the Islamic world and the importance of the fast as a marker of Islamic identity. If this interpretation is correct it may help to explain the importance of the fast in Indonesia which is located on the eastern border of the Islamic world and where observance of the rites of Ramadan is clearly understood as a marker of Muslim identity.

[4]The other is *Id al-Adha*, the feast of sacrifice at which Muslims sacrifice goats and other animals to commemorate the Prophet Ibrahim's (Abraham) willingness to sacrifice his son. This rite is an integral part of the *Hajj* but unlike other components of the pilgrimage to Mecca, is performed throughout the Muslim world. Among the Habib, Malays of Hadrami Arab descent, of east Sumatra

concerning the importance of Ramadan, Javanese Muslims observe it in quite different ways. There are two basic contrasting understandings of the holy month, which are characteristic of *santri* and *kejawen* Muslim communities. *Santri* interpretations of Ramadan are firmly rooted in the Universalist textual tradition, though within the community there are serious disagreements about what is the proper way to understand scripture and to put them into practice.

Seemingly minor differences in the observance of the fast are significant symbols of both traditionalist and modernist Muslim identities. These "minor" differences include the question of whether the statement of intention (A. *niyah*) required prior to the beginning of the fast should be verbally articulated or only mentally formulated, the number of prayers to be performed each evening, and whether the *Id* prayers at the conclusion of the month are best performed in a mosque (the traditionalist Shafite position) or in an open field (the modernist view), continue to be the subject of considerable debate.[5] There are however signs that these debates have become less acrimonious. Moller who conducted fieldwork in Yogyakarta between 1999 and 2003 writes that traditionalists and modernist are now more inclined to agree to disagree about these matters than they were in the past.[6] My own observation of the two communities over the past three decades supports his interpretation. In the late 1970s when the in initial field work upon which this chapter is based was conducted, members of both communities often resorted to *takfiri* (denouncing their opponents as non-Muslims) rhetoric in discussions of ritual matters. This is much less common today. *Kejawen* interpretations of Ramadan are elements Local Islam in which elements of religious belief and practice drawn from the Universalist textual corpus are inputs to a process of *bricoulage* from which culturally specific modes of religious belief and behavior emerge. This style of Islam emphasizes the Local side of the scripture/culture dichotomy. Consequently, the modes of ritual behavior practiced by *kejawen* Muslims in the observance of Ramadan, while clearly derived from trans-cultural Muslim scripture, are, at the same time uniquely Javanese. They share many of these with traditional *santri*. In

it is called *Lebaran Hajj*. In Java, and in Indonesia more generally, even non-Muslims celebrate the Id because it is a national as well as religious holiday.

[5]In *Muslims through Discourse*, Princeton: Princeton University Press, 1993, John Bowen has shown that similar questions of ritual detail are basic to the distinction between traditionalist and modernist Islams among the Gayo of North Sumatra. Many Javanese Muslims maintain that even given convergence within the Muslim community on issues concerning politics, the economy and social welfare, that there is little, if any, sign that divisions concerning ritual practice are diminishing, but simply that they are not worth fighting about. It is now a live and let live stand off rather than a life and death struggle for the heart and soul of Javanese Islam. Today, the most salient division within the *santri* community is that between traditionalists and modernists who have somewhat different views of the relationship between *Agama Islam* and *Kebudayaan Islam* and neo-Wahhabis who seek to replace Javanese Islamic culture with a new Wahhabi-Arab inspired *bricolage*. This new bifurcation with the Javanese Muslim community is described in the conclusion to this chapter.

[6]A. Moller, "Islam and Traweh Prayers in Java: Unity, Diversity and Cultural Smoothness," *Indonesia and the Malay World,* vol. 33, No. 6, 2005, pp. 1–20.

Yogyakarta the character and rituals of Local *kejawen* Islam have been greatly influenced by the mystical and ritual traditions of the *kraton*, which continue to serve as a model for popular Muslim piety in the *kejawen* and portions of the traditional *santri* communities.

The fast of Ramadan is particularly important in Javanese Islam because of the shared belief that it is a rite of personal and social renewal which cleanses the individual of sin and which binds the community together, regardless of theological, social and political differences. In this Chapter I will be concerned as much with these shared understandings as with the conflicting interpretations of Ramadan and divergent modes of ritual practice they motivate. In an attempt to understand what is shared, I will employ theoretical approaches to the study of ritual developed by Mircea Eliade and Victor Turner. In The *Myth of Eternal Return* Eliade argues that calendrical rituals are religious universals and that among the purposes of these rites is what he terms "the regeneration of time."[7] He shows that in a wide variety of religious traditions calendrical rituals replicate or reenact the creation of the world. He concludes that by symbolically recreating the world, participants in these rituals restore it to its original, pure and pristine condition, which he describes as "a concrete realization of the rebirth of man and the world."[8] Eilade's interpretation of calendrical rituals as cosmic renewal requires some modification in the case of Islam. Eliade is concerned primarily with relationships between ritual and cosmogonic mythology. Clearly the rites of Ramadan do not repeat or replicated the genesis of the Islamic cosmos. Because Islam presumes a linear rather than cyclic notion of time, creation is a singular event which can not be repeated. What Ramadan is said to accomplish is the restoration of the individual to his/her original sinless condition and, in principle at least, the Muslim community to its pristine condition of purity and unity. Many Javanese, of almost all religious orientations say that on *Lebaran* at the end of the fast, they feel that as individuals they have been "born again" and that the community is as pure and holy as that of the Prophet Muhammad and his immediate companions.

It is at this juncture that Turner's discussions of the ritual process become important for understanding the performative structure of the rites of the fast. Turner is concerned with the sequential ordering of rites of passage, calendrical and other ritual events. In *The Ritual Process* he argues that rites of passage and many other rituals include three distinct phases: separation, margin or *limen* and reaggregation or reincorporation. For Turner the middle phase is crucial. It is marked symbolic reversal and status ambiguity. It is period during which many of the normal structures of social life absent or even reversed. It is also a period of *communitas*. *Communitas* is a social state or condition in which humans interact, not on the basis of clearly defined roles or status hierarchies, but rather on the basis of a common humanity. Turner maintains that in all human societies there is an alternation between the

---

[7]M. Eliade, *The Myth of the Eternal Return or, Cosmos and History*. Princeton: Princeton University Press, 1954, pp. 49–73.

[8]Ibid., pp. 58.

states of *communitas* or anti-structure and structured social relations and that peri-odic moments of *communitas* are essential for the establishment and maintenance of structured social relations.[9]

Taken together, these approaches to the study of ritual help to explain the sig-nificance of Ramadan in Yogyakarta. Textual and ethnographic data indicate that Ramadan can be understood as a rite of spiritual and social renewal. It is, however, not the world, but rather the individual and the Muslim community (*ummah*) that are renewed. Buitelaar argues that in Morocco the month of Ramadan can be under-stood as a period of liminality, and that discussions of the meaning of the fasting month emphasize the notion of *communitas*.[10] Here I will expand upon this anal-ysis, arguing that the ritual complex formed by the months of Shaban (J. Ruwah), Ramadan and Sawal can be understood in terms of Turner's theory of the three phases of the ritual process. Ceremonies at the end of Ruwah are rites of separation. Those of Ramadan itself are marked by marginality or in Turner's usage liminality. Characteristically they include element of symbolic reversal and intensified reli-gious, as opposed to secular, action. The celebration at the end of the fast (A. *'Id al-Fitr*) and the *Sawalan* ceremonies which follow reconstitute the community of believers in a more perfect form.

This combination of approaches allows us to understand how it is that Ramadan is of great religious and social significance even to those who do not observe the fast strictly. While *santri* and *kejawen* Muslims have similar understandings of the religious importance of Ramadan, they observe the fast in strikingly different ways. Javanese Muslims of both orientations hold that Ramadan is 'God's month' and that religious observances during Ramadan 'burn off' sin accumulated during the previous year. Many also believe that it purges the body of "toxins" and brings relief from chronic and even infectious diseases.[11] They differ primarily concerning the steps required to accomplish this transformation.

Ramadan in the Islamic Scriptural Tradition

The fast (A. *sawn*, J. *pasa*, I. *puasa*) of Ramadan is the fourth of the five pillars of Islam. According to the Shafite law school, which is recognized by almost all Indonesian and other Southeast Asian Muslims, with the exception of modernist organizations such as *Muhammadiyah* which does not recognize any of the Sunni legal schools, anyone who denies the fast is an unbeliever (*kafir*). One religiously conservative, but politically liberal, friend told me that anyone failing to keep the fast

---

[9] V. Turner, *The Ritual Process. Structure and Anti-Structure*. New York: Aldine Publishing Company, 1969, pp. 94–130.

[10] Op. cit., pp. 159–177.

[11] When I contracted Hepatitis shortly before the beginning of Ramadan in 2008 many Javanese and Malay friends told me that fasting would help me to recover more quickly. Some advised me to fast during the day and drink *jamu* at night. My doctor told me that I would not feel like eating and that fasting would be easy and to get plenty of rest, which would also be easy.

with out a good excuse, or to make up for missed days by fasting later or feeding the poor would definitely go to Hell.

The basic requirements of the fast are outlined in *Surah al-Baqarah* (183–187) of the *Qur'an*:

> O believers, prescribed for you is the Fast, even as it was prescribed for those that were before you – haply you will be god-fearing-for days numbered; and if any of you be sick, or if he be on a journey, then a number of other days; and for those who are able to fast, a redemption by feeding a poor man. Yet it is better for him who volunteers good, and that you should fast is better for you, if you but know;

> The month of Ramadan, wherein the *Qur'an* was sent down to be a guidance to the people, as clear signs aof the Guidance and the Salvation. So let those of you, who are present at the month, fast it; and if any of you be sick, or if he be on a journey, then a number of other days; God desires ease for you, and desires not hardship for you; and that you fulfill the number, and magnify God that He guided you, and haply you will be thankful.

> And when My servants question the concerning Me – I am near to answer the call of the caller, when he call to Me; so let them respond to Me, and let them believe in Me; haply so they will go aright.

> Permitted to you, upon the night of the Fast, is to go in to your wives; they are a vestment for you, and you are a vestment for them. God knows that you have been betraying yourselves, and had turned to you and pardoned you. And eat and drink, until the white thread shows clearly to you from the black thread at the dawn; then complete the fast unto the night, and do not lie with them while you cleave the mosques. Those are God's bounds; keep well within them. God makes clear His signs to me; haply they will be god-fearing.

The *Qur'an* emphasizes the importance of the fast of Ramadan and outlines the most basic requirements for observing it Both of these themes are elaborated upon in Hadith, which Muslims consider to be the Prophet Muhammad's commentary on the Quranic text and in subsequent legal and spiritual commentaries.

Bukhari's collection of Hadith is the largest and most systematic in its presentation of materials about the fast and about Ramadan in a more general sense. His "Book of Fasting" includes 224 Hadith There are numerous others concerning the practice of seclusion in the mosque during the fasting month (A. *I'tikaf*, J. *Halwat*), the Night of Power which falls near the end of the month and on which it is believed the *Qur'an* was first sent down from heaven, the night prayers conducted throughout the month (*tarawih*) and the festival at the conclusion of the fast (A. *Id al-Fitr*, J. *Lebaran*). Some of these will be cited in conjunction with discussions of Javanese observances latter in this chapter. There are, however, two general themes that run through the Hadith literature concerning the observance of the fast of Ramadan. One group of Hadith is concerned with the details of ritual performance. Another explains the spiritual benefits and blessing derived from it:

> The Prophet said: "There is a gate in paradise called *Ar-Raiyn*, and those observe fasts will enter through it on the Day of Resurrection and none except them will enter through it. It will be said: 'Where are those who used to observe fasts?' They will get up, and none except them will enter through it. After their entry the gate will be closed and nobody will enter through it." (Bukhari: 31, 120).

> I heard God's Apostle saying: "When you see the crescent [moon] (of the month of Ramadan start fasting, and when you see the crescent (of the month of Shawwal), stop

fasting; and if the sky is overcast (and you can't see it) then regard the month of Ramadan as of 30 days." (Bukhari: 30, 124)

Some Hadith include passages emphasizing both themes:

God's Apostle said: "God said," All the deeds of Adam's sons are for them, except fasting which is for Me, and I will give the reward for it.' Fasting is a shield of protection from the fire and from committing sins. If one of you is fasting, he should avoid sexual relations with his wife and quarrelling, and if somebody should fight or quarrel with him, he should say, "I am fasting." By Him in Whose hands my soul is, The unpleasant smell coming out from the mouth of a fasting person is better in the sight of God than the smell of musk. There are two pleasures for the fasting person, one at the time of breaking his fast, and the other at the time he will meet his Lord; then he will be pleased because of his fasting. (Bukhari 31, 128)

Legal and theological texts from the classical period expand further on both the requirements and merits of the fast of Ramadan. The eleventh century Shafite scholar Abu Shudja described in great detail the pillars (A. *arkan*) of the fast, who is required to abide by them, and the conditions which break or invalidate it (A. *mufti-rat*).[12] For the fast to be valid it must be preceded by the formulation of intention. This statement can be formulated on the night before the beginning of Ramadan, in the evening after the *tarawih*, prayers or, alternatively, before dawn on every morning of the month.[13] All adult Muslims are required to observe the fast. Exceptions are made for menstruating or pregnant women and those who have recently given birth or who are nursing a young child, old people, the sick who have no hope for recovery or whose condition would be worsened by fasting, those of unsound mind and travelers who have set out on a journey before sunrise. Those who must perform heavy labor should formulate an intention in the morning and attempt to fast, but may break it if necessary.

The age at which children begin to observe the fast varies considerably. Some as young as six or seven *want* to fast, but usually find it too difficult. For them there is a custom known as "*Puasa Bedug.*" The *bedug* is an oversized drum, the beating of which, accompanies the call to prayer in traditional Javanese mosques. Children observing this practice begin fasting when they hear it, or the call to prayer, and may break it when they hear it again. In general young people begin to seriously observe the fast at approximately the age of puberty.

Fasting is negatively defined. It is commonly understood as avoiding activities which would break the fast. The most basic rule is the prohibition of allowing any

---

[12] For an English summary of this text see C. Berg "Sawm" in H. Gibb and J. Kramers, *Shorter Encyclopedia of Islam*, Leiden:E.J. Brill, 1974.

[13] The Shafi'i legal texts commonly used in Indonesia state that the intention to fast must be formulated prior to dawn on each day of the month. Conservative Muslims insist that the statement of intent be verbally articulated, while modernists maintain that it should be formulated in the heart. See Ahmad ibn Maqib al-Misri, '*Umdat al-salik* (*The Reliance of the Traveller. A Classical Manual of Islamic Sacred Law.*) Translation by N. Keller, Evanston: Sunna Books, 1991 p 277. Many Javanese Muslims formulate an intention to fast for the entire month, or for a specific number of days on the final day of *Shaban* and repeat it prior to dawn on the days of Ramadan during which they plan to fast.

substance to enter the body so long at it is preventable. This includes eating, drinking, the use of medicines or illegal drugs, swallowing spittle, sexual intercourse etc. Vomiting, child birth, the onset of menstruation, insanity and intoxication all render the fast invalid. Other regulations concern the determination of the beginning and end of the fasting month and how missed days are to be made up for.

The legal tradition also specifies recommended pious acts such as breaking the fast with ripe dates, eating immediately prior to dawn, avoiding rude behavior and actions, even those which are not technically forbidden but which might anger others, reciting the *Qur'an* and thanking God at the end of the day.[14] It is believed that there is blessing (*pahala*) in all of these acts. In a more general sense it is believed that almost everything one does during Ramadan, even sleeping, is a form of *ibadah* (ritual performance). One informant explained that if you sleep during the day it is impossible to break the fast or to be angry and that God will bless you as a result.

The purpose of these and other regulations is to provide Muslims with proper guidance and to ensure that the fast is acceptable to God. Scholars of the classical period attempted to provide complete guidance for human behavior in these and other areas. Modernity has, however, created new social, cultural and technological contexts within which the fast of Ramadan and other Muslim rituals must be conducted. Among the questions contemporary Muslims must confront are those of blood transfusions, the use of calendars and technological means to determine the beginning and end of the month, the use of toothpaste, eye drops etc. These are questions which are currently debated by Muslims in Indonesia and elsewhere.[15] The movement of Muslims into high latitude regions presents particularly difficult problems. Islam began as a mid latitude religion. The vast majority of Muslims continue to live in mid to low latitude regions. For those who find themselves in extreme northern or southern regions, the extreme length of summer days can pose serious problems when Ramadan falls during that time of the year. Indonesian students at universities in the northern regions of the United States often experience serious difficulties when the normative regulations require them to fast from 4:30 in the morning until after 10:00 at night. Various solutions have been developed for this problem. One is that the discomfort must simply be endured. Another is that the period of fasting should be recalculated based on day length in either Indonesia or Saudi Arabia. Others define themselves as travelers and make up the missed fast days or feed poor people upon their return home, still other contribute to "food banks" and other charitable organizations in the United States or to Islamic charities

---

[14]For a detailed discussion of these regulations refer to '*Umdat al-salik* op. cit., pp. 299–296.

[15]For a discussion of these and other similar questions see T. Shu'aib, *Essentials of* Ramadan, *The Fasting Month*. Los Angeles: Islamic Book Center, 1991. The author of this work is a native of Nigeria, who was educated in Medina and currently resides in the United States. Similar issues arise in Indonesian texts. The modernist organization *Muhammadiyah* has stated that swallowing pills and other medicines breaks the fast even if ordered by a qualified Muslim doctor, and that diabetics are not able to conduct the fast at all because of the medical necessity of eating several times per day. See Tim PP Muhammadiyah Majlis Tarjij, *Tanya-Jawab Agama*. Yogyakarta: Penerbit Suara Muhammadiyah, 1992, p. 150.

that provide relief for Muslim refugees and internally displaced people in the Middle East.[16]

Theological works, while often concerned with the legal requirements of fasting, also focus on the spiritual dimension of the fast. Many of these have been influenced by Sufi concerns with the purification of the heart. Among the most famous of these and the one which has had the greatest impact on Indonesian Islam is al-Ghazzali's "Secrets of Fasting" a chapter of his *magnum opus The Revival of Religious Learning*.[17] In this work al-Ghazzali summarizes Shafite regulations concerning the fast, but emphasizes what he calls "the fast of the mind" which he describes as being the highest lrvel of fasting. Ghazzali is known as both a theologian and as a Sufi. His purpose *in Ihya 'Ulum-Ud-Din* and many of his other work is to strike a balance between dry legalism which would define Islam in almost exclusively behavioral terms and the more extreme forms of Sufi mysticism which emphasize personal religious experience but have little regard for the requirements of the law. Ghazzali's works are commonly studied in Java. His views of the fast continue to exert a profound influence on Local understandings of Islam in Yogyakarta and elsewhere in Indonesia.

> Know, O-dear readers, that there are three classes of fast. (1) fast of the general Muslims. It is to restrain oneself from eating and drinking and from sexual passion. This is the lowest kind of fast. (2) Fast of the few select Muslims. In this kind of fasting, besides the above things, one refrains himself from sins of hands, feet, sight and other limbs of body. (3) Fast of the highest class. These people keep fast of mind. In other worlds, they don't think of anything else except God and the next world. They think only of the world with the intention of the next world as it is the seed ground for the future. A certain sage said: One sin is written for one whose efforts during the day are made only to prepare for breaking fast. This highest class of people are the Prophets and the near ones of God. This kind of fast is kept after sacrificing oneself and his thoughts fully to God. This is the meaning of the verse: Say God and then leave them sporting in their vain talks (6:91).

> The fasting of select few pious men rests on six duties for gaining perfection. (1) To restrain eye sight from what is evil and from things which divert attention from God's remembrance. The Prophet said: Eye sight is a poisonous arrow out of the arrows of the devil. If a man gives it up, God gives him such a faith of which the taste is tasted by his mind. The Prophet said: Five things destroys fasting-falsehood, back-biting, slander, perjury and sight with sexual passion.

> (2) To restrain the tongue from useless talk, false-speaking, back-biting, slander, abusive speech, obscenity, hypocrisy and enmity, to adopt silence and to keep the tongue busy with the remembrance of God and reciting the Quran. The sage Sufiyan Saori said: Back-biting spoils fast. Hazrat Muzahed said: Two things spoil fast, back-biting and falsehood. The Prophet said: Fast is like a shield. If a man keeps fast, let him not rebuke and dispute. If a man wants to assault or make quarrel, let him say to him: I am fasting. There is in

---

[16] A common joke among Indonesian students at the University of Wisconsin is the question: "Why are there no Muslims in Alaska?" to which the reply is "They would starve when Ramadan comes in June!" Even in Madison, where the sun does not set until nearly ten at night, the fast can be quite difficult when it fall in the summer months.

[17] For an English translation of this work see Ak-Haj Maulana Fazal-Ul-Karim (translator*) Imam Gazzali's IhyA' 'Ulum-Ud-Din (The Revival of Religious Learning Books I&II)*. Lahore: Kazi Publications, nd., 222–231.

Hadis: Two women kept fast at the time of the Prophet. They were so much overstricken with hunger at the end of the day that their lives were about to end. They were sent to the Prophet so that he might order them to break fast. He sent a cup for them telling them that they should vomit in it what they ate. One of them vomited fresh blood and fresh flesh which filled up half of the cup. Another vomited similarly and filled up the cup. The Prophet then said; The two women fasted with lawful food but broke it with unlawful food. The two women back-bited the people and ate their flesh.

(3) To restrain the ear from hearing the evil talks because what is unlawful to utter is also unlawful to hear. For this reason, God placed the eater of unlawful food and the hearer of unlawful words on the same level. God says: the hearers of falsehood and eaters of unlawful food – 5:46. God says: Why do not the God-fearing men and the worldly renunciated men prohibit talking sinful words and unlawful eating – 5:68? To remain silent at the time of back-biting is unlawful. God says: You are then like them – 9:139. Thus said the Prophet: The back-biter and the hearer of back-biting are equal co-sharers in sin.

(4) To save hand, feet, and other organs from sins, from evil deeds and to save belly from doubtful things at the time of breaking fast. There is no meaning of fasting if it is kept with lawful food and broken with unlawful food. He is like a man who destroys a town for constructing a building. It is also injurious to eat lawful food in excess and not to eat it little. He who fasts and does evil deeds is like a patient who restrains himself from eating fruits for fear of disease but who swallows poison. A sin is like eating poison. He who drinks this poison is a fool. An unlawful thing is like poison and it destroys religion and a lawful thing is like a medicine. Its little does benefit and its much spoils. The Prophet said: there are many fasting men who do not gain by fasting except hunger and thirst. On being asked the reason, he said: He refrains from eating lawful food and breaks fast by eating human flesh by back-biting. That is unlawful.

(5) To eat even lawful food so much at the time of breaking fast that it fills up the belly. A belly filled up with too much lawful food is hated more than all other reservoirs. A fasting man eats in full at the time of breaking fast what he could not eat during day time. He prepares different kinds of foods. The object of fast is to keep belly vacant in order to control passion and to increase God-fear. If the belly remains full from morning to evening, sexual passion rises high and greed and temptation reign supreme.

(6) To keep the mind of a fasting man between fear and hope, because he does not know whether his fast will be accepted or not, whether he will be near God or not. This should be the case for every divine service. Once Hasan Basri was passing by a party of men who were playing and sporting. He said: God made this month for Ramadan for running in which the people will be running for good deeds and competing with one another. The object of fast is to anoint one with one of the divine attributes. That attribute is *Samadiat* meaning to be bereft of hunger and thirst and to follow the angles as far as possible being free from passion. The rank of a man is far more superior than that of a lower animal as he can control his passion by dint of his intellect, but his rank is lower than that of an angel as his passion is strong and he is tried by it. Angels are near God. This nearness keeps connection with attribute but not with space. The Prophet said: Fast is a trust. Let everyone of you keep that trust. When he read this verse: "God orders you to give trust to its rightful owners (4:61)," he placed his hands on his ears and eyes and said: Ear is a trust and eye is a trust. If it had not been a trust of fasting, the Prophet would not have said: I am fasting. In other words, I have kept my tongue as trust for saving it. How can I give it up for replying you? So it appears that for every affair there are secret and open matters. It is now open to you to observe both the secret and open matters or to observe either of them.

In his treatise on fasting al-Ghazzali emphasizes both the "open" and the "secret" matters. It is clear that his own view is that a Muslim should attend to both. His discussion very closely resembles the range of interpretations of the fast one encounters in Yogyakarta. Almost all Javanese Muslims are concerned with what al- Ghazzali terms the "secret" or internal (J. *batin*) matters of the fast. The fact that these are emphasized so often in speeches and sermons indicates that there is a concern that some fall into error because they pay strict attention to the behavior rules of the fast, but ignore its spiritual components. *Santri* Muslims of both traditionalist and modernist orientations believe that there is a necessary connection between strict compliance with the "open" requirements of fasting and the "secret" or spiritual observance of the rites of Ramadan. Their *kejawen* neighbors are deeply concerned with the "secret" matters of the fast, but place less importance of strict observance of "open" *Shari'ah* regulations.

Ramadan in Javanese Islam

The *Hadith* 367 al-Ghazzali' quoted at the beginning of this paper is often mentioned by Javanese Muslims of diverse theological orientations and social positions to explain the religious meaning of Ramadan. It is quoted in Arabic, Javanese and Indonesian language religious texts and in sermons and other forms of oral Islamic discourse. For Javanese Muslims familiar with the textual corpus of normative or Universalist Islam, this statement is understood as being the speech of the Prophet Muhammad. For others it is a Javanese proverb. Even those Javanese Muslims who know little, if any, Arabic and are generally lax in their observance of the devotion program mandated by the *Shari'ah* mention it when asked to explain the religious significance of the fast.

I first encountered this statement concerning Ramadan and the gates of heaven in the in Yogyakarta in 1979. At the time I was struck by the fact that one of my informants, a leader of the Local branch of the modernist Muslim organization *Muhammadiyah* mentioned it as a Hadith, and referred me to the classical *Hadith* collections of Bukhari and Muslim for further details, while another, a self described "Javanese Muslim" described it as a "Javanese proverb" that he learned in his youth. Very many Javanese Muslims take it completely literally. In Yogyakarta, and especially in rural areas surrounding the city, children rarely play outside after dark because dangerous spirits are especially active after dark. This is not true during Ramadan. Then it is safe to be out in the evenings and very large numbers of children are – because as one young boy put it: "the devils are in jail so we can play"

The remainder of this chapter examines the ways in which these religious concepts are articulated in the performance of what will be referred to as the "Ramadan ritual system." This complex of rituals includes those associated with the months of Shaban which precedes the fast and Sawal which follows it as well as the total ritual and other religious acts conducted during Ramadan.[18]

---

[18]Many contemporary Javanese Muslims comment on the time consuming character of this ritual complex. One friend explained that given everything that must be done before and after Ramadan,

Ruwah (*Shaban*) – Rites of Separation

Turner describes rites of separation as being symbolic behavior signifying the detachment of the individual or group from an earlier fixed point in the social structure, from a set of cultural conditions (a "state"), or from both.[19] They are the ritual means through which the existing qualities of persons and social groups are symbolically dissolved so that they may be reconstituted in subsequent stages of the ritual process. Shaban is the eighth month of the Islamic year.[20] According to Hadith it was the custom of the Prophet Muhammad to fast during this month.[21] Many pious Muslims fast during part of the month as part of a more general attempt to live in accordance with the *sunnah* (A. practice) of the Prophet. In Java and throughout the Muslim world it is also common for people to use the month of Shaban to "make up" days they were not able to fast in the previous Ramadan.

Shaban is also associated with death and the spirits of the dead. In Java Shaban is more commonly known as Ruwah. The term Ruwah is sometimes said to be derived from the Arabic *ruh* meaning "spirit" and at others from *arwah* meaning "spirits of the dead."[22] The night of the fifteenth of *Ruwah* is known in Arabic as *Lailat al-Bara'a* and in Javanese as *Nifsu Shaban*. It is believed that on this night the tree of life is shaken. The names of all humans are written on the leaves of this tree. People whose names are written on the leaves that fall will die in the coming year. It is also believed that on this night God descends to the lowest level of heaven and calls on people to repent their sins so that they may be forgiven. Many Javanese Muslims fast on this day and recite *Surah Yasin*, the chapter of the *Qur'an* most commonly associated with the souls of the dead. This *Surah* is often said to be the "heart of the *Qur'an*" and is expressly concerned with the central Islamic teachings of revelation and the afterlife. Throughout the Muslim world it is considered to be appropriate to recite it to those who are near death, and in all ceremonies in which the dead are remembered or commemorated. Many Javanese Muslims believe that it has great spiritual power and that reciting it at graves or in honor of the dead is a source of God's blessing and mercy for themselves as well as the departed. At almost all tomb shrines one can find "Yasin Books" in Arabic and Roman script and increasingly in Indonesian translation. It is customary to bring on with you on a pilgrimage to a saint's tomb, and to exchange it for one that has been left by a previous pilgrim. They are often left on top of, or beside graves. The book that one takes is thought to have some of the blessing (*barakah*) of the saint.

In South Asia and Sumatra and most other Malay societies, as well as in Java, ritual meals are prepared and prayers said for the benefit of the dead during Shaban.

---

it was mistaken to think of it as the "Fasting *Month*." He said "A month and a half, maybe even 2 months, that would be more like it."

[19] Turner, op. cit., pp. 94

[20] See A. Wensinck, "Sha'ban", in: SIE p. 508.

[21] Bukhari 30., 53.

[22] See Wensinck, op. cit., p. 508 and Muhaimin, op. cit., p. 185.

During the month of Ruwah sermons in Javanese mosque focus on the coming fast. There are also billboards posted throughout the city and announcements on Television urging people to prepare for the fast and reminding them that it is a month filled with God's blessing and mercy. People are urged to contemplate the meaning of the fast and to perform it with sincerity and proper intention. It is explained as a duty to God and as a source of blessing, religious and social renewal. The purpose of *Ruwah* observances is to cleanse and purify the physical body in preparation for the fast. They also honor saints and deceased family members who, in Java, are treated as saints by visiting graves.[23]

Traditional *santri* and *kejawen* Muslims perform an elaborate series of rites in the last half of the month. The fifteenth of *Ruwah* is believed to be the day on which God decides who will die during the coming year. Many *kejawen* and traditional *santri* Muslims hold a *slametan* known *Ruwahan* on this evening. Many traditional and reformist *santri* spend the night in the mosque reciting the *Qur'an*, especially *Surah Yasin*. This is also a time for family gatherings. Many people say that the purpose of these rituals is to reunite living and deceased members of extended bilateral kin groups. Many believe these rites are obligatory for anyone who has lost a parent, spouse or child. Others explain that it is necessary to visit the grave of parents and grandparents and as many other relatives as possible. Some *kejawen* informants explained that the dead somehow are pleased by the aroma of the food prepared for the *slametan*.[24] Others stated that the purpose of these rites was to honor the ancestors and to pray for them. Numerous informants explained that rituals for the dead conducted during the month of Ruwah differ from the normal pattern in that during Ruwah one does not ask for favors or blessings from the dead. In Yogyakarta these rites range in size and complexity from small gatherings in private homes to large-scale ceremonies sponsored by the *kraton*. In 1979 I attended two *Ruwahan Slametan*. One was conducted by my neighbor, who invited only his children and grandchildren and the visiting anthropologist. The other was sponsored by the Yogyakarta *kraton* to honor Sultan Hamengkubuwana VII. The Sultan had 78 children and by that time thousands of descendants. The ritual was conducted in the *kraton* and attended by more than five hundred people. In addition to a very large and elaborate *slametan* there were *gamelan* (percussion orchestra) and *wayang* (shadow play) performances.

There is not a clear connection between the *Ruwahan* observances and the coming fast of Ramadan. The emphasis on the dead is, however, continued in the *Nyadran* rites conducted at the end of the month, which are clearly linked to the

---

[23] Modernists, of course, do not visit graves at this or any other time.

[24] The view that food should be prepared for and offered to the dead is also common among Sufi orders in South Asia. An eighteenth century manual for the veneration of Chisti saints entitled "Introduction to the Treasury of Death Anniversaries" states: "Know seeker of God that the perfectly guided ones, sincere disciples and trustworthy adherents out to present food to the spirits of the elders, their masters, and their guides, as much as possible without objection. Thus by their blessing, the benefits and good fortune of both worlds are increased." translation by Carl Ernst in "An Indo-Persian Guide to Sufi Shrine Pilgrimage." ms. n.d.

beginning of the fast. *Nyadran* rites include a *slametan*, recitation of *Surah Yasin*, cleaning and repairing graves, and scattering flowers on them. *Nyadran* is observed during the last week of *Ruwah*. These rituals focus on the tombs of saints and family members. The visitation of graves is an important part of Javanese Muslim piety, but is generally not practiced during Ramadan by Yogyakarta Javanese with strong ties to *kraton* tradition. They royal cemeteries at Imo Giri and Kota Gede are closed for the entire month. There are two explanations. The first is that the dead, like the living must fast. Because ritual meals and food offerings are major components of pilgrimage it would be an affront to the pious dead to present them during the fasting month. The second is that during Ramadan one's attention should be focused only on God. Consequently it is considered inappropriate to seek blessing from saints. Yogyakarta and other Javanese more strongly associated with traditional *santri* culture have an entirely different view. Their position is that is appropriate, and indeed, desirable and beneficial to visit graves located in mosque compounds during *Ramadan*. Some spend most of the nights of the fasting month in cemeteries praying and reciting *Surah Yasin*. Cemeteries located at the rear of *kraton* mosques are often filled during *Ramadan*. Reformist Muslims, who regard the visitation of graves as sinful innovation, never do this.

There is another explanation for *Nyadran* rites which is in closer accord with scriptural understandings of death and the afterlife. Many traditional s*antri* Muslims explain that the dead are subject to some combination of pleasure and torment in the grave depending upon the nature of their faith and deeds in life. It is often stated that during Ramadan the punishments of the grave come to a halt. Prayers are said, the *Qur'an* recited and alms distributed on the behalf of the deceased in the hope that God will show mercy on them and permanently end the torment of the grave.[25] This understanding of the importance of Ramadan for the dead builds upon and extends the traditional Shafi'i view that pious works including the recitation of *Surah Yasin*, fasting and pilgrimage can be dedicated to the deceased and that they will receive the benefit of them.[26] The exception to this rule is that it is considered appropriate, and indeed, desirable and beneficial to visit graves located in mosque compounds. Reformist Muslims, who regard the visitation of graves as sinful innovation, never do this.

The composition of the *slametan* offered on this occasion vary considerably, but always include *apem* a rice flour pancake which is strongly associated with death

---

[25]For a discussion of the punishments and pleasures of the grave see J. Smith and Y. Hadad, *The Islamic Understanding of Death and Resurrection*. Albany: State University of New York Press, 1981, pp. 31–62.

[26]See '*Umdat al-salik* op. cit., pp. 929–930. The modernist organization Muhammadiayah takes a different view of the matter particularly with regard to fasting. Their position is that it is not possible for the living to carry out religious obligations for the dead, although in keeping with a literal reading of the *Qur'an* and Hadith they maintain that it is possible for a child to dedicate the merits of pilgrimage to his/her parents if the parent has formulated the intention to perform the *haj* but is unable to make the journey to Mecca. See Tim PP Muhammadiyah Majlis Tarjih, op. cit., p. 151.

and the spirits of the dead. *Apem* are so strongly associated with death that many Javanese, particularly the elderly, will not eat them. They are, however, an essential component of mortuary rituals and are distributed in traditional village mosques immediately prior to the ritual washing of a corpse.

The scale of *Nyadran* ceremonies, like those of the Ruwahan vary greatly. Some people visit only the graves of their parents or grandparents. Others who are more concerned with genealogy as a source of prestige and social status may visit the graves of as many of their ancestors as possible. This practice is particularly common among upper class people and those descended from Javanese kings or Muslim saints. One informant, a high ranking official in the Yogyakarta court, who numbers both Sultan Hamengkubuwana III and the *wali* Sunan Kalijaga among his ancestors, explained that he should visit seven different cemeteries in central and east Java, but that this would take so much time that he often relied on the *juru cunci* (care taker) at one or more of them to perform the rites for him. This is an increasingly common practice as many Javanese now live very far from the graves of their ancestors. Many feel profoundly guilty that they are not able to visit as many graves as they would like to.

For some families *Nyadran* is almost as complicated and difficult to organize as the *mudik* journeys at the end of the month. Families who can afford to often come from all over Indonesia to celebrate this occasion. Many hold elaborate *slametan* attended by fifty or more members of extended families at one or more cemeteries and distribute the food to *Juru Cunci* and families living in the vicinity. One of the consequences of this is that poor people living near cemeteries eat very well at this time of year.

The *Nyadran* of the Yogyakarta *Kraton* are conducted at the two royal cemeteries at Kota Gede and Imo Giri and at tomb shrines administered by the *kraton* scattered throughout the Sultanate. The participants include representatives of the court and the cemetery care takers. Letters are sent to the *juru cunci* well in advance instructing them as to exactly when and how the rites should be conducted. [27] The Sultan does not attend either of these ceremonies because he is, according to Javanese custom, not allowed to visit the graves of his ancestors because to do so would hasten his own death. He delegates this responsibility to senior members of the court who are accompanied by servants and guards. They bring large quantities of red and white flowers and incense from the *kraton*. Food for the *slametan* is prepared at the cemetery by the wives of the *juru cunci*, who act on orders of, and receive compensation from the *kraton*. The grave of Sultan Agung is the primary focus of the Imo Giri *Nyadran*. Sultan Agung is widely regarded as the greatest of the kings of Mataram. He is also the most senior of the kings and nobles buried at Imo Giri. His grave is located at the highest level of the central courtyard of the ceremony. Those of the Susuhunans of Surakarta are located to the left of the central complex and those of the Sultans of Yogyakarta to the right. All of the participants in the

---

[27] Ironically these letters are sent by the *Penghulu* or chief ritual official who as a member of *Muhammadiyah* does not approve of the practice of visiting graves.

Nyadran pay homage to the grave of Sultan Agung. Incense is burned and flowers placed on the tomb. Similar rites are performed at other graves by people descended from subsequent kings. After the grave has been cleaned a *slametan* is held in a pavilion located outside of the cemetery complex. Yogyakarta and Surakarta hold separate *slametans*. I attended the Yogyakarta *Nyadran slametan* in 1979 and, like all others, Received a portion of the food to take home with me. I genuinely did not know what to do with it and asked my landlady, who was very excited and immediately organized a *slametan* so that we could share the blessing with others in the *kampung*.

In Kudus and other areas in East Java where the *Wali Sanga* are the most important saints there are often night markets at which flowers, incense and other materials for *Nyandran* offerings are sold. People who can afford to send uncooked food to the *Juru Cunci* of the tombs of all of the major and many of the minor saints of the region. It is used for the preparation of very large and elaborate *slametan* held at these shrines.

Nyadran ceremonies are also conducted by informal mystical associations lead by *kejawen* religious teachers and *dukun*. In the late 1970s there were many of these organizations in Yogyakarta, few of which were officially recognized as *aliran kebatinan* (mystical societies). Many of these organizations are based on devotion to regional saints, some of whom are known only to the leaders of the organization. Others claim to be able to establish direct contact with some of the most famous saints and spirits in central Java. I worked closely with one of these organizations, which was based on devotion to a saint known as Prabu Lingasari. Pak Mul, the leader of the group explained that he had discovered the grave of this saint and several of his relatives while meditating in a remote mountainous area.[28] The organization's rituals included *slametan* and healing rituals at which mediums were possessed by Prabu Lingasari and other, better known figures in the *kejawen* spirit world including Gusti Kanjeng Ratu Kidul, the spirit queen of the southern ocean who is believed to have been married to all of the Sultans of Yogyakarta. Pak Mul, the leader of this group used, *Nyadran* as an opportunity to repair and expand the grave complex which is the central symbol of his organization. Over the years he and his followers have replaced deteriorated tombstones, dug wells and constructed a set of buildings resembling a miniature Imo Giri. In 1979 Pak Mul organized an elaborate *Nyadran* for which he rented ten mini-vans to transport more than one hundred of his followers to the grave site. The pilgrimage lasted for 4 days and included elaborate *slametan*, recitation of *Surah Yasin*, and trance sessions in which he and his followers communicated directly with the spirits upon whom his teachings are based.[29]

---

[28] See Chapter 2.

[29] Trance performances play a very important role in *Shaban* observances in Morocco, for a discussion of these rites see Buitelaar, op. cit., pp. 49–50. While most Javanese informants understood the logic of Pak Mul's Shaban performance many found it to be highly unusual, if not inappropriate.

The cleansing and repair of graves is a central element of *Nyadran* rituals. Most people first remove any grass and weeds that have accumulated since their last visit. Next they sweep the grave and the area surrounding it. Finally there are offerings of incense and flowers and food is distributed to *juru cunci* and people living in the vicinity of the cemetery. Then they sweep the grave and the area surrounding it. It is often said to be similar to the purification rites and ritual baths (J. *padusan*) many Javanese Muslims perform on the final night of Ruwah. On this might many *kejawen* and some traditional *santri* Muslims visit as many as seven sacred springs or tanks to cleanse themselves before the beginning of the fast.[30] Some *kejawen* informants explained that at this time at least some of the springs and rivers of Java contain *zam-zam* water.[31] The practice of bathing before the beginning of Ramadan is not mentioned in the classical *fiqh* (law) books used by traditional Javanese Muslims or in the ritual manuals of contemporary modernist organizations. It is an aspect of *Kebudayan Jawa*, but one which builds on and extends basic Islamic concerns with purity, cleanliness and ritual performance. A state of ritual purity is not required for the fast to be valid, but is required for all of the other ritual activities associated with Ramadan.[32] Many Javanese Muslims believe that it is necessary to cleanse the physical body prior to any ritual act, even those, such as fasting, not specifically mentioned in the books of law. Bathing before the beginning of Ramadan also extends the Shafite tradition which recommends, but does not require, bathing on holy days including *Id al-Fitr* at the end of the month. In this respect Javanese custom is similar to that of Moroccan Muslims, who as Buitelaar has shown, regard the cleansing of houses and cooking utensils and purification of the body as essential

---

[30]Many say that is principle one should visit seven springs or holy wells in a single night, but because this is usually not possible the ritual is most often spread over several days. Others say that walking through even one of the moats which surround traditional mosques is sufficient. In 2008 I noticed that some people now simply sprinkle themselves with *zam zam* water that is available in shops throughout the city.

[31]*Zam-zam* refers to a well located near the *Kab'ah* in Mecca. Water from this well is often used to break the fast in the great mosque of Mecca. It is believed by many to have curative and other magical powers. Javanese and other pilgrims bring gallons of *zam-zam* water back from Mecca to share with family, kin and neighbors. In the 1970s *zam-zam* water was a rare commodity. Today pilgrims bring large pre-packaged containers when the return form Mecca. Small bottles can be purchased at any number of shops that sell Muslim religious items. In Java the term *zam-zam* is used for holy water in a more general sense. Water from tanks at Imo Giri and that which is left over from the washing of sacred heirlooms (J. *pusaka*) is often called *zam-zam* by *kejawen* Muslims. *zama zam* water of either variety is often said to have medicinal qualities. See Chapter 2 for details.

[32]There are two types of ritual impurity. Minor impurity is caused by "anything that exists from the front or rear private parts"; "loss of the ability to distinguish, whether through insanity, unconsciousness, sleep or other [reason]"; "when any, no matter how little, of the two skins of a man and a woman touch" or "touching human private parts with the palm or the inner surface of the fingers." One in such a state may not pray, or carry the *Qur'an*. Minor impurity is removed by ritual ablutions (*wudhu*) in which the face, arms, head and feet. Major ritual impurity is caused by sexual activity, menstruation and child birth. Restrictions in addition to those required by minor impurity include remaining in a mosque and reciting the *Qur'an*. For a detailed discussion of these matters see *'Umdat al-salik* op. cit., pp. 49–99.

for the conduct of the fast.[33] Many Javanese however, consider both *Nyandran* and *Padusan* to be obligatory (*wajib*) element of the fast. Many traditional *santri* who are aware that they are not *sunnah* still consider them to be essential. This is congruent with a more general attitude that if a ritual innovation is in keeping with the spirit of Islam, that it is a good thing to do. *Muhammadiyah* Muslims and others concerned with the "problem" of *bidah* in Javanese culture consider these rites to be reprehensible if not actually sinful.

Many modernists Muslims, particularly those influenced by the teachings of organizations like *Muhammadiyah*, strongly disapprove of the *Nyadran* complex because of the emphasis it places on visiting graves and communicating with the dead. Some, however, continue the custom of visiting graves during the days before the beginning of Ramadan. They are, however, careful to explain the practice in congruence with *Muhammadiyah's* understanding of Islam. One explained that visiting graves at this, or any other time in the hope of obtaining blessing was pointless, not really Islamic and would not work. He explained that the real purpose of visiting graves was to remind us that no matter how great and powerful we may be in this world that death is inevitable. He continued that knowing this can lead to greater concern with religion and a better understanding of the greatness and power of God. He concluded that this was particularly important at the beginning of Ramadan because fasting can be hard and many Javanese need extra motivation. In general modernist Muslims are as concerned with preparing for the fast as are their more traditionally inclined and *kejawen* neighbors. For them, however, preparations more frequently take the form of sermons and religious lessons (*pengagian*) explaining the importance of fasting than with ritual performance.

As a whole, Ruwah rituals mark a departure from normal social life and the beginning of a period of liminality and *communitas*. They are based on two basic concepts: First the establishment of the condition of *slamet* (J. tranquility) which that is characterized by the absence of status distinctions, social and psychological harmony.[34] Ruwah ceremonies reestablish the unity of social groups including ancestors as well as the living. Pilgrimage to the graves of saints brings them into the community as well. The extensive use of mortuary symbolism also calls attention to the importance of religious devotions, upon which the nature of the afterlife depends. Informants often state that *Nyadran* reminds them of death and the afterlife. This is thought to encourage piety during Ramadan because it reminds people that this life is transient and only a preparation for death. In a social sense these rites mark the transition from normal life to the intense religious observances of Ramadan They establish the state of ritual purity many think are required for religious devotions and mark the transition from profane to sacred time.

---

[33] Buitelaar, op. cit., pp. 38–39.

[34] See Chapter 3

Ramadan, Liminality and Symbolic Reversal

The fast and other rites conducted during Ramadan cleanse and purify the spiritual body. Passion (J. *nepsu*) is purged and replaced by faith. The result is blessing in this world and the rewards of paradise in the next. It is often said that everything that one does during Ramadan, is filled with blessing, *if you are fasting*. The conduct of the fast is governed by *Shari'ah* regulations. As is other Muslim cultures it is forbidden to eat, drink, smoke or have sexual contact between the hour in the morning when a white thread can be distinguished from a black one and that in the evening when this distinction can no longer be made.

For Javanese who fast, time is reversed during Ramadan. Most wake up between 3:30 and 4:00 in the morning. In many *kampung* it is almost impossible *not* to wake up because *Qur'an* recitation is broadcast from the mosque and young people run through the neighborhood banging pots and pans and playing (very loud) recorded music. *Sahur* is the last meal before the fast begins. Like almost everything else one does during the month it is thought to be a source of blessing. It is especially important because with out eating and drinking it is difficult to maintain tranquility through the day.[35] It is a normal Javanese meal consisting of rice, vegetables, and for those who can afford it fried bean curd, chicken, fish and occasionally beef or mutton. Some people, especially students, eat "energy bars." Some people go back to sleep after eating, others go about their daily business. Both sleeping during the day and conducting business as usual are sources of blessing – sleeping because it makes acts that would break the fast impossible and doing what one usually does because it is a sign of devotion and perseverance. Many people nap in the afternoon when hunger, and especially thirst, become troublesome.

Almost all *santri* and many *kejawen* Muslims observe the fast. Those who do not are of two minds. One explanation for not fasting is that one does not feel strong enough in either the spiritual or physical sense to undertake it. Those who must perform heavy labor in the fields or in urban occupations such as construction find it impossible to abstain from eating and particularly from drinking water during working hours.[36] Another view is that the fast of Ramadan and other forms of piety mandated by Islamic law are optional for travelers on the mystical path. Some *kejawen* Muslims fast for a few days at the beginning or end of the month, others fast some years and not others. In recent decades the percentage of Javanese who observe, or at least try to observe, the fast has increased significantly as concern with the outward forms of Islamic piety has increased. I know many people who did not fast in the late 1970s but now do so on a regular basis. There are, however, still many Javanese Muslims who do not fast, or who do so for less than the entire month. Despite uneven participation in the fast itself, almost all Javanese Muslims

---

[35] This is correct.

[36] Many people feel guilty about doing this and try to avoid being seen drinking, and especially eating.

participate in devotional practices which, according to the law, are optional and in Local, Javanese forms of Muslim piety are traditional.

Ramadan is "God's month." It is often stated that people are free to use other months for their own purposes, but that the fasting month should be devoted to religious concerns. It is sacred time. Many Javanese believe that is especially important to avoid sinful acts during Ramadan because they would invalidate their fasts. This is an element of what al-Ghazzali called the "secret" fast, but the growth of Islamism has brought the secret into the open. Attempts to enforce piety or at least abstinence from sin, on the community as a whole are increasingly common. In Yogyakarta local authorities go to extra lengths to crack down on sex workers and drug dealers during Ramadan. In parts of Java where such work is legal, including Malang and Surabaya, brothels are required to close during Ramadan. In 2008 in Surabaya sex workers were taught how to make hand rolled cigarettes and supplied with corn husks and tobacco. Social workers involved with the project said that it had no lasting effects. In many parts of Indonesia bars, discos and other "entertainment places" are now encouraged, if not required, to close for the month. Some people think that this is a good idea, because they would like to see them closed permanently and think that closing one month per year is better than nothing. Others find it silly and even hypocritical, explaining that people who are genuinely committed to fasting are unlikely to be tempted by alcohol or elicit sex, especially if they are not generally inclined towards such vices.

It is now very difficult to find *warung makan* (I. food stalls) that are open during the day except restaurants, hotels and other establishments frequented by foreigners. Most that do remain open cover windows and open spaces with curtains. In 2008 in Jakarta, members of the radical Islamist group *Front Pembela Islam* (Front for the Defense of Islam) served as "Ramadan Enforcers." They ransacked food stalls that did remain open and beat up the owners. Most Javanese Muslims found this behavior reprehensible and definitely not in keeping with what is, or at least should be, the spirit of Ramadan. Some also expressed the opinion that requiring eating establishments to close during the day was an extremely negative commentary on the Muslim community. One friend explained: "What are they thinking? If you have the intention to fast, you will, and the sight of other people eating will not bother you." Others commented that only Muslims are required to fast during Ramadan and that there should be places where Christians and others can eat and drink if they choose to.

Breaking the fast (*Iftar/ Buka Puasa*) is the most common ritual observance during Ramadan. It is considered *Sunnah* or the custom of the Prophet Muhammad to break the fast with a ripe date. This practice is far more common today than it was 30 years ago. One rarely sees dates in Yogyakarta except during Ramadan. Immediately after Lebaran the price drops by as much as 75% because many Javanese are not that fond of them. Most Javanese break the fast with a glass of sweet tea or with *kolak,* a sweet dink made with coconut milk, cassava, bananas and sugar. In villages and *kampung* young men and boys gather at mosques to listen to sermons and to break the fast collectively. This is sometimes referred to as a *slametan*. Wealthy members of the community provide meals on a rotating basis. This is said to result in a blessing from God equal to that of keeping the fast for the entire month, but does not excuse one from observing it. In recent years fast breaking buffets at fashionable restaurants and hotels have become increasingly common.[37] Other restaurants, including McDonalds, offer discount *paket buka puasa* (fast breaking packages).

Often prominent *ulama* are invited (and usually paid) to deliver sermons at *iftar* gatherings. Because there are *never* enough *ulama* during Ramadan, students from *pesantren* and Islamic universities are sometimes invited to speak and lead prayers at these events. Sometimes they are paid; sometimes they are only given free meals. Many are glad to receive either or both. Muslim charities including some from the Middle East also distribute food baskets and sponsor *Iftar* gatherings for the poor. Following the collapse of the New Order and the reinvigoration of Islamic political parties many adopted the customs of sponsoring *Iftar* gatherings and distributing food baskets to the poor during Ramadan.[38] Businesses, government offices and even the United States Embassy also sponsor *Iftar* gatherings.[39] Others prefer to break the fast at home with their families and a few friends. On university campuses large numbers of food vendors appear as the day draws to a close. There are often live bands, or at least recorded, and generally secular, music from sound trucks sponsored by radio stations. After sundown many venders ply the streets offers a wide variety of high sugar and/or fat foods some of which are sold only during Ramadan. Not surprisingly many people actual gain weight during the fast. On the other end of the economic spectrum *Iftar* meals are very simple, as are most all meals. It one gathering I attended in a remote area in the hills of Wonosari in 2008, only a dish prepared from steamed cassava and peanuts, and of course sweet tea, were served. All would agree that there is blessing in *Iftar*. Some say that God looks with special favor on the poor at these times. Many of the same people question the intention (*niyat*) of those attending elaborate and expensive *Iftar* Buffets.

Pesantren students often travel for the entire month, visiting famous teachers and graves and attending sermons. Their places in dormitories are often occupied by pilgrims who seclude themselves in *pesantren* for periods ranging from a few days to nearly the entire month during the fast. Many *kejawen* Muslims attend services at the mosque more regularly during Ramadan. Until 1979 government schools were closed. Children, even those of *kejawen* parents, attended classes on *Qur'an* recitation and ritual performance at local mosques.

---

[37] This practice is now common throughout the Muslim world.

[38] In 2008 the Islamist political party *Partai Keadilan Sejahtera* (PKS) made a systematic attempt to "capture" or as many in Yogyakarta put it "steal" Ramadan. Television and print advertisements made much of the party's offers to provide "reduced price" *Iftar* meals for the poor. Others, who were not trying to politicize the fast, simply gave them away. For a more detailed account of PKS's ritual-political strategy see M. Woodward, "Resisting Wahhabi Colonialism in Yogyakarta," *COMOPS Journal*, October, 2008.

[39] These upscale events are priced at a minimum of five US dollars and in "five star" hotels may cost as much as fifty. They provide opportunities, much like weddings, for political elites to mingle in "non-political" contexts.

Charity, *Qur'an* recitation and other devotional acts performed during Ramadan are believed by many to be of greater value than those performed at other times. Beggars who normally just approach cars on the streets carry paper signs asking for alms. According to some Hadith ritual devotions performed during Ramadan yield ten to seven hundred times the blessing of those performed at other times. There is, in both the Hadith literature and in Javanese sermons and religious discourse, a clear connection between religious observance during Ramadan and material well being. The following Hadith is an example.

> Ibn Abbas relates that the Holy Prophet was the most generous of men and that he was at his most bountiful during Ramadan when Gabriel visited him every night and recited the *Qur'an* to him. During this period the bounty of the Holy Prophet waxed faster than the rain-bearing breeze.[40]

There are special prayer services (J. *trawèh/* I. *tarawih/*A. *salat tu'ttarawi*) and *Qur'an* recitations at night. Modernists perform eleven prayers, traditionalists twenty two. According to *ulama* traditionalist practice is in keeping with the *sunnah* (tradition) of the Companions of the Prophet Muhammad, while modernist practice is in keeping with the *sunnah* of the Prophet himself. There are other differences. Modernists and traditionalist pray in slightly different ways and in slightly different directions: traditionalists towards the west reflecting pre-modern geographic knowledge and modernists towards the north-west, reflecting twentieth century knowledge of the direction of Mecca. Modernist prayers are typically restrained, while those of traditionalists are punctuated with ecstatic cries of "ALLAH!!!!" and "AMIN!" Generally speaking modernist prayers are performed in unison with all of those participating performing the required prostrations at the same time. Traditionalist prayers are less uniform. The pace flows from the worshippers' spiritual states. Traditionalists perform more prayers, but perform them more quickly.

Many observers say that these differences reflect more general theological orientations. The practice of *Muhammadiyah* and other modernists reflects a concern with the unity of the Muslim community (*ummah*). That of more traditionalist Muslims reflects concern with the individual's relationship with God. Prayers of both numbers and in both directions are sometimes conducted in the same mosque. This is always the case at the Grand Mosque of the Sultanate.

There are also recitations praising the Prophet Muhammad (*shawalat*), *zikir* or remembrance of God by reciting portions of the *Qur'an,* and sermons at almost every mosque. After the *traweh* prayers many men and boys sit in the mosque, alternatively reading or reciting the *Qur'an*, talking about all manner of things and, of course snacking on all manner of fried things, sweet things and fired sweet things. Women congregate in separate spaces and, I presume, also spend much of the night talking and snacking. Some mosques hold *slametan* for the entire community.

Several Hadith mention that the Prophet Muhammad retreated to the mosque and was particularly devoted to prayer during the last 10 days of Ramadan.[41]

---

[40]M. Kahn, *Gardens of the Righteous (Rdyadh as-Sahlahin)*. London: Cruzon, 1975, p. 213

[41] Kahn, op. cit., p. 208

Consequently some traditional *santri* seclude them in the mosque during this period or even for the entire month and spend much of the time reciting the *Qur'an*. Many stay in vacant dormitories in *pesantren* for the first 10 or 20 days of Ramadan and return home near the end of the month to prepare for *Lebaran*. The last five odd numbered nights in Ramadan are particularly important because one is the "Night of Power" known in Javanese as *malem selikur*. This is the night on which the *Qur'an* is believed to have descended from the highest to the lowest heaven. It is described in the *Qur'an* as follows.

> Behold, We sent it down on the Night of Power; And what shall teach thee what is the Night of Power? The Night of Power is better than a thousand months; in it the angels and the Spirit descend, by the leave of their Lord, upon every command. Peace it is, till the rising of dawn. (97:1–5)

It is thought that on this night angels visit the earth. Anyone praying or reciting the *Qur'an* at the exact moment they arrive receives a special blessing. It is commonly believed that this blessing is the same or greater than that which could be attained by praying and fasting continually for 1,000 months. Others say that if you are praying at the time the Angel appears you, "get whatever you want."

On these evenings mosques are filled. One man explained that the angels arrives between midnight and three A.M., but that they had to return to heaven before dawn. He continued that if one is praying or reciting with proper intention and sincerity the sound of a great wind will be heard, but the trees will remain still. Others say that at this time even plants and animals prostrate themselves. *Kejawen* Muslims hold *slametan* on these nights and hope to accomplish the same ends. In some villages near Yogyakarta farmers place lanterns in their fields to attract the angels and the blessing they bring. Prior to the Second World War the *kraton* staged elaborate *slametan* on the square in front of the *kraton*. These were hosted by the Sultan, the vizier and other *kraton* officials and were thought to yield blessing for the state as well as for the host. Even Dutch officials were invited.

Reformist Muslims have problems with the ritual complex attached to the Night of Power. It is impossible for them to reject it because it is clearly motivated by the *Qur'an* and Hadith. On the other hand they want to discourage concern with blessing and with angels and other spiritual beings. One explained that it is true that the angels come on this night but that they do not dispense blessing, they only notice who is praying and then pray to God that he forgive their sins and bless them. When I mentioned this interpretation to a traditionalist he replied that it was factually incorrect and not supported by either the *Qur'an* or Hadith.

Sawal: Rites of Reaggregation

Id al-Fitr (J& I. *Lebaran*) comes at the end of Ramadan. It celebrates the successful completion of the fast and is marked by communal prayer and the collection of the *zakat al-fitr* (A. alms tax) which is distributed to the poor.[42] In Java *Lebaran* is the single most important religious (and secular) holiday. It is an occasion for rejoicing and the exchange of gifts and salutations. It marks the return to secular time and the reconstitution of society in a purified state. *Antri* and *kejawen* informants agree that the purpose of *Lebaran* and the *Sawalan* ceremonies is to cleanse and purify social relations.

The fast ends at sunset on the eve of *Lebaran*. Later in the evening there are torch light processions, *Qur'an* recitation contests as well as night markets and all forms of secular entertainment. Thousands of young people march through the streets chanting *"Allah Akbar"* (God is great). This is called *Takbir Keliling* which means literally "walking around praising God." The streets are filled with motorcycles and trucks carrying loudspeakers from which blare (at maximum volume) the divine speech of the *Qur'an*.[43] The atmosphere combines that of a religious celebration and carnival. *Muhammadiyah* sponsors a procession of illuminated floats in which hundreds of children and teenagers participate In 2008 the spirit of this festival was clearly Yogyakarta nationalism and the unity of the Muslim community. There were floats that were replicas of the Grand Mosque, and even of a Chinese mosque. Marchers were dressed in costumes resembling those of palace guards and very strangely Pharonic Egyptians and Chinese Dancers. There was even a float of a giant *bedug* the oversized drum that accompanies the call to prayer in traditionalist mosques, the use of which *Muhammadiyah* strongly opposes. People explained that the purpose was to celebrate the unity of the Muslim community and to oppose attempts by Islamist *Partai Keadilan Sejahtera* or PKS (Justice and Prosperity Party) that would eliminate Yogyakarta's status as a "special region" and the Sultan's hereditary right to the office of governor. This was the most amazing thing that I have seen in Yogyakarta in 30 years. One would think that neo-Wahhabi reformist piety and Sufi royalist nationalism do not mix. In Yogya, they do. PKS supporters were noticeable absent.

The following morning the atmosphere is more sedate. Rice from *zakat* funds is distributed to the poor. Many people visit cemeteries early in the morning before attending the communal prayer which is held in mosques (by traditional *santri*) or in open fields (by reformists). It is often stated that every one should be happy on *Lebaran*, that they should have enough to eat, and if at all possible more than enough, and new clothes. Millions of Indonesians travel long distances (I. *Mudik*) to be with their families on *Lebaran*. Flights are full, train and bus tickets expensive, hard to come by and always over sold. Even Christians travel for *Lebaran* because it is a national as well as a Muslim holiday.

---

[42] In addition to offering of rice *Shari'ah* requires that 2.5% of accumulated wealth be donated to the poor or to religious scholars and institutions. Today many Islamic banks and charitable organizations offer on line and text messages ways to make the contribution. Most people continue to contribute to funds at Local mosque and to poor people directly.

[43] One of the most striking examples I observed in Yogyakarta in 1979 was a group of approximately 50 motorcycles ridden by young men dressed in Arabic garb. They followed a jeep equipped with a loudspeaker and chanted in union as the drove (at high speed) through the streets of the city. It would pass almost unnoticed today.

In Yogyakarta tens of thousands of people gather at the Grand Mosque and *Alon Alon* and other locations scattered throughout the city for the morning prayers. Following this the *kraton* stages a *Garebeg* similar to that described in Chapter 5. However, because the *kraton* and the mosque use different calendars, in 2008 the *Garebeg* was held the following day.

Perhaps the most striking aspect of the Javanese celebration of the *Id* is that everyone, young and old, rich and poor, noble and commoner, spends much of the day walking around apologizing to everyone they encounter asking forgiveness for external (*lahir*) and internal (*batin*) faults. In the afternoon there are family gatherings at which younger family members beg forgiveness and blessing from their elders. For much of the next month similar ceremonies, which often include *slametan,* are held in villages, urban neighborhoods, schools, mosques and offices. The *kraton* host separate events for male and female nobles and retainers. *Bupati* host similar ceremonies in their respective domains, some of which are also attended by the Sultan. There are similar gatherings at *pesantren* to offer respect to *Kyai*. Community organizations and cultural groups host similar gatherings for much of the month. Some people place notices in the classified advertisement sections of newspapers and send text messages on their mobile phones and e-mails to discussion lists and chat rooms they participate in.[44] Perhaps the most unusual and certainly one of the most touching and widely circulated *Id* greetings I have ever encountered was neatly printed on a one thousand Rupiah (0.01 USD) bank note.

Informants of all theological orientations state that the purpose of these rites is twofold. The first is that because Islam includes duties to humans as well as to God, God will not forgive sins unless one asks pardon from those one has wronged. The second is that *Sawalan* rites purify social relations and reconstitute society as a sacred, tranquil (*slamet*) community. It is often stated that what Ramadan does for the individual, *Sawal* does for the community.

This custom is also known by the Arabic phrase "*HalalBihalal*" which means "to gather together to ask forgiveness for mistakes and sins." But the expression is ungrammatical and by all accounts it is *not sunnah*. It cannot be justified on the basis of either *Qur'an* or Hadith. It is generally believed to have originated in Java and spread to the rest of Indonesia, Malaysia and Singapore in the 1940s.[45] It is not observed anywhere in the Muslim world outside Southeast Asia. But almost no one objects to the practice or considers it to be *bidah* or "un-Islamic." In *this* case Local Islam trumps Universalist Islam and *Kebudayaan Muslim* trumps *Agama Islam*.

Conclusions

Javanese observances of the rites of Ramadan fall into three general categories. Those of reformists which are limited to rites prescribed by Islamic law (with the except of *Halal Bihalal*,) those of traditional *santri* add a complex set of locally defined devotional acts and finally those of *kejawen* Muslims who often neglect

---

[44] I receive, and send, several hundred such e-mails every year.

[45] *Republika*, October 12, 2008.

Shari'ah regulations but who join enthusiastically in superogatory acts of piety. Despite these differing performance styles, Ramadan observances are motivated by a common understanding of the purpose and benefits of the fast and share a common ritual structure, i.e., that Ruwah purifies the physical body, Ramadan cleanses the spiritual body of sin and that Sawal transforms social relations.

The degree to which these understandings are shared is illustrated by the following examples. The first is taken from a *pengajian* (religious talk) by Pak Hassan at the *Muhammadiyah* mosque in the *kampung* where we both lived in 1979; the second is drawn from an interview with Pak Muci, one of my *kejawen* neighbors who fasted for only 3 days at the beginning of Ramadan and two at the end.

First the pengagian:

> The month of *Sawal* is for cleaning relationships between people. The real meaning of *zakat* is to make the community pure and holy. Also if you are old or sick and can't fast, paying extra can be substituted for fasting. The *zakat* and asking forgiveness from people are really very similar. God orders us to be on good terms with our neighbors. We aren't asking them to forgive us in the same way that God does, but it is necessary to repair our social relations before God will pardon us. This is possible only because of the fast of Ramadan, in which we withdraw from social relations and concentrate on religion. You use the faith and devotion that fasting builds to rebuild social life. Fasting is also a religious duty which is commanded by God. God did not require it to make things difficult for use because Islam is an easy religion which does not impose burdens on people. He commanded us to fast because it builds our faith in Him and teaches us to live together as members of the great family of Islam.

Second: Pak Muci's interpretation of Ramadan:

> Everyone must fast for at least part of the month. In reality the fast is three things: First cleaning the physical body, the house and the neighborhood of physical impurities. Fasting won't work if you don't do this first. Second cleaning the spiritual body by fasting which burns up sin and passion. Third cleaning social relations is the family, the neighborhood, the city and the whole Muslim world. Number two depends on number one and number three depends on number two. (He then explained) Fasting during Ramadan, and fasting in general, is not just not eating. It is withdrawing from social relationships. It breaks bonds between humans. This lets you develop faith and trust in God. Number three is based on number two. It is rebuilding social connections but based on faith. It makes society calm is the same way that fasting makes the spirit calm. You should also make offerings to spirits at this time because it makes them calm and they won't harm you for the rest of the year. God has ordered us to do all of these things. It is important that they be done with real feeling and sincerity. It is hard to tell who is sincere, but God knows and judges you on what your inner (*batin*) states are. It's almost like the judgment day, but it comes once per year.

Pak Muci did not feel that the *Shari'ah* was the truly important part of Islam. He prayed and fasted when his heart told him to. Pak Hassan lived next door to him.[46] He never missed any of the five daily prayers and found Pak Muci's views to be impious at best. But despite their very real differences, the two men believed that the rites of the Ramadan are among the most important parts of Islam. In spite of their theological difference, their interpretations of the structure of ritual performances of

---

[46]This account is based on fieldwork conducted in 1979. I refer to them both in the past tense because both men are now deceased.

Ramadan and its transformative ends were strikingly similar. They also asked each other for forgiveness on *Lebaran*. Some years later Pak Hassan prayed at Pak Muci's funeral. This was beautifully constructed *bricolage*.

Photos

Ramadan Devotions

Women reading the Qur'an   **Men reading the Qur'an**

Ramadan Devotions

Qur'an class for children   ***Ziyarah – Visting graves***

Buka Puasa – Breaking the Fast

Local Mosque -- Yogyakarta   **Grand Mosque -- Yogyakarta**

Buka Puasa – Breaking the Fast

Ramadan Buffet   **Village mosque**

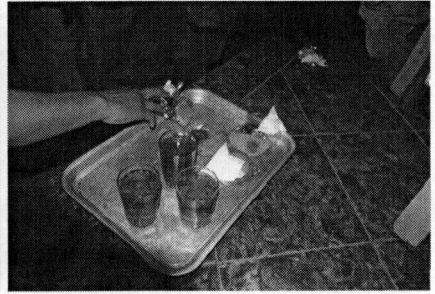

Traweh Prayers

Takbir Keliling

Majorette Muhammadiyah Drum Band

Children dressed as palace guards

Lebaran

Id prayers

Id prayers

Lebaran

Asking forgiveness

Asking forgiveness

Chapter 7
The *Kraton* Revolution: Religion, Culture, Regime Change and Democracy in Yogyakarta

> *Hamengku means to give more than you receive. Hamengku means to act as a loving parent, giving peace, protection and security to the heart. Regardless of how much state power it is given, Kraton Yogyakarta has a strong desire to be a lamp in the center of society with the values, vision and history of leadership. Suharto ruled the nation with a concept of political leadership rooted in Javanese culture, that of Yogyakarta. However, in many cases he acted on the basis of his personal interpretation.*
>
> – Sultan Hamengkubuwana X

This chapter explores the interplay of *kebudayaan* and *agama* in Yogyakarta at the end of the New Order and the ways in which Sultan Hamengkubuwana X used the *kraton* as a stage for cultural/religious/political drama that figured significantly in the process of *Reformasi* that led to the democratic transformation of 1998.[1] It has been argued throughout this volume that in societies that adhere to any of the great trans-cultural religions there is an inherent tension between culture and religion. Religion seeks to transform culture, while culture seeks to domesticate or localize religions originating in other times and/or places. Cultures and religions change over time, despite claims of some religious and cultural conservatives to the contrary. As they change the relationship between the two is renegotiated. Over the past three decades much of what scholars of religion and Javanese of previous generations would have called "religion" – the veneration of sacred graves, state ceremonies, the *slametan*, sacred geography, the theory of power (*kesekten*) and the like have come to be known as "culture" rather than "religion." While much of this cultural/religious

---

[1] *Reformasi* refers to the movement for political and moral change that emerged in response to the economic crisis of 1997 and 1998 and culminated in the resignation of President Suharto on May 21, 1998. It can be translated in two ways: "Reform" and "Reformation." Indonesians used both terms. The English "reform" emphasizes the political dimension of the process, "reformation" the religious aspect. In the late 1990s Ohio State University Political Scientist William Liddle and I often appeared together on panels devoted to the Indonesian political crisis and subsequent democratic transition. It was very nearly a standing joke that Bill referred to it as "reform" and I called it "reformation." As much as anything else, this choice of words reflects alternative disciplinary orientations.

complex is shared with believers throughout the Muslim world, many modernists and Wahhabi influenced Islamists denounce it as *bidah*, *kufarat* and *shirk*. Defining "religion" as "culture" serves to isolate traditional Javanese Islam and Muslims from these charges. The central thesis of this chapter is that in May of 1998 this linguistic shift enabled *kejawen* and *santri* Muslims to unite in a common struggle against the Suharto regime in much the same way that they did in the struggle against the Dutch half a century before under the combined banners of nationalism and *jihad*. This allowed Yogyakarta to remain peaceful while Jakarta the capitol and the neighboring royal city of Surakarta went up in flames. In this chapter it is argued that this was possible because Yogyakarta's history as the "mother city" of the Indonesian revolution and the charisma of the Yogyakarta throne enabled Hamengkubuwana X to draw on a mix of religious, cultural and nationalist symbols of legitimacy in defiance of a regime that by May of 1998 could rely only on brute force to remain in power. This *bricolage* enabled the Sultan to work together with *ulama* and Muslim politicians of diverse theological orientations to maintain peace and order in a time of chaos. It enabled him to define what began as an economic and political crisis as a cosmic struggle between good and evil; between Yogyakarta and Jakarta and between himself and President Suharto.

My use of the concept of charisma differs some what from that of Max Weber who defined it as:

> A certain quality of individual personality, by virtue of which s/he is set apart from ordinary people and treated as endowed with supernatural, superhuman, or at least specifically exceptional powers or qualities. These are such as are not accessible to the ordinary person, but are regarded as of divine origin or as exemplary, and on the basis of them the individual concerned is treated as a leader.[2]

Ernst Gellner, has argued that among Berber Muslims of the Atlas Mountains of Morocco, charisma is inherited in saintly lineages.[3] This is also true in Java, where "exceptional powers" are believed to be transmitted in both royal and *Kyai* lineages. Even individuals, including the Susuhunan of Surakarta, who personally exhibit none of the qualities of charisma are believed to posses them to some extent, simply because of the positions they occupy. This is also true in Yogyakarta, where even powerless Sultans of the era of "high colonialism" were treated almost as gods by their subjects. They possessed the charisma of the office or throne of the genuinely charismatic Sultans of the past. By virtue of his role in the Indonesian Revolution Sultan Hamengkubuwana IX established his personal charisma and reinvigorated that of the Yogyakarta throne. For the first decade of his reign it was not clear that his son and successor possessed anything more than the residual charisma of his ancestors. This was, however, sufficient to place him on center stage in the Indonesian political dramas of May 1998, to establish his personal charisma and further enhance that of the Yogyakarta throne.

---

[2] See S. Eisenstadt (ed.) *Max Weber, On Charisma and Institution Building: Selected Papers*, Chicago: University of Chicago Press, 1977.

[3] E. Gellner, *Saints of the Atlas*, London: The Trinity Press, 1969, p. 70.

As the nation fell into chaos, this combination of inherited and acquired charisma made possible a moment of what Victor Turner called Spontaneous Communitas that made violence impossible, and transformed what were potentially "leveling crowds" into masses of peaceful devoted subjects. While Jakarta and many other cities burned tranquility reigned in Yogyakarta. This precipitated a complex series of events that can be aptly termed the "Kraton Revolution."

The analysis presented here builds on that of the symbolism of the Yogyakarta *kraton* presented in Chapters 4 and 5 and on the discussion of power and morality included in Chapter 2. It focuses on the ways in which sacred space can be used in social and political drama for which it was not specifically intended. Again, the concept of *bricolage* holds the key to understanding the transformation of concepts religion, culture and nationality at the end of the New Order period. In this case it was *bricolage* in real time. During the political crisis of May 1998 what had been cultural space very rapidly became Yogyakarta and Indonesian political space. While indexical symbols of nationalism and revolution had been memorialized in Kraton Museums they had been largely dormant since the New Order came to power in 1966 and especially for the first decade of Hamengkubuwana X's reign. My primary concern in this chapter is with how they were reinvigorated and the ways in which the *kraton* was used as a stage for a hybrid form of religious, cultural and political conflict in which Javanese concepts of kingship were employed in the service of democratic reform. The events of May 1998 show that despite centuries of colonial rule and more than half a century of Indonesian independence and nation building, notions of Javanese-Islamic sacred geography and the charisma of the Yogyakarta throne remain potent forces in Indonesian politics.

The New Order was an authoritarian military regime that based its religious, nationalist and cultural legitimacy on an assemblage of neo-liberal economic policies, Javanese notions of authority and whispers that it had absorbed the symbols and substance of the power of the Javanese Islamic kingdoms, i.e. the Surakarta *pusaka*, in much the same way that Mataram, and its' successors Surakarta and Yogyakarta had absorbed the power of earlier Hindu-Javanese states and their *pusaka*. This too was *bricolage* At least as seen from Yogyakarta; it was unequal to the task of confronting the combination of a national economic crisis and the nationalist/royalist/Islamic/democratic *bricolage* that emerged in and around the *kraton*.

Yogyakarta and Indonesian Political Culture

Of the approximately 350 traditional states that existed in the Netherlands Indies at the beginning of the Second World War, Yogyakarta is the only one to have survived as a viable political entity.[4] It is one of three "Special Regions" in the Indonesian

---

[4] Wirabhumi (et al.) state that in 1945, "Overnight the courts were reduced to political irrelevance. Their rulers lost both inherited power and traditional sources of income. Many simply disappeared, while others clung to a preacrios existence as tourist attractions or cultural centers." E. Wirabhumi

Republic largely because of the central role that Sultan Hamengkubuwana IX played in the Indonesian revolution.[5] It is also the cradle of Indonesian nationalism. Yogya, and its' place in the Indonesian struggle for independence also figure significantly in mythological narratives constructed to establish the legitimacy of the New Order and President Suharto.

Much of Suharto's political legitimacy derived from his purported role as a revolutionary hero and especially his role an aid to the two legendary leaders who organized the "general uprising" of March 1st 1949 in which Republican forces recaptured Yogyakarta from the Dutch for six hours. This led the United Nations and the United States to push for international recognition of Indonesia's independence. These leaders were the General Soedirman and Sultan Hamengkubuwana IX. Soedirman, more than any other figure in modern Indonesian history, embodied the warrior ethos of the Javanese past.[6] He refused to leave his troops during the darkest days of the revolution, even when he was dying from tuberculosis and had to be carried over mountainous terrain in a sedan chair. Sultan Hamengkubuwana IX is widely regarded as having been among the greatest kings in Java's long history and as a Muslim saint. Approximately a million people lined to road leading to the royal cemetery Imo Giri when he died in 1988. He is known for his early and unbending support for the revolution and for staring down a Dutch tank when it attempted to enter the *kraton*. *Kraton* tradition maintains that when the Dutch commander offered the Sultan the throne of a reunited kingdom of Mataram in return for his allegiance, he replied that the only thing that he was willing to discuss was "When and how you are going to leave?"[7]

Accounts of this incident I first heard in 1978 maintain that Suharto was the messenger who kept the two leaders in contact by masquerading as a peasant bringing vegetables to the *kraton* and one of several field commanders on the day of the uprising. These accounts systematically under estimate the role that Suharto played in the attack. They can be understood as counter-hegemonic discourse contesting heroic New Order Narratives.

Throughout the New Order period the official "Indonesian" version of history maintained that the attack was Suharto's idea that he played a major, if not the leading, role in planning it and personally led the attack. *Jalur Kunning*, a semi-official and extremely controversial film about the uprising produced in 1978, portrayed

---

(Project Director), *Karaton Surakarta*, Jakarta: *Yayasan Pawiyatan Kebudayaan Kraton Surakarta*, 2004, inside front dust jacket. This is true of Surakarta and most of the other traditional courts, but is most certainly not the case in Yogyakarta.

[5] The others are Aceh in North Sumatra and Jakarta.

[6] On General Soedirman and his role in the Indonesian Revolution see: S. Said, *Genesis of Power: General Sudirman and the Indonesian Military in Politics, 1945–49*, Singapore: Institute of Southeast Asian Studies, 1991.

[7] I can not independently confirm the veracity of this tradition.

Suharto in heroic terms.[8] Similar versions of the story are included in school history textbooks and Suharto's autobiography and were memorialized in monuments, celebrated and reenacted in New Order state ceremonies. In Yogyakarta most people have always thought the official accounts to be lies concocted by Suharto to bolster his personal legitimacy and that of his regime. The Yogyakarta account of the uprising is among the events depicted in the relief carvings on the *Pagelaran* wall in the *kraton*. It depicts Suharto receiving orders from the Sultan. The fact that this "text" was constructed during the period of Suharto's rule is a stunning display of resistance to New Order hegemony. Hamengkubuwana IX never spoke publically about these events. K. P. H. Poerwokoesoemo did in a 1985 interview in which he explained that the uprising was the Sultan's idea and that he worked closely with General Soedirman.[9] Since the fall of the New Order the events of March 1st 1949 have received renewed attention from Indonesian historians. There is now a consensus among Indonesian scholars that the official account is exactly what people in Yogyakarta have long believed it to be, lies intended to establish Suharto as a revolutionary hero of mythic proportions.[10] These lies were told so often and on such a grand scale that millions of Indonesians continue to believe them. They have become mythology. It is impossible to know how long these lies/myths will endure.

The *Kraton* and *Reformasi*

The symbolism of the *kraton* was discussed in Chapters 4 and 5. In this Chapter I will be concerned primarily with the large square (*Alon Alon*) at the northern end of the *kraton*. The *Alon Alon* is the place where regional officials and the common people gather for major state ceremonies. It is, in this respect, an extension of *Siti Inggil* and *Pagelaran* audience halls where higher ranking officials assemble. The highest position is the Sultan's throne, which is described as a "seat in heaven." This complex represents the hierarchical organization of the traditional state.

The symbolic meanings of the *Alon Alon* are complex. Its expanse represents the shoreless ocean seen by the mind in meditation that, in turn, is a common image for the infinity of God. *Kyai Dewadaru* and *Kyai Jagadaru*, the banyan trees located at the center of the *Alon Alon*, depict the identity of microcosm and macrocosm. *Kyai*

---

[8]I and other foreigners living in Yogyakarta at the time were offered roles as extras in this production. Military officers came to our houses to "invite" us to "help" with the film. *Kraton* officials told me that it would be most inappropriate for me to appear riding on a tank dressed as a Dutch soldier and advised me to decline the offer. I did.

[9]http://id.shvoong.com/books/1755952-kontroversi-serangan-umum-maret-1949/ Pak Poerwo provided me with this information in 1978 and asked that it remain confidential for as long as Suharto was president.

[10]H. Putra, "Remembering, Misremembering and Forgetting: The Struggle over 'Serangan Oemoem Maret 1949' in Yogyakarta Indonesia," *Asian Journal of Social Science*, vol. 29, no. 3, 2001, pp 471–494.

Dewadaru represents God and the Sultan; *Kyai Jagadaru* represents humanity in general and the population of the Sultanate in particular. Together they are symbolic of the concept of the "union of servant and lord" that is the lynchpin of Javanese mystical and political thought. Just as nobles come to the *kraton* to petition the Sultan, commoners – if they wish to bring an injustice to his attention – may perform a rite between the two trees known as *pepe*. In this rite the petitioner dresses in white (a symbol of purity), makes small offerings (*sajen*) to each of the trees, and sits motionless until he/she comes to the attention of the Sultan who is required to decide the case without regard to the status or social position of the petitioner.

The traditional mystical symbolism of the *Alon Alon* and the more "modern" form of sacred geography apparent in Poerwokoesoemo's writings, which describe Yogyakarta as the symbolic center of Indonesia, were combined in the political dramas of 1998 and 1999 that led to the fall of the Suharto government and the rise of Sultan Hamengkubuwana X as an important and powerful national leader – and contender for the Indonesian presidency.[11]

Yogyakarta, Sacred Geography, and the End of the New Order

It is generally accepted that modern Indonesian political culture has been profoundly shaped by traditional Javanese notions of kingship and authority.[12] One of the central tenets of Javanese political theory is that heads of state, be they *rajas*, sultans or presidents possess and embody esoteric knowledge that allows them to mediate between God and their subjects/citizens. This mediating process is widely understood as an important conduit through which the blessing and mercy of God are conveyed to the general populace. In an exoteric sense, peace, social harmony and prosperity are among the consequences of this mediation. Traditional Javanese of all religious orientations maintain that if the chief executive maintains a proper relationship with God and lives a moral life; the state will be peaceful and prosperous. Should he, or she in the case of today's Indonesia, fall from this state of grace, chaos, famine, plague, and pestilence, are among the predictable results.

The Crisis

In the spring of 1998, Indonesia was in chaos. The economic crisis that began in 1997 led to widespread student demonstrations, violence by mobs and the security forces, and demands for an end to the New Order government.[13] The Sultan did

---

[11]On Poerwokoesoemo's understanding of the sacred geography of Yogyakarta see Chapter 1.

[12]T. Sarsito, "Javanese Culture as the Source of Legitimacy for Soeharto's Government," *Asia Europe Journal. Intercultural Studies in the Social Sciences and Humanities*, July 2006, pp. 1–16 and W. Liddle "Suharto's Indonesia: Personal Rule and Political Institutions," *Pacific Affairs*, vol. 58, no. 1, 1985, pp 68–90.

[13]On the history of New Order Indonesia and the *Reformasi* movement see A. Schwarz, *Nation in Waiting: Indonesia's Search for Stability* (2nd edition), London: Allen and Unwin, 2000 and

not sit on the "seat in heaven" in silent meditation as he does during the *Garebeg* ceremonies. He stood in front of the people at the bottom of the steps leading from the *Pagelaran* to the *Alon Alon* wearing Indonesian attire, trousers and a *batik* shirt, rather than the traditional *kraton* garb required for Javanese ceremonial occasions and spoke of the need for *Reformasi* – in both the political and religious senses of the term.

Those who remember Indonesia in the mid – 1960s speak of shops with empty shelves and villages filled with naked children. People who had the money to buy cloth simply could not find any. They also speak of political chaos and living in constant fear.[14] After coming to power following the abortive coupe of 1965 Suharto began a relentless program of economic development and enforced political stability.[15] The result was nearly three decades of sustained economic growth and very real improvement in the quality of life for most Indonesians. These gains were not, however, with out cost. Suharto's "New Order" was a rigid administrative state in which parliament did little more than confirm executive decisions and re-elect the president. Political dissent was tolerated, but only within vaguely defined limits. Insulting the president or his family was a criminal offense. No one knew exactly what this meant.

Suharto also cultivated a cult of personality that built on traditional Javanese theories and symbols of legitimacy. Deference towards and respect for authority are among the central values of Javanese and Indonesian political culture. Hildred Geertz has argued that respect for social hierarchy is among the most basic aspects of Javanese culture and that hierarchy is understood as being "a good in itself."[16] Throughout the New Order period Suharto demanded, and generally received, gestures of respect and deference appropriate for a father figure and not unlike those traditionally accorded to Javanese kings and nobles. He also cultivated a culture of fear. Unknown numbers of leftist and Islamist opponents were jailed or simply disappeared. Many were tortured. People were afraid to speak with those who had been labeled "communists" even when they were close relatives. Even the descendents of dissidents were denied access to public higher education and employment.

K., O'Rourke, *Reformasi: The Struggle for Power in Post Suharto Indonesia*, London: Allen and Unwin, 2003 and K.Va n Dijk, *A Country in Despair, Indonesia between 1997 and 2000*. Leiden: KITLV press, 2001. On the religious and ethnic violence of the period see M. Woodward, "Religious Conflict and the Globalization of Knowledge: Indonesia 1978–2004," in Linell Cady and Sheldon Simon (eds.) *Religion and Conflict in South and Southeast Asia. Disrupting Violence*, London: Routledge, 2006. This chapter is not intended as a comprehensive analysis of the role of religion and culture in the *Reformasi* movement. Accounts of the economic impact of the crisis and of political struggles and violence in Jakarta are included to provide contexts for the dramatically different course *Reformasi* took in Yogyakarta.

[14] I would like to thank Professor Clark Cunningham, Professor Emeritus, Department of Anthropology, University of Illinois at Urabana-Champaign for this observation.

[15] See J. Bresnan, *Managing Indonesia. The Modern Political Economy*, New York: Columbia University Press, 1993.

[16] H. Geertz, *The Javanese Family. A Study of Kinship and Socialization*, Glencoe: The Free Press, 1961 p. 147.

The ban, which has since been lifted, was to last seven generations. In the Javanese system of kinship reckoning this is the number of generations for which descendants of a common ancestor are considered to be related. A decade after Suharto's fall, people remain reluctant to discuss their experiences of this aspect of the New Order. In Java kinship ties are enormously important. Some now speak in shame of avoiding family members for decades in fear of being labeled "Communists" themselves, and describe their efforts to rebuild family ties with joy mixed with tears.

For most of the New Order era Indonesians tolerated the authoritarian nature of the regime because of substantial improvements in material welfare. Through about the 1970s and 1980s it was widely believed that Suharto and the state ideology of *Panca Sila* was extremely *sakti* (powerful) because together they had be able to defeat the Indonesian Communist Party following the 1965 coup attempt and that his rule was based on *Wangsit Keprabon* (J. divine appointment).[17] All but the bravest dissidents feared to publicly challenge authority. All of this changed in the early months of 1998. The Asian financial panic of 1997 hit Indonesia harder than any of its neighbors.[18] On January 1st 1998 the value of the Indonesian *Rupiah* stood as 2,361 to the US Dollar. By January 25th it had fallen to 14,800. As the value of the *Rupiah* plummeted, a sense of panic gripped Indonesia's cities and towns. Large numbers of middle class consumers rushed to supermarkets buying basic commodities such as rice, sugar, milk and cooking oil in enormous quantities. Some stores reported completely depleted stocks and others limited purchases of rice to twenty kilograms. The panic spread rapidly to traditional markets frequented by less affluent Indonesians. One merchant in central Jakarta's *Pasar Senin* reported selling his complete stock of 7,500 kg of rice in less than two hours. Initially there was fear, though no actual reports, of looting. In some places angry crowds attacked shop owners accused of raising prices to profit from the crisis. Some merchants specializing in imported luxury goods closed temporarily for "re-pricing" to avoid losses. Many cancelled or sharply curtailed orders. "Import substitution" began almost immediately as locally made "designer clothing" appeared in markets at a fraction of the cost of the "re-priced" genuine articles. In Jakarta, Yogyakarta and other cities many gold dealers closed up shop because the market was so unstable. The feared that either buying or selling could result in enormous losses. This was particularly critical because many Indonesians, especially the lower classes, do not trust banks and keep their savings in gold or silver jewelry. It prevented them from

---

[17] In Javanese mystical thought *Wangsit Keprabon* can be distinguished from *Wahyu Kedhaton* as the former refers to political authority in a general sense and the later to kingship in specific. For understanding the role of Javanese culture and religion in the New Order legitimation strategy, the distinction is of only marginal significance because Suharto never claimed to be king. While *Wangit Keprabob* was most commonly used in reference to Suharto, *Wahyu Kedhaton* was also used. See M. Mubarok and A. Rasyidin, *Soehatro Tak Pernah Mati*, Surabaya, Institute for Development Economic, 2008, pp. 125.

[18] J, Sachs, "The East Asian Financial Crisis: Diagnosis, Remedies, Prospects", Brookings Paper, vol. 28, no. 1, 1998.

converting the tumbling currency into more tangible assets. Some, particularly those with limited assets, bought rice instead.

The sense of panic was enhanced by cultural and religious factors. The crisis began during the Islamic fasting month of Ramadan, a time when many Indonesians purchase larger than normal quantities of food and clothing in preparation for the feast of *Id al-Fitri*. Many feared, correctly as it turned out, that they would not have sufficient funds to celebrate the holiday in the customary way.[19] For many in Jakarta and Yogyakarta *kampung*, this meant that they could not afford the chicken traditionally prepared for the feast. The dominance of ethnic Chinese in the retail sector of the economy heightened ethnic tensions. As the crisis deepened rumors spread that many Chinese business people had known about the collapse of the *Rupiah* in advance and had moved enormous sums off shore or converted *Rupiah* to dollars or gold. Some Indonesians believed that they had deliberately engineered the economic collapse in order to acquire property at vastly deflated prices. The fact that many Indonesian Chinese are Christians only exacerbated the tension. Concern about these developments prompted some shop owners to post signs reading "*Toko Islam*" (I. Islamic store) or "*Toko Pribumi*" (I. indigenous store). These signs saved some, but not all, from looting and arson in the violence that was soon to follow.

Unemployment and underemployment skyrocketed. The tourist industry, upon which many in Yogyakarta depended for their livelihoods, collapsed almost completely. The main streets of the city are usually crowded with foreigners. In May of 1998 I could wander the streets for half a day and not see another "*bule*" (I. foreigner). Many who could no longer find work turned to (very) petty trading in attempts to make ends meet. The peripheries of markets soon became crowded with people selling all manner of used goods, ranging from motorcycle parts to antiques at bargain rates. The number of *warung* (I. small shops) selling sundries, cigarettes, snack foods and drinks in Yogyakarta *kampung* increased dramatically, but not because of rising demand. People simply had no other way of making a living. In the *kampung* which I have called home for the past three decades, the number increased from two before the crisis to more than twenty in May of 1998. Even more tragic was the increase in the number of girls and young women forced into prostitution. They sold their bodies so that they and their families could eat. Young people, who could remember nothing other than the New Order, and who were used to nearly continuous economic improvement, could scarcely believe how far and how fast their standards of living fell. While they suffered financial losses, the life styles of the elite, including of course Suharto and his family, were not severely affected. Those who had dollar or other hard currency assets actually prospered. As one friend put in early June, "The people who were having parties before are still having parties." She was right. I was invited to more than one lavish wedding that summer. Suharto's son Tommy continued to cruise the streets of Jakarta in his pink Rolls Royce.

---

[19] See Chapter 6 for an account of *Id al-Fitri* celebrations.

Efforts by the government and the international community, most notably the International Monetary Fund, did little to stop the economic hemorrhage. Some, especially the "Love the *Rupiah*" movement supported by Suharto's daughter Siti Hardiyanti Rukmana or Tutut as she is commonly known, were absurd. There were numerous calls, some of them on the Inter-Net, for collective action to "save" the *Rupiah* by selling dollars at a loss. There were popular songs about it, and even pleas to pray for it. The "Love the *Rupiah* Movement" was often mentioned in the press and in statements by government officials. Prominent people, including Tutut, who was at the time often referred to as the *Putri Mahakota* (Crown Princess) because of her close relationship with her father and obvious political ambitions, were photographed selling dollars or gold or donating them to the treasury. Tutut flamed ethnic tensions by appearing on television talk shows and suggesting that Chinese businessmen had worsened the crisis by moving money overseas[20]. Some *dukun* were reported to have used black magic to counter their efforts.[21] These theatrics did nothing to resolve the monetary crisis. Very few Indonesians took them seriously and many were bitterly critical of the "movement." Many observed that the wealthy made shows of selling very small percentages of their hard currency assets while ordinary people were forced to pay dramatically higher prices for life's necessities.

Austerity measures required by the International Monetary Fund as a condition for emergency credits may have contributed to long term economic stability. They did nothing to help the poor in the short term. Indeed dramatic increases in fuel and electricity prices are among the factors that contributed to the spasms of violence that rocked Indonesia's cities later in the year.[22] They also sparked feelings of economic nationalism and resentment against the Suharto regime and the international community. Letters of intent signed by IMF representatives and Suharto were often compared with the "political contracts" the Dutch required Javanese monarchs to sign at the beginning of their reigns. A photograph of Michael Camdessus of the IMF standing with his arms crossed beside a seated Suharto signing one such document was widely seen as a national humiliation.

In late 1997 and early 1998 economic conditions could barely have been worse, particularly when seen from the *kampung*. As Suryopratomo subsequently put it, "All of the results of development were destroyed."[23] Those old enough to remember the hard times of the mid 1960s feared that they would return, with perhaps even worse political repercussions, because, as one put it: "In those days all we had ever known was poverty, first from the Dutch, then the depression and then the Japanese

---

[20] R. Simanjorang (ed.) *Kurusuhan Mei 1998. Facta, Data dan Analisa*, Jakrta: *Solidaritas Nusa Bangsa*, 2007, p. 19.

[21] *Tajuk*, vol. 1 no. 14, September 1998, pp. 20–21.

[22] Simanjorang, op. cit., pp. 224–228 and M. Woodward,"Rice, Chickens, Politicians and the IMF: Politics, Morality and Food in Indonesia," *Suvanabhumi*, vol. 11, no. 1, 1998, pp 9–13.

[23] Suryopratomo, *"Sekapur Sirih"* in, J. Luhulima, *Hari-Hari Terpanjang. Menjelang Mundurnya Presideeetn Soeharto dan Beberapa Peristiwa Terkait*, Jakarta: Kompas, 2001, p. vii.

War, the Revolution and Sukarno. But now that people know what development is, they won't tolerate this for long." They didn't.

There were soon calls for Suharto's resignation or at least that he not seek a seventh five year term as president in elections scheduled for March of 1998. For several years there had been rumors that Suharto planned to retire at the end of his sixth term because of his advanced age (77). These were fueled by the death of his wife in 1996. These rumors proved to be false. On January 20 it was announced that he would be, as usual, the only candidate. As usual he was unanimously re-elected by the *Majelis Perwakilan Rakyat* (the upper house of parliament).

There had been anti-government demonstrations on university campuses since early January. After Suharto announced his candidacy, and especially after his election on March 11th, the scale and intensity of the protests increased dramatically. In January demonstrators numbered in the hundreds. By April they numbered in the tens of thousands.[24] There were powerful symbolic statements that contributed to the de-legitimation of the regime. Suharto's official portraits were frequently defaced and he was burned in effigy at a demonstration at Gadjah Mada University in Yogyakarta.[25] Such acts are of much greater significance in Indonesia than in western countries. Deference towards and respect for authority are among the central values of Javanese and Indonesian political culture The fact that there were so many blatant public acts of disrespect was taken by many as a sign that power, in both the Javanese and western senses was slipping from Suharto's grasp. The public expression of discontent fostered its growth. The inability of the regime to command respect suggested that it no longer deserved it and that its' *wangsit* or *wahyu* had been withdrawn by God as well as the people.

Many religious leaders and public intellectuals joined with the students in calls for radical political change. They were generally far more *halus* (J. refined) than student demonstrators, but clearly supported their agenda. Many engaged in "indirect speech," being *harshly* critical of the regime without being *overtly* critical.[26] Nurcholish Madjid, for example, advocated a US style two party system and a district based electoral system. The implementation of such a system would have dramatically undermined the power of the Jakarta based elite and increased that of local and provincial leaders. It was also an implicit call for the end of the "floating mass" concept that prevented political parties, other than the government party GOLKAR, from organizing on district or village levels. Intellectuals and student leaders spoke privately, and as time progressed, publicly about bringing Suharto and his family to justice and confiscating their fortunes. Religious leaders including Amien Rais and Deliar Noer supported this view. Amein Rais stated: "What the

---

[24] Simanjorang, op. cit., p. 37.

[25] Luhulima, op. cit., p. 84. Official portraits of the president and vice president are displayed in virtually every office and school in Indonesia.

[26] On "indirect speech" in Indonesian and Javanese religious and political discourse see, M. Woodward, "Textual Exegesis as Social Commentary: Religious, Social and Political Meanings of Indonesian Translations of Arabic Hadith Texts". *The Journal of Asian Studies*, vol. 52, no. 3, 1993, 565–583.

students say is the voice of the people." He also explained that the students had no trust in the government and what was taking place was not simply and economic and political crisis but a crisis of belief *(krisis kepercayaan)*. This term generally refers to religious belief. Noer stated that "the aspirations of the students are those of the greater portion of the people" and that the students were not likely to ignore the problems confronting the people.[27]

Diagnosing the Crisis

Indonesian understandings of the economic collapse of the New Order and the subsequent political crisis were often works of *bricolage* melding political, religious and political reasoning. There were numerous esoteric accounts of the crisis. Some believed that God was punishing Indonesia for arrogance, pride and impiety. There are two basic versions of this interpretation. The first was that society as a whole was to blame and that because of increased levels of prosperity and consumerism the nation had fallen from grace. Professor Komarudin Hidayat of Syarif Hidayatullah State Islamic University in Jakarta called on Muslims to be particularly concerned with the fast of Ramadan in 1998 to atone for their sins and short comings. He explained that fasting cleanses the soul allowing it to receive the blessing and mercy of God. He concluded that God helps those who perform the duties of the fast with sincere and pious intention. He concluded that the divine blessing acquired from it would aid not only individuals but Indonesian society as a whole. In short his argument was that if Indonesians paid sufficient attention to their religious duties that they would develop the moral and spiritual qualities upon which peace, prosperity and social harmony depend.[28]

Islamist Indonesians attributed the crisis to Suharto's moral failings and subsequent loss of divine grace. Many believe that the collusion, corruption and nepotism of which Suharto was routinely accused were not simply political crimes but also sins for which God was punishing the entire nation. They argued that the crisis could only be "overcome" and prosperity restored with the emergence of a leader whose moral character and commitment to *Shari'ah* and would re-establish the flow of divine blessing on which the well-being and perhaps survival of the nation depends. Some *kejawen* Muslims offered even more esoteric interpretation according to which Suharto had sought and acquired sources of power associated with Javanese kings and *dukun* and that his wife, Siti Hartinah, or Bu Tien as she was commonly known, held the "*wansit keprabon*" (J. divine appointment) that enabled Suharto to hold on to power for so long. These sources state that with her death on April 28, 1996, his mystical power began to slip away.

---

[27] *Forum Keadilan April 20th 1998* Noer is a prominent modernist Muslim intellectual and author. Rais is a University of Chicago trained Political Scientist and at the time was the General Chairman of Muhammadiyah. Madjid held a Ph.D. in Near Eastern Studies from the University of Chicago and was among Indonesia's most prominent Islamic theologians.

[28] *Suara Pembaruan*, 18 December 1997

Both explanations circulated widely as rumors throughout the crisis. They began to appear in print shortly after Suharto's resignation and more than a decade later remain extremely popular. These works merit discussion here because they provide insight into the ways in which religious concepts of authority and leadership shaped the discourse surrounding the crisis of 1997–1998 and the ways in which they contributed to political action in the closing days of the New Order.

15 Dalil Mengapa Suharto Masuk Neraka (*15 Religious Proofs that Suharto will Go to Hell*) by Khairil Ghazali al al-Husni is an Islamist critique of the New Order.[29] The text is located within a larger Islamist discourse system that seeks to explain Indonesian history in terms of anti-Islamic and anti-Indonesian conspiracy theories.[30] It is also an example of how critiques of the Suharto regime shared by many Indonesian of all religious persuasions are viewed through an Islamist lens. In a broader sense it is a contemporary example of a classical discourse which speaks of denouncing the transgressions of rulers as being among the greatest of Muslim virtues. In an analysis of the place of "forbidding the wrong" in Muslim discourse Cook mentions the following *Hadith*:

> The finest form of *jihad* is speaking out in the presence of an unjust ruler and getting killed for it.[31]

By publishing this work, al-Husni clearly spoke in the virtual presence of the ruler he denounced. He did not risk "getting killed" because his book was published after Suharto's fall, but then most versions of the *Hadith* omit the concluding phrase.[32]

The alleged "sins" of President Suharto described reflect the concerns of Muslims associated with *Dewan Dakwah Islamiyah Indonesia*, the successor of the Sukarno era Muslim political party *Masyumi*. The text is also what Azyurmardi Azra, the former rector of Jakarta's State Islamic University calls, a "death *fatwa*."[33] It states explicitly that Suharto should be killed. "Death to Suharto!" was one of rallying cries of the *Reformasi* movement. Attempts to bring him to trial continued until his death in 2007. In this respect al-Husni's critique does not differ significantly from those of other Indonesians. He simply locates it within an Islamist framework.

The introduction summarizes Suharto's "sins" including: restricting the power of the *ulama*, paralyzing the economy, encouraging family planning, manipulating history, jailing political opponents, bringing about a decline in social values, looting natural resources and installing himself as a dictatorial tyrant. Al-Husni explains that current criticism does not mitigate support in the past, and that Suharto's supporters, past and present are *munafiqh* While it is often translated "hypocrite" this is a technical term in Islamic law meaning "one who pretends to be a Muslim but

---

[29] Jakarta: Pustaka Muthmainnah, 1999.

[30] In this respect its' discourse style resembles tht of the popular Islamist periodicals *Media Dakwah* and *Sabali*.

[31] M. Cook, *Forbidding Wrong in Islam*, Cambridge: Cambridge University Press, 2003, p. 75.

[32] Ibid., p. 75.

[33] Arzyumardi Azra "Death of Religious Tolerance?" Jakarta Post January 3, 2003

who is actually working for the destruction of Islam and the Muslim community."
According to Indonesian and other Islamist understandings of *Shari'ah, muafiqh*
should be executed and will subsequently burn in Hell.

In the following chapters al-Husnsi summarizes common Islamist complaints
about the New Order and others that are shared with non-Islamists. These include
complicity with the US Central Intelligence Agency in masterminding the 1965
coupe, enriching himself and his family and suppressing dissent. He also exposes
more explicitly religious sins: links with the Anti-Christ, child abusers and sorcerers, forsaking Islam and persecuting the Muslims. He makes frequent uses of
passages from the *Qur'an* and Hadith as proof texts, the most damning of which is
the following passage from the *Qur'an*.

> The hypocrites will be in the lowest depths of the fire: no helper wilt thou find for them.
> (*An-Nissa*, 145).

The *kejawen* literature is more nuanced than the Islamist because power, unlike
sin, is morally ambiguous. Accounts of the *gawat* (J. powerful but dangerous) character of Suharto's regime began to appear in the tabloid press shortly after his fall
from power. There is now an extensive literature on the subject.[34] These books are
enormously popular and are sold in most major bookstores. They focus on both the
ways in which Suharto acquired the power, in the Javanese sense, to rule Indonesia
for more than 30 years, and how he lost it. This literature is almost exclusively
concerned with the mystical and religious foundations of the New Order and the
crisis that brought it to a close. Very little, if any, mention is made of the currency
crisis and outside factors contributing to it or about western notions of power and
politics. The epistemologies used in their diagnoses of the crisis are almost exclusively Javanese. Artha, at least, is clearly aware of this distinction. He argues that
there are two "doors" to understanding Suharto and the New Order. The first is that
of politics. He finds this approach deficient because, even though it is open and
transparent, it focuses of the strategies employed by "particular groups" to advance
their own interests. He characterizes these as rotten, scheming and manipulative
even if true.[35] The second door is that of *kebatinan* (mysticism) which, in his view,
provides a more holistic understanding that all Javanese can appreciate. His view
is that *kebatinan* provides a more profound, though often less direct explanation of
political events. In Artha's and other works of this genre there are four basic themes.

- Suharto's origins as a "child from a village."
- His quest for "magical power" through asceticism by the acquisition of *pusaka*.
- His relationships with *dukun* and *paranormals*.

---

[34] A. Artha, *Dunia Spiritual Soeharto. Menelusiri Laku Ritual, Tempat-Tempat dan Guru Spiritualnya*, Yogyakarta: Galang Press, 2007 and *Bu Tien, Wangsit Keprabon Soeharto*, Yogyakarta: Galangpress, 2007, M. Shoelhi, *Rahasia Pak Harto*, Jakarta: Grafindo, 2008 M. Mubarok and A. Rasyidin, op. cit., F. Soempeno, *Prabowo Titisan Soeharto? Mencari Pemimpin Baru di Mada Paceklik*, Yogyakarta: Galangpress, 2008, K. Pamungkas, *Rahasia Supranatural Soeharto*, Yogyakarta: Penerbit Narasi, 2007.

[35] Artha, *Dunia Spiritual Soeharto*, op. cit., pg. mentions Luhulima's work as an example of this style of analysis.

• The importance of his wife, Siti Hartinah (Bu Tien) as the *wangsit keprabon* or spiritual power behind the throne.

Suharto's fall is attributed to a combination of Bu Tien's death and the subsequent withdrawal of divine authority and the inappropriate, if not evil, intentions motivating his quests for *kesekten* or power in the Javanese sense.

Suharto was proud of the fact that he was a "child of the village" (*anak desa*). He and Bu Tien were often photographed standing in rice fields wearing the cone shaped straw hats favored by Javanese farmers.[36] And yet, for many Javanese it was more than something of a mystery that an *anak desa* managed to become president, let alone remain in power for more than 30 years. Suharto had none of the characteristics that, from a Javanese perspective, would have prepared him for leadership. He was from a poor family, and not particularly well educated in either modern or Islamic tradition.[37] As Artha puts it he was "not an important person."[38] Suharto did have one personal characteristic that could have contributed to his accomplishments, and it was Javanese. He was born on the day *kliwon* of the 5-day Javanese market week.[39] People born on this day are believed to have hearts that are as hard as stone. These factors led many to search for mystical explanations.

Suharto is often said to have employed a variety of strategies in a systematic quest for "magical" (I. *magis*) power. These included: "fasting, not eating, not drinking and not abandoning the customs of the ancestors such as conducting *slametan* for his family."[40] He also practiced another form of asceticism that is believed to be particularly potent and associated with the great kings of the past inducing Sultan Hamengkubuwana I. This is *kungkum* a form of meditation practiced while sitting nearly submerged in a river.[41] These are entirely normal mystical practices. But Suharto also engaged in others that are known as *klenik*. These are mystical practices motivated by a selfish desire for power and which sometimes border on sorcery. Suharto is said to have consulted as many as 1,000 *dukun,* and *kyai* with similar abilities, from various parts of Indonesia. According to some accounts he had at least one from every province. Even a report that refuted this allegation claimed that at most he had 200 who "actively helped him."[42] In either case it is an astounding number. He is also said to have acquired at least 2,000 *pusaka,* also from every part of Indonesia. His acquisition of *pusaka* from the Javanese court of Surakarta is discussed in Chapter 2. He is said to have tried, but failed, to "borrow" *pusaka* form Yogyakarta. It is not surprising that Bu Tien plays an important role in oral traditions

---

[36] See Mubarok and Rasyidin, op. cit., p. 124.

[37] This is true not only in an absolute sense but also in comparison to other nationalist leaders, many of who were educated in Dutch schools.

[38] Artha, *Dunia Spiritual Soeharto,* op. cit., p. 14.

[39] The Javanese calendar is extremely complex. It includes 5 day and 7 day weeks and Islamic and international months. This yields a large number of unique days, each of which is said to have its own mystical association.

[40] Artha, *Dunia Spiritual Soeharto,* op. cit., p. 14.

[41] Ibid., p. 179. Hamengbubuwana I's practice of this form of meditation is depicted in the reliefs and the *Pagelaran* wall of the *kraton.*

[42] Pamungkas, op. cit., pp. 8–9.

concerning the "first family" and Yogyakarta *pusaka*. It was Bu Tien, not Suharto, who is said to have asked to "borrow" some of the most important Yogyakarta. Hamengkubuwana IX is said to have remained straight faced and silent, as was his practice when he disagreed with a proposal, and escorted her to the room where they are kept. She promptly fainted and had to be carried from the room. Suharto is said never to have asked to "borrow" a Yogya *pusaka* again.

It is widely known that Suharto regularly visited graves and other holy places associated with the Mataram dynasty particularly those where Javanese kings are said to have performed asceticism in their own quests for power. Among these is the stone seat in *Kota Gede* where the founder of the Mataram dynasty, Panembahan Senopati, is said to have performed austerities. Some speculate that Suharto tried to make up for his humble origins by these pilgrimages to royal holy sites. An alternative explanation is that by "seizing" the regalia of kingship, including both heirlooms and holy places, Suharto attempted to seize the mantel, if not the titles of kingship. Heine-Geldern has suggested that in pre-modern Malay cultures, seizing the royal heirlooms was the equivalent of seizing the throne.[43] It would seem that this is exactly what Suharto tried to do. Actually he attempted to seize the heirlooms of many traditional states with out actually claiming to be king of any of them. His quest for spiritual counsel and heirlooms from throughout Indonesia is among the clearest examples of the nationalization of Javanese concepts of power and authority.

Suharto's reliance on Bu Tien's reputed spiritual powers was a less problematic element of his quest for power and legitimacy. Javanese culture includes conflicting, and indeed contradictory, understandings of the religious qualities and social roles of women. A clear distinction can be drawn between woman as obedient companion and woman as powerful partner. On the one hand, women are expected to be passive and subservient to their husbands to the point of accepting polygamous marriages solely at their discretion. They should be concerned exclusively with maintaining harmony and tranquility in family life and not be concerned with affairs other than those of hearth and home. This view is rooted in what contemporary Muslim feminists hold to be a deeply flawed understanding of Islamic scripture and in older Hindu-Javanese traditions. A fifteenth century Hindu-Javanese text analyzed by Noorduyn mentions a princess as being: "serene in uninterrupted meditation on her husband," who is likened unto a god.[44]

Citing examples for Javanese Islamic texts, Rohmaniyah describes religious dimensions of the marriage relationship as follows:[45]

---

[43] R. Heine-Geldern, "Conceptions of State and Kingship in Southeast Asia," Far Eastern Quarterly, vol. 2, no. 1, 1942, pp. 15–30.

[44] J. Noorduyn, "Majapahit in the fifteenth century," *Bijdragen tot de Taal, Land en Volkenkunde*, vol. 134, no. 2/3, 1978, pp. 207–274, p. 220.

[45] I. Rohmaniyah, "Religion, Culture, the State and Women: Women's Issues and Polygamy in Indonesian Legislation" For a literary and historical account of the ways in which this ideology informed social life among the Javanese elite of the early twentieth century see P. Ananta Toer, *The Girl for the Coast*, New York: Hyperion Books, 2002.

A woman's subservience and devotion to her husband is a sacred duty *(wedi lan bekti ing laki)*. The feeling of scariness and the obligation to obey the husband are implemented in the wife's willingness to submissively accept her husband's commands and desires, and never ever hamper them intentionally or unintentionally. The *Serat Centhini pupuh 360 Dhandhanggula* highlights that there are two things the wife has to remember: to be afraid of Allah, and of her husband. Similarly, *Serat Wulangreh Putri* confirms that a wife has to remember three things: (1) *bekti* (devotion); (2) *nastiti* (obedience); and (3) *wedi* (fear). In this context the wife has to regard the husband as her master to whom she has to listen, accept and never reject his orders.

The status of woman as a wife is clearly lower than her husband. A woman, as a wife, has to regard and treat her husband as an adorable, scary, and as an honored god *(dewa),* as mentioned in *Serat Candrarini:*

Sungku sungkeme ngawula maring kakung, pangrengkuhe Bathara Di, ngudi kawidadanipun, jrih terus ing lair batin, sundhuk cumadhong ingkarsa.

(The devotion and obedience of a wife to her husband is just like the devotion to god, being physically and psychologically happy, obeying him totally and being ready to do whatever he wants).

Even in aristocratic circles this idealized, from a male perspective, depiction of women is more of a "model for" than "model of" social reality. During the late colonial era there was also a maxim according to which is was "the husband's responsibility to maintain the honor of the family, and the wife's to provide for and maintain it."[46] Many Javanese women have extraordinary business acumen. They manage enterprises ranging from market stalls to major commercial and industrial concerns. It is not uncommon for male politicians to be financially dependent on business concerns managed by their wives. Women are also understood as being the source of order and stability in the Javanese family, values which, as Hildred Geertz has observed, are of central importance.[47] This is an important consideration in evaluating Bu Tien's role in the New Order, because she and her husband were raised in this environment. Bu Tien is said to have exemplified this ideal, and to have maintain a tranquil and orderly family life that was a "source of blessing" and a "model for Indonesian families."[48]

There is also a deeply seated notion that women, or at least some of them, are sources of power. Ratu Kidul, with her legions of spirit soldiers is best known example in contemporary Java.[49] But she and the larger tradition of the "magical woman" are rooted in a much older tradition reaching deep into the Hindu past. Ken Dedes of the Old Javanese text *Pararaton* is the prototypical magical woman. She is described as having been strikingly beautiful and to have been the "princess with the flaming womb," whose genitals glowed with a divine light.[50] It is said that any man who

---

[46]This observation is based on field work conducted in Yogyakarta in the late 1970s.

[47]Op. cit., pp. 145–150.

[48]Artha, *Dunia Spiritual Soeharto,* op. cit., p. 93.

[49]Ratu Kidul is very rarely mentioned in discussions of Suharto's quest for magical power. To have done so would have risked a public confrontation with the Yogyakarta and Surakarta *kraton.*

[50]See B. Andaya, *The Flaming Womb. Repositioning Women in Early Modern Southeast Asia,* Honolulu: University of Hawaii Press, 2006.

married her would become a great king. According to the *Pararaton*, Ken Arok, upon learning this, murdered Ken Dedes' husband, married her and founded the kingdom of Majapahit.[51] This tale is often cited in reference to Bu Tien and her marriage to Suharto.[52]

The magical woman is can also be a source of prosperity. The Old Javanese text discussed by Noorduyn describes a Majapahit queen as follows:

> She was the living image of the daughter of the Lord of the Mountain [Siva] and whose body was created by Lokesha, Keshava and Mahaeshvara (Brahman, Vishnu and Shiva) to be embraced by the king, the Lord of Java, to increase the prosperity of mankind to everyone's delight.

In his analysis Noorduyn observes that:

> The religious and magic function of the royal marriage which was conceived of as a genuine source of prosperity for the people clearly emerges from these verses.[53]

Like the concept of *kesekten*, that of the Hindu-Javanese magical woman has been transformed by Islam and acquired distinctively Muslim meanings. It is said that one of the ways in which women establish the harmony and tranquilities of their households and families is through praying, fasting and performing austerities, not for their own benefits but for those of their husbands and children. The magical woman, in this case Bu Tien, remains a source of authority and prosperity. She is the bearer or embodiment of God's *wangsit* or *wahyu* and the vehicle through which his blessing is conveyed, not the divine consort of a divine king.

Bu Tien's status as the magical woman of the New Order derives primarily from the fact that she was a fourth generation descendant of Mangkunegara III (reigned 1835–1853) of the secondary court of Surakarta.[54] This is a rather distant genealogical connection. Given the fact that during the eighteenth and nineteenth century Javanese aristocrats commonly had as many as fifty children there are likely tens, if not hundreds of thousand of Javanese with similar royal connections. Many higher ranking members of the royal families in both Yogyakarta and Surakarta were singularly unimpressed with her pretensions. Had she not be married to the president her ancestry would have counted for very little. But as she was Suharto's wife it contributed significantly to the mythology he constructed to establish cultural and religious legitimacy. Artha describes her as having been: "A very holy *pusaka* because within her was the fire of sacred kingship, through which an ordinary person could become king."[55] Elsewhere Artha explains that Bu Tien inherited many

---

[51] This complex of belief can be traced to Indian Tantric Hinduism and Buddhism and to the more general Hindu notion that divinities come in male and female pairs. From this it follows that if the king is an incarnation or manifestation of a Hindu god or Mahayana Buddhist celestial Buddha or Bodhistava, that his queen must be a manifestation of the femine aspect of divinity. Here see W. O' Flartey, *Eroticism and Aeseticism in the Mythology of Siva*, Chicago: University of Chicago Press, 1976 and R. Heine-Geldern, op. cit.

[52] Artha, *Dunia Spiritual Soeharto*, op. cit., pp. 87–89, Soempeno, op. cit., pp. 83–84.

[53] Noorduyn, op. cit., p. 212.

[54] Artha, *Bu Tien*, op. cit., p. 51.

[55] Artha, *Dunia Spiritual Soeharto,* op. cit., p. 89.

of the moral qualities of her royal ancestors including the ability to ensure the tranquility of her marriage and family and that she did not need to rely on black magic or sorcery.[56]

Given this understanding of the origins of Suharto's authority the conclusion that when Bu Tien died, his aura began to fade in entirely logical. Her departure left him with possibly ill-gotten *pusaka* and a squadron of *dukun* but without the moral authority Bu Tien brought to his regime. It is widely believed that in the years following her death Suharto became increasingly out of touch and unable to control his own family, let alone the nation. Artha and Soempeno both conclude that given this set of circumstances it was a mistake for Suharto to have stood for election in 1998 and that "a period of disharmony and instability" was inevitable.[57] That is exactly what happened in May of 1998.

12 –20 May 1998 – *Zaman Endan* – Crazy Time

This is where things stood on 11 May. Things were bad and seemed likely to only get worse. Hopes that the New Order would overcome what was by then was called the "multi-dimensional crisis" and regain its cultural and religious legitimacy were dim and fading fast. In Javanese political thought the "period of disharmony and instability" between the collapse of one governmental system and the appearance of its successor is known as "*Zaman Endan*" or crazy time. For the next nine days things were to become much crazier than anyone could have imagined. On 12 May security forces opened fire on a peaceful student demonstration at Jakarta's elite Tri Sakti (Trinity) University.[58] Four students were killed. They were proclaimed *Pahlawan Reformasi* (Heroes of the Reformation) by the press and the public. The term *pahlawan* is the same one used to describe those who died in the Indonesian revolution and is strongly associated with the Islamic concept of martyrdom. Their deaths galvanized the opposition. Faculty and administrators at universities through out the country, intellectuals and many New Order insiders joined the students in their call for Suharto's resignation.[59]

Suharto was in Cairo when the killings occurred. He appears to have been deeply troubled by the bloodshed. Late at night (Jakarta time) on May 12th he gave a rambling unscripted speech to the local Indonesian community in which he stated:

---

[56] Artha, *Bu Tien,* op. cit., pp. 89–90. Many Javanese are not convinced and believe that she did use black magic and sorcery to enrich her family. Among dissidents she was often referred to as "Ibu 10%," for the commissions she allegedly extracted from government contractors.

[57] Artha, Ibib., pp. 93–93 and Soempeno, op. cit., pp. 83–84.

[58] Tri Sakti is a private, primarily Chinese and Christian university. The fact that the killing of Chinese Christian students led to the massacre of Chinese Christians in many parts of Indonesia is among the appalling paradoxes of the crisis of 1998. If, as appears likely, the killings and the riots that followed were planned by the government, they were a betrayal of almost unfathomable proportions because the Chinese business community was the New Order's chief partner in the development program on which its legitimacy rested.

[59] See Lululima, op. cit., pp. 112–120.

In truth, if the people no longer believe (*memberi kepercayaan*) in me, that does not matter. I have already said, that if they no longer believe, they don't. I will not reign by relying on the power of weapons. It's not like that. I will become a sage and draw close to God.[60]

This is a sanitized/secularized Indonesian version of the statement reported by the Catholic paper *Kompas*. On May 16th the paper issued a version retaining more of the Javanese that Suharto used and which resonates much more strongly with traditional Javanese concepts of authority. Here it was reported that Suharto explained that he was prepared to "*Lengser Keprabon*" (renounce the throne.) He spoke not in Indonesian, the national language and the language of politics, but in Javanese, the language of mysticism and political authority. He explained it was not a problem for him to resign if the people no longer believed in him. He stated that he was prepared to "step aside, to become a sage and grow close to God, encourage his children and grandchildren to become responsible citizens and give advice to the nation."[61] He offered no indication of when, or from where his journey to God would commence. This was a graceful, self serving exit strategy that was not without precedent in Javanese history. Sultan Hanengkubuwana VII (reigned 1877–1921) is an example. He renounced the throne and the title Sultan, and for the remainder of his days lived is ascetic seclusion in a palace to (what was then) the north of the city. As Soempeno observes the word *lengser* carries with the connotations that the leader's departure from power is voluntary, honorable and perhaps only temporary.[62] When coupled with the phrase "*madeg pandhito*" (become a sage) it suggested that Suharto was responding to a divine calling and that he might become the *dalang* (puppeteer) who rules from behind the scenes. This prospect was particularly frightening because Habibie, Suharto's hand picked Vice President, was a political neophyte and widely considered to be a buffoon. Many believed that he has been chosen as Vice President because he was clearly unqualified to be President.

The Jakarta elite and the people as a whole would have nothing of it. Many did not believe that Suharto meant what he said. Most found the idea that he could grow close to God or that he had any reasonable advice to give the nation absurd. *Reformasi* supporters found the idea that Tommy and Tutut could become productive citizens laughable. Nevertheless, the phrase "*Lengser Keprabon*" became the slogan of the day. The military, speaking through General Wiranto, the chief of staff, claimed that the president had been misunderstood and that he did not intend to step down. Leaders of the *Reformasi* movement seized the opportunity to hold him to his word, but not before the situation became *much* worse.

The following day massive rioting erupted throughout Jakarta, and soon spread to other cities. There were 3 days of arson, looting and rape. Security forces stood by as large areas of Jakarta, Surakarta and other cities burned. Tens of thousands roamed the streets pillaging and burning Chinese businesses and others identified with the Suharto family. The homes of several prominent Chinese businessmen with ties to

---

[60]Ibid., p. 123.

[61] *Kompas* May 16, 1998

[62]Op. cit., pp. 47–48.

the government were burned while rioters holding their portraits posed for pictures. The primary aims of most of the participants were economic. Supermarkets, banks, ATMs, appliance and electronics stores were particularly hard hit. The poor used the opportunity to grab anything they could carry and burned what they could not. More than a thousand people died; most of them looters unable to escape from fires that other, more sinister, elements in the crowds set.

While most of the rioters were motivated by desire for short term economic gain, others were organized gangs intent on terrorizing the Chinese community. Accounts of the riots describe provocateurs yelling anti-Chinese, anti-student and anti-opposition slogans and posting signs reading "destroy Chinese property."[63] Chinese were denounced as "pigs, lice and dogs," suggesting that they are defiled beings. There were reports that military vehicles were used to transport these gangs and that some of the buildings looted and burned were tear gassed to disable security guards. What are even more insidious are numerous, well documented accounts of gang rapes of Chinese women by men yelling "*Allah Akbar*" (God is great). Many were assaulted in front of their families. Some of the rapists justified the attacks by stating that "At least they will have Muslim babies." An unknown number were murdered, some beheaded or burned alive. Many of the bodies were mutilated. Some of the victims suffered such shame that they killed themselves by drinking insecticide. Others were hospitalized for psychological trauma as well as physical injuries. Still others we ashamed that they had survived: some by pretending to be dead and others by sheer chance. Friends and relatives who escaped, but often witnessed, the violence often blamed themselves for not being able to prevent it. Several weeks later it was common to see survivors picking through the rubble or sitting on street corners sobbing or staring blankly into space. Many suffered emotional wounds from which they will never recover.

While riots and looting occurred in many parts of the city, almost all of the rapes occurred in Chinese neighborhoods.[64] *Asia Week* reported that at least 468 women were raped.[65] The total was probably much higher because victims are often reluctant to discuss abuse, let alone report it to authorities many knew to be the perpetrators of the crimes. Many victims subsequently received letters threatening them with further abuse or death if they spoke with investigators. This almost certainly contributed to the undercount.[66] This indicates that the perpetrators of the violence

---

[63] See BBC online http://news.bbc.co.uk/1/hi/events/indonesia/special_report/118576.stm, Associated Press online http://members.tripod.com/~reformasionita/ap071098.html and *Tim Relawan untuk Kemanusiaan*, "The Rapes in the Series of Riots" http://www.huaren.com/Indo/atrocities.html

[64] See *Tim Relawan Untuk Manusia (The Volunteers Team for Humanity)*," The Rapes in the Series of Riots: The Climax of an uncivilized Act of the Nation Life." (sic) http://www.geocities.com/CapitolHill/4120/tim1.html

[65] *Asia Week*, July 24, 1998

[66] J. Herman, *Trauma and Recovery: The Aftermath of Violence from Domestic Abuse to Political Terror* , New York: Basic Books, 1997, p. 67 observes that many rape victims have difficulty even

had planned carefully, both the cover their own tracks and to perpetuate trauma and fear.

It is clear that the Tri Sakti killings and the riots that followed were planned. Ballistics tests revealed the weapons used to kill the students were 5.56 mm assault rifles of a type widely used by the Indonesian military and some police units.[67] Most analysts and witnesses I interviewed in early June were convinced that the killings were carried out by military forces. It is clear that soldiers actively encouraged the riots that followed. Military vehicles were used to transport gangs of rioters and supplied them with incendiary materials. Some buildings were tear-gassed to disable security guards before they were looted and burned. Soldiers laughed, joked and shared looted drinks and snacks with rioters.[68]

On the basis of an extensive surveys and special analysis Daihani, Purnomo and Simanjorang determined that riots broke out in many locations almost simultaneously.[69] These were what Stanley Tambiah has called "leveling crowds."[70] Their purpose was to destroy property, lives and honor. While the riots and the rapes were certainly planned, the ability of provocateurs to organize such extreme violence speaks to the intensity of tension between Chinese and "indigenous" Indonesians and of the power security forces still had at this time. The ultimate goals of the perpetrators of these horrendous acts may never be known. It is widely speculated that the waves of violence and ethnic cleansing that appeared to be sweeping the country were intended to convince the public that only a reinvigorated military government could bring the country back from the brink of disintegration.

For eight days in mid May of 1998 one small city stood for the hope of the nation. That city was Yogyakarta.

Yogyakarta, the *Kraton* and the Fall of Suharto

The Yogyakarta *kraton* played a pivotal role in averting even more tragic violence and in facilitating the end of the New Order. On three occasions, the *Alon Alon* was the site of massive rallies that contributed significantly to national level political developments. The first occurred on 20 May 1998, when the Sultan called on Suharto to resign. The second occurred in July, when the parliament and people of Yogyakarta demanded that the Sultan be appointed governor of the special region.

---

naming their experience, let alone discussing it authorities who may have well been complicit in the crime.

[67] Luhulima, op. cit., p. 115.

[68] A report by Radhika Coomaraswamy the United Nations Special Rapporteur on Violence Against Women included as an appendix in Simanjorang, op. cit.), pp. 397–416 confirms this analysis.

[69] D. Daihani and A. Purnomo, *Lansekap Berbagai Kerusuhan da Potensi Disintegras,* Jakarta: Lembaga Penelitian Universitas Trisakti, 2000.

[70] S Tambiah, *Leveling Crowds, Ethnonationalist Conflicts and Collective Violence in South Asia,* Berkeley: University of California Press

The third occurred in February 1999, when the people of Yogyakarta nominated the Sultan as a candidate for the presidency.

In his coronation address, Hamengkubuwana X indicated that his understanding of the role of the monarchy was similar to that of his father: "For what purpose would one reign as Sultan other than to benefit the people?"[71] For the first decade of his reign, the Sultan maintained a relatively low profile. He was deputy governor of Yogyakarta but did not play a major role in national politics. He explained that it was necessary to refrain from public statements about political matters because of his position as Sultan. Prior to the advent of the economic crisis, he described himself and the *kraton* as symbols and guardians of Javanese culture (*kebudayaan*), but rarely mentioned religion (*agama*). He stated that because his father had declared that the Sultanate was a part of the Republic of Indonesia, he had a duty to restrict his activities to cultural and ritual performances.[72] He did, however, continue his father's policy of serving as an advocate for the poor, and was critical of development projects that did not benefit the communities in which they are located.

When the legitimacy of the government of the Republic came into question, the Sultan rethought his position and became a national political figure. He clearly understood the symbolic power of the charisma he had inherited from his ancestors and particularly his father. Like his father, Hamengkubuwana X is devoted to the Indonesian nation, and is, at the same time, willing to employ traditional Javanese notions of kingship and authority when the Republic is in danger. The days leading up to what was subsequently referred to as the "great uprising" of 20 May 1998 are clear examples of the ways in which symbols of Javanese culture and religion can be powerful weapons in a political struggle.

Suharto was often described as a pseudo-Javanese king; the Sultan is a genuine Javanese king. In May 1998, when the Suharto government faltered and allowed the nation to slip into chaos, the Sultan used the charisma of his throne to preserve peace and order. Unlike Jakarta – where there was arson, looting, pillage, and rape – in Yogyakarta, a million of the Sultan's subjects visited him at the *kraton* in a massive act of *pepe*. The Sultan "went public" by sending flowers to the funeral of Mozes Gatotkaca, a businessman who became the first martyr of the reformation movement when he was killed in a clash between students and security forces. In part because of this public expression of sympathy for Mozes' family, the Sultan became one of the most visible and vocal leaders of the reformation movement.[73] He proved to be remarkably adept in speaking the complex symbolic language of the Indonesian/Javanese reformation. His position as Sultan enabled him to speak in four voices – those of Islam, Javanese culture, political reform, and critic of the New Order. Often these voices were masterfully intertwined, each reinforcing and legitimizing the others.

---

[71] *Kedaulatan Rakyat*, 6 October 1989

[72] *Suara Pembaruan*, 11 December 1996

[73] *Kompas*, 14 May 1998

On May 11th, the Sultan and Amien Rais announced their intention to conduct a dialog on the nature of reformation with student leaders to be held at the headquarters of the Yogyakarta branch of the Indonesian Hajji's Association, which is located on the Northern *Alon Alon* inside the *kraton* walls. Concerns about planned increases in fuel and electricity prices were on the agenda; so was the need for "peaceful reformation" not only of the political process but also of the human spirit. In announcing the meeting the Sultan and the Modernist Muslim leader spoke as one, in the language of *bricolage*. Press reports indicated that the students had pushed for a meeting with the Sultan and responded favorably to his announcement.[74]

The events of May 12th pushed the Yogyakarta *Reformasi* in new and unanticipated directions. The possibility that the skies of Yogyakarta would soon be filled with smoke was very real. On May 13th, the Sultan stated that he was not willing to comment on the current state of the crisis, fearing that people would blindly follow his lead, but that he was willing to take action. He refused to elaborate other than to say that he had chosen the role of "*nglakoni*" – a Javanese expression meaning to follow a predetermined course. It usually refers to a combination of fasting, pilgrimage and asceticism. He declared that he was not interested in "popularity," and that the *kraton* was open to establishing a dialog with the students, whom he again invited to meet with him either at the *kraton* or at Gadjah Mada University. He stated that what was important was that their "aspirations should continue and that violence and destruction must be minimized."[75] He concluded that he knew that life had become difficult for the people and that he would "take a message" from this. He refused to answer further questions concerning his plans, simply stating that he would "resolutely carry out whatever became his duty." The word he used for "duty" was *wajib*, a technical term in Islamic law meaning religious obligation.[76]

Several days later, in a more reflective moment, the Sultan explained that *kepercayaan* (belief) is an inter-subjective phenomenon that involves sentiments of honor in those who believe. He explained that people believe (*percaya*) in a government only if it maintains clear lines of communication. He cited a Javanese proverb – "the loss of belief means that all is lost" – and said that, in Javanese culture, *kepercayaan* is the foundation of humanity and social life. If people lose their belief, they also lose their sense that social life should be based on a common humanity. His conclusion was that the government had lost its legitimacy because the people no longer believed in its wisdom and authority. All that was left for the government now was power (in the Western, material sense of the term). He cited the example of the Islamic Prophet Yusuf (Joseph of the Hebrew Bible) as a leader who was able to resolve problems because he encouraged the king to listen to the voice of the people. He explained that he planed to attend a meeting of central Javanese *ulama* (Muslim scholars) to encourage them to play a more active role in public life and

---

[74] *Kedaulatan Rakyat*, 12 May 1998
[75] *Kedaulatan Rakyat*, 14 May 1998
[76] *Kompas*, 14 May 1998

live up to their responsibility to obey to Quranic injunction to "command the good
and prohibit the evil" According to Islamic law, "commanding the good and pro-
hibiting the evil" is the most important task for both rulers and *ulama*.[77] This was a
masterful *bricolage* of Javanese and Islamic ethics and concepts of authority. It was
spoken in Indonesian – the national language.

Like other proponents of *Reformasi*, the Sultan understood Indonesia's economic
and political failings as being the result of a religious and moral crisis. He made it
extremely clear that he was prepared to use the moral force and authority of the
Yogyakarta *kraton* to bring about political and spiritual *Reformasi* that by time had
come to mean both "reform" in the political sense and "reformation" in the religious
sense.[78] In September 1998, the Sultan provided an explanation of his actions even
more deeply rooted in Javanese culture and religion. In an interview published in
the news weekly *Forum Keadilan*, he stated:

> I saw that Pak Harto was out of control. Because of this I fasted for an entire month. I chose
> this *cultural* (my italics) path because he too had chosen to follow it. He knew and so did
> I. In this ritual (fasting) there is the belief that wherever there are two identical bee hives,
> thousands of white flying ants will come. Based on this belief I fasted for an entire month.
> Between the 19th of April and the 19th of May I remained in ascetic seclusion. On May
> 20th, the people assembled on the *Alon Alon* of the *kraton*. The explanation is as follows:
> The two bee hives are the *waringan* trees. The people are the flying ants. This was the end
> of Suharto.[79]

This relatively brief statement requires a somewhat lengthy exegesis. In traditional Javanese Islam, fasting, other than that required by Islamic law during
the month of Ramadan, is understood as a source of spiritual power (*kesekten*). It is referred to by the Sanskrit (and Javanese) term *tapas*. In the late
1970s this was often described as being an element of Javanese Religion (*Agama
Jawa*). In the late 1990s it was commonly referred to as an element of Javanese
culture.

By describing the events of May 1998 in these terms, the Sultan suggested
that the fall of the New Order was the result of a personal struggle between himself and President Suharto and, in a more general sense, between Yogyakarta and
Jakarta. This recasts the history of the late twentieth century in terms of that of the
eighteenth, which, in Yogyakarta, is understood as a military, political, and spiritual struggle between the Javanese court of Yogyakarta and the Dutch East India
Company at Batavia – now Jakarta. It portrays the spiritual powers of the Sultan and
Suharto as opposing forces that gave definition to the crowds that filled the streets
of the two cities. Put simply, the claim was that political legitimacy and the grace
of God are not to be found in the modern world of Jakarta, but among the people
and in the *kraton*, mosques and *kampung* of Yogyakarta. It is also interesting to
note that one of the relief carvings on the *Pagelaran* wall depicts the first Sultan

---

[77] *Kompas*, 17 May 1998

[78] *Kompas*, 17 May 1998

[79] *Forum Keadilan*, 7 September 1998

performing this type of asceticism in preparation for his struggle against the Dutch. It also resonates strong with the account of the efforts of *dukun* and other healers against sorcery presented in Chapter 2. There it was argued that the Sultan and healers share the common goal of purging their "patients," individuals and the Sultanate of the forces of evil. In May of 1998 Hamengkubuwana IX stretched the limits of his domain to include the entire nation of Indonesia.

On May 13th, *kraton* announced that an extraordinary night prayer service referred to as *Salat Lail Reformasi* (The Night Reformation Prayer) would be held at the Grand Mosque of Yogyakarta. The purpose of this prayer service was to ask God for a change in national leadership. The service was planned for 2:30 A.M. on Friday, which Javanese believe is the most effective time and day for extraordinary prayers. It was sponsored by the *kraton* and the *Muhammadiyah* youth organization. Officials of the Grand Mosque, who are also *kraton* officials, explained that revolution would require great loss of life, so they hoped to achieve the same ends with "moral force." The chairman of the Yogyakarta branch of the Indonesian Council of Islamic Scholars (a semi-governmental organization) stated that what the students hoped to gain through demonstrations, the rest of the Muslim community would seek through prayer. He encouraged other mosques to follow in their footsteps.[80]

Approximately ten thousand people attended. Amien Rais planned to deliver a sermon but was unable to find a way out of Jakarta because of the continuing violence. He sent a fax apologizing for his absence. Worshipers were asked to pray that God would save the nation from destruction and bring calm both to society and to the campuses. Abunda Farouk, who spoke in the absence of Amien Rais stated:

> We do not have rifles, tanks or other weapons. Our only weapon is resolute faith in God the almighty. Pray that God will deliver us from this moral, political and economic crisis and bring us tranquility so that society can once again be calm, peaceful and friendly.[81]

He continued by saying that the Muslim community has always been in the vanguard of the struggle against oppression, injustice, and hypocrisy, and he called on the government to act wisely in the conduct of reformation and to avoid harsh responses to students and others engaged in the struggle for the betterment of the nation.

The gathering dispersed peacefully after the dawn prayer. In the afternoon more than five thousand people gathered in front of the mosque to express support for the student demonstrators and for the *Muhammadiyah* youth movement. Prince Joyokusumo, the Sultan's younger brother, was the main speaker. He explained that he and the Sultan were prepared to stand behind the students and the people in the struggle for reformation. He stated:

---

[80] *Kedaulatan Rakyat*, 14 May 1998

[81] *Kedaulatan Rakyat*, 15 May 1998

As long as the students and the people avoid acts of destruction, I promise that I and the Sultan will shelter you. In your struggle choose the path of peace, not that of harsh action. The path of destruction will bring only pain and tragedy to our people.[82]

His speech was welcomed with loud applause. After a break for prayers at 3:00 there was a march similar to those of election campaigns, but no acts of violence. The Sultan was not present at the prayer service or the rally that followed, but did participate in a meeting of 250 Muslim scholars the next day, the purpose of which was to arrive at a religious solution to the problems facing the nation.[83] In an indirect way, the Sultan called for regime change. He explained that the people no longer respected the government and that, "This has happened because the people no longer see wisdom or justice in the government"[84]

Once he publicly declared himself in support of the student demonstrators, the Sultan rapidly took charge of the *Reformasi* movement in Yogyakarta. He made it clear that he would not tolerate violence by either security forces or looters in his realm, and he promised to "go down into the streets" to maintain peace and order. On 14 May, he promised that he would, if necessary, "go into the streets to preserve order and support *Reformasi*"[85] He did exactly as promised on May 16th, leading what had been an angry crowd bent on destruction to the Gadjah Madah University campus for a peaceful rally. Yogyakarta papers reported that the crowd was almost hypnotized when the Sultan seized a megaphone and encouraged them to support the reformation movement in the "Yogya style of struggle." In response to "the charisma of the throne of Yogyakarta," members of the crowd dropped the hundreds of rocks they had planned to throw.[86] The choice of words here is significant. It suggests that the crowds responded not to Hamengukuwana X's *personal* charisma, but rather to the *institutionalized* charisma of the office of Sultan. This is most likely an indirect reference to Hamengkubuwana IX's status as a revolutionary and national hero. It is significant to note that Pakubuwana XII of Surakarta attempted something similar when he addressed a crowd of "hot-tempered demonstrators" at the Seblas Maret State University in Surakarta. He spoke not in the capacity of reigning monarch, but as a member of the university's advisory committee. His efforts were not successful. Much of the city's business district was subsequently burned and an untold number of people, many of them ethnic Chinese, killed, raped and/or beaten by angry crowds.[87] This suggests that the charisma of the throne of Yogyakarta is rooted in a unique combination of royalist, revolutionary and nationalist histories that its neighbor and long term rival Surakarta tragically could not match in this period of crisis.

---

[82] *Jawa Pos*, 16 May 1998

[83] *Kedaulatan Rakyat*, 14 May 1998

[84] *Forum Keadilan*, 7 October 1998

[85] *Kedaulatan Rakyat*, 15 May 1998

[86] *Kedaulatan Rakyat*, 16 May 1998

[87] E. Wirabhumi (Project Director), *Karaton Surakarta*, Jakarta: *Yayasan Pawiyatan Kebudayaan Kraton Surakarta*, 2004, p. 22.

The *Reformasi* movement in Yogyakarta reached its climax on May 20th. Massive demonstrations at the National Monument in Jakarta were canceled for fear of violence. Amien Rais and others surveyed the area late on the night of May 19th, and found streets blockaded and filled with tanks.[88] At 1:15 on the morning of May 20th he held a press conference at which he announced that the march would be canceled because the security forces appeared to be preparing for all out war and that he wished to avoid unnecessary casualties. He concluded by urging his supporters to join together in prayer.[89] There were no tanks or barbed-wire barricades on the streets leading to the *kraton*. Demonstrations continued as planned. The Sultan announced that he would lead the "Long March" from campuses around the city that would end on the *Alon Alon*.[90] This came to be known as the *Pisowan Agung* or great visitation.[91] On the morning of May 20th, Yogyakarta newspapers published a list of eleven routes leading to the *kraton*. According to some reports as many as a million people followed them. The *kraton* had prepared fifty thousand meals, probably the largest number in its' history. They were far from sufficient but the intention was clear. It was as if the demonstration has become the "*Slametan Reformasi*." The crowd gathered on the *Alon Alon* to listen to popular music, participate in collective prayers, and listen to a speech and proclamation by the Sultan. The Sultan described the rally as a symbol of peaceful reformation. He explained that his participation in the *Reformasi* movement was in keeping with the spirit of his father, who had struggled in the cause of the people, and that this was a duty (*wajib*) he owed to God. He stated that, since the time of the revolution, power had rested in the hands of the people, and that he was acting to help them reclaim it – that it was his duty as Sultan to aid in the process of *Reformasi*. Yogyakarta would be the city of *Reformasi* in the same way that it had been the city of the revolution. He concluded by saying that he was not a politician who had to negotiate, but rather the representative of a moral force.[92] He summarized his view of *Reformasi* as follows:

> We are now at a turning point in history. God has given us two choices, the path of good or that of destruction. If we choose goodness, *Reformasi* is the only road. *Reformasi* is the desire of the people. We are not simply a movement seeking food, clothing and shelter, but also one [seeking] for the return of the rights of the people that [have] been stolen. No longer will the people be subjected to tyrannical power and injustice.[93]

---

[88] Luhulima, op. cit., p. 223.

[89] Ibid., pp. 223–224.

[90] The term "Long March" was used for demonstrations or "*demos*" as they were commonly referred to that began on university campuses and culminated with rallies at off campus locations. During this period the government tolerated student demonstrations, but only on campus for fear that off campus events would incite the "masses." This was a high risk strategy that could have easily failed. Had the crowds turned violent, or been broken up by security forces, I do not care to think about what Indonesia might be like today.

[91] *Sowan* is a Javanese term for a courtesy call on a person of high status.

[92] *Kompas*, 21 May 1998

[93] *Forum Keadilan*, 7 October 1998

The Sultan read a proclamation which he described as being similar to that signed, in 1945, in support of the Indonesian revolution by his father and Paku Alam VIII (the prince of a royal house subordinate to the Yogyakarta *kraton*). As reported in *Kompas* on May 21st 1998, it read:

> We, Sultan Hamengkubuwana X and Paku Alam VIII, in the name of the tradition of struggle and the spirit of the people expressed in the Declaration of Independence of 17 August 1945, and the Proclamation of Sultan Hamengkubuwana IX and Paku Alam VIII of 15 September 1945, state that:
>
> 1. We join the people of the Special Region of Yogyakarta together with all of the people of Indonesia in their support of the Reformation Movement and the establishment of a national leadership which supports the people.
> 2. We encourage the armed forces in their powerful attempts to support the people and the Reformation Movement in the spirit of establishing the unity of the people and the Armed Forces.
> 3. We encourage the people of the Special Region of Yogyakarta and of all Indonesia to establish the unity of the people and to reject every sign of anarchy that is not in accord with the moral philosophy of *Panca Sila* [the national ideology based on belief in God, national unity, social justice, democracy, and human rights].
> 4. We call on the people of the Special Region of Yogyakarta and all of Indonesia to pray, according to the dictates of their own religions, for the peace of society and the nation.

When he finished reading the proclamation, the Sultan stated, "I am ready to join the people in the process of reformation."[94] The fact that the text of this statement mirrored the 1945 proclamation symbolically underscored the belief that the reformation movement was a repetition of the revolution, a period of time considered to be sacred by most Indonesians. It was as if the spirit of 1945 had been recaptured, and that the Yogyakarta *kraton* was once more the spiritual center of the nation.

The rally began at 7:00 in the morning with marches from university campuses; it ended at 1:45 in the afternoon with prayers, the singing of patriotic songs, and cries of "Long Live the Sultan." The crowd dispersed peacefully – many sang and danced in the streets as they returned home. In Yogyakarta the message of "peaceful reformation" took hold. Papers throughout the country encouraged the people to take heed of the Sultan's message. The geography faculty at Gadjah Mada University suggested that Yogyakarta once again become the capitol of Indonesia in the Era of Reformation. They described Yogya as the city of struggle and the center of moral and spiritual purity, and suggested that by distancing the economic power of Jakarta from politics, the goals of the reformation movement could be achieved.[95] Regional military commanders supported and encouraged the Sultan's efforts. Even Suharto appeared to listen. Following an intense period of negotiations with cabinet

---

[94] *Kedaulatan Rakyat*, 21 May 1998

[95] It would be only a slight exaggeration to refer to it as the Department of *Sacred Geography*.

members, members of parliament, generals and *ulama*, he announced his resignation at 9:00 A.M. on May 21st. On May 25th *Forum Keadilan* reported that news of the contrast between the peaceful demonstration in Yogyakarta and the violence in Jakarta was among the factors that led to Suharto's decision to step down.

Yogyakarta was a miracle in a time of crisis. It showed, as it had in 1945, that traditional notions of authority and kingship could be strongly linked with modern concepts of nationalism, egalitarianism, social justice, and economic reform. Western critics of Indonesian politics have often blamed the country's problems on the traditional, feudalistic character of the Suharto government. One week in Yogyakarta showed that this same traditional and deeply religious system is capable of speaking for the needs of the people and of restraining them from violence, even in the face of dire economic circumstances. Since May 20th 1998, the Sultan has become an important national figure.

The Sultan as Governor – The *Kraton* and the *Patihan*

The death of Paku Alam VIII sparked the Sultan's first major political crisis. Paku Alam VIII was the titular head of a principality subordinate to the Yogyakarta Sultanate. He had been a close associate of Sultan Hamengkubuwana IX. From 1945 to 1988, he was deputy governor of the special region of Yogyakarta. Upon the death of the Sultan, he became governor. Sultan Hamengkubuwana X was the clear choice to succeed him – the question was how, and on what terms. What followed was a confrontation with the national government, not unlike that between Hamengkubuwana IX and the Dutch at the beginning of his reign.

During the colonial period, succession was the vehicle through which the Dutch came to dominate the political and economic life of the central Javanese states. Monarchs were installed by the colonial government. A political contract, drawn up and signed prior to coronation ceremonies, dictated the terms of this relationship. Over time, the Dutch used this process to severely limit the authority of the Javanese courts. In 1939, Hamengkubuwana IX attempted to use the process to enhance his authority. The result was months of deadlock. Finally, the Sultan is reported to have received a clear message from his late father that he should sign anything the Dutch wanted because they would be leaving shortly.

The conflict between Hamengkubuwana X and the Indonesian government was nearly as intense. The questions at issue concerned the legal procedures through which the Sultan would become governor of the Indonesian Special Region of Yogyakarta. The larger issue at stake was the same as in 1939 – the balance of power between Jakarta and Yogyakarta. Yogyakarta became part of Indonesia as the result of an exchange of letters between President Sukarno and Sultan Hamengkubuwana IX. The Sultan stated that, "The State of Ngayogyakarta Hadiningrat is a Kingdom that is a special region of the Republic of Indonesia." The second paragraph states that all authority in the area of internal affairs is in the hands of the Sultan. The third states that relationships between Yogyakarta and the Central Government of the Republic of Indonesia will be conducted directly between the Sultan and the

President. The Sultan's proclamation was dated 5 September 1945. Soekarno's response was to send a charter confirming the Sultan's position in office dated 19 August 1945. It is very vague, stating that, "We, the President of the Republic of Indonesia, confirm Ingkang Sinuwun Kanjeng Sultan Hamengkubuwana Senopati Ing Ngalaga Abdurrakhman Sayid Panatagama Kalifatullah ingala kaping IX [the Sultan's full title] in his position with the belief that he will expend his thoughts, powers, spirit and body for the well being of the area of Yogyakarta as a portion of the Republic of Indonesia."[96] Yogyakarta has rarely enjoyed as much autonomy as the Sultan claimed in 1945. The installation of Hamengkubuwana X as governor presented an opportunity to renegotiate the Indonesian variant of the "political contract."

The Sultan and his supporters based their arguments on a 1950 law that gave the governorship to him for life by virtue of his position as Sultan. The government preferred the 1974 local government act that provided for governors to be elected by provincial legislatures. However, the Yogyakarta legislature voted *not* to vote. The conflict was eventually resolved by a presidential decree that mentioned both documents. It was stated at the time that the issue would be resolved by a new law on the status of the "Special Region" of Yogyakarta to be considered by parliament. In July of 2008 the issue had not been resolved. The Yogyakarta legislature requested that the president to issue a decree reconfirming the positions of Hamengukuwana X and Paku Alam IX as governor and deputy governor because it was unlikely that a new law could be enacted by the times their terms expire in October 2008.[97] The Sultan had stated in late June that he would not take a public stand on the issue and would leave it to the people's representatives to decide. Much of the debate surrounding the Sultan's appointment concerned the autonomy of the "special region." It also should be understood as Yogyakarta nationalism – as an attempt to unite the throne (the *kraton*) and the day-to-day administration of the Sultanate.

Seemingly in keeping with these concerns, the Sultan made it clear that as governor he would continue to work for the well-being of the people. The *kraton* webpage includes the following statement:

> Sri Sultan Hamengkubuwana X shall do necessary things, so that the city of Yogyakarta remains calm and peaceful as the seedbed of [the] pure idea of reformation, a place of crystallization of ideas and leaders trusted by the vast society, not only trusted but also highly adored. As a Governor he shall remain close to the people and open to any critic. He shall fight for a greater autonomy for Yogyakarta Special Region.[98]

This statement implies that the *kraton* is the sacred center not only of Yogyakarta but of Indonesia as a whole, and that the Sultan, as the representative of God

---

[96] As quoted in S. Kutoyo, *Sri Sultan Hamengkubuwana IX: Riwayat Hidup and Perjuangan*, Jakarta: PT. Mutiara Sumber Widya, 1996, pp. 128–129. The full texts of both statements are preserved on marble plaques displayed in the *kraton* museum memorializing Hamengkubuwana IX.

[97] *Koran Tempo*, 9 August 2008.

[98] *Selamat Datang di Kraton Ngayogyakarta Hadiningrat*. Website homepage for Kraton Ngayagyakarta. http://kraton.yogya.indo.net.id.

on earth, holds the key to the welfare not only of Yogyakarta but of the nation as a whole. In September of 2009 the crisis has still not been resolved. On the 64th anniversary of Hamengkubuwana IX's proclamation Yogya TV held a special talk show hosted by a *kyai* and professors from Gadjah Mada University. They described that document as having the same legal status as a treaty between two sovereign nations. The Sultan and his wife sat in the audience nodding in agreement.

The Sultan for President

Even before the fall of Suharto, the burning political question in Indonesia was, "Who will be the next president?" In Yogyakarta, there was, and still is, considerable support for Hamengkubuwana X. In part, this movement is, based on reverence for Sultan Hamengukuwana X and his as a hero of the *Reformasi* movement. It is also based on the inherited charisma of the throne of Yogyakarta and the desire to reshape Indonesia in the image of the sacred geography of the Sultanate. His election would make the *kraton* the sacred center of the nation. In 1999 he was officially nominated by the small Republic of Indonesia Party and, surprisingly, by the Yogyakarta branch of the National Salvation Party (PKB), which is associated with *Nahdlatul Ulama*. He was also courted by the ruling GOLKAR party as an alternative to Suharto's unpopular and eccentric successor, Habibie.

On 8 February 1999, the Yogyakarta branch of the PKB held a mass rally on the *Alon Alon* to announce the selection of the Sultan as their candidate for president. This is illustrative of the link between the *kraton* and the mosque. It points to another of the symbolic meanings of the *Alon Alon*. As part of the stage for the performance of state ceremonies, it lies between the *kraton* and the mosque. It is also used for the performance of public prayers on the feast of *Id al' Fitr* at the end of the fasting month of Ramadan. The Sultan did not decline these nominations but he also did not actively seek the office, choosing not to enter the rough and tumble arena of Indonesian electoral politics. He stated that he was prepared to accept the office if it was offered to him by parliament, but that he would not campaign. In an interview published in *Gatra* on 17 April 17th 1999, he stated that he would not become involved in party or electoral politics because parties could withdraw their nominations at any time, and that, "Once you slip up, you are finished."

Indonesians chose a president by direct popular vote for the second time in 2009. The Sultan was again mentioned as a potential candidate for either president or vice president. He floated a trial balloon early in the year, but never formally campaigned. It was clear that while he had considerable support in Yogyakarta that there was substantially less support for his candidacy in other parts of Indonesia and especially among non-Javanese. Even some of his most devoted subjects thought that he should not run for president because to be elected to national office would limit his ability to serve as Sultan.

Conclusions and Implications for the Understanding of "Non-cases" of Ethno-Religious Conflict

Historically, sacred geography has played a very basic role in the legitimization of Javanese and other traditional polities in Southeast Asia. In Yogyakarta at least, it continues to inform political discourse and action. What is important is not so much the details of what Tambiah describes as "Galactic Polity," in which the state is conceived of as a *mandala*, but a more generalized notion that Eliade describes as the symbolism of the center, in which sacred space is the locus of spiritual purity and piety.[99]

Few genuinely expect that the Sultan will ever redefine Indonesia as a Javanese/Islamic state with the *kraton* as its sacred center. Many in Yogyakarta do believe in the sacredness of their center and its potential to redefine the moral and political life of the nation. Finally, it is, perhaps, interesting to note that the Yogyakarta daily, *Kedaulatan Rakyat*, defines world news as that of the *Manca Negara*, a term used in traditional Javanese sacred geography to refer to "outlying provinces." Newscasts on Yogya TV conclude with an anchorperson dressed in *kraton* garb saying "*Sallam Indonesia.*" This is an ambiguous statement, perhaps deliberately so. I could be understood as greeting to Yogyakarta as a part of Indonesia. It could also be the Sultanate of Yogyakarta greeting and conferring blessing on Indonesia.

Much has been written over the last decade about the correlates and causes of ethno-religious violence and strategies for healing the physical and emotional scars it causes. It is more difficult to theorize "non-cases." It is also not clear that conclusions derived from the analysis of one non-case are applicable in others. These caveats not withstanding, four generalizations can be drawn from Yogyakarta's "Kraton Revolution."

- Violence is less likely if there is a broadly based elite coalition opposed to it. In Yogyakarta this consensus was cultivated among traditional aristocrats, religious leaders of all theological orientations, and leaders of educational institutions and NGOs.
- Encouraging alternative action among the masses likely to participate in violence reduces the probability that it will occur. The Kraton Revolution did not simply advocate restraint from violence, it provided a non-violent alternative.
- Depicting the struggle against violence a cosmic struggle between good and evil reduces the likelihood of violence. This leaves no place for ambiguity, or striking at selected targets that could lead to counter violence. It is also the inverse of one of the most commonly used tactics to promote or justify ethno-religious violence.

---

[99]M. Eliade, *The Myth of Eternal Return or Cosmos and History*, Princeton: Princeton University Press, 1954. S. Tambiah, *World Conqueror and World Renouncer: A Study of Buddhism and Polity in Thailand Against a Historical Background*, Cambridge: Cambridge University Press, 1976.

- The direct involvement of socially recognized religious/cultural leaders helps to reduce the likelihood of violence. Orchestrated, artificial personality cults such as that promulgated by the New Order do not work in times of crisis. In Yogyakarta what did work was the appeal of the Sultan and others, including Amien Rais, whose credentials and legitimacy were beyond question.
- Finally, when the state or its representatives are the actual or potential perpetrators of violence, security forces have to be convinced not to fire on peaceful crowds or to incite mob violence. This happened in Yogyakarta on 20 May 1998. It other cases, notably in China and Burma in 1988 and again in Burma in 2007, it regrettably did not.

Photo

Chapter 8
Conclusions: Nationalisms and Post-coloniality

Robert Heine-Geldern's "Conceptions of State and Kingship in Southeast Asia" is the most influential study of religion, the state and political authority in the region ever written. In just fifteen pages he established a paradigm that has guided the work of generations of scholars for more than 60 years. He was concerned primarily with the ways in which classical Hindu and Buddhist states were constituted as cosmic models, or what Eliade would refer to later as the "replication of archetypes." It is as relevant for the analysis of state-religion relationships in traditional Southeast Asian Muslim states as it is for that of Hindu and Buddhist kingdoms. I first read Heine-Geldern's article in 1971 when I was an undergraduate at the University of Illinois. It has profoundly influenced almost everything that I have written about Southeast Asia.

What is less commonly understood is that he also anticipated much of the discourse of what has come to be known as "Post-colonial Studies." "Conceptions of State and Kingship" appeared during the darkest days of the Second World War when Japanese had replaced European colonialism in Yogyakarta and most of the rest of Southeast Asia. At the time, it was not clear that there would be a post-colonial future, at least any time in the foreseeable future. "Indonesia" was then only a nationalist dream.

Heine-Geldern anticipated what were to be some of the most important features of, and daunting challenges for Indonesia and the other post-colonial states in the region. Near the end of his analysis of the religious foundations of pre-modern Southeast Asian states he raised the question:

> Is all of this a crumbling structure giving way under the impact of modern civilization or may it still influence the political activities of the people concerned? This question is not easily answered.

He concluded with the observation that it would be a "grave mistake to disregard the importance of native culture and tradition for a future satisfactory reorganization of the region."

It is clear that both "modern civilization" and indigenous concepts of political and religious authority have figured significantly in the imagination of nationality in Yogyakarta and in Indonesia more generally. Indonesia is at once a colonial and a nationalist project and a hybridity of indigenous and European notions of nationality and authority. It began as a colonial project, was usurped by Indonesian nationalists in the early twentieth century and in the post colonial era became, depending on one's perspective a nation building or neo-colonialist project.[1] Territorially Indonesia comprises the territory of the former Netherlands Indies. It includes thousands of islands and hundreds of ethnic and religious groups of which Java and the Javanese are but one, albeit the most numerous and most powerful. In one of the last of his many books, Nurcholish Madjid, described Indonesia as a nation "in the making."[2] Benedict Anderson puts it somewhat less diplomatically when he writes that the dream of the "perfect Indonesia" is: "some short or long way down the yellow brick road."[3]

The preceding chapters tack between discussions of Indonesian and Yogyakarta nationalisms. *Kebudayaan*, *agama*, religion and culture figure significantly in both. Two complimentary theoretical perspectives on nationalisms and nations are useful for understanding the overlapping nationalist imaginations: Gellner's characterization of nation states as social formations characterized by uniform bureaucratic governance and technological communication populated by largely anonymous, replaceable citizens and sustained and reproduced by a (relatively) uniform educational system that instills common civic values as well as the knowledge necessary for sustaining the bureaucratic and technological "expert systems" on which modern industrial societies are based.[4] For Gellner, the ideologies in which nationalisms are rooted are equivalent in the sense that they are forms of false consciousness to the extent to which they seek to establish organic, primordial foundations for what are, in fact, modern social and political formations.

Anderson is concerned with the culturally and historically specific characteristics of nationalisms and the ways in which they shape the lives of nations and citizens. He described nations and nationalisms and nations as "imagined communities."[5]

---

[1] Separatist movements have often described Indonesia as a colonial power not unlike the Dutch. Members of *Gerakan Aceh Merdeka*, the Aceh Independence Movement or GAM as it is commonly, known I interviewed by e-mail in 1997 and in person in 2009 frequently referred to the Indonesian government as the "Javanese imperialists." While GAM is widely perceived as an Islamist movement it is, in fact, more nationalist than religious. GAM leaders and supporters often mentioned the fact that Aceh was never part of the Netherlands Indies or "The Javanese State" (Indonesia) and refer to an eighteenth century treaty with the British East India Company as "proof" of this position. GAM understands itself not as a separatist but as a nationalist movement. The people of Aceh have suffered horribly for imagining themselves as a nation apart from the Netherlands Indies and Indonesia. Indonesia's often brutal response has made a lie of the national motto "Unity in Diversity." For a sustained analysis of Acehnese nationalism see E. Aspinal, *Islam and Nation. Separatist Rebellion in Aceh Indonesia*. Stanford: Stanford University Press, 2009.

[2] N. Madjid, *Indonesia Kita*. Jakarta: Gramedia, 2004, p. 114.

[3] B. Anderson, *The Spectre of Comparisons: Nationalism, Southeast Asia and the World*. London: Verso, 1998, p. 130

[4] E. Gellner, *Nations and Nationalisms*. Ithaca: Cornell University Press, 2006, pp. 55–57.

[5] B. Anderson, *Imagined Communities: Reflections on the Origin and Spread of Nationalism*. London : Verso, 1983

Nationalisms, especially those located in colonial, and many post-colonial contexts, are dreams of nations that might yet be. Anderson has been especially concerned with the variety of ways in which Indonesia has been imagined. I am cognizant of the importance of bureaucratization and institution building in the process of nation building. In this book I have, however, been concerned primarily with the cultural and religious concepts that legitimize and guide the course of these processes. In this respect my analysis has built on foundations laid in Anderson's pioneering work more than it does on Gellner's.

My own view is that these theoretical approaches to the study of nationalism are complimentary. Nations are simultaneously social realities and imagined realities. The nation is a social reality to the extent that it exercises relatively uniform control over a bounded space and the population inhabiting it. It is an imagined community to the extent that culturally and/or religiously salient symbols and narratives are manipulated in ways that lead an often disparate peoples to accept the proposition that they have a unique heritage that establishes them as a clearly defined and bounded community the borders of which are co-terminus with those of the geographic space of the nation state. This is what distinguishes nations form empires, which define themselves as political and economic, but not cultural realties.

In many parts of the world colonial nationalisms and post-colonial states, including Indonesia, have attempted the often-gargantuan task of transforming colonial empires into more or less homogeneous nations. Tambiah has shown that in this process post-colonial states often discard or at least subvert European ideologies in favor of traditional religious concepts and narratives in attempts to establish the cultural authenticity of the social realities of new states.[6] Chatterjee describes this process as follows:

> The spiritual, on the other hand, is an "inner" domain bearing the "essential" marks of cultural identity. The greater ones success in imitating Western skills in the material domain, therefore, the greater one's need to preserve the distinctness of one's spiritual culture.[7]

Colonial and post-colonial nationalist narratives are often triumphalist and seek to establish the possibility of the future by retrieving the greatness and the cultural and/or religious distinctiveness of the past. Generally speaking this is an idealized or mythological past shorn of oppressive and often brutal social realities and portrayed in terms of cultural and religious grandeur. The remembered/imagined grandeur of the past is often larger than life or history. The Yogyakarta construction of Indonesian history as an unbroken line of divinely inspired development

---

[6]S. Tambiah, *Leveling Crowds. Ethnonationalist Conflicts and Collective Violence in South Asia*. Berkeley: University of California Press, 1996. In other cases, including China, Vietnam and Cambodia under the Khmer Rouge, variant understandings of Marxism-Lennism displaced traditional cultural and religious concepts in the imaginations of post-colonialities.

[7]P. Chatterjee, *Nationalist Thought in the Colonial World: A Derivative Discourse?* London: Zed, 1983, p. 6.

beginning with the construction of Borobudur in the eighth century and continuing until the present is an example. So is the Indonesian nationalist myth that the boundaries of the modern state are roughly conterminous with the fourteenth century Hindu-Javanese kingdom of Majapahit.

Recognition of the socially and politically constructed nature of nationality has led some critics of the Indonesian nationalist project, especially Pemberton, to decry its inauthenticity.[8] While I share his disdain for the violence and excesses of the New Order regime, I do not share the view that contemporary Javanese and Indonesian cultures and nationalisms are inauthentic because they differ from those of the past. They are the realities within which contemporary Javanese and other Indonesians live. Western (and other) scholars who bemoan the inauthenticity of post-colonial nations and cultures continue the Orientalist tradition of glorifying the past and condemning the decadence of the present.

Hidayah's critique of the Indonesian nationalist project is both more firmly grounded in present realities and more pointed in its analysis of the social and cultural inequities inherent in the New Order drive for national uniformity. She argues that nationalisms and nations can be colonial enterprises, especially in the case of nations characterized by ethnic and religious diversity.[9] In the context of diversity and in absence of genuine pluralism, the imposition of the religious concepts and narratives of a privileged majority, plurality or minority community on others deprives them of what she terms "discursive" as opposed to mere legal citizenship. Because, in such cases, the forces of domination are "indigenous" they have an aura of legitimacy impossible in cases of external colonialism, and are more difficult to contest. Unlike those of scholars who simply wring their hands over the "inauthenticity" of the present her critique is a corrective measure that points to possible improvements in the on going process of imagining Indonesia as a more just and equitable society and establishing these imaginations as social and political realities. Chief among these is decoupling nationality from *agama* in ways that make constitutional guarantees of freedom of religion meaningful for all Indonesians.

Post-colonial and other nationalisms can be over or under imagined, with equally tragic results. Burma is an example of an "over imagined" post-coloniality. The seemingly incongruous combination of Burman Theravada Buddhist xenophobia and 45 years, and counting, of brutal military rule have resulted in systematic oppression of the nation's ethnic and religious minorities that rises to the level of state terrorism and genocide.[10] In 2007 one Karen Burmese Baptist pastor I

---

[8] J. Pemberton, *On the Subject of Java.* Ithaca: Cornell University Press, 1994.

[9] Hidayah, op. cit., *passim.*

[10] I make this observation on the basis of having lived and conducted fieldwork in Burma for 18 months in the early 1980s and a for a shorter period in 2007 and among Burmese refugees in Singapore in 2007 and 2008. See M. Woodward, "On Monks and Mayhem: Dark Days in Buddhist Burma," Arizona State University, Center for the Study of Religion and Conflict, http://www.asu.edu/csrc/documents/Burma_Paper_Woodward.pdf 2007 and "Burma's Generals and Cyclone Nargis: Incompetence, Callous Indifference or Both?," *COMPOS Journal: Analysis, Commentary and News from the World of Strategic Communications,* May 2008,

spoke with put it this way: "What they [the Burma government] want is a country that is completely ethnically Burman and religiously Buddhist." If Burma is over imagined, the Democratic Republic of Congo and Rwanda are under imagined. In both cases the result has been failed states in which national identities transcending local ethnicities and religiosities have, tragically, failed to be imagined, much less established as social realities.[11] In all three cases hundreds of thousands have died and many more have been brutalized, raped and driven from their homes in part as the result of the failure of imagination by their nations' elites. Indonesia is somewhere in between, but has been closer to Burma than to the Congo or Rwanda for most of its history. The Acehnese critique of Indonesia as a Javanese colonialist enterprise is not without merit and is shared by many non-Javanese Indonesians. Government sponsored "transmigration" projects which have moved millions of Javanese to less densely populated provinces and the New Order practice of appointing Javanese to high level administrative positions in non-Javanese provinces are often mentioned as examples. At the same time, educational and language policies and national media have promoted the emergence of an Indonesian culture that, to some extent, transcends ethnicity. The emergence of national Muslim movements and consciousness serves a similar integrative function.

The imagination of Indonesia and of nations in general, is an ongoing process that is almost always contested and never finished. One of Indonesia's national myths explains that the imagination of the nation began on October 28, 1928 with the *Pemuda Indonesia* (Young Indonesia) conference at which young leaders from diverse regional and ethnic backgrounds swore an oath to support the concepts of one people, one country and one language.[12] In the more than eight decades that have followed Indonesia has been imagined as liberal democracy, a Marxist sate, Soekarno's "guided democracy" which sought to unite disparate elements of Marxism, nationalism and religion and the neo-traditionalist centralized authoritarianism of Suharto's "New Order" and as some combination of an Islamic State and Islamic Society.[13] Today it is officially imagined as an, as of yet imperfect,

---

pp. 1–18, (May 2008), http://comops.org/journal/2008/05/27/burma%e2%80%99s-generals-and-cyclone-nargis-incompetence-callous-indifference-or-both/

[11] I make this observation on the basis of having served on the US Government Political Instability (formerly State Failure) Taskforce for more than a decade. See, R. Bates, D. Epstein, J. Goldstone, T. Gurr, M. Woodward, B. Harf, M. Levy, M. Lustik, M. Marshall, T. Parris, K. Knight and J. Ulfelder, *Political Instability Taskforce PhaseIV Report*. McLean, VA: Science Applications International Corporation, 2006 and J. Goldstone, R. Bates, D. Epstein, T. Robert Gurr, M. Woodward M. Lustik, M. Marshall and J. Ulfelder, "A Global Model for Forecasting Political Instability," *American Journal of Political Science*, vol. 54, no 1, 2010, pp. 190–208.

[12] See G. Kahin, *Nationalism and Revolution in Indonesia*. Ithaca: Cornell University Press, 1952, p. 97. Anderson, op. cit., *Java in a Time of Revolution*, shows that it was this generation of young, western educated colonial subjects who, in terms that he would use later, "imagined" Indonesia and played the central roles in the cultural, political and military struggles that made that dream a social reality.

[13] R. Elson, *The Idea of Indonesia*. Cambridge: Cambridge University Press, 2008.

pluralistic democracy.[14] While this view is politically ascendant at the moment, Indonesia has been imagined in very different ways in the past and today is imagined by some as an Islamic state or as a portion of a regional or global Caliphate and by others as a far less integrated nation than the current "unitary state" in which regions have far more autonomy than they currently do.[15] In Yogyakarta, these centrifugal forces are often manifest as royalism. In other parts of Indonesia they take the demands for the local implementation of *Shari'ah* and in some Christian areas of eastern Indonesia, for the formal establishment of Christianity. There are also some who would see the nation dissolved and replaced by a constellation of ethno-religious states.[16] The current revival of interest in Indonesia's first president Soekarno can be understood as an Indonesian nationalist counter discourse to this cacophony of devolutionist tendencies.[17] These alternative imaginations of Indonesia continue to shape religious and political thought and praxis. They may lie dormant for decades only to emerge suddenly and dramatically when conditions

---

[14]During the period of "Guided Democracy" Soekarno attempted to build an Indonesia based on his ideological vision which combined elements of Nationalism, Socialism and Religion. This experiment in social and ideological engineering failed miserably in almost every way imaginable. At least two hundred thousand people died in the military reign of terror that brought the New Order to power in 1966 and millions more endured a terror of silence that lasted for 32 years. The New Order imagined Indonesia as paternalist authoritarianism beneath the façade of "*Pancasila* Democracy." See, D. Lev, *The Transition to Guided Democracy: Indonesian Politics 1957–1959.* Ithaca: Cornell University Modern Indonesia Program, 1965 and D. Weatherbee, *Ideology in Indonesia: Sukarno's Indonesian Revolution.* New Haven: Yale University Southeast Asia Program, 1966. On the ideological and political foundations of the "New Order: see E. Darmaputera, *Pancasila and the Search for Identity and Modernity in Indonesian Society. A Cultural and Ethical Analysis.* Leiden: E.J. Brill, 1998 and D. Rammage, *Politics in Indonesia: Democracy Islam and the Idea of Tolerance.* London: Routledge, 1995. On the re-imagination of Indonesia in the post-Suharto *Reformasi Era* see, D. Porter, *Managing Politics and Islam in Indonesia.* London: Routledge, 2002, B. Harymurti, "Challenges of Change in Indonesia," *Journal of Democracy*, vol. 10, no. 4, 1999, pp. 69–83, P. Tan, "Indonesia 7 Years after Soeharto: Party System Institutionalization in a New Democracy" *Contemporary Southeast Asia*, vol. 28, no. 1, 2006, pp. 88–114. D. King, *Half-Hearted Reform: Electoral Institutions and the Struggle for Democracy in Indonesia.* New York: Praeger, 2003. M. Woodward, "Imagining Indonesia: Democracy and Identity Politics in the Reformation Order," *Suvannabhumi*, vol. 10, no. 5, 1999, pp. 5–10.

[15]On contemporary Islamist imaginations of Indonesia see Z. Abuza, *Militant Islam in Southeast Asia: Crucible of Terror.* London: Lynne Rienner, 2002. M. van Bruinessen, "Genealogies of Islamic Radicalism in Post-Suharto Indonesia," *Southeast Asian Research*, vol. 10, no. 2, 2002, and N. Hasan, *Laskar Jihad. Islam, Militansi, dan Pencarian Identitas di Indonesia Pasca-Orde Baru.* Jakarta: LP3ES, 2008 and M. Woodward, "PKS Against the Rest. The Justice and Prosperity Party and the 2007 Jakarta Election." S. Rajaratnam School of International Studies Commentary no. 55, (April 2008) http://www.rsis.edu.sg/publications/commentaries.asp?selYear=2008 and "Indonesia's Religious Political Parties: Democratic Consolidation and Security in Post-New Order Indonesia," *Asian Security*, vol. 4, no. 1, 2008, pp. 41–60.

[16]See, H. Schulte Nordholt, "Renegotiating Boundaries: Access, Agency and Identity in Post-Soeharto Indonesia," *Bijdragen tot de taal-, Land- en Volkenkunde*, vol. 158, no. 4, 2003.

[17]The large number of books published about Soekarno in the last decade is one indication of the revival of popular interest in him since the democratic transition of 1998.

permit as they did following the economic crisis of 1997 that led to the collapse of the New Order, which suppressed, but did not eliminate alternative imaginations. Yogyakarta nationalism is different from most others because it is not separatist and does not seek to overthrow Indonesia as either socio-political or imagined reality. Rather it understands the Sultanate of Yogyakarta and Indonesia as being interdependent and inseparable.

The imagination of Indonesia remains a contested discourse. Just how contested it currently is became clear to me at a meeting of religiously conservative Muslim intellectuals who imagine Indonesia as a liberal religiously and ethnically plural democracy in Jakarta in November of 2008.[18] The purpose of the meeting was to discuss possible responses to a recent upsurge in Islamist violence associated with the Front for the Defense of Islam (*Front Pembela Islam*/ FPI) and the growing influence of the Islamist Justice and Prosperity Party (*Partai Keadilan Sejathera*/ PKS). Both of these groups imagine Indonesia as an Islamic state, though PKS does not state this publicly. Many Indonesians understand the recent passage of a draconian "anti-pornography" law, strongly supported by both groups, as an ominous and frightening step in that direction.[19] For nearly an hour the two Islamist groups were referred to by the common Indonesian euphemism *"kelompok yang tertuntu"* (a certain group.) Finally a spokeswoman for a Muslim feminist organization rose to her feet and in a passionate, extemporaneous address lasting nearly half an hour stated that it was time to stop talking indirectly and in symbols and being "so Javanese."[20] She stated that PKS and FPI are *the* problem facing Indonesia today and that they are attempting to steal religion (Islam) for political purposes.

---

[18] Because this meeting was, to use an American expression, "off the record and not for attribution," I can not identify the names of individuals present. The "anti-pornography" law also prohibits what is referred to as *"porno-aksii"* (Pornographic action). *"Porno-aksi"* is vaguely defined but would appear to include practices considered "normal" in many Indonesian cultures including young couples holding hands in public in Yogyakarta, to the "custom" of "wearing very little clothing" common among some non-Muslim and non-Christian communities in Eastern Indonesia. Even classical Javanese and Balinese dance could easily be deemed "pornographic." What many find even more alarming is that the act allows nongovernmental organizations to enforce its provisions. This would legalize the brutality of FPI thugs.

[19] On FPI see, A. Rossadi, *Hitam Puitih FPI. Mengunggggkap Rahasia-rahasia Mencengangkan Ormas Keagamaan Paling Kontroversial.* Jakarta: NUN Publisher, 2008. FPI is an organized band of Islamist thugs who use fear and intimidation in attempts to enforce their own moral standards on the Indonesian public. It bears a striking and disturbing resemblance to the Nazi Brown Shirts of the 1930s. It poses a clear threat to Indonesia's democracy and to religious, social and cultural pluralism more generally. On PKS see Woodward, op. cit., "PKS Against the Rest . . . ." and "Indonesia's Religious Political Parties . . . ." Many Indonesians believed that the "anti-pornography" bill passed because politicians were afraid of being labeled "pro-porno" by PKS's formidable propaganda mill. They are probably correct. Yogyakarta, Bali and some provinces in Eastern Indonesia immediately declared the legislation to be unconstitutional and made it clear that they would not enforce it.

[20] Javanese and especially those from Yogyakarta and Surakarta are well known for indirect speech and "talking in symbols." Other Javanese and non-Javanese Indonesians sometimes find this frustrating. There is no correspondence between this cultural/linguistic style and religious orientation.

She decried the tendency to allow "international debates about what is the correct Islam is" to dominate Indonesian discourse and declared the "issue is not what people in Cairo or Saudi Arabia think, but what the *Indonesian* vision of Islam is." She accused PKS of "creeping around" stealing the symbols of nationalism and even feminism.[21] She concluded that they are a dangerous threat to pluralism, without which the nation can not survive. In December of 2008 a friend who is a faculty member at Sunan Kalijaga State Islamic University in Yogyakarta made a similar observation after learning that PKS cadre must swear an oath of eternal loyalty to the party. She said: "These people are very smart and very dangerous. If they get their way, that will be the end of Indonesia. Ambon, Minahasa and all the other Christian areas won't stand for it, neither will Bali because they are Hindus and there will be a civil war. As for Yogya, Yogya people won't stand for it either. They will just go back to being a *kerajaan* (kingdom). That's what they really want anyway." My friend is Javanese, but not originally from Yogyakarta. On the opposite end of the political spectrum some Islamists deny their national and cultural identities altogether. In December of 2008 one told me: "I am not Javanese and I am not Indonesian, I am only Muslim. Indonesia is the problem, the Caliphate is the solution."

From all this we may conclude that religion, culture and nationality are as contested today as they were more than 60 years ago when Indonesia was founded and more than 80 years ago when it was first publicly imagined. The democratic transition of the last decade did not create these debates; it only allowed them to emerge from the shadows of the New Order.

More than half a century and several generations later, Heine-Geldern's speculations about the nature of post-coloniality seem prophetic. While the nations and nationalisms of Southeast Asia vary enormously, all are in some way hybridities in which, through a process of *bricolage*, traditional notions of polity and authority have been used in the imagination and construction of nationalisms and nations. What I have tried to accomplish in this volume is to show how this process of *bricolage* has and continues to operate in a place that is at once, Indonesia, Java and Yogyakarta and how all three are Islamic places but places in which the nature and meaning of Islam is also contested.

---

[21] PKS has attempted to appropriate many of the most important symbols of Indonesian nationalism, including Soekarno, Sultan Hamengkubuwana IX and the founders of the countries two largest Muslim organizations, both of which are unalterably opposed to the party's program and methods in a series of Television advertisements that featured their portraits. In September of 2008, PKS went so far as to attempt to make a symbolic claim that it somehow owned the Muslim fasting month of Ramadan in Yogyakarta. See, Chapter 6 and M. Woodward, "Contesting Wahhabi Colonialism in Yogyakarta," *COMPOS Journal: Analysis, Commentary and News from the World of Strategic Communications*, pp. 1–8 (November, 2008). They described support for the "anti-pornography" bill as a "feminist initiative." Almost all Indonesian women's organizations, most Muslim and almost all non-Muslim groups, strongly oppose it.

Index

A
Agama, 4, 7, 32, 55, 136, 170, 201, 206, 223, 253
Agama Jawa, 4, 136, 253
Agency, 4, 19–20, 156–157, 196, 242, 268
Al-Ghazzali, 78, 207–209, 218
Aliran Kepercayaan, 26
Alon Alon, 147, 150, 152–154, 158–160, 163, 169, 179, 185, 192, 194–195, 223, 233–235, 250, 252–253, 256, 260
Ambon, 5, 11, 270
Anderson, B., 12, 14, 20, 24, 59, 79, 264, 267
Animism, 10, 58, 113–114, 117–118
Anthropology, 2, 6, 28–32, 35, 37, 44, 53, 55–56, 64, 69, 80, 145, 173, 235
Apem, 124, 212–213
Arab, 6, 47–48, 63, 71–72, 83, 109, 184, 189, 200–201
Arabic, 11, 15, 23, 31, 41, 44, 49–50, 52–53, 58, 60, 63–67, 69, 71, 73–74, 77, 83, 93, 113, 118, 120–121, 126, 128–130, 143, 145, 151, 153, 155, 157–158, 170, 174–176, 180, 182, 189, 199–200, 209–210, 222–223, 239
Asad, T., 19, 29, 34–35, 53
Atoni, 104, 137–138, 163

B
Bali, 21, 43, 47, 52, 61, 72, 95–96, 105, 165, 187, 269–270
Barakah/berkat, 38, 69, 113, 176, 210
Batin, 60, 72–73, 86, 97, 121, 176, 209, 223–224, 245
Blessing, 38–40, 69, 75, 85, 98–100, 113–126, 129–132, 134, 137, 139, 149, 152, 154–155, 157–158, 165, 172, 176–179, 183–187, 190–192, 195, 198, 204, 206, 210–212, 214, 216–217, 219–221, 223, 234, 240, 245–246, 261

Bricolage, 9, 38, 67, 70, 105–106, 111, 114, 135, 140, 166, 173, 201, 225, 230–231, 240, 252–253, 270
Buddhism/Buddhist, 4, 7, 10, 13, 26, 30, 33, 36, 42–47, 56–59, 60–62, 94, 124, 135, 137–140, 153, 163, 246, 261, 263, 266–267

C
Charisma, 1, 12, 59, 101, 164, 192, 195, 230–231, 251, 255, 260
Charity, 114–115, 117, 123, 134, 150, 180, 220
Chittick, W., 141–142, 144
Christianity/Christian, 4–5, 7–8, 10–11, 19–20, 22–23, 25–26, 28–29, 31–32, 35–36, 42–47, 50, 59, 64, 108, 111, 120, 139, 149, 218, 222, 237, 247, 268–270
Colonial/colonialism, 2–6, 9, 11–12, 14–19, 26, 28, 36, 45–46, 49, 51, 53–55, 56, 59, 62, 76, 88, 100, 105, 138, 150–151, 156, 162–167, 172, 174–175, 177, 182–183, 186–188, 190–191, 194–195, 219, 230–231, 245, 258, 263–270
Communist, 7, 10, 19–21, 25, 135, 171, 235–236
Culture, 1–73, 75, 79, 83, 100–101, 104, 106, 108, 113–115, 117, 121, 123–124, 128, 135–136, 138, 163, 172, 178, 181, 188–191, 195, 199–201, 212, 216–217, 229–267, 269–270
Cunningham, C., 137–138, 163, 235

D
Demak, 39, 133, 171, 179–183, 187, 191, 194
Demit, 37, 87, 89
Democracy/democratic, 3, 8–12, 15, 19–20, 24–25, 27, 54, 67, 75, 89–90, 103, 108, 132, 165, 174–176, 187–188, 194, 229–270
Dewantara, 24–25
Dihkr, 43, 92, 119, 121, 129–130, 134

CPSIA information can be obtained at www.ICGtesting.com
Printed in the USA
LVOW10*1546191213

366065LV00011B/243/P